Royall Tyler
and Hungary

Royall Tyler
and Hungary

An American in Europe and the Crisis Years 1918–1953

Zoltán Peterecz

Helena History Press

Copyright © Zoltán Peterecz 2021
All rights reserved

ISBN 978-1-943-596-24-9

Official documents on page 318 and 322 are reproduced by permission of The National Archives, London, UK. All other illustrations are courtesy of Gwenyrth Todd, Thompson Todd Collection.

H P

KKL Publications LLC, Helena History Press
Reno, Nevada USA

Publishing scholarship about and from Central and East Europe

www.helenahistorypress.com

Distributed by IngramSpark and available through all major e-retail sites
info@helenahistorypress.com

Table of Contents

Introduction (by Professor Tibor Frank) vii
Preface xix

CHAPTER 1: A Young American in Europe 1
CHAPTER 2: World War I, Peacemaking, and the New Europe 19
CHAPTER 3: The League of Nations Years – Part I:
 the Hungarian Financial Reconstruction, 1924–26 39
CHAPTER 4: The League of Nations Years – Part II:
 The Post-Reconstruction Hungary under Tyler's Watch, 1926–1929 71
CHAPTER 5: The League of Nations Years – Part III:
 Out of and Back in the League of Nations 99
CHAPTER 6: The League of Nations Years – Part IV:
 Adviser to the Hungarian Governments 133
CHAPTER 7: The League of Nations Years – Part V:
 The Last Year of Peace 171
CHAPTER 8: World War II – An Intelligence Officer 197
CHAPTER 9: Tyler in the Early Cold War 247

Appendix
 – Royall Tyler to Henry Morgenthau, December 21, 1939. 267
 – Royall Tyler, "Treatment of War-Criminals and Propaganda
 for Axis Countries," Geneva, April 12, 1943. 272
 – Royall Tyler, "Feudalism in Hungary," December 1944. 276
 – Royall Tyler, "The Outlook for the Economic Issue,
 after San Francisco," Geneva, June 28, 1945. 283

Bibliography 299
Index 311

Tibor Frank

A Man for All Seasons: Royall Tyler (1884–1953)

It gives me great pleasure and satisfaction to introduce the new book by my erstwhile student Zoltán Peterecz at Eötvös Loránd University, Budapest, Hungary, who was awarded his PhD right there in 2010. Over the years Zoltán became a first rate US foreign-policy-history expert interested especially in Hungarian-American relations in the 20th century. An Associate Professor at the Institute of English, American and German Studies, Eszterházy Károly Catholic University, Eger, Hungary, Zoltán approaches some of the largely forgotten subjects of this area with an astute sense of scholarly eagerness, a stubborn search for the unknown and a visible happiness at investigating and solving great historical issues. I am very proud of him.

Zoltán Peterecz's new book is the logical continuation of his very successful monograph on Jeremiah Smith, Jr. (1870–1935), Commissioner-General of the League of Nations for the 1924 loan to Hungary. In his 2013 *Jeremiah Smith, Jr. and Hungary, 1924–1926. The United States, the League of Nations, and the Financial Reconstruction of Hungary,* Zoltán Peterecz dealt also with the economic and political problems associated with the post-World War I financial reconstruction of Hungary—both on the domestic and international scene.

That book by Zoltán already gave a valuable insight into the official and unofficial trends within the foreign policy of the United States after World War I. Set against the background of widely scattered international events, the author supported his narrative on Jeremiah Smith, Jr. with a large body of diverse sources, including archival materials, contemporary newspaper articles from a number of countries, and an impressive range of secondary sources. The result was a well-written and valuable work welcomed not only by scholars of the interwar period, but also by non-specialist readers.

In his present monograph, *Royall Tyler and Hungary: An American in Europe and the Crisis Years 1918–1953*, Zoltán Peterecz addresses the same period, witnessed this time, however, by somebody who worked closely with Jeremiah Smith, Jr. but also succeeded in an international career that encompassed financial, political, and diplomatic issues alike.

The result is a new book by Zoltán that became an important and complex contribution not only for those interested in Hungary or the international scene in the interwar years. Royall Tyler and his activities are integrated and, indeed, incorporated by this book into US history at large. We follow Tyler taking part in World War I, his activities at the Paris Peace Conference, his work of several years as an official US delegate on the Reparations Committee, before joining the League of Nations for the next twenty years. Zoltán Peterecz focuses on this latter aspect of Tyler's career as a diplomat in five great chapters 3 through 7.

Not every student of modern history would know today who Royall Tyler actually was. *Dumbarton Oaks*,[1] the newsletter of a Harvard University research institute, library, museum, and garden located in Washington, DC remembers him in a memorial article as "an historian, diplomat, economist, and art connoisseur", who spent most of his life in Europe. He was much more than that: he emerges from Zoltán Peterecz's breathtaking description and analysis as a serious historian of both Byzantine and Spanish art, and a diplomatic historian of the Tudor age, and a secret service wizard, and a highly important international financier who worked for top US diplomats—and much more. The discovery itself of this renaissance American and his dedicated achievements for Hungary alone is a tribute to a young and more than just promising talent. Zoltán Peterecz, whose presentations of Jeremiah Smith, Jr., Royall Tyler and, most recently, in an article in print,[2] of Theodore Brentano, the first US Minister to sovereign Hungary (1922–1927) mark what may in due course appear as an endeavor to reinterpret interwar and post-War US foreign policies, bringing fresh light to an entire

---

[1] https://www.doaks.org/resources/bliss-tyler-correspondence/annotations/royall-tyler (Downloaded 28.10.2021).

[2] *Hungarian Studies*, probably Spring 2022.

epoch which is usually catalogued as sheer Conservatism and insularization and the closing world of a seemingly disinterested America. This book not only sheds fresh light on a forgotten hero of American history but opens up the mediocre world of post-Wilsonian United States. Here is somebody of importance whose discovery by a Hungarian historian may be looked upon as an event of international scholarship.

A descendant of the American jurist and playwright Royall Tyler (1757–1826), Zoltán Peterecz's Royall Tyler married the Countess Elisiana de Castelvecchio, a great-great-granddaughter of Louis Bonaparte, descending from the prospective French emperor's illegitimate son François de Castelvecchio (1826–1869).[3] (This may not seem important, but it is, and it is very interesting.) Young Tyler moved to London in 1898, and was educated for the next 20 years at Harrow School, the New College, Oxford, the Universidad de Salamanca as well as the École des Sciences Politiques in Paris.

Peterecz makes it clear that Tyler had extremely strong and varied connections to Great Britain. He studied and lived there for many years; he received his first commission from the Public Record Office; he met his future wife there; he was almost in constant contact with various figures of the British political establishment throughout the interwar years.

Fluent in French, Spanish, and German and proficient in Italian, Hungarian, and Greek, Tyler authored *Spain: A Study of Her Life and Arts* (1909),[4] a facsimile reprint of which was published in 2010. Fifty years after the publication of his initial *Spain: A Study of Her Life and Arts* in 1909, the art historian Walter Muir Whitehill could still write that it "remains an unrivaled introduction to the subject."[5]

In 1911, the Public Record Office of the British Home Office appointed him editor of the *Spanish Calendar of State Papers,* collection of translations of the correspondence of diplomats posted in Spain with their English Monarchs.[6] Tyler completed five volumes (Vols. 9–13) of this tremendous

---

3   https://peoplepill.com/people/william-r-tyler (Downloaded 28.30.2021).
4   New York: M. Kennerley/London, G. Richards, 1909.
5   Dictionary of Art Historians. https://arthistorians.info/tylerr (Downloaded 29.30.2021)
6   "The complete series of the *Calendar of State Papers, Spain* is now alive. There are 19 volumes in all, covering the period from the accession of Henry VII to the death of Mary I. The calendar gives a summary, with extensive quotation, of the official papers of the Spanish court which relate to England and English affairs." https://blog.history.ac.uk/2009/03/calendar-of-state-papers-spain/ (Downloaded 30.10.2021). Tyler "published the first of the five volumes of these papers in 1913; the

undertaking between 1913 and 1953. He also authored, with Hayford Peirce, *Byzantine Art* (1926)[7] and *L'art byzantin*, Vol. 1 (1932) and Vol. 2 (1934), a series of catalogues in French, originally planned for five volumes with a thousand illustrations but stopped and left unfinished by the Nazi German occupation of Paris during World War II.[8] Tyler also edited, with R. R. Tatlock, *Spanish Art, an Introductory Review of Architecture, Painting, Sculpture, Textiles, Ceramics, Woodwork, Metalwork*,[9] in 1927.

In and after World War I, Tyler became an interrogator of German POWs (1918–1919) and a member of the US delegation to the Paris Peace Conference (1919). A delegate on the US Reparations Commission (1920–1924) he was to become a deputy commissioner general of the Economic and Financial Section of the League of Nations in Geneva (1924–1926), where he was particularly responsible for overseeing the economic reconstruction of post-War Hungary. He thus spent much of his time in Budapest, and learned even the proverbially difficult language of the Hungarians tolerably well—no easy task for even an already polyglot American.

Tyler continued to give much of his energy to his scholarly interest and was instrumental in organizing the first international exhibition of Byzantine art in Paris in 1931. In the same year, he became the League of Nations Financial Committee's financial advisor to the Hungarian government in Budapest (1931–1938). Between 1938 and 1943 he lent his expertise to the Economic and Financial Section of the League of Nations in Geneva, spending much of World War II in Switzerland. On unpaid leave from the League of Nations, he worked for the US intelligence network run by Allen Dulles. Between 1943 and 1949, Tyler served as the Swiss representative of the United Nations Relief and Rehabilitation Administration (UNRRA) and, in 1944, as the special attaché to the US Legation in Bern, Switzerland.

In 1923, Royall and Elisina Tyler acquired (and later restored) the historic garrison-castle, *Antigny-le-Château*, in Burgundy. He died early, at 68, in

---

last, completed just before his death, appeared in 1954." https://peoplepill.com/people/royall-tyler-1/ (Donwloaded 30.10.2021)

7   New York: F. A. Stokes, 1926.
8   https://www.doaks.org/resources/bliss-tyler-correspondence/annotations/lart-byzantin (Downloaded 30.10.2021)
9   London: B.T. Batsford, 1927.

A Man for All Seasons: Royall Tyler (1884–1953)

1953, in Paris, most probably by suicide. His last book, on the Holy Roman Emperor *Charles the Fifth* was published posthumously in 1956.

We find Royall Tyler first in Paris where he served as head of the Paris field office of the International Bank for Reconstruction and Development (1946–1949) and then as the European representative of the National Committee for a Free Europe. This US anti-Communist organization founded in 1949 by Allen Dulles, with whom he also helped found the Free Europe College in Strasbourg, France. It is not without relevance to Tyler's rise as an international figure that his son William Royall Tyler joined the United States Foreign Service after World War II, becoming a career diplomat. As to William R. Tyler, US President John F. Kennedy nominated him in 1962 as Assistant Secretary of State for European Affairs, and, after Senate confirmation, W. R. held this office from 1962 until 1965. In 1965, President Lyndon B. Johnson named W. R. Tyler United States Ambassador to the Netherlands: Tyler, Jr. served in The Hague from 1965 through 1969.[10]

Much to their dismay, Tyler and his wife Elisina arrived at Vienna in late 1920 only to find this beautiful city in miserable condition. Elisina Tyler described the scene in terms that were fitting for most of Europe in the aftermath of the Great War: "The smell of hunger pursues one everywhere, even in the hallway and stairs of the Grand Opera, that horrible unnatural smell of diminished vitality which human beings give out when the process of physical disintegration has been set up"—she complained in a 1921 letter to Mildred Barnes Bliss, an intimate friend of the Tylers.[11] "The whole vast city lay in darkness under a thick shroud of snow. Shadowy figures clad in worn-out army uniforms stood silently imploring by every doorway. Misery reigned supreme," she remembered in a 1941 diary entry.[12] This was true not only of the proud Habsburg capital but of most parts of Europe which the Tylers went to see. Elisina Tyler was not only a silent observer of the post-War scene.

> She stayed in the Austrian capital three weeks out of every two months for more than two years. She made use of the help of various diplomatic representations of the main powers, and built an excellent working re-

---

10 William R. Tyler, American Diplomat. https://peoplepill.com/people/william-r-tyler (Downloaded 30.10.2021).
11 Quoted by Peterecz, 34.
12 Quoted by Peterecz, 34.

lationship with local organizations and committees. She also founded the "Self Help for Austria" campaign, of which she was chairman and vice president. She donated more than 20 million Kronen ($10,000) for the University of Vienna, which made it possible to fund canteens where needy students could receive cheap meals. In addition, Elisina provided grants and scholarships and donated clothes, shoes, and books for Viennese students. In recognition of her commitment to alleviating the humanitarian emergency at the university, she was nominated for the Badge of Honor of the University of Vienna, and on March 24, 1922, its academic senate approved the award. Also in recognition of her work organizing this charity effort between 1920 and 1923, she was awarded the highest decoration of the Austrian Red Cross.[13]

As a recognition of their obvious generosity and good will, Tayler and his Elisina were made *chevaliers* of the Legion of Honor.

Apart from the laudable efforts of the Tylers to make Vienna (and Europe) "great again", Zoltán Peterecz provides a wealth of information on the horrible fate of Europe in ruins, from France to Russia and Italy to Belgium, as seen by these philanthropic Americans visiting Europe—who understood, more and more, their own post-War duties and obligations.

Tyler of course sensed the whole situation through the eyes of a historian and art-lover with great political connections. He met important political figures during Franklin D. Roosevelt's second administration, such as the President himself, Secretary of State Cordell Hull, Under Secretary of State Sumner Welles, Assistant Secretary of State George C. Messersmith, Treasury Secretary Henry Morgenthau, Jr., as well as officials and advisers at the State Department, for example, Herbert Feis and Harry C. Hawkins. His role became so important for his contemporaries, that the then well-known US journalist Jerome Beatty devoted an entire chapter to him among his stories of Americans working in various capacities around the world.

Zoltán Peterecz became interested in Royall Tyler due to his years devoted to the financial reconstruction of Hungary (1924–26) and the post-reconstruction period "under Tyler's watch," between 1926–1929.

---

13 Peterecz, 34–35.

A Man for All Seasons: Royall Tyler (1884–1953)

In the 1930s Tyler served as an adviser to subsequent Hungarian governments. These three chapters make up the very essence of this book where the author focuses on issues important also for Hungarian historians and, hopefully soon, Hungarian readers. Detailing Tyler's career, the book significantly contributes to our knowledge of the League of Nations' effort to reconstruct Europe.

Hungarians attributed great weight to the presence of both Jeremiah Smith, Jr. and Royall Tyler in Budapest as they considered them a special link between Hungary and the United States. This was not true as they represented the League of Nations. As Peterecz aptly puts it:

> Although both Smith and Tyler were officials of the League of Nations and did not have any formal ties to the American government, the Hungarian political leadership and the people in general regarded them not only as representatives of the overseas giant but also as a kind of bridge between the two nations. Despite their energetic efforts to deny that they possessed the influence contributed to them, in the eyes of the average Hungarian they did represent the United States. This had been a common phenomenon since the end of World War I. An American officer of the Coolidge Mission noted in 1919 that in Budapest "no amount of persuasion could convince the Hungarians that our mission was not political and did not carry great weight in Paris."[14] Another member of the same mission, writing basically about the whole Central European region, wrote in his diary that almost everybody was "looking to America as a composite savior, guardian angel, boundary commission, and food supply."[15] Coolidge himself wrote that Hungarians "look primarily to America for their salvation."[16] And since certain steps taken by Amer-

---

14 Peterecz (65) quotes Nicholas Roosevelt, *A History of a Few Weeks, Being an Account of Experience in Austria and Hungary during the Armistice*, Box 18, Nicholas Roosevelt Papers, Special Collections Research Center at Syracuse University Libraries, USA, 6, 32 229. For Captain Nicholas Roosevelt see Tibor Frank, Diplomatic Images of Admiral Horthy: The American Perception of Interwar Hungary, 1919–1941. In Waldemar Zacharasiewicz (ed.), *Images of Central Europe in Travelogues and Fiction by North American Writers* (Tübingen: Stauffenburg Verlag, 1995), 198–200.
15 Peterecz (65) quotes a diary entry of November 26, 1918, Charles Moorfield Storey Journal, 1918–1919, Massachusetts Historical Society, United States.
16 Peterecz (65) quotes Archibald Cary Coolidge to the American Mission in Paris, January 19, 1919, quoted in Harold Jefferson Coolidge and Robert Howard Lord, *Archibald Cary Coolidge: Life and Letters* (Boston and New York: Houghton Mifflin, 1932), 211.

icans, either private or governmental, only strengthened this prevailing sentiment, it was not within the power of Smith and Tyler to overcome it.[17]

Tyler had a sharp sight for some of the burning issues of Hungarian society. His views of a most controversial issue of Hungarian history, remained not quite uninfluenced by the Hungarian propaganda of Tyler's day, are summed up by Zoltán Peterecz in his balanced way:

> In one of his letters to Mildred Barnes Tyler,[18] Tyler wrote about the prevailing anti-Semitism in Hungary. Hungarians had for a long time showed antipathy toward Jews, but notwithstanding this widespread sentiment, the majority of the Jewish population had managed to climb the social ladder and they occupied a disproportionally large segment of the various free professions, such as doctors, lawyers, engineers, or musicians.[19] Many of them took part in trade or were bankers, and some became so rich that they could even buy their way into the aristocracy, another point causing animosity among most Hungarians. The Bolshevik coup in March 1919, in which many of the leaders were of Jewish origin, only heightened the prevalent anti-Semitism, and easily targeted Jews as scapegoats for the tragic postwar situation. This was both a result of, and further added to, what Paul Hanebrink called "the myth of Judeo-Bolshevism," which referred to the belief on part of many that Communism was brought on as a Jewish plot.[20] As he put it, and his observation was by all means true of Hungary, "Judeo-Bolshevism loomed in political imagination throughout the region as a powerful transnational enemy."[21] These circumstances consequently laid the groundwork for the first anti-Jewish legislation in Europe, the Numerus Clausus, in

---

17 Peterecz, 65.
18 Peterecz (66) quotes Royall Tyler to Mildred Barnes Bliss, April 5, 1926, Budapest, "Bliss–Tyler Correspondence," https:// www.doaks.org/resources/bliss-tyler-correspondence/letters/05apr1926, accessed December 7, 2015. "Hunk" was a typical term Tyler used for Hungarians. Zoltán Peterecz assumes this was not derogative on his part, rather a shortened term.
19 Peterecz (66) quotes Ezra Mendelsohn, *The Jews of East Central Europe between the World Wars* (Bloomington: University of Indiana Press, 1983), 100–102.
20 Peterecz (67) quotes Paul Hanebrink, *A Specter Haunting Europe: The Myth of Judeo-Bolshevism* (Cambridge, MA, London, England: Belknap Press of Harvard University Press, 2018).
21 Peterecz (67) quotes *ibid.*, 51.

1920, which law limited the number of Jews who were allowed to study in institutions of higher learning.[22] Tyler experienced this anti-Jewish atmosphere in Hungary, but in his opinion, the Jews had started to make a slow comeback, and this was due to their strong work ethic, while "the Hunk is not prepared to go to such heights."[23]

Notwithstanding this paragraph from a private letter to a friend, Zoltán Peterecz comes to the conclusion that

> Tyler avoided even the most remote thought of getting too close to political questions, and he focused strictly on the financial matter at hand and remained as impartial as could be expected from an American. Naturally, he kept in touch with a wide variety of people, many of whom were politicians, but he did not get enmeshed in the game of politics. He obviously did have a political opinion, but he kept that to himself and instead tried to pursue his intellectual interests in both Hungarian culture, mainly the language, and his ever-present passion for art history.[24]

Tyler was never uncritical of Hungary. He found the Hungarian environment self-centered, where "people usually imagine that the entire world has its eyes fixed upon their own particular little dump."[25] Though he remained away from local politics, Tyler met with the American minister of 1927 in Budapest, Joshua Butler Wright (1877–1939) quite regularly, and shared valuable information on both general conditions and finance-related subjects. As Minister Wright noted in his diary, "One always gleans much information from him for he knows everyone here. Has been particularly helpful to me and comments have been most valuable."[26] Tyler was convinced that "Horthy

---

22 Peterecz (67) quotes the text of the bill is in *Magyar Törvénytár*, 1920. évi törvénycikkek [Hungarian Law Collection, Law Bills of 1920] (Budapest, 1921), 145–46. See also, Gergely Egressy, "A Statistical Overview of the Hungarian Numerus Clausus Law of 1920—A Historical Necessity or the First Step Toward the Holocaust?" *Eastern European Quarterly* 34 (January 2001): 447–64.
23 Peterecz, 66–67.
24 Peterecz, 71.
25 Peterecz (80) quotes Royall Tyler to Jeremiah Smith, Jr. September 2, 1927, Budapest, OV 33/2, BoE.
26 Peterecz (85) quotes a diary entry by US Minister Joshua Butler Wright, of February 22, 1928, Series 4: Diaries, Minister to Hungary, 1 January–6 April 1928, Box 2, Joshua Butler Wright Papers, 1909–1938, Seeley G. Mudd Manuscript Library, Princeton, USA. See also diary entries of February 14, and March 19, 1928.

would remain governor for life," and appreciated Prime Minister Count István Bethlen's political acumen, going so far as to call him "a great man."²⁷

Contrary to his self-perception, however, he was not at all unappreciative of politics. During World War II, and specifically in 1943–45, Tyler was Allen Dulles' right-hand man in Switzerland. Among the varied secret negotiations with countries such as Hungary, Bulgaria, Romania, as well as Greece, Spain, and Italy, he worked closely with Dulles in his varied efforts to detach some or all of these countries from the Third Reich. Thanks to Tyler's large web of acquaintances in all these countries, Tyler was Dulles' leading expert in many of his clandestine activities when it came to East-Central and Southern Europe. Zoltán Peterecz's book contains a most thorough and indeed pioneering research on Tyler's involvement in Hungary's half-hearted and ill-fated efforts to leave Hitler and Nazi Germany in World War II, particularly during the crucial years of 1942–43. Tyler did not share the general sentiment of successive Hungarian governments and the general attitude of the Hungarian nation, confessing "I'm not very keen on revision, myself; I fear it would create as much trouble as it would settle, and I'd rather see progress on the economic plane—bigger units and lowering of barriers."²⁸

His private opinions help us understand how the US tried to get involved in the top-secret political battlefield in Europe, well before D-Day and the military efforts of 1943–44. Peterecz recalls a well-known 1941 anecdote to discuss how Hungary declared war on the United States—indeed one of the stupidest things to do in a year when Hungary already attacked the Soviet Union. Britain brought it to the attention of Hungary that as of December 6, 1941 a state of war existed between Britain and Hungary, followed by a declaration of war by Canada, Australia, New Zealand, and South Africa. Rulers of Hungary may not have known the school globe in their school years.

Peterecz makes it very clear how Hungary got into the war and especially against the US, particularly in a year when absolute giants such as the Soviet Union (one sixth of the globe) and the British Empire (one fourth of the

---

27 Peterecz (97) quotes Royall Tyler to Mildred Barnes Bliss, May 29, 1929, Budapest, "Bliss–Tyler Correspondence," https:// www.doaks.org/resources/Bliss-Tyler-correspondence/letters/29may1929, accessed December 16, 2015. For the perception of Adm. Horthy and Count Bethlen by US diplomacy see Tibor Frank: A Vermont Yankee in Regent Horthy's Court: the Hungarian World of a U.S. Diplomat. In Tibor Frank, ed.: *Discussing Hitler. Advisers of U.S. Diplomacy in Central Europe 1934-1941* (Budapest—New York: CEU Press, 2003), 23–70.

28 Peterecz (139) quotes Royall Tyler to Mildred Barnes Bliss, January 17, 1933.

A Man for All Seasons: Royall Tyler (1884–1953)

globe) were already included as enemies of Hungary in the greatest global conflict of human history. Says Peterecz:

> With the German occupation still a few days away, Tyler compiled an intelligence report outlining how Hungary got into the war and what were then the relations with the surrounding countries. This report was probably ordered by the State Department, wishing to explain the contours of Hungary to Americans. No one else on the American side at the time could have provided such a thorough examination of the Hungarian situation. [...] The long report had two sections of 23 and 14 typed pages, respectively. In the first, titled "How Hungary Got into the Second World War," Tyler meticulously summarized Hungarian history from 1918 up to the present, with an emphasis on how Hungary became involved in the war on Germany's side. He started with a very well-known and much quoted anecdote on how President Roosevelt may have received the news of the Hungarian declaration of war. "Indeed," Tyler appended sarcastically, "Alice never met anything more wonderful in Wonderland than this Hungary, a kingdom without a king, headed by an admiral without a fleet, declaring war on the U.S.A. because of territories annexed or occupied by the U.S.A.'s enemies, in association with whom Hungary had just joined in a crusade against the Soviet Union, which power had nothing to do with the case."[29]

Tyler's role as a cold warrior is also introduced by Peterecz's book through his connections of the National Committee for a Free Europe (NCFE).

"All this," Peterecz concludes, "naturally provides the basis of a good story that needs to be told, and through Tyler's career, if it can be called that, the European story between World War I and the early Cold War can be revisited."[30] Justly put and very well done.

Tibor Frank,
Professor Emeritus of Eötvös Loránd University Budapest,
Full Member of the Hungarian Academy of Sciences,
Fellow of the Royal Historical Society

---

29 Peterecz, 234–5.
30 Peterecz, xi.

Preface

When in 2008 I was close to completing my PhD dissertation on Jeremiah Smith, Jr.'s work in the financial reconstruction of Hungary in the mid-1920s, I had already begun doing research on Royall Tyler. It was not only logical since he was Smith's deputy during those two and half years in Hungary, but I also had the sense and sporadic evidence that he was much more involved with Hungary and Europe than his fellow New Englander.

The problem of doing research on Tyler stemmed from his stature being not a prominent target for historians for the mainly behind-the-lines efforts he always practiced. He was not a primary player, ergo interest in him was relegated to occasional mentions and footnotes in historical works. Also, his talents and activities were manifold, therefore one had to cover a wide array of scenes and times in order to present him faithfully. This process meant that instead of one exhaustive collection at one of the major archives, I had to carry out my research at many institutions, and try to cover his tracks in secondary works as well. After ten years of on and off research, I felt the time had come to start writing the story of the man that was in many ways unique: an American who was almost European, a self-taught art historian who became a name to reckon with in the field of Byzantine art history, an amateur historian with a superb organizing faculty of mind, a League of Nations officer who became intimately involved with Central Europe but mainly with Hungary, an OSS officer and right-hand man of Allen Dulles during World War II, a Cold Warrior until his premature death in 1953. All this, I believe, naturally provides the basis of a good story that needs to be told, and through Tyler's career, if it can be called that, the European story between World War I and the early Cold War can be revisited.

Preface

There were many people who helped me through the decade's work at various institutions that came my way, and it would be almost impossible to list them all, but wherever I turned to help, I almost always received a fair portion of it. There were other colleagues and friends who aided me in various ways, and I would like to mention at least a few names to whom my gratitude flows to: András Joó, Miklós Lojkó, András Becker, Katharina Kniefacz, Robert Nelson, James Carder, Mark Weiner, Kriszta Kaló, Petra Hamerli, and Róbert Kerepeszki. I also need to mention Professor Tibor Frank, my long-time mentor with whom I discussed the project early on and who encouraged me to follow this path. There are two special mentions. I was extremely lucky to get to know Royall Tyler, the grandson of the subject of this book. He helped me so much to understand the "old" Tyler with his reminiscences and insights. We also could meet in person at Princeton, where he was teaching at the time I was there on a short research stint. The other person is Gwenyth Todd, great-granddaughter of Royall Tyler's, who let me use her private collection about her family, which proved to be a treasure trove. But above all I must thank my family (Rita, Tomi, and Gergő) for the patience they exercised when I chose researching and writing over them. I can only hope they are satisfied with the result.

Budapest, March 23, 2021.

Chapter 1

A Young American in Europe

What could a young American man from a long-prominent New England family do with his life in the latter part of the nineteenth century? Go to a prestigious East Coast university like Harvard, Yale, maybe Princeton, and then moving into either law or business? Toy with the idea of entering politics? Become a professor at a university and author scientific theses or write novels, or work as a journalist for a prominent magazine, for instance *The Atlantic Monthly*? Royall Tyler chose none of the above avenues, although the path to many of them were paved for him from birth. In the end, life had different callings in store for him.

Royall Tyler was born in Quincy, Massachusetts, in 1884, a place that had in earlier times given unforgettable names to American history, outstanding among them the Adams clan with two presidents, John and John Quincy, and politicians and writers such as Charles Francis Adams and Henry Adams. The place, Quincy, for a long time had been country to Boston, but that city of Puritan ancestry was starting to creep ever closer.

Tyler's great-grandfather was also born in Quincy and was also named Royall Tyler (1757–1826). He was supposed to graduate from Harvard in July 1776, but the War of Independence intervened. He joined the Continental Army, and initially served under Colonel John Hancock. Two years later he returned to Harvard to finish his studies and received his master's degree the next year. He was romantically interested in the daughter of John Adams, who at this time was serving in Europe, but the future president and his wife were against a more serious relation between the two because they did not wholly approve of Tyler's character, for Tyler had squandered half of his inheritance during and immediately after college. After moving to Vermont and building a successful career in law, in 1794 Tyler married Mary Hunt

Chapter 1

Palmer Tyler (1775–1866). The marriage proved long-lasting and mutually satisfying. It produced eleven children, four of whom became clergy members, two became merchants, one a lawyer, and two, both women, worked with children. The others did not survive. The couple remained together until Tyler's death.

In 1807, after working as a member of the Vermont Supreme Court for six years, Tyler became the first chief justice of Vermont, and was elected to that position six times. He is sometimes dubbed the "first American playwright" for *The Contrast*. Penned in 1787, the play, a comedy, put into the focus the differences between European and American culture—and by a strange twist of fate, the amalgam of the two cultures would be embodied by his eponymous great-grandson. Although it is not accurate to label it the first play written by an American, it was, however, "the first native comedy to be professionally produced," and "perhaps the most famous American play before the twentieth century."[1] Tyler's wife, Mary Palmer, also achieved a first. In 1811, she anonymously published the first childcare manual that was both comprehensive and written by an American woman, *The Maternal Physician*. The well-received book also strengthened the idea of "Republican motherhood," that is, women's role in educating their children for the virtuous young republic in order to prevent possible mobocracy and chaos. Throughout Vermont Royall Tyler became a household name as a chief justice, and he was also a trustee of the University of Vermont, where later he taught as professor for three years. He even ran for Senate in 1812, but he lost.[2]

There is not much known about Tyler's grandfather, yet another Royall Tyler.[3] His father, William Royall Tyler, was born in 1852 and was a well-known teacher specializing in classical studies. He taught Greek and Latin

---

1 G. Thomas Tanselle, *Royall Tyler* (Cambridge: Harvard University Press, 1967), 53, 81.
2 The paragraph was based upon the following sources: Tanselle, *Royall Tyler*; Susan Clair Imbarrato, "Royall Tyler (1757–1826)," *The Heath Anthology of American Literature*, Fifth Edition, Paul Lauter, General Editor, https://college.cengage.com/english/lauter/heath/4e/students/author_pages/eighteenth/tyler_ro.html, accessed September 6, 2018; Catherine E. Kelly, "Between Town and Country: New England Women and the Creation of a Provincial Middle Class, 1820–1860," (Ph.D. diss., Rochester, NY: University of Rochester, 1992), 20–29; Catherine E. Kelly, *In the New England Fashion: Reshaping Women's Lives in the Nineteenth Century* (Ithaca, NY: Cornell University Press, 1999), 47–58; for Tyler's childcare manual, see Marilyn S. Blackwell, "The Republican Vision of Mary Palmer Tyler," *Journal of the Early Republic* 12 (Spring 1992): 11–35.
3 He nonetheless authored a book compiling legal texts in Vermont, mainly for law enforcement officers. Royall Tyler, *A Book of Forms, with Occasional Notes* (Brattleboro, VT: Joseph Steen, 1845).

at Adams Academy, Massachusetts, where he later served as principal, 1893–1897, until his untimely death due to pneumonia. "The cruelest blow I have ever suffered"— Tyler recalled decades later.[4] As an adult, Tyler recalled his father to have been gentle and sweet but lacking in vitality, the reason for which was that "he was the product on both sides of half-a-dozen generations of Bostonians, unrefreshed by so much as one drop of other blood."[5]

Tyler's mother, Ellen Curtis Krebs (18??–1904), was the daughter of a Slovak immigrant by the name of Rak—meaning crayfish, a close equivalent of Krebs (crab), the name Tyler's maternal grandfather promptly adopted in the hope of being more accepted in Boston. In fact, he became a successful homeopathic doctor. His daughter, Ellen, married William Royall Tyler in 1883. It was a love match, although thanks to her father's marriage to the daughter of a Boston shipbuilder, she also came into a sizeable fortune. Not long after the marriage, Ellen converted to Christian Science, which ruled her life from then on. In fact, the disease that killed her husband might have been curable, but Christian Science barred the use of any medicine. This approach to sicknesses endangered Tyler's life as well when, at the age of nine, both measles and pneumonia sickened him at the same time. He survived, which must have strengthened his mother's belief in Christian Science as the true faith.

Tyler's father did not fight the question of religion in the household for "the sake of a quiet life," and Tyler, for as long as her mother was alive, also chose the easy way out of the domestic religious dilemma and did not rebel either.[6] He later described her mother as someone who "possessed vivacity, a sense of fun, Danubian charm and good looks in a blend to which Boston was unaccustomed," and was "the most positive influence my formative years knew."[7] However, soon after Tyler's father died in 1897, his mother moved to Europe and in 1900 was remarried to Josiah Huntington Quincy (1859–1919), a former Boston mayor and an old acquaintance of the family. This caused young Tyler to further drift away into his independent and self-centered world. As he saw in hindsight, the "isolation did not often weigh on

---

4   Royall Tyler, "Autobiography," in Royall Tyler, *One Name, Two Lives* (Charlie's Forest, NSW, Australia: Blue-Tongue Books, 2017), 15, 17. Since the latter work appeared in print, hereafter I will give it as reference. Also, "William Royall Tyler '74," *The Harvard Crimson*, November 3, 1897.
5   Tyler, *One Name, Two Lives*, 20.
6   Ibid., 17.
7   Ibid., 15, 18.

me, but there were moments when the sense of problems altogether beyond me grew oppressive."⁸ Her mother bore another child from her second marriage in 1903, Edmund Quincy (1903–1997), whom she endowed with more wealth than Tyler after her untimely death of cancer in 1904. Tyler always resented this, because despite the inheritance he himself received, he was still forced to earn his living as well.⁹

Royall Tyler was an only child, and thanks to his lineage, he carried both traditional New England blood and a Danubian immigrant strain—a combination that he put to use in his mature years. He looked back on a happy childhood that was full of gaiety, in which he usually got what he wanted and carried no strict religious atmosphere. He had a great love for birds and for historical stories ("local antiquities") either in book form or from old relatives.¹⁰ However, he did find the town of Quincy undesirable, since it witnessed "decline…from a staid rural community to an unsightly suburb."¹¹ His father died when he was fourteen, and his mother succumbed to cancer a few years later, so for the greater part of his life he was without parents and parental love, which he tried to discover elsewhere. In 1897, Tyler was enrolled in Milton Academy, where he liked to be left alone, a trait that remained with him for the rest of his life, even as he became to be a man of the world in many respects. His father's death just a few weeks after his enrollment meant that "the little world in which I had been brought up fell to pieces."¹² He was not able to fit in at Milton afterwards, he hoped to finally be able to see England. This wish was triggered by his mother having previously travelled to Europe and by his father's influence. His early joy in reading Izaak Walton's book, *The Compleat Angler*, his father's love for England, and also that of the parents of one of his friend, made him "long to know that land and silently to disregard the anti-English talk that was rife in America in the nineties."¹³ The following year he did move to Europe with his mother and never again lived in the United States aside from short visits. Europe became his permanent home.

---

8   Ibid., 50.
9   Ibid., 154.
10 Ibid., 15.
11 Ibid., 45–46.
12 Ibid., 33.
13 Ibid., 25. Izaak Walton was an English writer in the seventeenth century. *The Compleat Angler*, the first edition of which came out in 1653, was his most famous book.

He went to a series of good schools in the country that he had loved from boyhood. First, he entered Harrow School in London in 1898, a public school where he spent four years. "I just barely managed to scrape through the entrance examination into the lowest form," he remembered later.[14] But he liked the institution, where education was of a much higher quality than at Milton. Although in his first semester he struggled and needed to adjust to the differences such as heavy emphasis on Latin and Greek, a special branch of football played there, and corporal punishment – he later found that though there were not many lectures, "they are all interesting, and thank heaven I am no more frenzied by mathematics."[15] In the course of four years he managed to climb the rungs, and spent most of his time reading. His efforts paid off when he won the Lord Charles Russell's Shakespeare Prize, both in Lower and Upper school.

The composition of the student body also taught him something about the British Commonwealth. He had expected to be around various squires' sons, but instead there were "princes from India and Siam, Egypt and Persia. There was the Sultan of Zanzibar, as black as one's hat and reputed to have a harem at home. There were Jews of all descriptions, ranging from the orthodox, ministered to in the 'Ghetto' by a Rabbi, through various shades of Christian converts, to those who were merely suspected of having a drop of Jewish blood. There were colonials, as they were called before the days of Dominions, including some Cape Dutch while the Boer War was actually being fought. Apart from these British subjects and feudatories, there were Greeks and a couple of Poles, Hungarians and Germans, but no Frenchmen. There were perhaps half-a-dozen Americans. All in all, a sizable percentage of Harrow's six hundred boys must have been non-British."[16] Looking back, he was happy with Harrow School: "I came out of my four years there with a thirst for learning, albeit of an unorthodox kind, and with glimmerings of an art that is of inestimable value in life: how to go one's ways while remaining on terms with the community one has to live in, and to discover some common ground with people whose favorite pursuits one may be determined to shun."[17]

---

14 Ibid., 33.
15 Royall Tyler to Mildred Barnes, October 29, 1902, New College, Oxford, "Bliss–Tyler Correspondence." https://www.doaks.org/resources/bliss-tyler-correspondence/1902-1908/29oct1902 accessed October 4, 2015.
16 Tyler, *One Name, Two Lives*, 45.
17 Ibid., 49.

Chapter 1

Through a friend of his mother's, the suggestion came that he should try to enter the Foreign Office. When his mother died, he was doubtful as to this Foreign Office career, but as a possible way of preparation, he decided to master French, German, and Spanish. His Majesty's Principal Secretary of State for Foreign Affairs Sir Eric Barrington gave him an interview and basically said he could not pursue such a career. "He told me plainly that the Foreign Office preferred young men as true as possible to the John Bull type, adding that he detected a trace of Yankee twang in my speech."[18]

He often spent Christmas and Easter holidays in Biarritz, France, with her mother and some friends of hers. There he had a glimpse into southern France and even neighboring northern Spanish regions, with occasional trips to Italy. This latter provided the stage for an important moment in 1900, on a family Easter vacation. In San Marco Basilica, in Venice, sixteen-year-old Royall experienced "a revelation comparable with that I had experienced on encountering the liturgy."[19] What he saw inside that church filled him with elation and a newly felt purpose that lasted for the rest of his life. "Domes, pendentives, marble wainscoting, porphyry columns, carved capitals, mosaic pavements and the light in which they bathed suddenly made me feel that these things were for me," and "I turned eagerly to Byzantine color and form."[20] The beauty he experienced among those walls made him a lifelong admirer or and later expert on Byzantine art.

He decided against spending a final year at Harrow and moved to New College, Oxford, for four semesters. It was not a happy and fulfilling period for the young American. The whole milieu and the subjects were not what he would have cared for. His intellect had been more or less gratified at Harrow but was "now starved, and when sober I was thoroughly dissatisfied with myself and my surroundings."[21] Not surprisingly, he moved on. His education took him to continental Europe, when at the age of nineteen, with his mother's consent, he travelled to France. A geological expedition into the Pyrenees made him fall in love with Spain, first with the Basque region, and the "effect of this experience on my health and spirits was almost miraculous."[22] Other

---

18   Ibid., 44.
19   Ibid., 55.
20   Ibid., 55.
21   Ibid., 60.
22   Ibid., 61.

trips to Spain followed immediately. The influence was so strong and irresistible for Tyler, that he decided to leave Oxford and enroll for a year in the Universidad de Salamanca. the University of Salamanca, learning Spanish and studying about Spain. This plan coincided with her mother's passing away in January 1904, and her second husband, his legal guardian until Tyler reached age twenty-one, did not question the wisdom of the Salamanca plan.

So, a new chapter in another country began for Tyler on his long educational path. His curiosity about old churches and the liveliness with which people frequented these places in Spain turned Tyler "into a passionate antiquary."[23] His earlier distaste for the deadened style of museums' exhibits suddenly disappeared, and he started to seek out every opportunity to study old art forms, and he "gulped down the heady Spanish atmosphere as a boy drinks champagne," and "sucked in Spain through every pore."[24] He particularly was enchanted by the Spanish people, for they possessed "self respect, tolerance (!) and courtesy that I have never seen elsewhere. It must have been civilized out of other peoples."[25] His feelings did not change years later, when he confirmed the above mentioned sentiments about Spain: "the Spaniards have more personal dignity than any nation I know ... they are the finest gentlemen in Europe."[26]

The University of Salamanca "formed a striking contrast with Oxford."[27] The students were less wealthy than those in England, the collegiate life was not centered around sports, and entertainment was restricted mainly to arguments about various subjects. Still, Tyler found that "the students were a vivacious lot, far less often bored than their contemporaries at Oxford."[28] He also welcomed the "free and unconstrained exchange between students and professors."[29] Almost as proof of this observation, at Salamanca he became close friends with the president of the university, the philosopher

---

23 Ibid., 64.
24 Ibid., 64, 61.
25 Royall Tyler to Mildred Barnes, January 5, 1904, Villa Aritzari, Biarritz, "Bliss–Tyler Correspondence," https://www.doaks.org/resources/bliss-tyler-correspondence/1902-1908/05jan1904, accessed October 5, 2015.
26 Royall Tyler to Mildred Barnes Bliss, April 12, 1910, Seville, "Bliss–Tyler Correspondence," https://www.doaks.org/resources/bliss-tyler-correspondence/1909-1919/12apr1910, accessed October 7, 2015.
27 Tyler, *One Name, Two Lives*, 69.
28 Ibid., 71.
29 Ibid.

Don Miguel de Unamuno, and with a few other people. Tyler felt almost at home there. At that time, he did not fully realize how important Spain was in shaping his character. But as he reflected on it more than a decade later, he believed it was for him "the discovery of a new world," mainly in the metaphysical sense.[30] With the carnage of World War I, Tyler was perhaps even more convinced than ever that Spain represented "a permanent and irreplaceable value for Europe."[31]

As a testament to Unamuno's role in his life, he wrote to him: "I am of a Spanish formation, you were my teacher, you sent me to other countries and you directed, albeit from a distance, my studies."[32] Unamuno's patience and the care with which he took Tyler under his intellectual wing had a lasting effect on the American. He felt he owed Unamuno "infinitely more than any other of the professors and distinguished professors that were in charge of my initiation into the spiritual life."[33] Tyler also believed the Spanish professor was responsible for giving him the chance "to glimpse the possibility of peace through inner discipline, finally accepting what I instinctively fled from as an adventurous and restless child—family duties and the like, etc."[34]

What made him relocate once again was a thirst for more knowledge. Although he loved Spain and could imagine living there a whole lifetime, he wanted to learn German and was not satisfied with the level of his French either. After a short visit back to America, he "took the plunge into the family of a retired Prussian Lieutenant-General, at Cassel. I chose Cassel because I had never heard of an English-speaking youth going there. A sobering experience after Salamanca!"[35]

"I don't like the Germans and don't believe I ever shall" was one of the first conclusions he drew about the people he encountered.[36] Although he came to the conclusion in Cassel that "the German system made for monot-

---

30 Royall Tyler to Miguel de Unamuno, February 21, 1918, in William Royall Tyler, "A Young American Friend of Miguel de Unamuno," in *Homenaje a Julian Marías* (Madrid: Espasa-Calpe, S.A., 1984), 732.
31 Ibid.
32 Ibid.
33 Ibid., 733.
34 Ibid. I want to thank Isaiah Romo for the translation of the letters.
35 Tyler, *One Name, Two Lives*, 79.
36 Royall Tyler to Mildred Barnes, November 1, 1904, Cassel, "Bliss–Tyler Correspondence," https://www.doaks.org/resources/bliss-tyler-correspondence/1902-1908/01nov1904, accessed October 5, 2015.

ony and boredom," he was nonetheless struck by their meticulous and systematic life as well as by their love of classical music.[37] Soon, however, he was complaining of the pervasive dullness he experienced: "I have discovered in the last four months that no one has any right to talk about being bored unless he has undergone the experience in Germany. It is not boredom alone. It is the impotent rage that the sight of so many Germans produces, and the everlasting effort to explain to one's self how the creatures came to write music or poetry."[38] This view that there were two Germanys seemed typical back in the United States as well, and up until the first year of World War I, it remained the prevailing sentiment.[39] Berlin made a much better impression on Tyler, with its air of relative freedom and as a stronghold of the arts, but of course the social hierarchy and the military caste was strikingly different to what Tyler's Anglo-Saxon mind was used to. In his overall observations, he found that "the German senses of discipline remained unimpaired," but in the realm of politics "Germany had no public opinion in the sense given to the term in the Western countries."[40]

After almost a year in Germany, and now fluent in both German and Spanish, he moved back to Paris in order to become truly proficient in French so that he could attempt the exam at the Foreign Office in London. In the fall of 1906 he enrolled in a two-year course on political philosophy at the École des Sciences Politiques in Paris. This soon paid dividends with respect to his thought processes, since a "living view of political trends throughout Europe began to take shape before my eyes."[41] After his experience in Germany, he was not wholly pleased with the French either. He found himself "so much out of temper with the French that I don't care to play with them."[42] However, what he found worse than either Germans or the French seems to have been the American tourists in Paris. He was anxious to avoid them, since these compatriots, if we can speak in such terms in Tyler's case,

---

37 Tyler, *One Name, Two Lives*, 82.
38 Royall Tyler to Mildred Barnes, February 16, 1905, Cassel, "Bliss–Tyler Correspondence," https://www.doaks.org/resources/bliss-tyler-correspondence/1902-1908/16feb1905, accessed October 6, 2015.
39 Michael S. Neiberg, *The Path to War. How the First World War Created Modern America* (Oxford: Oxford University Press, 2016), 9–18.
40 Tyler, *One Name, Two Lives*, 85.
41 Ibid., 92.
42 Royall Tyler to Mildred Barnes, February 20, 1906, Paris, "Bliss–Tyler Correspondence," https://www.doaks.org/resources/bliss-tyler-correspondence/1902-1908/20feb1906, accessed October 6, 2015.

Chapter 1

"take up my time and who bore me hideously, and have to be asked to tea, and who don't at all fit in with my Spanish things."[43]

No wonder, he felt he did not really belong to a certain place; he was more or less drifting between the cultures of Europe's countries and his sentiments about those cultures. At the age of twenty-two, he came to the sober conclusion that he had no home country. "I am an outcast, a *sans patrie* [stateless]—and as little or as much at home here or anywhere else as in London. It is a bad business, but something odd may come of it yet."[44] This perspective was not restricted to other cultures or peoples but was an overall trait in his personality: he preferred to shun people altogether. He did not like to be in the limelight, hated speaking in front of others, and did not make friends easily. "I can't be anything like intimate with a lot of people," he wrote once to Mildred Barnes, his lifelong friend. "I tried once, at Oxford, and it made me sicker than any other external circumstances ever have. I have always been so—from childhood, and good fellowship is hideous to me."[45] All this gave him forebodings about his future, and he was unsure if he was heading toward being a dismal failure in life.[46]

In the fall of 1906 he took an apartment in Paris, and although he may not have realized it at that time, he would reside in France for the rest of his life. He grew increasingly involved in the business of dealing in art and became well acquainted with the market. Due to his love of Byzantine art and his knowledge of it, others soon came to trust his judgment—occasional mistakes notwithstanding—but his only real profit was that he became fluent in French. His self-taught knowledge was acquired through reading, travel, and personal experience there, and the pieces he occasionally collected started to pay dividends in world of art dealers. His linguistic abilities and honest moral code made him a welcome member of the dealers' close circle, so he knew what was on the market and could be among the first to see precious pieces.

---

43 Royall Tyler to Mildred Barnes, April 11, 1906, Paris, "Bliss–Tyler Correspondence," https://www.doaks.org/resources/bliss-tyler-correspondence/1902-1908/11apr1906, accessed October 6, 2015.

44 Royall Tyler to Mildred Barnes, June 23, 1906, Paris, "Bliss–Tyler Correspondence," https://www.doaks.org/resources/bliss-tyler-correspondence/1902-1908/23jun1906, accessed October 6, 2015.

45 Royall Tyler to Mildred Barnes, November 12, 1906, Paris, "Bliss–Tyler Correspondence," https://www.doaks.org/resources/bliss-tyler-correspondence/1902-1908/12nov1906, accessed October 6, 2015.

46 Royall Tyler to Mildred Barnes, September 1, 1906, Seville, "Bliss–Tyler Correspondence," https://www.doaks.org/resources/bliss-tyler-correspondence/1902-1908/01sep1906, accessed October 6, 2015.

One of the most important persons in Royall Tyler's life was Mildred Barnes. It is not clear where and when they first met, but it is beyond doubt that by the time Tyler moved to Europe, a strong bond had been forged between the two. It is not wholly out of line to surmise that Tyler was in love with the somewhat older Barnes, and the profusion of letters he wrote to her throughout his life might well be a manifestation of suppressed romantic love. He was usually the initiator of the correspondence, even after Barnes' marriage in 1908 to Robert Bliss of the American Foreign Service. Bliss was also her stepbrother. Although the marriage might have put a stop to such a relationship between Tyler and Barnes, their friendship lasted for another 45 years, until Tyler's death. Robert Bliss also formed a friendship with Tyler, and often it was he who kept up the family correspondence with Tyler. The Tyler-Bliss correspondence is a trove of information about Tyler, his activities, and perhaps most importantly his thoughts and feelings about certain events and personalities. This epistolary connection helps us draw a more intimate portrait of Royall Tyler, and since the correspondence went on throughout his life, the letters help one follow Tyler's multidimensional career.[47]

After his mother's death, Tyler could rely on financial stability if not wealth, and he seems to have decided on following where his intellectual curiosity led him rather than building a traditional career. This path led to a book in 1909. His attraction to art and Spain, together with the self-education that he had pursued paid off when, somewhat by chance in 1908, he received an offer to write a book on Spain. He heartily accepted and chose not to finish his studies in Paris, although only a few months were left to complete them. This is again evidence of his somewhat capricious personality, impatience, and always present eagerness to learn more and do what his heart and soul dictated. In his own wry words later on, he described his younger self and years, writing, "Vagrancy has been my lot, and I am not sorry I did not draw another."[48] The book, *Spain: A Study of Her Life and Arts*, was written at the request of a London publisher, and it took up most of his time and energy, but it was a happy undertaking, and also a life-changing event from more than one perspective. Not only was the actual job of writing

---

47 Robert Nelson and James Carder transcribed all the letters, and they can be read as the Bliss–Tyler Correspondence site, https://www.doaks.org/resources/bliss-tyler-correspondence.
48 Tyler, *One Name, Two Lives*, 99.

it "one of the greatest experiences of my life," as he recalled years later, but also the book "had a very enthusiastic reception in England."[49]

The general praise the book received played a part in an offer from the Public Record Office of the British Home Office to Tyler to complete the Calendars of State Papers, the so-called Spanish series. The former editor had just died, and Tyler was selected to fill the sudden void.[50] As he chronicled the event: "I sent in my name without so much as hoping that they would give me the post. A couple of months ago they sent for me, and after an interview with the head of the department I received the appointment. It was a surprise, for I had no backing at all except a letter from Unamuno saying I knew Spanish well, and no references except my book."[51] What Tyler found most gratifying was that it was "really madly interesting work, and I am given absolute freedom."[52] After being selected, he plunged into the work, which took him to Vienna for several months in 1911, then to Paris and Simancas in Spain. In the latter town he spent weeks on end at the local archives. Having visited several archives, he did the actual writing in Paris, where his afternoons were spent with various art dealers. The finished work contrasted him positively with the former editor's, Hume's effort. Although the last volume Tyler edited would not be published in his lifetime, the reviewer's words are valid for the earlier Tyler volumes as well: "The contrast with the Elizabethan Calendar is striking. Not only was Martin Hume's search for documents defective: he did not know of the existence of dispatches actually in print when he compiled the Calendar. Neither criticism can be made of Royall Tyler."[53] It is easy to detect a note of pride on his part as well when recalling the work he had done: "In less than four years I had published three stout volumes," and he had collected enough material for

---

49 Ibid., 100; Royall Tyler to Mildred Barnes Bliss, April 12, 1910, Seville, "Bliss–Tyler Correspondence," https://www.doaks.org/resources/bliss-tyler-correspondence/1909-1919/12apr1910, accessed October 7, 2015. Later on, excerpts from this book were used as guidebooks promoting the various provinces in an effort to promote tourism in Spain. Eugenia Afinoguénova, "An Organic Nation: State-Run Tourism, Regionalism, and Food in Spain, 1905–1931," *The Journal of Modern History* 86/4 (December 2014), 763.
50 H. C. Maxwell Lyte to Royall Tyler, December 21, 1910, Thompson Todd Collection.
51 Royall Tyler to Mildred Barnes Bliss, March 5, 1911, Paris, "Bliss–Tyler Correspondence," https://www.doaks.org/resources/bliss-tyler-correspondence/1909-1919/05mar1911, accessed October 7, 2015.
52 Ibid.
53 J. E. Neale, "Calendar of State Papers Spanish. Vol. xiii, 1554–1558, by Royall Tyler," *English Historical Review* 72, no. 282 (January 1957): 113.

two more.⁵⁴ Although he was not well compensated for the work financially, from his personal point of view, it was profoundly gratifying. At the age of twenty-eight, he was starting to become somewhat of a well-known name in certain circles in London and elsewhere, although it was still not clear under what rubric he would really fit.

Spain: A Study of Her Life and Arts had something of an intriguing afterlife for Tyler in the form of his relationship with the wife of its publisher, a literally life-changing experience. Elisina Grant Richards was born Elisina Palamidessi de Castelvecchio in Florence, Italy, in 1875, although officially the date was given as 1878. Her mother, Joséphine Marie Suzette Juliette de Castelvecchio (1857–1932), was a grandniece of Napoleon III and was married to an Italian musician of great promise, whom she divorced at the age of twenty-four with four children in her care, Elisina being the eldest. Joséphine decided to move to England and tried to pursue an acting career, with mild success. Eventually, she moved to the United States, in 1898, and later became an American citizen. A highly intelligent and independent woman, Elisina was editor of *The Englishwoman*, a progressive art and sociopolitical periodical. She spoke all the major European languages and was highly engaged in everything she undertook. Her younger sister, Linetta, was a renowned Italian language and literary scholar in the interwar years.⁵⁵ After a short engagement, Elisina married Richards in 1898 and bore four children. The talented publisher was not a good business man, and he went bankrupt in 1906. Although Elisina did all she could to revive the business, Richards went bankrupt again.⁵⁶

Interestingly, or perhaps inevitably, shortly after Barnes married Bliss, Tyler fell in love with Elisina. Perhaps, after his tender feelings for Barnes had been rejected, the pent-up romance building up in him had to find an

---

54 Tyler, *One Name, Two Lives*, 101. Volume nine, his first, was published in 1912, volume ten in 1914, and volume eleven in 1916. Volume twelve did not appear until 1949, while the last volume edited by Tyler, volume thirteen, was published posthumously in 1954.

55 "Linetta Richardson," *University of Birmingham Gazette*, 1977, in William R. Tyler, *The Castelvecchio Family*, Form. and suppl. Royall Tyler (New South Wales, Australia, 2014), 214–19. On the official papers, Elisina's birth date appears as March 18, 1878 – she lied about her age. On Elisina, also see, James N. Carder, "Brussels, Buenos Aires, and Paris (1909–1919)" in Robert S. Nelson and James N. Carder, "Bliss–Tyler Correspondence. An annotated transcription of the correspondence between Mildred Barnes Bliss, Robert Woods Bliss, Royall Tyler, and Elisina Tyler between 1902 and 1953." https://www.doaks.org/resources/bliss-tyler-correspondence/1909-1919, accessed June 14, 2015.

56 William R. Tyler, *The Castelvecchio Family*, 205.

outlet. Naturally, he may simply have fallen in love regardless of what had happened with Barnes. But the proximity of the two events suggests that disillusionment with one love paved the way for quickly finding another outlet for his deep feelings of longing. Tyler and Elisina seemingly hit it off right away, despite the fact that she was nine years his senior. Eventually, in 1909, she left the four children with her husband and secured a divorce from him in 1914. She married Tyler in the fall of that year. In their separate letters to Mildred Barnes the couple confessed their true feelings about one another. Tyler believed that "the hardest of things are possible with her," while Elisina admitted that her "life was all wrong before I met Royall, and is all right now."[57] In hindsight, they seem to have made the right decision: they spent more than four decades together. Their child, William Royall Tyler, was born in the fall of 1910, right after the couple's romance began and four years before they could legally be married; Mildred Barnes became his godmother. At first, Tyler and Elisina lived in Paris, although naturally they spent some time in Italy and Spain. Then, before World War I broke out, they first saw their "dream-house," Antigny-le-Château, but the couple would only acquire the property ten years later, in 1923.[58]

Tyler's education—in the broad sense of the word—had already been rich when he married and became a father. Sometime in the 1940s Royall Tyler undertook to write an autobiography. Unfortunately, the date of this cannot be stated beyond doubt. Although he received a request for an autobiography in 1947 to which he responded positively, still there is strong circumstantial evidence that the surviving manuscript was penned in 1942, but possibly rewritten later (perhaps in 1947), before typed out in the form available today.[59] It is not clear why he started to write it in the first place, but with the help of this writing, one can get a certain amount of insight into Tyler's personality. Unfortunately, the autobiography records his life and adventures only up until 1910, still, it opens up the past and one can gain insight into

---

57 Royall Tyler to Mildred Barnes Bliss, June 10, 1910, Cauterets, France, and Elisina Tyler to Mildred Barnes Bliss, August 20, 1910, Bourron France, in "Bliss–Tyler Correspondence," https://www.doaks.org/resources/bliss-tyler-correspondence/1909-1919/10jun1910, and https://www.doaks.org/resources/bliss-tyler-correspondence/1909-1919/20aug1910, accessed October 7, 2015.
58 Elisina Tyler to Mildred Barnes Bliss, December 1, 1913, Paris, "Bliss–Tyler Correspondence," https://www.doaks.org/resources/bliss-tyler-correspondence/1909-1919/01dec1913, accessed October 7, 2015.
59 Simon Michael Bessie to Royall Tyler, January 22, 1947, and February 10, 1947, Thompson Todd Collection, Tharwa, Australia; Tyler, *One Name, Two Lives*, 7–8.

the early years of Tyler's life, which played an important role in his later years as well. It is also instructive that in his writing Tyler did not delve into his memories after his marriage with Elisina. This would be too speculative as to why but it is perhaps an indication of how difficult he may have found to grapple with so personal a topic.

In his autobiography Tyler mentions that, at the age of six or seven, he had his first dose of Central European culture in the form of music and language. We do not know whether his mother, who arrived in the United States in 1870, used her native language at home, but he did have some musical upbringing and was attuned to music. He heard Hungarian gypsies play while on a visit to Newport as a child, and it had a lasting impression on him: "The echo of those fiddles and that cymbalom [sic] has never faded from my ears, nor have I ever forgotten how, when the Gypsies were not playing, I stole up near them, drank in the deep accents in which they spoke, and marveled at the slow rhythm of their movements when they rose from their chairs or sat down, so unlike the jerky gestures of Yankeedom."[60]

He was also drawn to history early on. First it manifested mainly as an interest in hearing stories of colonial and early nineteenth-century events from the older generation, but Tyler grew more interested in the palpable version of history, and in hindsight it is not surprising that art history became his calling, where he could take the objects of history in hand. "Apart from outdoor pursuits and reading," he recalled, "the only occupation that appealed to me was writing. I filled many notebooks with my observations of birds, of old buildings, pre-revolutionary tomb-stones, sites where Indian arrow-heads were found, and even with little essays and doggerel. Stories I cannot remember attempting. There was always something or other to record."[61]

Although he did not become a graphomaniac, Tyler wrote profusely throughout his life, either in private letters or in official notes and reports. Religion was always a subject of the young boy's curiosity. In New England, his mother's strict following of Christian Science often made him wonder, and his slight exposure to Catholicism awoke his interest in that denomination. Eventually, Roman Catholicism appealed to him more and more, and in Paris in 1902 he converted, together with his lifelong friend, Mildred Barnes.

---

60 Tyler, *One Name, Two Lives*, 20.
61 Ibid., 32.

Chapter 1

Tyler had mixed feelings about his home country. Not long after moving to Europe, he confessed that "I don't believe in American moral breadth, and I don't like Americans."[62] The comparison was especially sharp with England: "And I do love England. I can't forget how intolerant everyone was to me in America and how kind in England."[63] Although he toyed with the idea of taking British citizenship after reaching adulthood, he soon had second thoughts and retained his American one. This ambivalent feeling about his birth country remained with him for a long time, and changed somewhat only with World War I. But his European centeredness endured and became the vantage point from which he observed the old continent that was being reshaped in those years and remained turbulent as a consequence for the rest of his life.

Throughout the years, Tyler's erudition concerning art grew. Next to Byzantine art, his unrivaled favorite, he also acquired a deep knowledge of Persian and Spanish pottery and French medieval sculpture. His knowledge guided the Blisses in creating their collection. Mildred Barnes inherited a fortune before the war, and the already well-off couple became quite wealthy and could devote their time, energy, and money to collecting valuable art. Or, it would be more correct to say, art that Royall Tyler believed to be valuable, since he was their point man in the art world. As one researcher wrote, "Tyler's influence on the Blisses' taste in art and on their collecting preferences in this period is nothing less than remarkable, and he was instrumental in formulating the Blisses' collecting interests for the remainder of their lives."[64] Tyler not only knew art dealers but also made friends with prominent museum curators whom he judged experts in the field, and who also helped him in various ways over the years. With Tyler's intimate knowledge of many fields in art, the Blisses sought Tyler's help not only to find quality art works but to judge their authenticity, help he was eager to provide. Later, Tyler expanded his expertise to include Gothic sculpture and Chinese ceramics. His knowledge, which was really a passion, was of great

---

62 Royall Tyler to Mildred Barnes, August 19, 1903, Dinard, France, "Bliss–Tyler Correspondence," https://www.doaks.org/resources/bliss-tyler-correspondence/1902-1908/19aug1903, accessed October 4, 2015.
63 Ibid.
64 James N. Carder, "Brussels, Buenos Aires, and Paris (1909–1919)" in Robert S. Nelson and James N. Carder, "Bliss–Tyler Correspondence. An annotated transcription of the correspondence between Mildred Barnes Bliss, Robert Woods Bliss, Royall Tyler, and Elisina Tyler between 1902 and 1953," https://www.doaks.org/resources/bliss-tyler-correspondence/1909-1919, accessed June 14, 2015.

service to the Blisses, and the well-known Bliss Collection at Dumbarton Oaks bears Tyler's imprint.

So, on the eve of World War I, by the age of thirty, Royall Tyler had gained a lot of knowledge and experience on the European continent, had married and become a father, and yet still did not possess a clear idea as to what his future line of work might be. World War I and its aftermath would inevitably play a significant role in shaping his views and opportunities.

CHAPTER 2

World War I, Peacemaking, and the New Europe

When the United States stepped into the international arena around the turn of the century, the main geopolitical aim was to strengthen its positions in Latin America and Asia, especially in the Philippines and China, but Europe was a taboo. Not only was a long-time American political aversion toward Europe and European political institutions palpable, but also, in the military field the traditional European powers represented so much might that it was made impossible for America to think of meddling in any European affairs. The United States was satisfied to have millions of European immigrants—many of whom caused internal frictions among Americans—but the country wished to do nothing when it came to Europe and its political entanglements. When the Great War started soon after Archduke Franz Ferdinand was assassinated and the Austro-Hungarian Empire declared war on Serbia, closely followed by Germany's declaration of war on Russia and France, the United States unsurprisingly chose to stay away from what was seen as a European war, and, accordingly, President Woodrow Wilson was quick to reinforce traditional neutrality. He called on Americans to be "neutral in fact as well as in name" and "impartial in thought as well as in action."[1]

However, the war offered a unique opening for American exports to Europe and for various loans that later would put virtually all the major European countries in debt to the United States. For a long time, despite occasional German atrocities against neutral American ships or American passen-

---

[1] Congressional Record, 63rd Congress, 2nd Session, 14042, August 20, 1914.

Chapter 2

gers on other's ships, the American government remained officially neutral. Of course, the majority of the loans and material going to Great Britain and France questioned true neutrality. The Wilson campaign slogan in the elections of 1916 was "He kept us out of war," and his subsequent victory at the polls well summarized the overall attitude within the United States. Only a small minority in the northeast wanted to see the United States join the war against Germany. However, the trampling of the rights of neutral countries, increasing American casualties as a result of more and more reckless German submarine warfare on the high seas, the Zimmerman telegram that brought national security questions to the table, the financial commitment, and, last but not least, the desire on Wilson's part to shape the postwar world all led to the American war declaration on April 6, 1917. To emphasize the difference of American aims and posture to the European fighting partners, or Allies, the United States became only an Associated Power to the Entente Powers.

When World War I broke out, the Tylers were in France. Then in October they moved to London, where Tyler had an engagement with historical documents (the Spanish series). They returned to Paris in 1915, and both became busy with work. Tyler found it imperative to earn some money given the circumstances. Despite his yearly allowance, he almost constantly worried about his, and now their, financial situation. Initially, he wanted to provide a decent life to Elisina, then with the birth of their son in 1910, to provide for his family. Being short on funds seems to have been one of his great fears throughout his career. In his younger years he had led an affluent life, and getting accustomed to more constrained circumstances was sometimes harsh. Throughout his life, he often voiced his pecuniary worries, indicating that it was a frequent fear.

For her part, Elisina became involved in American novelist Edith Wharton's widespread charity program that tried to provide work for unemployed women, later for refugees, at several hostels throughout France. Elisina was asked to serve as vice president of the organization in the fall of 1915. Wharton also founded the Children of Flanders Rescue Committee in 1915, of which Elisina served as director. In recognition for their refugee work, in the course of which they managed to raise more than 9 million French francs, both women received the Medal of Queen Elisabeth from the Belgian government in September 1918. They were also both awarded the Legion d'Honneur, and, in a report read before the French Academy by

Raymond Poincaré on November 25, 1920, the two were jointly awarded the gold medal of *Le Prix de Vertu*.[2]

The Tylers often rented a chateau in Burgundy during the war years—Antigny-le-Château. "I am living a real country life," wrote Tyler, "swimming, fishing walking and now and then reveling with Monsieur le Curé, as fine a specimen of Burgundian priesthood as one could wish to see."[3] Meanwhile, one of Elisina's three sons from her earlier marriage, Gerard, died in an accident in 1916, an event that placed her under considerable stress, and she needed to take extended rests and cures.

Unfortunately, the informative letters between Tyler and Mildred Barnes came to a virtual standstill between mid-1917 and 1920, so it is hard to know exactly what and how Tyler did during that time. From the beginning of the war, Royall Tyler wanted to serve in some useful capacity, and with the United States' entry in April 1917, he soon joined the army. He was commissioned as lieutenant, and by the end of the war he had risen to the rank of major. His language skills came to the forefront once more, and he was tasked with interrogating prisoners of war.

One gain that occurred in the war years was his rediscovered love, or at least appreciation, for his country of birth. "The life that I have now, the military life that I would never have been able to imagine, has its rewards," he wrote to his old professor in Spain. "Above all else, I who always felt somewhat strange and uncomfortable with my contemporaries of the Anglo-Saxon race, now love and appreciate them, and this has taken a weight off my heart."[4] The last part of the sentence clearly shows the inner dilemma and anguish that he must have felt on account of being an American but not really belonging to that nation.

Tyler worked during the war as an intelligence officer in the G-2 section of the U.S. Army. His main task was to provide information on various issues concerning the war effort and the war situation. In the spring of 1918, once again thanks to his language skills, Tyler became to head the Inter-Allied Bureau, a group sharing information among the Allied and

---

2   William R. Tyler, *The Castelvecchio Family*, 206.
3   Royall Tyler to Mildred Barnes Bliss, April 29, 1916, Seville, "Bliss–Tyler Correspondence," https://www.doaks.org/resources/bliss-tyler-correspondence/1909-1919/29aug1916, accessed October 9, 2015.
4   Royall Tyler to Miguel de Unamuno, February 21, 1918, in William Royall Tyler, "A Young American Friend of Miguel de Unamuno," 732. I want to thank Isaiah Romo for the translation of the letter.

Chapter 2

Associated Powers. Information was exchanged on economic issues regarding the enemy's strength, also trying to ferret out suspected spies, or assessing public opinion in Germany and France. Various documents regarding such issues filled his daily reports and were forwarded to the headquarters of the Intelligence Section in Paris. The workload was immense, and there was a grave need for more American officers with language skills, first and foremost in French and German. It fell to Tyler to examine the candidates, and a good indicator that American intelligence work at that time was in its infancy is that he found about two-thirds of the possible recruits to be unqualified. Important information had to travel fast, and Tyler sent any that came into his possession through a special and expedited system of delivery.[5] Crucially, while doing this work he met Hayford Peirce, who would become his collaborator on works dealing with Byzantine art for the better part of the next three decades.[6]

In November 1918 the Great War came to an end, leaving unprecedented carnage in its wake, and the most significant and urgent task was to create a lasting peace that would thwart any similar such devastation. The United States, and Woodrow Wilson personally, came to the peace talks with an agenda that he had formulated earlier, in his famous Fourteen Points of January 8, 1918. It was based on free trade, open diplomacy, democracy in general, and national self-determination in creating new and restructuring older countries. The pragmatic, or cynical, European heads of states applied these goals only tepidly, and, as a consequence, the idealistic aims of this Wilsonian program were never fully implemented. Since Wilson's dream was to establish the League of Nations—a new international body to be responsible for keeping the peace and ensuring international cooperation—the Europeans gave him that in exchange for settling many other questions primarily according to their own taste. At first the American president was adamant that his way should prevail, but in the end, the League of Nations proved to be of more significance to him than some of his earlier-declared principles. As a result, issues concerning how to draw the borders, how to

---

5   Source for this paragraph: Noah J. Delwiche, "Major Royall Tyler and Military Intelligence during the Great War," in "Bliss–Tyler Correspondence, https://www.doaks.org/resources/bliss-tyler-correspondence/major-royall-tyler-and-military-intelligence-during-the-great-war-1, accessed June 14, 2015.

6   James N. Carder, "Brussels, Buenos Aires, and Paris (1909–1919)," in "Bliss–Tyler Correspondence, https://www.doaks.org/resources/bliss-tyler-correspondence/1909-1919, accessed June 14, 2015.

implement national self-determination, or how to ensure minority protection were often settled according to various interests and not in line with Wilson's lofty aims. Wilson exchanged his hard currency of high moralism to European selfishness and game of hard interest.

Although the Europeans managed to have their interests prevail in many cases during the Peace Conference, they were not actually responsible for thwarting Wilson's aims regarding the peace. In the United States the general attitude was to stay away from Europe and out of its problems. Under the leadership of Henry Cabot Lodge, the Republicans, who became the majority party in the Senate in the 1918 midterm elections, made sure that the Senate did not ratify the Versailles Peace Treaty. The Republican antagonism stemmed in part from Wilson's political blunder of including no prominent Republicans in the American delegation to Paris, because he wanted the glory of peacemaking to be attributed himself and the Democratic Party. Also, the antagonists of Wilson chose to interpret the League Covenant in a way that implied a danger of American involvement in European conflicts in the future. The Republicans simply took revenge and did not vote for ratification of the Peace Treaty. As a result, the United States did not become party to the European postwar world, to reconstruction, and, first and foremost, to the League of Nations.

Despite Wilson's appeal that "every territorial settlement involved in this war must be made in the interest and for the benefit of the populations concerned, and not as a part of any mere adjustment or compromise of claims amongst rival states," in the final outcome the peace settlement provided the basis for creating new states among those that had been fighting on the side of the Allies and to punish the defeated parties, rather than establish peace and harmony to everyone's benefit.[7] Wilson's rigidity and self-acclaimed status as a world savoir alienated many within his political base and his administration as well. For example, Secretary of State Robert Lansing did not agree with many of Wilson's sweeping ideals, and in the diary he kept during the Peace Conference he wrote, for example, concerning the notion of national self-determination: "The phrase is simply loaded with dynamite. It will raise hopes which can never be realized. It will, I fear, cost thousands of lives. In the end it is bound to be discredited, to be called

---

7   Congressional Record, 65th Congress, 2nd Session, 1937, February 11, 1918.

the dream of an idealist who failed to realize the danger until too late to check those who attempt to put the principle in force. What a calamity that the phrase was ever uttered! What misery it will cause!"[8] Although Lansing may have been motivated to write the book in which this excerpt appears because he had fallen out of favor with Wilson, this fact does not diminish his keen observation.

The American press played its role in whipping up anti-treaty sentiment. William Randolph Hearst helped create and maintain an atmosphere inimical to the United States joining the League of Nations, and his considerable readership agreed with the fear he expressed that war might come to America precisely because of League membership: "I do not consider it a league to keep us out of war but a league to get us into war," he wrote. "A man does not keep himself free from the small pox by going to bed with four other people who have it; and we cannot keep free from war by tying ourselves up with nations like England, France, Italy and Japan, which have the war disease in its worst form."[9] It seemed that aside from an East Coast globalist elite, as one would call them now, the overall sentiment in public opinion and political circles was against joining the League of Nations. Right from its inception, as a key figure in of the organization later recalled, the League was facing a "grave handicap" because "America's abstention changed fundamentally the League's ability to enforce its policy."[10]

By the end of the war, Tyler held the rank of major in the army intelligence establishment, and the United States, which was preparing for the Peace Conference, could not afford to dispense with skills such as his.[11] Accordingly, in late 1918, Tyler, together with Peirce, became members of the American Commission to Negotiate Peace, and he gained immense experience in international diplomacy and its related subjects. He also proved to be a very efficient organizer.

---

8   Lansing's diary entry, December 30, 1918, in Robert Lansing, *The Peace Negotiations: A Personal Narrative* (New York: Houghton Mifflin, 1921), 97–98.
9   William Randolph Hearst to Harry Hay Tammen, March 29, 1919, quoted in David Nasaw, *The Chief. The Life of William Randolph Hearst* (Boston and New York: Houghton Mifflin Company, 2000), 271.
10 Arthur Salter, *Security. Can We Retrieve it?* (London: MacMillan and Co., Ltd, 1939), 139, 145.
11 His proper status was "field observer." American Commission to Negotiate Peace, *Composition and Functions*, Paris, May 1, 1919. Box 75, Folder 39, Pamphlets for the American Commission to Negotiate Peace: miscellaneous information, Charles Seymour Papers, Manuscript and Archives, Yale University Library (hereafter Yale Archives).

In the turbulent preparatory days of the Paris Peace Conference, the American groups were disorganized and did not function well. In the confusion at the Hotel Crillon, headquarters of the American delegation to the Peace Conference, the success of the effort to lay the groundwork for the January start of the conference with Woodrow Wilson and other prominent Americans attending sometimes seemed uncertain. Tyler gradually took over the job of organizing the intelligence service and soon "established order" and "was achieving headway" concerning the various field parties.[12] This was the first time he had worked together with Allen Dulles (later the first civilian director of the CIA) on gathering and furthering intelligence—sent at that time to Joseph Grew, the secretary of the American delegation, and to Commissioners Frank Lyon Polk, Tasker Howard Bliss, Robert Lansing, and Henry White.[13]

As head of the intelligence section, important news regularly reached Tyler first, so that he could synthetize and forward such information, in whatever abbreviated form he deemed necessary. For instance, when the communist takeover in Hungary took place on March 21, 1919, the news reached Tyler the very next day, and he passed it on up the chain. The news came to him from Nicholas Roosevelt, who at that time was staying in Budapest as a member of the Coolidge Mission, which was entrusted with gathering information in Central Europe. The conclusion of Roosevelt's message to Tyler boded ill for the already contentious and problematic peace conference: "General impression that nationalists have resorted to Bolshevism in hopes of being able to preserve integrity of country. Public opinion apparently favors armed aggression towards neighbors."[14] In the end, the Hungarian situation and the Bolshevik threat, both perceived and imagined, decided Hungary's already bad fate with respect to the outcome of the Peace Conference: among the losing parties, Hungary was punished the most severely. Despite observations from UK Prime Minister Lloyd George to the effect that the Little Entente countries, especially the Romanians and

---

12 Nicholas Roosevelt, *A History of a Few Weeks. Being an Account of Experience in Austria and Hungary during the Armistice*, Box 18, Nicholas Roosevelt Papers, Special Collections Research Center at Syracuse University Libraries, USA, 6, 32.
13 Allen W. Dulles to Archibald C. Coolidge, March 1, 1919, Box 5, Folder 254, Dulles, Allen (1919–1920, 1922, 1934, 1936–1938, 1940, 1956), Charles Seymour Papers, Yale Archives.
14 Nicholas Roosevelt to Royall Tyler, Fiume, March 23, 1919, in Arthur S. Link, ed., *The Papers of Woodrow Wilson*, vol. 56 (Princeton, NJ: Princeton University Press, 1987), 241.

the Czechoslovaks, were "all little brigand peoples who only want to steal territories," the final peace treaties favored them almost exclusively.[15] The proclaimed national self-determination was to be understood as helping the Allies' partners to determine their territories, and the defeated countries were left to wonder if Wilson's high-minded notions had any meaning at all.

Tyler was only a small cog in a sometimes grinding machine that often showed signs of impotence and childish bickering. A few months after the Conference, Major Tyler was at the Military Information Division, in charge of the military personnel. Tyler was also the sieve through which intelligence reports on Germany went on to the higher echelons, and he acted as the American representative on the Liaison Commission with the German delegation.[16] Similarly to Hungary, Germany was also severely punished, but in its case not only with regard to territory but also the maiming reparation was to play a major and devastating part.

When the Versailles Peace Treaty was signed in June 1919, many things were still not settled. There was, for instance, the question of the peace treaties of the smaller enemy states: Austria, Hungary, Bulgaria, and Turkey. It was obvious that those treaties would resemble the one just concluded with Germany, but the measure of punishment—both territorial and financial—was at that time not wholly decided. Also, nobody was certain whether the United States would become and official party to the treaty. Although Woodrow Wilson was an architect of the peace, the results of the 1918 midterm elections did not augur well for the ratification debate that lay ahead. The League of Nations appeared the only stable point, but there were many lingering questions even regarding that organization of collective action and security in order to maintain the peace. For one thing, it was far from clear which countries could or could not be members. Would the United States join? Would the international pariah Soviet Russia be allowed to join? How about Germany? If these countries stayed outside the League of Nations, the international body would face an uphill battle. In the end, of course, the above mentioned three large powers stayed outside the League.[17] As a result, the League was not able to

---

15 Mantoux's Notes of a Meeting of the Council of Four, June 9, 1919, in Link, *The Papers of Woodrow Wilson*, vol. 60, 314.
16 Robert Lansing to Woodrow Wilson, Paris, June 5, 1919, in Link, *The Papers of Woodrow Wilson*, vol. 60, 178.
17 Germany was a member from 1926 to 1933, while the Soviet Union gained membership in 1934 but was expelled in 1939.

carry out a hoped-for global agenda and instead focused mostly on Europe. Also, the smaller European countries would have liked to see the United States in European politics because, based upon their experience, they feared the traditional big powers and their biased politics that was so well known to them. The defeated countries especially looked with hope to possible American participation in Europe's political life, and those nations were perhaps the most disappointed when finally they had to realize that the overseas power would remain outside the League and outside European politics.

The largest question in European–American relations focused on the debts that had accumulated throughout the war. The staggering amount that the Allies, mainly Great Britain and France, owed to the United States was about $10 billion.[18] The European countries, in the wake of the devastating war, were not in a situation to repay such a sum, and to complicate things further, there was a high intra-allied debt as well: Britain often passed on loans to France and other countries, and believably claimed that until it was paid back, it could not satisfy its debt to the United States. Both on practical and moral grounds—there being not enough cash and having fought and sacrificed so many lives partly for American values and security—the Allies wanted America to cancel the debts, or accept the fact that substantial reparations needed to be collected from Germany. Only once they were endowed with those sums would the debtor countries be able to repay their respective debts.

The subject of German reparations was the center of attention for a number of years in contemporary Europe—and in certain circles in the United States as well. Reparations were not only to provide enough money to repay the United States, as was often proclaimed, but also such a scheme had a security dimension: it would ensure that Germany would be kept on its back for a long time to come, and thereby ensure that it could not start a war of revenge. The United States argued that the debt question had nothing to do with reparations: the first was a business transaction, while the latter a politically

---

18   George Soule, *Prosperity Decade. A Chapter from American Economic History, 1917–1929* (London: The Pilot Press Limited, 1947), 255; Cleona Lewis, *America's Stake in International Investments* (Washington, D. C.: The Brookings Institution, 1938), 447; Howard H. Quint and Robert H. Ferrel, eds., *The Talkative President. The Off-the-Record Press Conferences of Calvin Coolidge* (Amherst, MA: The University of Massachusetts Press, 1964), 175. The value of the U.S. dollar went through little change in the 1920s after World War I. At the time of this writing (2020) an average dollar of that era would be worth approximately $17, counting only inflation. With other aspects involved and computed, it would be much more.

motivated punitive measure. Although it was clear that the two issues were closely related, and one could not possibly be realized without the other, the successive American governments were adamant in their refusal to negotiate reparations and debts along the same line. President Calvin Coolidge, in his trademark style, expressed the official American point of view succinctly and unambiguously: "They hired the money, didn't they?"[19] In prominent U.S. banker Thomas Lamont's opinion, "reparations caused more trouble, contention, hard feeling, and delay at the Peace Conference than any other point of the Treaty of Versailles."[20] In the end, as a substitute for a real solution, Congress created the World War Foreign Debt Commission in early 1922, which negotiated debt settlements with debtor countries with a view to a given country's ability to pay.

A Reparations Commission was called into being by the League of Nations to deal with that intricate problem. It was the responsible body regarding the amount and pace of payments coming from Germany and other countries punished by the imposition of reparations. Representatives of nine countries made up the Commission, and they followed the strict political agendas of their various governments. This did not augur well for reaching easy settlements. As a contemporary British diplomat noted, "instead therefore of becoming, as had been intended, an impartial, judicial and independent body, the Reparations Commission became a body sensitive to French political pressure."[21]

Since the United States did not become a party to the Versailles Peace Treaty, consequently it was not a member either of the League of Nations or its Reparations Commission. However, despite all the official rhetoric and the general sentiment of the American populace, the U.S. government always wanted to know as much as possible about the unfolding events in Europe, many of which now fell under the aegis of the League. As a consequence, an unofficial American representative was appointed to the Reparations Commission accompanied by a small delegation. Albert Rathbone was the first appointee, followed by Roland Boyden. The latter saw his job as

---

19 It cannot be proven whether Coolidge really uttered such a sentence. His wife said it sounded like her husband, and a member of the president's press team believed it did happen, but it appears nowhere in the transcripts or any other source. Quint and Ferrel, *The Talkative President*, 176.
20 Kenneth Paul Jones, ed., *U.S. Diplomats in Europe, 1919–1941* (Santa Barbara, CA: ABC-Clio, 1983), 43.
21 Harold Nicolson, *Curzon: The Last Phase* (London: Constable & Co., 1934), 219.

being practically the same as that of the official European representatives.[22] Although President Coolidge, who succeeded President Warren G. Harding upon the latter's death in 1923, may have spoken for the large majority of Americans in declaring that the United States was "better off out of the League," successive American governments closely followed what was taking place at Geneva.[23] Charles Evans Hughes, Secretary of State under both Harding and Coolidge, defined the status of the various Americans delegated to the League of Nations as "official representatives acting in an unofficial capacity."[24] The American ambassador to Switzerland was also entrusted with the task of collecting material on and about the League and maintaining the possible best relations with other countries' League representatives, but he was to carry out such a task in the most concealed way.[25]

These were the circumstances under which, in 1920, Royall Tyler was appointed to sit on the U.S. delegation of the Reparations Commission in the League of Nations. We do not know much about his work in that body, but if later years and events are an indicator, he unquestionably made himself useful and was liked by many in the League. In the end, Tyler spent four years representing the United States on the Commission. As he summarized those years, "as Establishment Officer of the post-World-War I Reparations Commission in Paris, I had to examine hundreds of young men of various nationalities, to allot them to various jobs and closely follow their performances."[26] This was an important continuation of his war service, and this gave a more substantial meaning to his life. In reality, one might be tempted to say that service for an ideal greater good was necessary to give a framework to Tyler's meandering life. Was it age and increasing maturity, or simply dissatisfaction with what he had achieved in the first three decades of his life that led him on that path? It is hard to say, but in all likelihood it was both. Despite himself, Tyler came to embody, to an extent, American foreign policy in Europe. He was one of those American citizens who toiled in

---

22 *In Memory of Roland William Boyden* (Boston: Commonwealth of Massachusetts, 1933), 10.
23 Calvin Coolidge, *The Autobiography of Calvin Coolidge* (New York: Cosmopolitan Book Corporation, 1929), 150.
24 Clarence A. Berdahl, "The United States and the League of Nations," *Michigan Law Review* 27/6 (April 1929): 629.
25 Waldo H. Heinrichs, *American Ambassador. Joseph C. Grew and the Development of the United States Diplomatic Tradition* (Boston and Toronto: Little Brown and Company, 1966), 52–53.
26 Tyler, *One Name, Two Lives*, 41.

a private capacity to preserve a semblance of the Wilsonian dream when, for domestic reasons, the United States refused to undertake such a role.

The first post-war steps toward an appearance of large-scale cooperation with a view to reconstructing much of the continent were taken in 1920. It was a multidimensional effort. On the one hand, there were major gatherings of various heads of state to discuss a possible solution to Europe's acute financial and economic problems. Many countries, and Central Europe in particular, lay in ruins, and without outside assistance they had little hope of regaining financial and economic health. The first such undertaking was the Brussels Conference held in the fall of 1920. This meeting of thirty-nine states, including defeated countries like Germany, Austria, and Hungary, sorely missed the United States, which was represented only in an unofficial capacity because the conference was convened by the League of Nations.[27] (Unofficial representation concerning European issues was the American custom in these years.[28]) Even worse, the reparation issue, although it was discussed, was raised too early for meaningful debate, because at that time no nation was ready to give up its claims. Still, the gathering was not held in vain. It laid down some of the most important principles that would guide the European reconstruction schemes in the interwar years. As the ter Meulen Plan, named after Dutch banker Carel Eliza ter Meulen, argued, the affected countries needed: budget equilibrium, a halt to inflation, setting up a central bank of issue, and providing external credits in the form of bonds to be secured out of the revenues of the assigned assets.[29] This was a forerunner of the plan that would later become known as the League reconstruction loans throughout Central, Eastern, and Southern Europe. Soon the League of Nations created its Financial Committee and Economic Committee, each consisting of impartial advisers, a major difference to the Reparations Commission with its various state representatives and their pronounced political interests. The way was paved for financial reconstruction as far as the League of Nations was concerned.

---

27 For the correspondence concerning the Brussels Conference, the League invitation, and the U.S. refusal to it, see Foreign Relations of the United States (hereafter cited as FRUS), vol. 1 (Washington, D.C.: U.S. Government Printing Office, 1920), 88–107.
28 This task fell to Roland Boyden, the American unofficial representative on the Reparations Commission. FRUS, vol. 1, 1920, 95–96.
29 League of Nations, *The League of Nations Reconstruction Schemes in the Inter-war Period* (Geneva, 1944), 8. On the Brussels Conference also see, Patricia Clavin, *Securing the World Economy: The Reinvention of the League of Nations, 1920–1946* (Oxford: Oxford University Press, 2013), 17–22.

The next momentous meeting was held at Genoa, Italy, in April and May 1922.[30] In sharp contrast to the Brussels Conference, the Soviet Union was invited—and when it eagerly accepted the opportunity, the number of participant countries reached thirty-four. Although, in Lloyd George's propagandistic terminology, all these countries were there and took part in the meetings on "equal terms," the traditional big countries played the main role, in part because they wanted to settle their arguments with the Soviets.[31] The smaller nations were, in practice, relegated to being spectators only. The beginning looked promising, however, and, being a continuation of the Brussels Conference, expectations were high, and such issues as foreign loans for reconstruction efforts and central banks' roles were also on the agenda.[32] The Soviet Union's presence offered an opportunity to discuss debts and reparations, and the Russian issue was deemed very important by Great Britain and France. Since this question received disproportionate emphasis, with the political underpinnings—a gently euphemistic term for debts and reparations—that it was to create, the United States chose to be officially absent one more time.[33] The U.S. government allowed only James Addison Logan, assistant U.S. unofficial delegate to the Reparations Commission, and the new ambassador to Italy, Richard W. Child, to attend in the now-well-known, strictly unofficial capacity and then inform Washington about the outcomes.[34] Actually, the somewhat selfish attitude on the part of Britain and France led to the creation during the conference of the separate Rapallo Treaty between Germany and the Soviet Union.[35]

Even if it did not meet expectations, the Genoa Conference managed to pass a series of resolutions regarding financial, economic, and trade issues,

---

30 For more detail on the antecedents of the conference, the political strife among the chief players, and the postponement of the most vital issues, see Carole Fink, *The Genoa Conference: European Diplomacy, 1921–1922* (Chapel Hill: University of North Carolina Press, 1984), 3–142.
31 Minutes of the First Plenary Session of the Genoa Conference, held at the Palazzo San Giorgio, April 10, 1922, at 3 p. m., Documents on British Foreign Policy (hereafter cited as DBFP), First Series, vol. 19: 340.
32 For more detail about the events during the conference, see Fink, *The Genoa Conference*, 143–280; FRUS, 1922, vol. 2: 770–813.
33 The correspondence about the attitude of the U.S. toward the conference and its refusal to take part in it, see FRUS, 1922, vol. 1: 384–96. See also Fink, *The Genoa Conference*, 47–49, 97–98.
34 Charles Evans Hughes to Richard W. Child, March 24 and 31, 1922, and Charles Evans Hughes to Myron T. Herrick, April 8, 1922, FRUS, 1922, vol. 1: 394–96. In addition, two more Americans were present at Genoa. William B. Causey and Alvin B. Barber were technical advisors of the American Relief Administration to Austria and Poland, respectively.
35 Fink, *The Genoa Conference*, 126–33.

Chapter 2

and in doing so created the basis on which further international cooperation might commence—a task that fell to the League of Nations. Various nonbinding recommendations also touched upon currency stabilization, preferably based on a gold standard, balanced budgets, and central bank cooperation. One resolution called for foreign loans as insurance for stability in various countries facing the need for reconstruction and where the possibility of additional taxation and expenditure could not show a further increase.[36] Although economic in name, in the end, the Genoa Conference assumed a too political nature, a fact that did not escape the American observers' attention and shaped their opinion accordingly. Child categorically labeled the conference as "confusion," while Logan came away with the conviction that Genoa represented a "cess-pool of Machiavellian political intrigue and machinations."[37] And not only the Americans were critical of the gathering. Arthur Salter, soon to be the head of the Financial Committee of the League of Nations, also looked back on Genoa and thought—although with the benefit of hindsight—that it "failed completely [because] each official was the prisoner of his own national system."[38] He added that the result was "rather to endorse and consolidate a system of trade barriers [...] and those passages in them which recommended reductions remained as merely pious hopes without practical effect."[39]

Parallel to such efforts as the conferences, central banks also worked on an overarching scheme to put continental financial order in place. The unquestionable leader of that effort on the European continent was Montagu Norman, the new governor of the Bank of England. He was an internationalist who knew that a healthy world economy was to Britain's advantage. He firmly believed in the sovereignty of central banks instead of puppets of governments, and also that cooperation among such institutions was the secret to achieving the desired financial stability. He believed in the sanctity of the gold standard and was very much against war debts and reparations,

---

36 Second Plenary Session of the Genoa Conference, held at the Palazzo San Giorgio, May 3, 1922, at 10 a. m., DBFP, vol. 19: 705–10; Tamás Bácskai, ed., *A Magyar Nemzeti Bank története* [The History of the National Bank of Hungary], vol. 1, (Budapest: Közgazdasági és Jogi Könyvkiadó, 1993), 501, n. 2; György Péteri, *Global Monetary Regime and National Central Banking. The Case of Hungary, 1921–1929* (Boulder, CO: Social Science Monographs, 2002), 10.
37 Quoted in Fink, *The Genoa Conference*, 207.
38 Salter, *World Trade and Its Future*, 39.
39 Ibid., 41.

which he saw as a hindrance to his goals. Lloyd George characterized him as "the high priest of the golden calf" whose "main preoccupation was to keep his idol burnished and supreme in the Panthéon of commerce. In his honest view it was the only god to lead the nation out of the wilderness."[40]

Next to adopting the gold standard, Normal also felt that there were other preconditions for financial stability in a given country: primarily, a well-managed bank of issue that, together with a politically-backed balanced budget, might ensure a stable currency.[41] These views largely corresponded with the recommendations reached at Brussels and Genoa, which is not surprising. These people knew each other and tried to influence the outcome of such cooperative work with their prestige and with the wherewithal that, for example, was at Norman's and the Bank of England's proposal. But one more link was needed: an overarching structure that might undertake the task actually at hand.

The third tier of this multifaceted effort for European financial reconstruction was the League of Nations, which initiated the Brussels Conference in the first place. The new and groundbreaking international organization's putative role in world affairs was to ensure peace and stability. Although not all the major powers were members in the organization, and the mechanism set up to deal with disputes was rather too weak to achieve any real and significant changes, it was nonetheless a bold new attempt to bring thorny issues before the various members and try to take the venom out of the often nasty disagreements. The League, which became more or less a "Europe first" club, had to deal with the issue of financial reconstruction on the continent. It was a task that called for action in the wake of widespread postwar devastation, especially in some of the defeated countries. There was also a political element underpinning such efforts, in which it was reasoned that if these countries were not put on a road to stability, they might be lost to Bolshevism. The events in Germany and Hungary in 1919 seemed to emphasize the reality of that fear.

This then was the European milieu in which Royall Tyler found himself in the early 1920s. As always, he tried to be a useful and reliable figure,

---

40   Lloyd George, *The Truth about Reparations and War-debts* (London: William Heinemann Ltd., 1932), 116.
41   On Norman's views and work in more detail see Sir Henry Clay, *Lord Norman* (London: Macmillan & Co. Ltd., 1957); György Péteri, *Revolutionary Twenties. Essays on International Monetary and Financial Relations after World War I* (Trondheim: University of Trondheim, 1995).

and although we do not know much about his work on the Reparations Commission, various allusions by others seem to prove that he was a popular and trustworthy man. As an unofficial American delegate to a League Commission, Tyler must have followed closely all the international steps taken toward ensuring a brighter economic and financial future, and, as a consequence, he gained knowledge —political, financial, and economic— about the European continent that few Americans at this time possessed. In this environment, Tyler embodied the typical American attitude regarding Europe: not to assume any responsibility, but to keep a close eye on the workings of the League of Nations and the various European countries. In light of all this, it is not surprising that from the time he joined the U. S. Army in 1917, Tyler's art collecting activities took a back seat. This period lasted until roughly the end of the Paris Peace Conference, the summer of 1920. After that he was again active in seeking out pieces, often suggesting that the Blisses buy certain ones.

Tyler's wife was also active in postwar activities. Much of Central Europe was devastated, and, with American help, mostly of private nature, relief was poured into the region.[42] From 1920 Elisina worked for the Viennese Children's Relief. After the General Relief Committee of New York offered her a $120,000 fund and the responsibility to disburse it, she traveled to Vienna in December 1920, where she saw devastation—both material and to the human body and soul—that was almost beyond belief. She chronicled her observations in Vienna, noting that "the smell of hunger pursues one everywhere, even in the hallway and stairs of the Grand Opera, that horrible unnatural smell of diminished vitality which human beings give out when the process of physical disintegration has been set up."[43] As she later remembered, "The whole vast city lay in darkness under a thick shroud of snow. Shadowy figures clad in worn-out army uniforms stood silently imploring by every doorway. Misery reigned supreme."[44] She stayed in the Austrian capital three weeks out of every two months for more than two years. She made

---

42 On the international politics on trying to help Austria, and with an emphasis with American involvement, see Patricia Clavin, "The Austrian Hunger Crisis and the Genesis of International Organization after the First World War," *International Affairs* 90, no. 2 (March 2014): 265–78.
43 Elisina Tyler to Mildred Barnes Bliss, March 5, 1921, Paris, "Bliss–Tyler Correspondence," https://www.doaks.org/resources/bliss-tyler-correspondence/letters/05mar21, accessed November 6, 2015.
44 Diary entry of June 13, 1941, *Elisina Tyler's 1940–41 Diary*, unpublished journal, access courtesy of Royall Tyler.

use of the help of various diplomatic representations of the main powers, and built an excellent working relationship with local organizations and committees. She also founded the "Self Help for Austria" campaign, of which she was chairman and vice president. She donated more than 20 million Kronen ($10,000) for the University of Vienna, which made it possible to fund canteens where needy students could receive cheap meals. In addition, Elisina provided grants and scholarships and donated clothes, shoes, and books for Viennese students. In recognition of her commitment to alleviating the humanitarian emergency at the university, she was nominated for the Badge of Honor of the University of Vienna, and on March 24, 1922, its academic senate approved the award.[45] Also in recognition of her work organizing this charity effort between 1920 and 1923, she was awarded the highest decoration of the Austrian Red Cross.[46]

As mentioned earlier, the Genoa Conference did not solve Europe's acute problems—perhaps even worsened some of them—but the effort was not wholly in vain. Especially with respect to the financial questions, the ideas of cooperation that were urged at Brussels were elevated into the political realm at Genoa. Maybe on account of the reparation question, the timing of these two conferences was precipitate; however, a design as to possible financial reconstruction did emerge. From that year on, Central Europe, and later other parts of the continent, saw a string of financial reconstructions based upon the ideas and recommendations reached at Brussels and Genoa, and initiated by the League of Nations. The first country to be tested, or helped, was Austria.

The Austrian Reconstruction was the first financial rehabilitation of a European country undertaken by the League of Nations.[47] Austria had lost many of its former provinces and, as a consequence, agricultural and industrial output together with the level of finished products fell sharply. The fact

---

45 Katharina Kniefacz, "Elisina Tyler, geb. Contessa di Castelvecchio," https://geschichte.univie.ac.at/de/personen/elisina-tyler-geb-palamidessi-de-castelvecchio, accessed August 17, 2019. See also, *Neue Freie Presse*, Nr. 20820, August 16, 1922, 5.
46 Diary entry of March 6, 1940, *Elisina Tyler's 1940–41 Diary*.
47 For a succinct summary of the Austrian financial reconstruction see, Zoltán Peterecz, *Jeremiah Smith, Jr. and Hungary, 1924–1926: the United States, the League of Nations, and the Financial Reconstruction of Hungary* (London: Versita, 2013), 63–79. For a more comprehensive and technical outline see, League of Nations. *The Financial Reconstruction of Austria. General Survey and Principal Documents* (Geneva, 1926).

that the newly created independent states, especially Czechoslovakia, were not on good terms with Austria in the immediate postwar years further aggravated the already difficult situation. An unnaturally swollen population in Vienna contributed to the country's lack of adequate food supplies, and in the wake of such conditions, social tensions ran high. Austria had to accept the Treaty of Saint-Germain-en-Laye, signed on September 10, 1919, which forbade the Anschluss, that is, the union of Germany and Austria. Austria suffered not only a huge loss of territory but also faced harsh reparation payments that were to be determined by the Reparations Commission. The new republic in the heart of Europe was an unstable startup, and the regular rioting and looting in the capital city sent ominous signals. In effect, Austria was sustained by foreign charity provided foremost by Great Britain and the United States. However, such efforts could, at best, only alleviate the ongoing crisis that was characterized by lack of raw materials, food and coal, and by runaway inflation.[48]

Austria was also seen as key to South-Eastern European trade, therefore British interests dictated that the country be helped to put its finances in order. The United States, for its part, considered Austria to be on "the verge of a reign of anarchy," and said "rumors of bolshevist plots [we]re rife." It wanted to assume no responsibility for the region, and wished to leave the troublesome continent to European governments to tackle.[49] So what official American policy avoided was taken up by private charity. For political reasons, Austria was a darling child of the Allies and the private sphere of the United States, so Vienna and Austria received proportionally larger sums of relief money than, for example, its neighboring pariah, Hungary.[50]

This situation led to the League of Nations as the only possible institution to undertake solving Austria's woes. Norman was a primary mover behind a possible financial reconstruction for Austria, and first he came up against a lack of willing investors who would take on a loan for that Central European country. The British government had grown tired of providing small amounts of money to a seemingly lost cause and had come to the conclusion that "no

---

48 League of Nations, *The Financial Reconstruction of Austria*, 11.
49 Robert Lansing to Richard Crane, January 23, 1920, FRUS,1920, vol. 1: 249.
50 On the general Central and Eastern European relief work, which in the greatest part was provided by American sources, see Herbert Clark Hoover, *The Memoirs of Herbert Hoover*, vol. 1 (New York: The Macmillan Company, 1951–1952), 282–430. On relief provided for Austria see, ibid., 392–95.

more good money is going to be thrown after the bad which has already been doled out."⁵¹ With Ignaz Seipel's appearance at Austria's helm in May 1922, the domestic scene there acquired relative serenity. The British chargé d'affaires in Vienna characterized the new chancellor as "a man of intelligence, tact and moderation [...] confident and determined [...] not sit[ting] with crossed hands waiting for something to happen," and indeed, he proved to be a dynamic leader who created favorable circumstances, and the possibility of an outside loan began to seem like more than a dream.⁵² In August, Austria officially asked the League for help, and, with British initiative, the wheels were slowly set in motion. In early October the Protocols were signed by the participating powers, these ensured Austria's territorial integrity, and the conditions for a loan not to exceed $125 million were guaranteed. Outside financial control also had to be accepted by the Austrian government. Initially, this commissioner-general was to be an American. Roland William Boyden was chosen. Like Royall Tyler, he was an unofficial American delegate on the Reparations Committee, and his choice would have meant some cooperation between the League of Nations and the United States. In the end, however, due to misunderstandings with the U.S. State Department, Boyden was asked not to accept the post, and Alfred Zimmermann of the Netherlands became the League's controller in Austria.⁵³

The United States government may have officially stayed away from the League of Nations and Austrian reconstruction, however, in launching the Austrian reconstruction loan, America took on an important role through its private banking sphere. The League was of the opinion that if American banks took part in the long-term loan, a precedent might be established "involving far-reaching consequences."⁵⁴ J. P. Morgan & Co. eventually decided in favor of participating, as did Kuehn, Loeb, & Co., and the loan

---

51 Montagu Norman to Benjamin Strong, July 6, 1922, G35/3, Bank of England Archive, London, UK, (hereafter cited as BoE).
52 Aretas Akers-Douglas to Lord Curzon, June 1, 1922, C8134/396/3, 7349, FO371, The National Archives, London, UK, (hereafter cited as TNA).
53 William Boyden to Jean Monnet and Arthur Salter, November 8, 1922, No. 3. Austria. Correspondence concerning appointment of Commissioner General. Telegrams dispatched and received, S. 106, Salter Papers, League of Nations Archives, Geneva, Switzerland, (hereafter cited as LNA); Arthur Salter, *Personality in Politics* (London: Faber and Faber, 1947), 167; *In Memory of Roland William Boyden*, 14.
54 Jan de Bordes' memorandum, April 27, 1923, C. 6. 4–8c. Dr. Zimmermann's mission to the U.S.A., Financial Reconstruction of Austria, LNA.

looked to be secured. On June 11, 1923, a successful subscription did take place both in England and the United States, with the two countries taking the lion's share, while other European countries provided the remainder. The successful launch of the reconstruction program with the long-term loan marked an historic moment: the League led an effort aimed at rehabilitating a former enemy country in Central Europe. Although not without obstacles, the next three years produced a financially stable Austria. The balanced budget and stabilized currency stood out as the most important features, but a general rise in the living standard compared to just a few years earlier was also measurable among the working classes. In the end, an important step was taken toward a hoped-for working economic block in Central Europe.

The end of the summer brought two important changes for the near and distant future for the Tylers as well. In August 1923, at the height of the initial phases of the Austrian reconstruction, Tyler, as an unofficial member of the Reparations Commission, visited Arthur Salter at Geneva. Salter was by then head of the Financial and Economic Section of the League. The two already knew each other, but soon became life-long friends, and Tyler was "very much interested in comparing the organization of the only other big international body with our own."[55] Largely because of this association, the League of Nations would appoint him deputy commissioner general to Hungary in the very near future.

Also, as Tyler proudly announced to Mildred Barnes Bliss, "We've bought Antigny, and have paid for it."[56] The purchase took place after a long haggle with the chateau's owner, but the Tylers' decade-long dream had finally become a five-hectare reality. This would be their real home and source of recharging their physical and intellectual compartments due to various jobs and travels across Europe in the next three decades. The price tag was $3,000, which would come to $45,000 in 2020 dollars, counting only inflation.

---

55 Royall Tyler to Mildred Barnes Bliss, undated (winter 1923), Paris, "Bliss–Tyler Correspondence," https://www.doaks.org/resources/bliss-tyler-correspondence/letters/undated-05, accessed March 20, 2019.
56 Royall Tyler to Mildred Barnes Bliss, September 5, 1923, Paris, "Bliss–Tyler Correspondence," https://www.doaks.org/resources/bliss-tyler-correspondence/letters/05sep1923, accessed November 7, 2015.

CHAPTER 3

The League of Nations Years Part I: The Hungarian Financial Reconstruction 1924–26

The next big League of Nations project in the financial realm was Hungary. It was clear from the start that Austria was only a first, albeit very important step, after which other countries should also be reconstructed financially. Logic dictated that the approach ought to be geographical, that is, Austria's neighbor to the east should be next. Not only were the two countries adjacent but both were also defeated in World War I, and in its aftermath revolution, or the fear of it, swept through both. As a consequence, they became geopolitically sensitive spots. The idea was that if both of these countries could be helped back on their feet, they could become important and valuable assets for a healthier and expanded European trade community—an especially important point in British strategic thinking. As Montagu Norman of the Bank of England famously put it, "If we can thus set up Austria, we must tackle Hungary next, so as to establish one by one the new parts of Old Austria. & then perhaps the Balkan Countries. Only by thus making the various parts economically sound & independent shall we reach what I believe to be the ultimate solution for Eastern Europe viz an Economic federation to include half a dozen countries on or near the Danube free of customs barriers &c."[1] Therefore, in British opinion Austria

---

[1] Montagu Norman to Benjamin Strong, April 9, 1923, G35/4, BoE. Also quoted in Clay, *Lord Norman*, 189–90; Péteri, Global Monetary Regime, 51; Péteri, Revolutionary Twenties, 168; Miklós Lojkó, *Meddling in Middle Europe* (Budapest: Central European University Press, 2006), 71.

Chapter 3

and Hungary were to be the first two positive dominoes in a line that was to reach all the way to Greece. Since Hungary would offer Royall Tyler his first involvement in a League of Nations reconstruction project, it is worth taking a closer look at that country's situation in the postwar years and what led to the financial reconstruction conducted by the League.

Hungary's position after the conclusion of the Great War was to be mourned. As part of the Austro-Hungarian Monarchy, Hungary fought as member of the Central Powers and was defeated. After the bloodshed was over, Hungary, now an independent country, found itself surrounded by new, inimical states. The relationship with Austria had always been burdened, but the main tension arose from the animosity on the part of the newly created successor states, Czechoslovakia, the Kingdom of Serbs, Croats, and Slovenes (later Yugoslavia), and an enlarged Romania. These countries' main aim was "a common policy against Hungary," which "must be merely part of a broader political conception."[2] By 1921 the three countries had formed the Little Entente, a political formation with strong French backing to keep a check on "the Hungarian menace."[3] What partly fueled these efforts was not only the traditional anti-Hungarian sentiment in the successor states but also the fact that on March 21, 1919, a short-lived Soviet Republic was established in Hungary under the Bolshevik leader Béla Kun.

A few years after the Kun takeover, the West's worst fears were realized when it saw the westward expansion of Bolshevik ideology in Hungary. A common platform needed to be found against this threat, and Hungary became an international pariah overnight. The real anxiety sprang from the fact that Hungary's example might spread even further westward, mainly to Germany, the most important country with respect to a peaceful postwar Europe. As an American observer reported from the scene of Kun's and the communists' takeover in Budapest, "the great significance of this revolution is that [...] the precedent set by this action will offer an encouragement to the Germans which may be disastrous. [...] The conclusion of the matter is that unless immediate and vigorous action is taken the Allies will be met with a disastrous state of affairs in Central Europe which it may take years to straighten out. Hungary has defied the Peace Conference and allied her-

---

2   Eduard Beneš, "The Little Entente," *Foreign Affairs* 1, no. 1 (September 1922): 69.
3   Ibid., 68.

self with the Bolsheviki. It is Germany's turn next."[4] The Bolshevik government in Hungary was overthrown after just four months in power by outside intervention in the form of mainly Romanian troops, which occupied the eastern half of the country and Budapest for months.

Perhaps the Western powers should have taken into account that to a large degree the reason the Kun regime could grab power was largely owing to the punitive measures taken by the Paris Peace Conference, which ordered the remaining Hungarian army units back to a now very small territory. This clearly foreshadowed what to expect in the formal peace treaty later on. With all the harmful ideology underpinning the short-lived Bolshevik government in Hungary, it was nonetheless a somewhat nationalistic movement to defend what it considered the rightful borders. As the above mentioned American on-site observer also noted, "The Hungarians are united in their conviction that Hungary must not be dismembered, have made use of Bolshevism as a last desperate resort to preserve the integrity of their country, and have openly defied the Allies."[5] But the stigma remained and was kept alive by the surrounding countries, and the general fear of Bolshevism and the instability that it might create did not help the Hungarians when it came to drawing up the Hungarian peace treaty—largely a replica of the Versailles Peace Treaty with Germany.

The Treaty of Trianon, signed on June 4, 1920, was a fatal blow to Hungary and its aspirations for both the present and the future, and it defined Hungary's fate and opportunities for the next two decades.[6] Perhaps no Hungarian held too rosy a view as to the final outcome of the peace treaty, but the extremely harsh measures often went against the Wilsonian principle of national self-determination, which the Hungarians had hoped would

---

4   Captain Nicholas Roosevelt to the Commission to Negotiate Peace, March 26, 1919, FRUS:1919, PPC, (1947), vol. 12: 418–19. Substance of this report was transmitted to President Wilson by Secretary Lansing the next day.
5   "The Hungarian Revolution," N. Roosevelt's report to the American Delegation at the Paris Peace Conference, March 26, 1919, *A History of a Few Weeks*, 367.
6   For the Treaty of Trianon in English see, H. W. V. Temperley, ed., *A History of the Peace Conference of Paris* (London: Henry Frowde and Hodder & Stoughton, 1921); Deák, Francis, *Hungary at the Paris Peace Conference. The Diplomatic History of the Treaty of Trianon* (New York: Columbia University Press, 1942); Sándor Taraszovics, "American Peace Preparations during World War I and the Shaping of the New Hungary," in Ignác Romsics, ed. *20th Century Hungary and the Great Powers* (Boulder, CO: Social Science Monographs, Atlantic Research and Publications Inc., 1994), 73–97; Bryan Cartledge, *Mihály Károlyi & István Bethlen: Hungary* (London: Haus Publishing Ltd., 2009).

Chapter 3

prevail in Paris. As a result of the Trianon Treaty, purely Hungarian ethnic blocs were detached from Hungary, which served strategic purposes and strengthening the successor countries. Hungary lost two-thirds of its former territory and about 3,000,000 ethnic Hungarians found themselves suddenly in other countries. As a further consequence, Hungary lost most of its raw materials and industry and became a tattered remnant from an economic perspective.[7] In addition, a stream of refugees arrived from the now separated regions, which put an extra burden on the postwar, post-revolution, post-treaty country.

The Treaty of Trianon contained the war guilt clause, and Hungary also faced reparations commencing in 1921. Article 180 of the treaty declared that "the first charge upon all the assets and revenues of Hungary shall be the cost of reparation."[8] Hungary reluctantly accepted the new reality, but the next twenty years of Hungarian foreign and domestic policy were largely aimed at the peaceful revision of the Trianon Treaty. Nearly every foreigner visiting the country witnessed the Hungarians' determination not to accept the treaty as final. As an American diplomat noted, "This idea germinated and fermented in the blood stream until it developed into a well-defined disease whose first symptom was the passionate 'Nem, Nem, Soha'."[9]

From March 1920 until 1944, Admiral Miklós Horthy was Hungary's leader, although the everyday political work was left to the various prime ministers, outstanding among them István Bethlen.[10] Both Horthy and Bethlen were Protestant, or rather Calvinist. This fact, at least on the subconscious level, must have helped their case in connection with the United States. With Bethlen's rise to the premiership in April 1921, a pragmatic, intelligent, and farsighted politician took political matters in hand. Bethlen

---

7   See, for instance, Joseph Rothschild, *East Central Europe between the Two World Wars* (Seattle: University of Washington Press, 1974), 156, 167; C. A. Macartney, *Hungary and Her Successors. The Treaty of Trianon and Its Consequences, 1919–1937* (London: Oxford University Press, 1937), 463; Derek H. Aldcroft, *From Versailles to Wall Street, 1919–1929* (London: Allen Lane, Penguin Books Ltd., 1977), 28; M. C. Kaser and E. A. Radice, eds., *The Economic History of Eastern Europe, 1919–1975* (Oxford: Clarendon Press, 1985), 227.
8   Temperley, *Peace Conference*, 235.
9   No, No, Never! – the Hungarian interwar slogan concerning the Treaty of Trianon. Joshua Butler Wright to Henry L. Stimson, May 10, 1929, 864.00 PR/18, M. 708, Roll 10, National Archives and Records Administration (hereafter cited as NARA), Washington, D. C., USA.
10 The best biography on Bethlen is Ignác Romsics, *István Bethlen: A Great Conservative Statesman of Hungary, 1874–1946* (Boulder, CO: Social Science Monographs, 1995).

came from a traditional Transylvanian family, and to illustrate his pragmatic political approach it is enough to recall his statement, "What I say and what I do depend on the requirements of foreign and domestic policy. My policies are shaped by the circumstances."[11] Bethlen tried to follow a British approach in his foreign policy, because, quite sensibly, he realized that only with British support could Hungary hope to withstand the pressure exerted by the Little Entente and backed by the French. He shrewdly understood that Great Britain would not allow France to create hegemony in the Danubian Basin, which region was important for British strategic thinking at this time. After Charles IV's two failed attempts to regain the Hungarian throne, the Hungarian Assembly passed the dethronement bill in November 1921, which officially excluded the possibility of a future Habsburg king in Hungary. This was an important step, and it made Hungary more presentable to the West and preempted the recurring Little Entente political attacks on this ground. But in order to acquire the much-needed British help—political and financial—Hungary first had to become a member of the League of Nations.

Although the League was an open society, the defeated countries were not at first invited to join. However, based upon these countries' attitude toward the vision of a more cooperative Europe drawn up by the organization, they were slowly accepted as members. Austria and Bulgaria were admitted in December 1920, and it was obviously only a matter of time before Germany and Hungary were going to be invited as well. Being in the League automatically meant much closer supervision over these countries' affairs, but it was also to their benefit, because certain advantageous avenues became opened to them.

Hungary's first two attempts to become a member failed. In May 1921, Hungary asked for admittance only to request a postponement on account of Charles IV's return to Hungary and the havoc it created.[12] When the question of Hungary's possible admittance was on the agenda again in the fall session of 1922, the situation was more favorable. Of the three members of the Little Entente, Yugoslavia was the most opposed to Hungarian

---

11 Ibid., 156.
12 Nicolas Bánffy to Eric Drummond, May 23, 1921, File 13039, Report of the Sixth Committee to the Assembly, September 26, 1921, and Resolution adopted by the Assembly, September 30, 1921, File 16180, Section 28, Admissions to the League, Box 1453, LNA, 1919–1927.

membership. But the unofficial leader of that alliance, Eduard Beneš, the Czechoslovakian foreign minister and an influential diplomat in western countries, supported Hungary because he knew that supposedly its place was already assured.[13] Great Britain exerted pressure on the Little Entente countries, and on September 18, 1922, the Assembly voted unanimously to admit Hungary to the League.[14] It is crucial to emphasize the importance of this membership from the Hungarian point of view. Not only did the country escape the isolation that had been its fate since November 1918 but membership also promised some defense against the Little Entente, and the important minority question—a vital issue for Hungary—could now be pursued in front of the international body. The Hungarians from the beginning bet on the British horse, and they kept trying to find support from London. Not only was Britain the logical and real counterweight to French schemes in Central Europe, a part of which was the Little Entente, but perhaps London was the only place from which financial help might have arrived. And to strengthen this view, unbeknownst to Hungarians, in British foreign policy circles there was a desire not to allow Hungary to "go under financially."[15]

Naturally, the Hungarian government tried to establish good relationship with the other Anglo-Saxon country overseas as well. Since the United States Senate did not ratify the Versailles Peace Treaty America remained outside the League of Nations, so it had to conclude separate peace treaties with the defeated countries. The clear signal that the United States was treating these countries as one group became evident when it concluded the following peace treaties within just a few days: on August 24, 1921, with Germany, on August 25, 1921, with Austria, and on August 29, 1921, with Hungary. The treaties came into force on November 8, November 11, and December 17, 1921, respectively. Diplomatic relations on the ministerial level were resumed between Washington and Budapest when Theodore Brentano

---

13   Árpád Hornyák, *Magyar-jugoszláv diplomáciai kapcsolatok, 1918–1927* [Hungarian–Yugoslav Diplomatic Relations, 1918–1927] (Újvidék: Forum Könyvkiadó, 2004), 115–16.
14   Report of the First Sub-Committee (of the Sixth Committee of the Third Assembly of the League of Nations), September 14, 1922, File 23483, League of Nations Archives. For more detail about Hungary's entry into the League of Nations, see, Mária Ormos, "Magyarország belépése a Nemzetek Szövetségébe" [Hungary's Entry to the League of Nations] *Századok* 91, no. 1 (1957): 235–49. Ádám Magda, *A kisantant és Európa 1920–1929* (Budapest: Akadémiai Kiadó, 1989), 215–16; Gyula Juhász, Magyarország külpolitikája 1919–1945 [Hungary's Foreign Policy 1919–1945] (Budapest: Akadémiai Kiadó, 1988), 89–94.
15   Lampson's minute February 22, 1923, C3081/942/21, 8861, FO371, TNA.

arrived in April 1922, and Count László Széchenyi presented his credentials in January 1922. Because the United States was considered the paragon of impartiality in diplomacy, from the start Hungary hoped to convince the Anglo-Saxon powers to help remedy the wrongs the country suffered by the Treaty of Trianon. The charity the Americans showed to Hungary in the early postwar years only enhanced that country's prestige, which was already high.[16] Hungary was in dire straits and in need of help.

The Hungary of the immediate postwar years was a devastated landscape both economically and financially, not to mention the psychological setback of the quick succession of revolutions, Romanian occupation, the harsh Trianon Treaty, and the Karlist coup attempts in 1921. Inflation was high, industrial production and agricultural output sharply diminished, and foreign trade showed negative numbers of between 200 and 300 million gold crowns ($40–60 million) yearly.[17] This was accompanied by a substantial budget deficit, and the "gloomy" economic situation, the "alarming rate of increase in the cost of living," and the general depression "in the hearts of most people" did not bode well for any immediate recovery.[18] The remedy seemed to be a foreign loan. As Prime Minster Bethlen argued: "Our financial situation is serious. From our revenues we cannot cover our expenditures. It will be a long time before we achieve this goal with hard work. In this work without foreign help we cannot reach the goal."[19] He knew very well that the reparations Hungary faced would make such a course impossible, so the balancing act was to find a way to receive a loan while avoiding or putting off reparation payments.

Hungary had tried to secure a private loan, but its endeavors on the American and British money markets failed to achieve any result. The advice came from British circles to turn to the League of Nations as a last resort,

---

16 On the American help for Hungary in the postwar years, see, Tibor Glant, "Herbert Hoover and Hungary, 1918–1923," *Hungarian Journal of English and American Studies* 8, no. 2 (2002): 95–109.

17 9/VIII/2/Appendix 12, Various Data on the Output of Hungary's Industries, 56, K 275, The Semi-official Papers of Finance Minister Kállay Tibor (hereafter cited as Kállay Papers), 1901–1941, Hungarian National Archives, Budapest, Hungary (hereafter cited as HNA); 6/V/7, The Volume of Foreign Trade, and the Industrial and Agricultural Output of Hungary, 1920–1923/1, Kállay Papers, HNA.

18 "Memorandum on Hungary" in Brentano to Hughes, October 1, 1922, 864.00/517, Microfilm Publications, Records of the Department of State Relating to Internal Affairs of Austria-Hungary and Hungary, 1912–1929. Roll 6, Microcopy No. 708, NARA.

19 *Magyar Hírlap*, March 28, 1922.

because it was the platform where the reparation question could be settled in favor of a loan. This course was unwelcome at first. Hungarians were interested in revision, not in taking steps that would further weaken their sovereignty. In the end, however, it was more important to try to make the most of the possibility of British backing than to insist on pipe dreams, given that the country was in such a shattered state. The British, for their part, supported tackling Hungary's situation, because they were pursuing their own interests in Central and Southeast Europe. Otto Niemeyer, Controller of Finance at the British Treasury and a member of the Financial Committee of the League of Nations, wrote an oft-quoted line in connection with this policy. It illuminates the British thinking very clearly: "If we could tie up another loose end in this way [League loan to Hungary along the lines of the Austrian scheme] we should I believe, extend and increase our consolidation in South East Europe. I hope the Foreign Office approve these notions and if so that you will do anything you can to push them."[20] That is the main reason why Great Britain was "prepared to support the scheme" and "genuinely anxious to set [Hungary] upon the right rails."[21] Hungary accepted the good advice, and the Bethlen government was willing to ask the League for help and was ready to accept its control.

Accordingly, Bethlen and Frigyes Korányi, future finance minister, appeared before the Reparations Commission on May 5, 1923, as Hungary's representatives. In a lengthy exposé about Hungary's woes and its efforts to tackle the situation, Bethlen asked the Reparations Commission to suspend the treaty charges, a move that would make it possible for Hungary to secure a loan and follow the advice of the Financial Committee.[22] For political reasons, the Reparations Commission decided against this request—the Little Entente, with French backing, prevailed, partly because Boyden, the unofficial American representative, hadn't the right to vote.[23] Given that it was a condition that some part of any loan should be spent on paying reparations, the whole plan was clearly unaccomplishable.

---

20 Otto Niemeyer to Miles Lampson, March 16, 1923, OV33/70, BoE. Also quoted in Péteri, *Revolutionary Twenties*, 168.
21 Butler's minute, March 21, 1923, C4996/942/21, 8861, FO371, TNA.; Curzon to Hohler, April 13, 1923, Documents on British Foreign Policy (hereafter cited as DBFP), First Series, vol. 24: 583.
22 Speech of Count Bethlen before the Reparation Commission, May 5, 1923, Communiqués from Kallay and Bethlen. Doc. No. 28903, Registry Files, R. 296, LNA.
23 Reparations Commission Minutes, May 23, 1923, OV9/430, BoE.

London came to the rescue. Even before Bethlen made his request of the Reparations Commission, Norman asked British political leaders to tackle Hungary as an overall piece of the British agenda in the region:

> I do indeed think that the position of Hungary needs to be tackled without delay. Czechoslovakia is more or less standing on her own legs; great efforts are being made to arrange for the Austrian Loan to be issued in a month or so, after which Austria should be able to regain stability; so Hungary is the next country to tackle both from the standpoint of her geographical position and her needs. I do not suppose that her condition is as serious as that of Austria, but I daresay some sort of foreign control will be essential in addition to a release of all Liens. Will you give this business a push in the right direction, and we will then try to get the question taken up by the League or through some other channel.[24]

Simply put, in the wake of the Reparations Commission's decision against Hungary, the British blackmailed the Little Entente countries financially—mainly Czechoslovakia, but all of them needed money in London.[25] Norman did not mince words: "There is no money for the Czechs (or Roumanians) till Hungary has release from reparation—which was prevented last month by Little Entente. Benes is free to come to London, but the City takes no part in his domestic politics and is not ready to talk future loans."[26]

The British government supported Norman, and Lord Curzon sent this message from the British Parliament: "We are giving our full support to the appeal of Hungary. [...] We desire to prevent the financial collapse of Hungary, with its incalculable consequences. We desire to see in force a complete scheme of reconstruction. [...] We earnestly hope, therefore, that the Reparations Commission will reconsider their decision of May last and

---

24   Montagu Norman to John Bradbury, April 28, 1923, G3/179, BoE. Also quoted in Péteri, *Global Monetary Regime*, 78, and Peterecz, *Jeremiah Smith, Jr. and Hungary*, 93.
25   Foreign Office Memorandum on Hungary, August, 24, 1923, C14677/942/21, 8865, FO371, TNA; Dering to Curzon, October 18, 1923, and Treasury to Foreign office, November 13, 1923, DBFP, First Series, vol. 24: 884; Memo of conversation between M. Milojevics, Yugoslav minister at Budapest and Sir William Goode at the S. H. S. Legation, Budapest, June 30, 1923, 9/VIII/5/95, K 275, Kállay Papers, HNA.
26   Norman's Diary Entries, July 5, 1923, ADM34/12, BoE.

will refer the question without delay to the League of Nations."[27] Curzon also warned Hungary to follow a more conciliatory policy toward its neighbors and facilitate whatever negotiations might take place.[28] The British simply wanted to see a stable Hungary as an integral piece to their continental trade in the Central European region. And if Bethlen could not secure the loan, his government might topple, which would mean the rise of "the most undesirable extremists [...] If this forecast should be true it would portend a period of inexpert adventure and experiment, which would be full of danger to the peace of Europe."[29] That is why the British were willing to use pressure, and this strategy proved useful: by mid-October the road was paved for the Financial Committee to deal with Hungary without the threat of reparation payments. Hungary had to accept less money and time, together with League control, but it managed to defer paying reparations.[30]

After a ten-day visit to Hungary in November 1923, the Financial Committee submitted its report, which contained the following recommendations: inflation must be stopped, which was to be achieved with the setting up of an independent Bank of Issue; by June 30, 1926, a balanced budget must be achieved; the main help to achieve these ends would come from a loan of 250 million gold crowns ($50 million); and the course of reconstruction would be controlled by a Commissioner-General delegated by the League.[31] In the following months two Protocols were drawn up. The words "treaty charges" were substituted in the protocols for the harsh-sounding term reparations, and these charges were not to exceed 10 million gold crowns ($2 million) on an annual average during the amortization of the loan, and in the first five years after 1926, the sum was to be substantially less in order to create more favorable chances of success for the reconstruction effort.[32] Therefore, the cloud of reparation still hung over Hungary, but for the time being it did

---

27 *British Parliament Diaries*, 32nd Parliament, 2nd Session, vol. 54, House of Lords (London: His Majesty's Stationery Office, 1922), 1364–65.
28 Ibid., 1365–66.
29 Thomas Hohler to Lord Curzon, January 3, 1924, DBFP, First Series, vol. 26: 10.
30 Peterecz, *Jeremiah Smith, Jr. and Hungary*, 95.
31 Report of the Financial Committee to the Council, November 30, 1923, Report to the Council on the 12th Session of the Financial Committee. Doc. No. 32475, Registry Files, R. 297, LNA. The *korona* (crown) was the currency of the new monetary system created in Hungary in March 1920. It was succeeded by the *pengő* from January 1, 1927.
32 1st Session of the Committee of the Council, Paris, December 1923. Doc. No. 32636, Registry Files, R. 297, LNA.

not represent a crushing burden, and the Bethlen government hoped that when the time came to pay it, it somehow might be overturned and nullified. Every party being satisfied, the final signatures on the Protocols were completed in the first half of March 1924.[33] The first Protocol was the political one, while the second contained all the technical details, including the question of control under the future Commissioner-General.[34] The Hungarian National Assembly passed the reconstruction bill on April 18.[35]

The next phase was to find a suitable person for the office of Commissioner-General, who would work in Budapest and would check how the Hungarians were working along the guidelines laid down in the reconstruction plan. This selection process has been presented in detail in another work, so here just a short summary is needed, with emphasis on Royall Tyler.[36] It was important that the person who was going to control the loan and the related financial issues represent an unbiased nation, and from the first the United States loomed large as a possibility. This was also the aim of the Hungarian government, because they hoped that if it were an American, the overseas money markets would respond favorably to a loan request. As Bethlen formulated this underlying concept, "In case an American specialist were sent to be the controller of the Hungarian loan, this would so much please the vanity of the Americans that the placing of our loan there would be much easier."[37]

The first serious candidate was William Procter Gould Harding, governor of the Federal Reserve Bank of Boston, but due to his state of health, and perhaps to financial considerations, he refused the job in early March. The next man was Roland Boyden, who, due to his experience in the case of the Austrian position, also refused the post. Boyden offered Jeremiah Smith, Jr. as the best possible choice, and Thomas Lamont of J. P. Morgan & Co. shared this view. Since the latter had been a principal actor in securing the American share of the Austrian loan, the League listened to his recommen-

---

33 Minutes of the meeting on March 14, 1924. Doc. No. 34921, Registry Files, R. 299, LNA.
34 League of Nations, *The Financial Reconstruction of Hungary. General Survey and Principal Documents* (Geneva, 1926), 80–92.
35 *National Assembly Diary, 1922–27*, vol. 22 (Budapest: Athenaeum Nyomda, 1924), 60–68, 237, 268–89, 299–315, 317–41, 343–97, 399–452; vol. 23:1–153, 163–241, 243–333, 335–426, 437–510.
36 On the selection of Jeremiah Smith, Jr. in more detail see, Peterecz, *Jeremiah Smith, Jr. and Hungary*, 100–117.
37 István Bethlen to Géza Daruváry and Károly Khuen-Héderváry, November 27, 1923, 123-6-54200/96618, K 69, Economic Policy Department, HNA.

dation. Smith had gained international financial expertise as a sidekick of Lamont, and he was accepted by the Hungarians as well. He was officially offered the Commissioner-Generalship on April 5, and he duly accepted. In this his being "a strong believer in what the League of Nations is trying to do" must have played a major role.[38] The Hungarians were satisfied with this outcome, and Bethlen well summarized the Hungarian point of view:

> Only an American could exert influence of quite the same independent and authoritative quality and could secure us against any external attempts which might be made to gain undue influence in Hungarian affairs [...] without American co-operation and active assistance, Europe can hardly hope to put itself on a stable basis [...] now we can hope that the confidence created by the appointment of Mr. Smith will attract to Hungary the private capital from America and elsewhere we need so much for our complete recovery.[39]

Smith's nationality was also important from a Hungarian domestic point of view, since the opposition attacked the government for entrusting the control to a foreigner's hand, which was tantamount to "financial dictatorship," and meant "the last nail in the coffin for the independent, free Hungary."[40] It was really true that the Commissioner-General possessed wide ranging powers: he supervised the whole reconstruction program; if he deemed the program to be in danger, he could require extra taxes be imposed by the Hungarian Government; no new loans could be taken up by Hungary without his approval; he was to inform the League Council through monthly reports; and he would stay in Hungary until the end of the program—planned for two and a half years.[41]

Smith was to have a deputy in order to facilitate the smoothest possible control even in his absence and to deal with the many tasks at hand. The Commissioner-General was not only the person in control but he was also to be the link between the League of Nations and the Hungarian government. He regularly had to appear in person in front of the League, and this required

---

38 Jeremiah Smith, *The Preservation of the Peace* (Cambridge, MA: Harvard Law School, 1927), 11.
39 *Christian Science Monitor*, April 10, 1924.
40 *National Assembly Diary*, vol. 22: 334, and vol. 23: 76.
41 League of Nations, *The Financial Reconstruction of Hungary*, 84–86.

someone to represent him in Budapest during his absences. Also, Smith was supposed to keep a close working relationship with the Hungarian Prime Minister, the Finance Minister, the National Bank, other financial institutions, not to mention the press and other actors. This would have been an overwhelming burden on one person, so it was deemed reasonable that he have a small staff and a reliable deputy. The post of Deputy Commissioner-General fell to Royall Tyler.

Tyler's presence, specifically, was required for a host of reasons. He had gained considerable experience concerning the postwar diplomatic merry-go-round of Central Europe during the Peace Conference. He had served as an unofficial American member on the Reparations Commission for almost four years, and in that capacity he had become familiar with the financial issues troubling the continent. He had been to both Vienna and Budapest, so he possessed some local knowledge of these places. He was an American citizen, which, as has been shown, was an important element in choosing various officers for the League, and he was also more than welcome in Budapest. But perhaps more than anything, his language qualifications made him indispensable. He had a command of all the continent's leading languages, and in Hungary one had to rely mainly on German in order to communicate with a vast number of officials and other members of society. Since Jeremiah Smith, Jr. could not speak German, it was essential to have someone close to him who could break through this language barrier. Also, since both Smith and Tyler came from New England, they had a bond, even if remote, which promised good cooperation between them. For all these reasons, together with his pleasant personality, Tyler proved to be simply "invaluable."[42] The Tylers led a life they enjoyed in Paris and at Antigny, so first he was not very excited about leaving France, but as he admitted to Barnes, "Elisina and I both feel I must take it."[43] Tyler did indeed become fast friends with Smith, whom he found "exceedingly attractive," and said he "liked him from the first moment."[44] So, on April 27, Tyler spent his last day at the Reparations Commission, with "really heart-rending partings," and the next day he offi-

---

42 Lord Cecil to Edward M. House, February 11, 1924, C2521/37/21, 9905, FO371, TNA.
43 Royall Tyler to Mildred Barnes Bliss, April 9, 1924, Paris, "Bliss–Tyler Correspondence," https://www.doaks.org/resources/bliss-tyler-correspondence/letters/09apr1924, accessed December 2, 2015.
44 Royall Tyler to Mildred Barnes Bliss, April 26, 1924, Paris, "Bliss–Tyler Correspondence," https://www.doaks.org/resources/bliss-tyler-correspondence/letters/26apr1924, accessed December 2, 2015.

cially became Deputy Commissioner-General of the League of Nations in the Hungarian financial reconstruction.[45]

The arrival of Smith's and Tyler's entourage in Hungary on May 1, 1924, began a period that would be important not only for Hungary's finances but also for the League of Nations' long-time plans concerning creating elements of a possible lasting peace on the continent. Smith strictly distanced himself from any political influences, and as the American minister reported to Washington, the Commissioner-General had apparently won "the general admiration of the Hungarian Government and people, due especially to his assiduity, modesty and courtesy."[46] Since Smith was in the spotlight, Tyler could work in the background, a situation that perfectly suited him. The American pair was assisted by Harry Siepmann of Great Britain, René Charron of France, and Livio Licen of Belgium, the last of which the Hungarians knew well. By the end of May, all interested countries had waived their priorities for a loan over relief bond charges, the Commissioner-General and his staff were on site, and so the raising of the loan funds could commence.

It is important to note that Hungary in the early 1920s was a virtual no man's land for Americans, and hardly a travel hotspot for Western Europeans, and not only because in the postwar years it had little to offer. Although on the map Hungary is located in Central Europe, in the mental mapping of Western Europeans and Americans it belonged to Eastern Europe. As historian Larry Wolff demonstrates, this mental mapping came into being during the Age of Enlightenment.[47] In the latter half of the eighteenth century, when real and imagined trips took place to the places situated east of Vienna, the resulting travelogues, letters, and reports described an area where less civilized, somewhat barbaric people lived with their alien culture and languages. "It was Eastern Europe's ambiguous location, within Europe but not fully European," writes Wolff, "that called for such notions as backwardness and development to mediate between the poles of civili-

---

45 Ibid.
46 Theodore Brentano to Charles Evans Hughes, June 11, 1924, 864.00/583, Roll 6, M. 708, NARA.
47 Larry Wolff, *Inventing Eastern Europe: The Map of Civilization on the Mind of the Enlightenment* (Stanford, CA: Stanford University Press, 1994). For a useful introduction to mental mapping, see, Norbert Götz and Janne Holmén, "Introduction to the Theme Issue: 'Mental Maps: Geographical and Historical Perspectives,'" *Journal of Cultural Geography* 35, no. 2 (2018): 157–61.

zation and barbarism."[48] Although not Slavic but still alien, Hungary and Hungarian culture struck travelers from France, England, and other places as unique but somewhat held back in time. The other picture that lived in Western minds was that Hungary had served as the bulwark against the heathen Turks, and as such it was defending Christian Europe.[49] This heroic trait was trumpeted by other Eastern European nations as well—the Poles being a good example—and it created a positive image for the nation living in the Carpathian Basin.[50]

But Hungary's real overseas claim to fame came with the freedom fight in 1848–49. Although the struggle for independence failed, Lajos Kossuth's subsequent appearances in England and the United States made Hungary and its unsuccessful fight for freedom a celebrated cause.[51] By and with World War I, however, this picture had become tarnished.[52] Hungary was now the junior member of the Austro-Hungarian Monarchy, and in that role a belligerent in the war against the Allied Powers, and on paper against the United States as well. What is more, its questionable minority policy fueled the flames of nationality in the oppressed minorities on its territory: Slovaks, Romanians, Croats, and the people of Bosnia-Herzegovina. The forcible Magyarization of the prewar period doomed any peaceful cooperation after Hungary emerged from the war as a defeated and weakened country. Its recent history, the successor states' propaganda against it, and the Hungarian Soviet Republic in 1919 all paved the way for the punitive Trianon Treaty.

By the early 1920s, therefore, the picture of Hungary held in the Anglo-Saxon mind was of a country situated between East and West, a somewhat backward country whose nobility had been trying to imitate English nobles,

---

48 Wolff, *Inventing Eastern Europe*, 9.
49 See, Enikő Csukovits, *Magyarországról és a magyarokról. Nyugat-Európa magyar-képe a középkorban* [About Hungary and Hungarians. The Hungary Picture of Western Europeans in the Middle Ages] (Budapest: MTA, Bölcsészettudományi Kutatóközpont, 2015).
50 For a summary of European travelers to Hungary up to 1848, see, Gyula Antalffy, *A Thousand Years of Travel in Old Hungary*, trans. Elisabeth Hoch (Budapest: Corvina Kiadó, 1980).
51 John H. Komlos, *Louis Kossuth in America, 1851–1852* (Buffalo, NY: East European Institute, 1973); György Szabad, *Kossuth on the Political System of the United States of America* (Budapest: Akadémiai Kiadó, 1975); Frank Tibor, "'...to fix the attention of the whole world upon Hungary.' Lajos Kossuth in the United States, 1851–52," *The Hungarian Quarterly* 43, no. 166 (Summer 2002): 85–98; Zsuzsanna Lada, "The invention of a hero: Lajos Kossuth in England (1851)," *European History Quarterly* 43, no. 1 (2013): 5–26.
52 See, Géza Jeszenszky, *Lost Prestige. Hungary's Changing Image in Great Britain 1894–1918* (St, Helena, CA: Helena History Press, 2020).

largely in vain. This East–West dichotomy seemed to be the dividing line, both geographically and psychologically: where did Western Europe and its culture and influence end, and where did Eastern Europe begin? The stereotypes concerning Hungary may have stemmed from eighteenth-century travelogues, but sometimes contemporary personal experience strengthened them. The first American diplomat in Hungary after World War I, Ulysses Grant-Smith, for instance, put forward his analysis that "Hungary is not a European but an Asiatic nation, and that in consequence the structure of her society resembles that of Turkey more than that of any of the western nations of Europe."[53] Hamilton Fish Armstrong, the editor of *Foreign Affairs*, opined, based upon his experience in Hungary, "Arriving in Budapest is like coming back to yesterday from tomorrow."[54] But he added that "Hungarian psychology is something entirely special and different from any other, in Europe or elsewhere. It is difficult for a visitor to understand it."[55]

In the years in question, Hungarians themselves debated what it meant to be Hungarian. Many thought of the country as a representative of both Eastern and Western values and inheritance. For instance, Prime Minister Bethlen, in his article informing the American readership about "the historical mission" of Hungary, described it as "the intellectual, political, and economic link between East and West."[56] The unfolding cultural propaganda and diplomacy that Hungary carried out from the mid-1920s in order to facilitate the revision of the Trianon Treaty remained, according to historian Zsolt Nagy, "a curious, often perplexing, combination of new and old, traditional and modern, in which the modern and progressive served as a proof of Europeanness while the traditional sought to depict uniqueness."[57]

Many people writing about Hungary found it "feudal" in its outlook and nature. This was so often mentioned that is must be considered a stigma that the country was labeled with. Its origin seems to be that these observers were really startled by the, to them, seemingly backward state of things in politics

---

53   Ulysses Grant-Smith to Bainbridge Colby, June 9, 1920, 864.4016/16, Records of the Department of State Relating to Internal Affairs of Austria-Hungary and Hungary, 1912–1929, Roll 20, Microcopy No. 708, NARA.
54   Hamilton Fish Armstrong, "Hungary Awaits 'Der Tag'," *Our World* 1, no. 6 (September 1922): 76.
55   Ibid., 77.
56   Stephen Bethlen, "Hungary in the New Europe," *Foreign Affairs* 3, no. 3 (April 1925): 454.
57   Zsolt Nagy, *Great Expectations and Interwar Realities. Hungarian Cultural Diplomacy, 1918–1941* (Budapest: Central European University Press, 2017), 106.

and especially the lifestyle in the countryside—all as compared to American or British standards. Hungary clearly did not strike them as a flourishing democracy. Despite describing Hungarians as "a refined and cultivated people," one author also wrote that Hungary represented an "incontestable danger to Europe," and that Hungarians were not real Europeans, and, to make things worse, "no country has remained more attached to feudalism."[58] And this was the general impression not only in the beginning but throughout the interwar period. The last American minister during World War II, for instance, said after he was forced to leave Hungary that although he was very sympathetic to Hungarians, he found that the country was still feudal.[59] This was Hungary through the lens of various Americans—a kingdom showing remnants of feudalism and touches of the East while striving to belong to the West. And this was the country—a multifaceted picture tainted with certain stereotypes—in which Tyler arrived in 1924.

Unlike Smith, however, Royall Tyler was not an average American. He had already had glimpses into Hungary and its culture. In Newport during his childhood, he heard Hungarian folk and gypsy music and the Hungarian language for the first time.[60] Also, he had a couple of Hungarian classmates at Harrow, and at least twice had traveled to Hungary prior to World War I: once in 1907, and at another time in the fall of 1912. Hungary and whatever glimpses into its culture Tyler may have experienced before 1924 must have made the country seem an exciting, perhaps exotic place to visit. Not only was he was open to other cultures, intrigued by the unique Hungarian language, and a fan of Hungarian folk and gypsy music, but his growing experience as a food and wine connoisseur also meant that he would have things to discover in his new surroundings. Tyler also carried with him a great sense of wanting to be useful and help others. In an important capacity and as a delegate of the League of Nations, Tyler must have felt that he was someone important who was doing an essential task for the betterment of Europe. And he was cut out for that work.

---

58 G. De Villemus, "Hungary To-day," *The Living Age* 332, no. 4305 (May 1, 1927): 785, 787.
59 Herbert C. Pell to Cordell Hull, February 26, 1942, 864.00/1037, Records of the Department of State Relating to Internal, Affairs of Hungary, 1930–1944, Roll 13, Microcopy No. 1206, NARA. For more detail about the British and American perception of Hungary in the interwar years, see, Zoltán Peterecz, "Reflection of and about Hungary in the English-speaking World in the Interwar Years," *Hungarian Studies* 31, no. 2 (2017): 237–49.
60 Tyler, *One Name, Two Lives*, 20.

Chapter 3

The purpose of what follows is not to give a detailed account of the financial reconstruction of Hungary, since the issue has been thoroughly dealt with elsewhere.[61] Therefore only a brief summary will be given of this League effort, with a special emphasis on Tyler's work in it and his experience in Hungary and elsewhere during this period.

The first critical step for Hungary was to establish an independent Bank of Issue. The institution was established on May 24, 1924, and opened a month later. Sándor Popovics, a conservative and competent expert, became its first president, a position he held until his death in 1935. Smith had to find an adviser to the Bank as laid out in the Protocols, someone who could communicate between him and the National Bank, and who was also trustworthy. After a few rounds, in the end the choice fell on a young protégé of Norman and a member of Smith's own staff, Arthur Siepmann. Siepmann also spoke German, a qualification crucial in Hungary. The ambitious Siepmann became a member of the triumvirate that practically governed the bank, the other two being Popovics and Dusán Tabakovics, the director of the banking and exchange department.[62] Siepmann had been a Treasury delegate under John Maynard Keynes at the Paris Peace Conference, worked under Salter at the Financial Committee of the League of Nations, and he was involved in Indian financial affairs before taking up the Hungarian job. A generally cynical person and fond of clear lines along which work should be done, Siepmann often voiced critical opinions about the reconstruction and never missed an opportunity to inform Norman about the situation as he saw it. René Charron replaced Siepmann on Smith's staff, doing work related to statistics and economics.

The other outstanding task was, naturally, to raise the reconstruction loan for Hungary. Britain, and in particular Montagu Norman, were to play the most crucial role. Britain had the biggest political influence on the continent, and through the Bank of England, British financial circles would provide the greatest share of the long-term loan, just as in the case of Austria. The United States was also expected to play a role similar to the case of the

---

61   For the history of the financial reconstruction of Hungary, see, League of Nations, *Financial Reconstruction of Hungary*; Mária Ormos, *Az 1924. évi magyar államkölcsön megszerzése* [Raising the Hungarian State Loan of 1924] (Budapest: Akadémiai Kiadó, 1964); Péteri, *Global Monetary Regime and National Central Banking*; Lojkó, *Meddling in Middle Europe*, 81–126; Peterecz, *Jeremiah Smith, Jr. and Hungary*, 118–204.

62   Lojkó, *Meddling in Middle Europe*, 120; Péteri, *Global Monetary Regime*, 97–98.

Austrian reconstruction loan, and now that the Commissioner-General and his deputy were Americans, and the Austrian scheme seemed to hop along without major disappointments, the League's not unfounded hope was that a similar scenario would play out again. Although things did not go as smoothly as had been hoped, in the end, the loan was successfully raised. The subscription started on July 2 in England and the United States, both places scoring a huge success resulting in oversubscription. Great Britain again subscribed the largest portion, and Norman basically became the dictator of the Hungarian financial reconstruction, while the United States had taken on less than in the case of Austria. The other countries taking part were Italy, Switzerland, Sweden, the Netherlands, and Czechoslovakia, while the Hungarian tranche was subscribed in early August. Henry Strakosch's message to Smith well summarized how relieved the League felt with the launch of the successful subscription in London and New York: "The League has done its duty, and now it rests with the Hungarians to make a real success of the plan of Reconstruction."[63]

Royall Tyler, together with Jeremiah Smith, Jr., arrived in Hungary on May 1, 1924. Both men shunned the spotlight, and if somebody was called on to speak to reporters, it usually had to be the Commissioner-General. At the very beginning, although Smith spoke in the first person singular, he summed up his own attitude and that of the whole staff: "My duties are financial, not political, and to them I shall devote all my energy, hoping to assist a people for which my country has always had a great admiration, to establish the conditions which are so necessary for their comfort and happiness."[64] Tyler obviously agreed with this statement. The two Americans especially wanted to lead an absolutely apolitical office, insofar as that was possible in postwar Central Europe, where every financial or economic decision had political significance and echoes. They, however, wished to concentrate only on the job in front of them: carrying out the reconstruction scheme to the best of their ability.

The financial reconstruction of Hungary as conducted by the League of Nations must be acknowledged as having been a success story in the short run.

---

63 Henry Strakosch to Jeremiah Smith, July 2, 1924, C.III (4) Correspondence - Sir Henry Strakosch, C. 111, Financial Reconstruction of Hungary, LNA.
64 Smith's press release in Budapest, May 2, 1924, P.III. Press communiqués, C. 117, Financial Reconstruction of Hungary, LNA.

The program and its achievements can be clearly discerned in the monthly reports the Commissioner-General had to submit to the League. Smith and his staff were in constant contact with the Hungarian finance ministry, the National Bank, the Prime Minister and his office, in addition to the League and the Bank of England. Throughout the period of the reconstruction effort, the Hungarian budget always reflected ever better financial figures, the National Bank of Hungary functioned successfully, the Hungarian currency became stable, trade moved to a more satisfactory level, and there were cuts in the too-numerous class of officials. Naturally, these results were not guaranteed at the outset, nor were the changes necessarily rapid.

The first period of the program was especially crucial and demanding. As Tyler wrote in a letter in mid-July, he had "a very busy time here." Despite the tangible results of the first two months—opening the national Bank, managing to raise the international loan—in his opinion, which, although admittedly exaggeratingly fairly reflects his ambition to succeed, "It seems to me now that hardly anything has been accomplished."[65] Smith seemed to be more optimistic, at least in his first monthly report in which he declared: "There is no reason apparent why the execution of the Reconstruction plan should not produce the expected results."[66] Tyler accompanied Smith to Geneva in June, where the Commissioner-General informed the Financial Committee about the state of affairs, and the gathering entertained Tyler. The job in Budapest, however, also meant regular separation from Elisina and young William for extended periods. Elisina sometimes joined him for weeks in Budapest, but he had a chance to see his son only in Antigny, and more typically during the summer, since the boy was being educated at Harrow, somewhat following his father's footsteps. Family reunions then could be arranged when he managed to take a few days off after a League meeting in Geneva, which town was somewhat nearer to Anitgny than to Paris.

Tyler also reflected on the cultural surroundings he found himself in. Languages being his soft spot, it was no wonder that the Hungarian tongue piqued his interest. Not only might being able to communicate in the host language have facilitated his everyday work to a considerable degree in the

---

65   Royall Tyler to Mildred Barnes Bliss, July 18, 1924, Budapest, "Bliss–Tyler Correspondence," https://www.doaks.org/resources/bliss-tyler-correspondence/letters/18jul1924, accessed December 11, 2015.
66   Smith's First Report, *League of Nations Journal* (hereafter cited as LNJ), 5th Year, No. 7, July 1924, 979.

long run, but he was also simply enchanted by Hungarian. Mastering the native tongue posed a significant challenge, but with it came the satisfaction of making progress. In two and a half months he managed to "read a paper with great labour and a dictionary," and he "vastly enjoy making the profound cavernous noises."[67] The intellectual joy was perhaps what really motivated this man of many languages. Learning Hungarian meant taking a different approach and was perhaps a more substantial test of his skills, since this language was "so vastly different from any other European language," but "the sound of the words is intoxicating."[68]

When Smith visited Geneva alone, typically every three months for the League sessions, Tyler was left in charge in Budapest. This pleased Tyler's ego. He seemed to enjoy the responsibility, and the multifarious approach needed meant he had to be on top of things. For example, in early September 1924, he proudly and excitedly informed Barnes that he had "a most interesting time here running the Loan Account (yes, me!). God evidently intended me to have a go at a variety of trades, and this one pleases me particularly. State budgeting, monopolies, railways, etc. are my daily fare and I eat thereof with delight."[69] Obviously, the job had drawbacks, mainly isolation. It was not the separation from family alone that hurt him but also his remoteness from the West in general. His cultural openness must have helped him through such rough times. He saw an exotic country, perhaps hovering on the borderline between Europe and Asia, and one carrying with it big city luxury and countryside poverty, refined culture in metropolitan Budapest and a charming barbarism away from it. Jeremiah Smith always spoke of the Hungarians and their government in the most polite terms, which is understandable due to his position. A few years later, however, while briefing a soon-to-be U.S. minister to Hungary, he unrestrictedly spoke of Hungarian "supernationalism and their sense of inferiority," highlighted their "energy" and "personal hon-

---

67 Royall Tyler to Mildred Barnes Bliss, July 18, 1924.
68 Ibid. Hungarian is challenging for English speakers. Naturally, it is impossible to measure the level of difficulty precisely and make a comparison with other languages, but according to a language test site, Hungarian is the third most difficult language for an English-speaking person to learn, while another put it in fourth place. https://www.telc.net/en/about-telc/news/detail/5-most-difficult-languages-in-the-world-to-learn.html, accessed December 4, 2020; https://unbabel.com/blog/japanese-finnish-or-chinese-the-10-hardest-languages-for-english-speakers-to-learn/, accessed December 4, 2020.
69 Royall Tyler to Mildred Barnes Bliss, September 3, 1924, Budapest, "Bliss–Tyler Correspondence," https://www.doaks.org/resources/bliss-tyler-correspondence/letters/03sep1924, accessed December 11, 2015.

esty," but also called attention to their "childishness."[70] Tyler's overall assessment after his first few months in Hungary was that the country and the situation were "a nut worth cracking, however hard."[71]

The situation of the Hungarian state's employees was a constant problem. On the one hand, these people earned barely enough to have a comfortable life; on the other, about 60 percent of the annual budget was for personnel and pensions, which obviously left little room for long-lasting and productive investments on the government's part. The pensioners can be said to have suffered proportionally more, since as of July 1, 1924, their pensions were cut by 40 percent.[72] The Commissioner-General was pragmatic and did not always insist on enacting or enforcing every point laid down in the program; he and his staff focused on the overall success of the program instead. They talked to the government and tried to find the golden mean in cases of disagreement, which was appreciated by the Bethlen government. In the meantime, the deficits proved smaller than expected while revenues rose to a very promising level. Bank deposits started to increase slowly, unemployment remained relatively low and stable, trade—previously languid—started to pick up, but as Smith pointed out, without foreign capital long-term investments and the wealth they might create were not possible to realize.[73] In November, the monthly budget showed a small surplus for the first time, but Smith kept warning that the favorable data should not encourage the government to start spending—an ever-recurring admonition from the Commissioner-General. At the close of the first half of the 1924/25 fiscal year, signs were promising as to the future, although there were indications that obstacles lay ahead.

December 1924 was both momentous and positive for Tyler. His wife and son joined him for Christmas in Budapest, obviously to his great satisfaction. This family reunion was in sharp contrast to how he personally felt about his situation in Hungary. He was forced to lead "a very monotonous life," from which only work and the ever-challenging Hungarian lan-

---

70   Nicholas Roosevelt's diary entry, October 15, 1930, Hungary 1930–1933, Box 19, Nicholas Roosevelt Papers, Syracuse, USA.
71   Royall Tyler to Mildred Barnes Bliss, September 17, 1924, Budapest, "Bliss–Tyler Correspondence," https://www.doaks.org/resources/bliss-tyler-correspondence/letters/17sep1924, accessed December 11, 2015.
72   Romsics, *István Bethlen*, 238.
73   Smith's Fourth Report, LNJ, 5th Year, No. 11, November 1924, 1741–48.

guage provided some escape.[74] He had made further advances in the new language—"I can talk it a little now, and read with the help of a dictionary"—but this was not sufficiently satisfactory, and Tyler kept expending energy on this challenge.[75] Aside from work and language studies, he found excitement in studying the archeological works and finds in Hungary, which bore a close resemblance to his encounters in Byzantine art history, and there was quality music available in nearby Vienna.

The year 1925, however, started badly from a personal point of view, because in the beginning of January Smith got seriously ill and stayed in a sanatorium for weeks. Tyler had to take the helm. His first act was to assuage the general worry in the wake of the Commissioner-General's illness.[76] Smith had traveled to Geneva in early February for a League meeting, so he could personally inform the organization about the status of the reconstruction program, but immediately afterward he began his extended rest and returned to Budapest only at the beginning of March. From then on, he had to work less, and in April he traveled home to the United States for a prolonged and badly needed respite. He returned to Budapest in mid-May, "not entirely recovered."[77] Tyler had to assume full responsibility of the controlling function in Smith's absence. For example, the report on the Hungarian financial situation for April was Tyler's work alone, and one might assume that various other monthly reports bore his stamp as well. Also, in lieu of the Commissioner-General, it was Tyler who conferred with Bethlen and agreed to an advance of 24 million gold crowns ($5 million) in light of the "extreme urgency to alleviate unemployment by carrying out certain public utility works in the Comitats and provincial towns."[78] Privately, he talked of a "lot of very difficult business coming on this summer," but he allegedly said to Salter that things were going really smoothly.[79]

---

74 Royall Tyler to Mildred Barnes Bliss, December 20, 1924, Budapest, "Bliss–Tyler Correspondence," https://www.doaks.org/resources/bliss-tyler-correspondence/letters/20dec1924, accessed December 11, 2015.
75 Ibid.
76 Press communiqué, January 17, 1925, P.III. Press communiqués, C. 117, Financial Reconstruction of Hungary, LNA.
77 Jeremiah Smith to Elliott Felkin, May 22, 1925, C.III (6) Correspondence - M. A. E. Felkin, C. 111, Financial Reconstruction of Hungary, LNA.
78 Royall Tyler to István Bethlen, May 14, 1925, Thompson Todd Collection.
79 Royall Tyler to Mildred Barnes Bliss, April 15, 1925, Antigny-le-Château, "Bliss–Tyler Correspondence," https://www.doaks.org/resources/bliss-tyler-correspondence/letters/15apr1925, accessed December 4, 2015.

Chapter 3

And indeed, in 1925 the reconstruction program continued its march toward a successful outcome. Revenue surplus was a constant feature, and despite the larger than expected and hoped-for expenditures, there was enough available money to implement what was intended. Being cautiously optimistic, Smith never failed to call attention to the fact that further steps toward reform and smaller spending on the part of the government were required. Hungary's economic nationalism, that is, trying to rely on being self sufficient, created problems and slowed progress toward signing commercial treaties with various countries, despite the fact that doing so was a fervent recommendation by the League. In addition, various increases in tariffs also contributed to weaker trade relations and a less healthy economic environment. But the Hungarian currency had at last become stable, and even the pessimistic adviser to the National Bank opined that it could be shaken by "nothing short of an international catastrophe."[80] With England returning to gold parity, the Hungarian crown—being pegged to the English pound—also found itself based on gold's value, which was a further stabilizing factor. Wholesale prices kept decreasing, unemployment remained relatively low, the National Bank's discount rate went down, and there was a strong prospect that further loans would arrive. An American rating group concluded that the Hungarian League bond was "the most attractive," partly because in-place supervision was carried out by Americans.[81]

Tyler complained that the Hungarian government, and basically everybody in Hungary, wanted more money. The reasoning was that since only roughly one third of the loan had been spent up until the spring of 1925 there was no need for extraordinary caution in spending and the government could use the remaining sum for various things, such as tax relief, tax burden being a recurring problem in the Central European country. Since Smith and the League resisted freeing this money to the Hungarian government, they were regarded "a nuisance" by many Hungarians.[82] But there was no denying that Hungary would "certainly get on her feet again, and to stay,"

---

80 Siepmann's memorandum on the Hungarian situation, March 15, 1925, C4189/260/21, 10772, FO371, TNA.
81 W. A. Harriman & Co. Analyses, June 5, 1925, L.V. (2) May 1925–Dec 1927, C. 114, Financial Reconstruction of Hungary, LNA.
82 Royall Tyler to Mildred Barnes Bliss, April 21, 1925, Budapest, "Bliss–Tyler Correspondence," https://www.doaks.org/resources/bliss-tyler-correspondence/letters/21apr1925, accessed December 4, 2015.

Tyler wrote. "Her fundamental position is stronger than Austria's."[83] When speaking of the government and its governing style, Tyler expressed mixed feelings. On the one hand, he admitted that a semi-democratic, somewhat authoritarian state form had "drawbacks," but at the same time "when it's a matter of putting through essential reforms one is deeply thankful for it."[84]

In June 1925, the meeting of the League Council in Geneva took place at what Tyler called "a critical juncture."[85] After all, this was the occasion to present the results of the first year of the reconstruction program—which were "far beyond the most sanguine expectations entertained by anyone a year ago."[86] In light of the good numbers concerning deficit and revenues, the League allowed the Hungarian government to draw 93 million gold crowns (almost $19 million) for productive purposes, subject to Smith's approval.[87] The Council also allowed some increase in the state officials' salaries, but there was no solution offered as to the high tax burden Hungarians had to put up with. In Tyler's unofficial words, "Our affairs are going quite well, but they need constant attention."[88]

The rest of that summer produced further promising signs. All indicators signaled positive results, all of which were substantiated by two foreign experts. Professor Allyn Young of Harvard and a Belgian financial expert, Maurice Frère, investigated the circumstances on the ground in Hungary for three weeks, and their findings were optimistic, although they called attention to such problems as low real wages, too much emphasis on industry instead of agriculture, heavy taxation, and the danger lying in "over-borrowing or in borrowing for non-productive purposes."[89] The harvest was an exceptional one, always a crucial aspect of the outlook for Hungary's well-being the following year. Tyler spent much of the uneventful summer in Budapest until he could escape to Antigny for a whole month in mid-August before returning to spend the rest of the year in Hungary.

---

83   Ibid.
84   Ibid.
85   Royall Tyler to Mildred Barnes Bliss, April 15, 1925, Antigny-le-Château, "Bliss–Tyler Correspondence," https://www.doaks.org/resources/bliss-tyler-correspondence/letters/15apr1925, accessed December 4, 2015.
86   Smith's Fourteenth Report, LNJ, 6th Year, No. 9, September 1925, 1242.
87   Report of the Committee, June 11, 1925, C. 335 (I). M. 116. 1925, LNA.
88   Royall Tyler to Mildred Barnes Bliss, July 7, 1925, Budapest, "Bliss–Tyler Correspondence," https://www.doaks.org/resources/bliss-tyler-correspondence/letters/07jul1925, accessed December 5, 2015.
89   Young- Frère Report, 3/1921–1928 B/2. 570/925, K 468, Bethlen Papers, HNA.

Chapter 3

Although the fall was uninteresting from the point of view of the program to which both Smith and Tyler devoted all their time and energy, at the end of October Smith once again traveled to the United States for health reasons. Tyler took over the job for another two months. Under his watch, the National Assembly passed the bill providing for the new currency unit, the *pengő*. The *korona* (crown) was the currency of the new monetary system created in Hungary in March 1920; the *pengő* would succeed it from January 1, 1927.

Tyler had to appear alone before the League Session in Geneva—the first time Smith had not attended. Facing the Financial Committee and the League Council may have seemed intimidating, but he had been there as Smith's sidekick quite a few times. All in all, Tyler "enjoyed it after the first emotion was over."[90] Similarly to the Financial Committee, which allowed the release of 50 million gold crowns ($10 million) for productive purposes, the Hungarian sub-Committee was satisfied with the results achieved, but pointed out that further steps were required in taxation and the tariff policy.[91] So, almost everything looked rosy regarding Hungarian finances, and the returning Commissioner-General boosted overall morale in an interview that he gave after his return to Hungary. Smith said that in American and other foreign countries, which must have meant mainly England, the Hungarian economy enjoyed trust, and those foreigners following the program of financial rehabilitation of Hungary "all share the same opinion that today the success of the reconstruction is a fact."[92]

Although both Smith and Tyler were officials of the League of Nations and did not have any formal ties to the American government, the Hungarian political leadership and the people in general regarded them not only as representatives of the overseas giant but also as a kind of bridge between the two nations. Despite their energetic efforts to deny that they possessed the influence contributed to them, in the eyes of the average Hungarian they did represent the United States. This had been a common

---

[90] Royall Tyler to Mildred Barnes Bliss, December 31, 1925, Budapest, "Bliss–Tyler Correspondence," https://www.doaks.org/resources/bliss-tyler-correspondence/letters/31dec1925, accessed December 6, 2015.

[91] Meeting of the Committee of the Council for Hungary, December 7, 1925, Financial Reconstruction of Hungary, Provisional minutes of the 9th Session: December 1925. Doc. No. 48287, Registry Files, R. 301, LNA.

[92] *Pesti Napló*, January 15, 1926.

phenomenon since the end of World War I. An American officer of the Coolidge Mission noted in 1919 that in Budapest "no amount of persuasion could convince the Hungarians that our mission was not political and did not carry great weight in Paris."[93] Another member of the same mission, writing basically about the whole Central European region, wrote in his diary that almost everybody was "looking to America as a composite savior, guardian angel, boundary commission, and food supply."[94] Coolidge himself wrote that Hungarians "look primarily to America for their salvation."[95] And since certain steps taken by Americans, either private or governmental, only strengthened this prevailing sentiment, it was not within the power of Smith and Tyler to overcome it.

The U.S. government concluded a Treaty of Friendship, Commerce, and Consular Rights with Hungary and signed it in Washington, D.C. on June 24, 1925, somewhat facilitating smoother relationship between the two countries. In trade the most-favored-nation principle prevailed, while the Hungarian consulates now could carry out their efforts based on a treaty, therefore they were able to better represent Hungarians' rights in the United States.[96] Hungary was in need of foreign capital, and loans were the only avenue to receive them. A week after the above mentioned treaty was signed, the $10,000,000 Hungarian Consolidated Municipal Loan was signed between the American Speyer & Co. and the Hungarian government.[97] Such events in the span of one week naturally boosted the already high prestige of the United States in Hungary.

In the days of sometimes difficult, but at other times smoother reconstruction, Tyler managed to find time and energy to focus on art history as well. It was more than pursuing intellectual curiosity; it also offered an

---

93   Roosevelt, *A History of a Few Weeks*, 229.
94   Diary entry, November 26, 1918, Charles Moorfield Storey Journal, 1918–1919, Massachusetts Historical Society, United States.
95   Archibald Cary Coolidge to the American Mission in Paris, January 19, 1919, quoted in Harold Jefferson Coolidge and Robert Howard Lord, *Archibald Cary Coolidge: Life and Letters* (Boston and New York: Houghton Mifflin, 1932), 211.
96   For the text of the treaty, see FRUS: 1925, vol. 2: 341–54. Soon after the signing of the treaty, the U.S. Senate added certain reservations concerning Hungarian immigration to the United States, which Hungary accepted. Kellogg to Széchényi and Széchényi to Kellogg, June 24, 1925, and Theodore Brentano to Lajos Walkó and Lajos Walkó to Theodore Brentano, September 4, 1926, ibid., 354–57.
97   *New York Times*, July 5, 1925. The different papers relating to the loan can be found in 332 and 334–38, K 269, Finance Ministry, General Papers, HNA.

escape from the daily routine of state finances and related chores. From the very first months he closely followed archeological diggings and the discoveries in their wake, and he sought out expert company in this field as well. Nándor Fettich became a regular companion, and although his specialty was not art history, his deep knowledge about early Hungarian history and even times before that must have appealed to the American.[98] Tyler was knowledgeable about Hungarian art collections both public and private, and he could inform the curious Blisses about certain pieces' exact whereabouts.[99] Also, Tyler was responsible for the chapter on architecture in a cooperative effort by many contributors that resulted in a book on Byzantine art.[100] But understandably, nothing brought as much pleasure as reuniting with his family. Both Elisina and young Bill came to Budapest for the Christmas vacation again in 1925, and they spent a brief but invaluable time together. Those days must have been special not only because he did not have to focus on the reconstruction program—although the overall indicators were good and the work was not as hectic as in the beginning—but also because only the school breaks offered these limited possibilities to be together with both his wife and son. The next such opportunity came in the spring, and although he could not escape to Paris and Antigny, the Dalmatian coast offered a venue in which to see Bill once more.

Concerning other aspects of Hungarian culture and ambiance, in one of his letters to Mildred Barnes Tyler Tyler wrote about the prevailing anti-Semitism in Hungary. Hungarians had for a long time showed antipathy toward Jews, but notwithstanding this widespread sentiment, the majority of the Jewish population had managed to climb the social ladder and they occupied a disproportionately large segment of the various free professions, such as doctors, lawyers, engineers, or musicians.[101] Many of them took

---

98 Fettich produced several books on history, and later became director of the Hungarian National Museum and a member of the Hungarian Academy of Sciences. Gyula László, "Fettich Nándor emlékezete" [Remembering Nándor Fettich], in *Cumania, 1, Archeologia*, eds. Attila Horváth and Elvira H. Tóth (Kecskemét: Bács-Kiskun Megyei Múzeumok Közleményei, 1972), 231–32; Kornél Bakay, "Fettich Nándor emlékére" [In Memory of Nándor Fettich], Életünk 18, no. 1 (January 1981): 55–62.
99 Royall Tyler to Mildred Barnes Bliss, April 5, 1926, Budapest, "Bliss–Tyler Correspondence," https://www.doaks.org/resources/bliss-tyler-correspondence/letters/05apr1926, accessed December 7, 2015.
100 *Spanish Art, An Introductory Review of Architecture, Painting, Sculpture, Textiles, Ceramic, Woodwork, Metalwork*, Burlington Magazine Monograph 2 (London: B. T. Batsford, 1927).
101 Ezra Mendelsohn, *The Jews of East Central Europe between the World Wars* (Bloomington: University of Indiana, 1983), 100–102.

part in trade or were bankers, and some became so rich that they could even buy their way into the aristocracy, another point causing animosity among most Hungarians. The Bolshevik coup in March 1919, in which many of the leaders were of Jewish origin, only heightened the prevalent anti-Semitism, and easily targeted Jews as scapegoats for the tragic postwar situation. This was both a result of and further added to what Paul Hanebrink called the "myth of Judeo-Bolshevism," which referred to the belief on part of many that Communism was brought on as a Jewish plot.[102] As he put it, and his observation was by all means true of Hungary, "Judeo-Bolshevism loomed in political imagination throughout the region as a powerful transnational enemy."[103] These circumstances consequently laid the groundwork for the first anti-Jewish legislation in Europe, the *Numerus Clausus*, in 1920, which law limited the number of Jews who were allowed to study in institutions of higher learning.[104] Tyler experienced this anti-Jewish atmosphere in Hungary, but in his opinion, the Jews had started to make a slow comeback, and this was due to their strong work ethic, while "the Hunk is not prepared to go to such heights."[105]

Given that all indicators showed a healthier economic and financial Hungary, the originally planned end of the reconstruction program was in sight. Already in April Bethlen asked the League of Nations to terminate the Commissioner-General's control, which was justified in the light of the results achieved, and which was a crucial point for perceived Hungarian sovereignty.[106] In the June Assembly at Geneva the major point was to terminate the direct League control in both Austria and Hungary. Although France and the Little Entente tried to postpone the decision on account of

---

102 Paul Hanebrink, *A Specter Haunting Europe: The Myth of Judeo-Bolshevism* (Cambridge, MA, London, England: Belknap Press of Harvard University Press, 2018).
103 Ibid., 51.
104 The text of the bill is in *Magyar Törvénytár, 1920. évi törvénycikkek* [Hungarian Law Collection, Law Bills of 1920] (Budapest, 1921), 145–46. See also, Gergely Egressy, "A Statistical Overview of the Hungarian Numerus Clausus Law of 1920—A Historical Necessity or the First Step Toward the Holocaust?" *Eastern European Quarterly* 34 (January 2001): 447–64.
105 Royall Tyler to Mildred Barnes Bliss, April 5, 1926, Budapest, "Bliss–Tyler Correspondence," https://www.doaks.org/resources/bliss-tyler-correspondence/letters/05apr1926, accessed December 7, 2015. "Hunk" was a typical term Tyler used for Hungarians. It was not derogatory on his part, rather a shortened term.
106 Jeremiah Smith to the Secretary General, April 24, 1926, Financial Reconstruction of Hungary, Cessation of the control of Hungarian finances. Doc. No. 51126, Registry Files, R. 301, LNA.

the franc forgery scandal earlier that year, the Financial Committee in the end agreed that the office of the Commissioner-General should be terminated as of June 30, 1926.[107] Smith was profusely praised by everybody; his pragmatic attitude, his ability to smooth rough waters, his relentless energy were all highlighted in various speeches at Geneva and Budapest alike.[108] Smith's final report to the League commenting on the Hungarian finances revealed spectacular results: the pledged revenues produced eight times the annual service charge in the last fiscal year; the same period boasted a substantial budget surplus; from the loan of 253 million gold crowns, only 70 million had to be spent on budget deficits, the larger part of the remaining amount had been authorized by the League for capital investments, while 81 million gold crowns ($16.2 million) still remained; the Hungarian currency was stable while inflation remained low; the National Bank reduced interest rate from 12.5 percent to 6 percent in the discussed period; trade relations improved greatly and commercial treaties had been concluded with several European countries; various domestic reforms had been carried out; continual growth of bank deposits was noticeable, while retail and wholesale prices had decreased; unemployment remained low.[109] It quickly has to be emphasized though that despite the many positive results, Hungary was still only approaching prewar levels, thus a long road lay ahead. The only thing Smith warned against was not to overburden the country with foreign loans, and although at present still under control, Siepmann had already complained about the Hungarian practice he characterized as a "free-lance campaign of borrowing."[110] The Hungarian prime minister also counseled "to take great care, despite the hard conditions, not to make this

---

107 Work of the Financial Committee during Its Twenty-second Session, June 3–9, 1926, C. 359. M. 127. 1926. II, LNA; Peterecz, *Jeremiah Smith, Jr. and Hungary*, 179–80. On December 14, 1925, a Hungarian officer was arrested in the Netherlands when trying to pay with a forged 1,000 French franc note. First, some officials in the French foreign political establishment wanted to exploit the scandal to cause a government crisis or change in Hungary, but nothing came of it, and during the League session in March, the franc forgery was not dealt with officially. Finally, the alleged perpetrators were given not too heavy sentences in the summer. For more about the scandal in detail, see Ignác Romsics, "Franciaország, Bethlen és a frankhamisítás" [France, Bethlen, and the Franc Forgery], *Történelmi Szemle* 26 (1983): 67–86; Balázs Ablonczy, "A frankhamisítás. Hálók, személyek, döntések" [The Franc Forgery. Networks, Persons, Decisions], *Múltunk* 53, no. 1 (2008): 29–56.
108 Peterecz, *Jeremiah Smith, Jr. and Hungary*, 181–82.
109 Smith's Twenty-fifth Report, League of Nations, *Financial Reconstruction of Hungary*, 164–87.
110 Harry Siepmann to Montagu Norman, May 19, 1925, OV33/39, BoE.

country deep in debt," which warning would prove interesting in light of later events.[111]

The League of Nations was satisfied that the first two reconstruction schemes it undertook in two defeated countries in Central Europe had finished on a high note. This outcome not only created prestige that was important for the organization from all angles but also meant that in the future the League-orchestrated financial reconstruction program would be welcome elsewhere and might offer a workable method for other financially wrecked countries. From another perspective, the financial-economic rehabilitation could not have taken place without political compromise, and it also produced a much larger degree of political stability in the region, parallel to the relative overall stability in most of Europe as well, certainly a key aspect to the League.

Understandably, the Hungarian government was pleased with the interim results and the final outcome of the reconstruction program, and despite its harmonious working relationship with Smith and his staff, it once more felt that it finally had a free hand after having been under League control for two and a half years. Therefore, it is significant to note that total control over the Hungarian finances did not cease. Supervision remained in place over the pledged revenues for the service of the loan and the balance of the League loan. The person to carry out this job and act as a contact and bridge between the League of Nations, the Trustees of the loan, and the Hungarian government was to be Tyler.[112] This was never really in question, and everybody heartily agreed to the nomination. His salary was to be $10,000 a year as representatives of the Trustees. He and the reduced staff of two in Budapest would receive $1,500 a month for expenses—the same as Smith had received as Commissioner-General. Tyler refused to accept any compensation for representing the Hungarian government before the Committee of Control, a job requested by the Bethlen government.[113] He thought that the job would require more than the anticipated two years—it would in fact turn out to be three years—and he would have to stay in Budapest more, in addition

---

111 *National Assembly Diary, 1922–1927*, vol. 45: 99.
112 Carel Eliza ter Meulen to Arthur Salter and Henry Strakosch to Arthur Salter, June 18, 1926, and István Bethlen to Arthur Salter, July 5, 1926, Financial Reconstruction of Hungary, Services and expenses of Mr. Tyler, a representative of the Trustees in Budapest. Doc. No. 52197, Registry Files, R. 302, LNA.
113 Royall Tyler to Arthur Salter, July 9, 1926, ibid.

to the required trips to Geneva and Paris. The latter two destinations made him keep in close touch with the Financial Committee, "a connection I greatly value," while allowing him to visit Antigny for extended albeit still too short periods of time.[114] He accompanied the Hungarian finance minister on his courtesy visit in July to Amsterdam to meet one of the Trustees, ter Meulen, then spent the next month at Antigny, and returned to Budapest in mid-August. With it Tyler began another chapter in his connection with Hungary and Hungarian finances.

---

114 Royall Tyler to Mildred Barnes Bliss, July 21, 1926, Antigny-le-Château, "Bliss–Tyler Correspondence," https://www.doaks.org/resources/bliss-tyler-correspondence/letters/21jul1926, accessed December 7, 2015.

CHAPTER 4

The League of Nations Years Part II: Post-Reconstruction Hungary under Tyler's Watch, 1926-1929

After the financial reconstruction of Hungary came to a successful end, Royall Tyler remained the link between Hungary and the League of Nations, and between the Trustees and the status of the League loan. He was also, inescapably, the private connection between the United States and Hungary, however vaguely and only symbolically in that capacity. As far as the work of supervising the Hungarian finances and the remainder of the loan went, Tyler did not need to worry: the League's reconstruction program had concluded successfully, and the additional three years that Tyler was to spend overseeing the loan account and the pledged revenues promised to be routine work. Also, the harmonious relationship that had been established with the Hungarian government and the National Bank of Hungary boded well for the remaining time under his control.

Following the attitude so conspicuously embodied by both Jeremiah Smith, Jr. and himself, Tyler avoided even the most remote thought of getting too close to political questions, and he focused strictly on the financial matter at hand and remained as impartial as could be expected from an American. Naturally, he kept in touch with a wide variety of people, many of whom were politicians, but he did not get enmeshed in the game of politics. He obviously did have a political opinion, but he kept that to himself and instead tried to pursue his intellectual interests in both Hungarian culture, mainly the language, and his ever-present passion for art history.

Chapter 4

Tyler officially visited Geneva for the League Council meeting in September 1926 in his new capacity, and also managed to spend some time to stay in Antigny before returning to Budapest at the end of the month. A few weeks later, he was due in Paris, then London to tend to additional business, among other things, before returning to Budapest to prepare his report for the December League meeting, which took him to Geneva again. This busy itinerary was proof that finances in Hungary were in good condition. Like Smith, Tyler submitted the required reports to the Financial Committee. These followed the structure of the earlier reports, but in view of the successful financial reconstruction program, Tyler prepared his every three months instead of once a month. His first report already contained news that reassured all concerned parties that the finishing touches of the rehabilitation program did not mean the end of the healthier financial atmosphere in Hungary. Bank deposits kept growing and reached the highest level since the beginning of the reconstruction period, the wholesale price index remained stable, the retail index was the lowest since March 1924, and foreign trade had increased a little, though production increase showed a slowing tendency.[1]

In November the revenue reached the highest point yet for any month, but Tyler also shared the older idea that taxation should be reduced. He reasoned that this was necessary because the increased revenue was not due to higher production and wealth in the country but rather to "the perfection of the fiscal machine, which is now being worked with deadly accuracy."[2] These good results only emphasized why control, if not scrapped entirely, was eased and put on an alleviated if still formal level. Hungary enjoyed positive figures in almost all categories, its credit was ensured in Western financial circles, and its relationship with the League was pleasant. Tyler's official position, Representative of the League of Nations to Hungary, reflected as much. He was not a controller like his predecessor but more of an observer and occasional advisor to Hungary.

Since the first long phase of his Hungarian stay had not allowed Tyler to get away for longer periods, the more leisurely pace of the second stage prom-

---

[1] Tyler's report to the Economic and Financial Section of the League of Nations on the financial position of Hungary between July 1, 1926, and November 24, 1926, November 24, 1926, OV 33/74, BoE.
[2] Royall Tyler to Harry Siepmann, December 3, 1926, ibid.

ised the chance "to catch up with a lot of things."[3] Some of his trips were related to art dealership. In Hungary he mainly could secure carpets, but he also made stops in Vienna, where he negotiated for the Niceforus Botaniates Medallion piece—a Byzantine art rarity—that was offered for sale by the Monastery of Heiligenkreuz.[4] His efforts on behalf of the Victoria and Albert Museum paid off, because early the next year the Museum secured the piece.

Conjoining semi-professional activities with personal pleasure, he managed to travel to Cairo, Egypt, with his son and wife for two weeks during Harrow's winter break. The journey was expensive, and Tyler could not afford it, but it was paid by the Blisses, for whom Tyler was carrying out art reconnaissance and negotiating possible purchases. This was not only a precious fortnight with his family, but it also offered a chance to instill some knowledge and hopefully passion into young William via first-hand experience in a land so rich in archeological treasures. Hayford Peirce also joined them in North Africa and remained there after the Tylers had gone. Tyler "enjoyed the visit to Egypt immensely," and altogether must have been satisfied with their progress there.[5] As Elisina conveyed it, "We bit deep into Egypt, in spite of the briefness of our visit."[6]

The following January the National Assembly of Hungary held a special session. It was the first time since the war that an Upper House had been called into being, and it was not clear whether the new session was to pass major resolutions. Obviously, these may have affected financial issues, so Tyler had to be in Budapest in case something momentous came up. He stayed in Budapest until the end of February, and Elisina joined him there, which happened infrequently. A period of travel followed. First, he was to appear at

---

3 Royall Tyler to Mildred Barnes Bliss, September 28, 1926, Budapest, "Bliss–Tyler Correspondence," https://www.doaks.org/resources/Bliss–Tyler-correspondence/letters/28sep1926, accessed December 8, 2015.
4 Royall Tyler to Mildred Barnes Bliss, July 21, 1926, Antigny-le-Château, "Bliss–Tyler Correspondence," https://www.doaks.org/resources/Bliss–Tyler-correspondence/letters/21jul1926, accessed December 8, 2015.
5 Royall Tyler to Robert Woods Bliss, January 13, 1927, Lloyd Triestino, Piroscafo "Helouan", Egypt, "Bliss–Tyler Correspondence," https://www.doaks.org/resources/Bliss–Tyler-correspondence/letters/13jan1927, accessed December 9, 2015.
6 Elisina Tyler to Mildred Barnes Bliss, January 25, 1927, Antigny-le-Château, "Bliss–Tyler Correspondence," https://www.doaks.org/resources/Bliss–Tyler-correspondence/letters/25jan1927, accessed December 9, 2015.

the meeting of the Financial Committee of the League of Nations at the end of February to inform the body about aspects of Hungary's finances. As he reported, everything went "smoothly here this time for me and my Hunkies."⁷ Thereafter, he stayed at Antigny, travelled back to Budapest, and later had some business in Rome in early April. After Rome, he proceeded to Belgrade, where he and Peirce gave a talk at the Byzantine Conference, following which he studied monasteries in Serbia.⁸ He also had a chance to meet there with his old colleague and friend, Charron, who was doing the League's work in Bulgaria at the time.⁹ To say that his itinerary was light would be an understatement. Tyler did not return to Budapest before May.

In 1927 signs appeared that not everything was all right, especially when compared to Tyler's earlier reports and the encouraging results of the reconstruction program. Hungary started to produce less than good overall performance results shortly after the conclusion of the reconstruction program. There was a negative trade balance, a restrictive trade policy and sometimes exorbitant prices, and in addition, some traditional Hungarian industries like milling were neglected in favor of other branches of industry, such as textiles. Also, high tariffs were restricting more plentiful trade, and two-thirds of the imports came from countries with which Hungary had no tariff agreement, and about half of Hungary's exports went to these countries as well.¹⁰ This was, of course, not a uniquely Hungarian phenomenon in tariff policy. The United States introduced high tariffs with the passage of the Fordney–McCumber Tariff Act of 1922, which raised the average tariff imposed on imported goods to almost 40 percent. The idea was to protect U.S. based industry and farmers, and for the United States, which provided loans throughout the world, the notion of higher tariffs made sense at the time. In Europe, a protectionist trade mentality also prevailed, despite the League of Nations' regular warnings and advice that tariffs ought to be lessened in order to facilitate freer trade. Especially in Central Europe, however, countries seemed to find short-term political and economic advantage

---

7   Royall Tyler to Mildred Barnes Bliss, March 9, 1927, Geneva, "Bliss–Tyler Correspondence," https://www.doaks.org/resources/Bliss–Tyler-correspondence/letters/09mar1927, accessed December 9, 2015.
8   Ibid.
9   Royall Tyler to Harry Siepmann, April 10, 1927, OV 33/2, BoE.
10 Arthur Salter to Royall Tyler, March 23, 1927, File 58698, Economic Situation of Hungary, Box 479, Registry Files, 1919–1927, Section No. 10, LNA.

in high tariffs, Hungary being no exception to this trend. Perhaps the burdened relationship with its neighbors only added impetus to take such a trade policy path.

What would have been needed, in both foreign and domestic economic and trade policies, was reforms. Not only administrative reforms, but also changing the existing dynamics of resorting to foreign loans. The financial reconstruction proved that Hungary was a safe place for long-term loans, and in the loan-giving environment of the 1920s, Hungary seemed to want more and more of them. The problem did not necessarily lie in the ability to secure fresh loans, but rather in how they were spent. The earlier trend of spending too much on various undertakings to boost the immediate living standard and overall morale rather than on productive investments did not augur well for long-term results. Historian György Péteri showed that hardly "more than one-third of the bond loans were invested in private enterprise, only about 11 percent in industry; the other two-thirds were absorbed by the investments and expenses of the public sector—the central government, the counties, the municipalities, communities and religious congregations."[11] Although Hungarian finance minister János Bud tried to stem the tide of loans, especially those of a municipal nature, alone he was too weak to facilitate a change.[12] There was still the remaining sum of the reconstruction loan that Hungary was supposed to receive and spend, but first the investment program had to be agreed by Tyler. With his consent, in March the Financial Committee, and consequently the League Council, agreed to release the remaining 50 million gold crowns ($10 million).[13]

At the same time, as if to echo Tyler's undesirable findings, evidence of Hungary's negative trend came straight from the horse's mouth. Béla Imrédy, who was head of the Intelligence Section of the National Bank of Hungary at the time, poured his heart out to Harry Siepmann, former adviser to the National Bank of Hungary and now with the Bank of England. Imrédy, like Tyler, stressed the growing debt and the negative trade balance, but the chief problem he identified lay in agriculture and the uncertain possibility that its products would be exported. Further increase in agricultural production, as

---

11   Péteri, *Global Monetary Regime*, 142.
12   Royall Tyler to Harry Siepmann, April 10, 1927, OV 33/2, BoE.
13   LNJ, 8th Year, no. 4 (April 1927), Forty-fourth Session of the Council, 514; Work of the Financial Committee during Its Twenty-Sixth Session, C. 152. M. 44. 1927. II, LNA.

he pointed out, was in itself no solution for Hungary. "What then remains?" he asked. "Are we to starve, or go about in rags, or dispatch the million superfluous Hungarians to a foreign country or to a better world?"[14] In his view, there were two choices: industrialization, which he admitted was a wasteful choice; or higher prices for Hungarian agricultural products, while offering imported industrial goods at a lower price. The overall stagnation in agricultural prices did not bode well, and, according to Imrédy, who by nature was a pessimist, this situation threatened "the very existence of a whole nation, and the whole structure of our State."[15]

Siepmann was in a key position at this time. The reputation that he had built in Hungary during the financial reconstruction made him a perfect intelligence officer for the Bank of England, whose governor, Norman, saw an important ally in the Hungarian National Bank and had been, of course, the key player in the loan for the financial reconstruction. Both Tyler and Imrédy regularly informed Siepmann about the state of Hungarian finances, so the Briton was as well informed as and perhaps more up-to-date than the League's Financial Committee. The Bank of England quickly reacted to this worrying information and sent an expert to investigate the financial and economic conditions in Hungary, but said expert "could find in Hungary no deep-seated troubles calling for diagnosis."[16] This conclusion is somewhat strange in hindsight. Still, the president of the National Bank of Hungary, Sándor Popovics, found it expedient to pay a short visit to London, which was telling. Popovics highlighted for Norman the discrepancy between agricultural and industrial price levels in favor of the latter, a feature that was hurting Hungary, but he added that lack of capital on the continent was playing a significant role as well, a situation that might change only after a transitional period. He saw the only possible solution for his bank to be that it play a more central role with respect to reducing foreign indebtedness and controlling monetary policy.[17]

To some extent, this revealed the weakness of the system. On the surface and after just a little digging, not even some of the expert eyes could detect fundamental problems in Hungary. After all, state finances were sat-

---

14 Béla Imrédy to Harry Siepmann, April 30, 1927, OV 33/2, BoE.
15 Ibid.
16 Harry Siepmann to Béla Imrédy, May 6, 1927, ibid.
17 "Memorandum. Hungary. Points which arose in conversation with Dr. Popovics," May 13, 1927, ibid.

isfactory, past harvests and the outlook for the 1927 harvest were excellent, business had picked up (mainly due to constructions in the country), and just like the year before, the government could boast of a sizeable revenue surplus, largely due to customs and the tobacco monopoly.[18] Still, the average Hungarian was poor, the standard of living far from adequate, the per capita tax burden very high. The composition of the Hungarian state did not help to alleviate these problems. Certain professions were overrepresented, such as merchants or lawyers. The overabundance of the latter category was connected to the too-large number of universities in Hungary producing them; not to mention the swollen state bureaucracy, which had also been a perennial shortcoming. As Tyler keenly observed, despite the government taking the overall right direction, these trends were really "the roots of the evil."[19] This combination of an unhealthy social composition, an adverse trend toward serving Hungarian needs in international trade, and regular borrowing on the international money market, mainly for consumption, really did produce symptoms of deep-seated difficulties, even if the surface may have seemed unruffled.

In the summer of 1927, after a short visit to London and Antigny, Tyler was asked by the League to use his experience and expertise elsewhere in Europe as well. It seems that the Financial Committee, too, judged the Hungarian state of affairs to be good enough to be able to dispense with Tyler for a while. He was sent to Greece to look around and talk to people, thereby gaining insight into yet another European country and culture known to few Americans. That South European country's situation was different than either that of Austria's or Hungary's.

Greece was experiencing a humanitarian crisis in the form of refugees. By the end of 1923, roughly one million Greek refugees fleeing Turkey had returned home. This wave represented about 25 percent of the whole Greek population, and the state was absolutely incapable of handling the situation. The Red Cross had tried to alleviate the crisis, but soon it faced such insurmountable difficulties that it chose to withdraw from the country. Under these circumstances Greece turned to the League of Nations for help, and

---

18 Royall Tyler to Henry Strakosch, May 13, 1927, ibid.; Tyler to ter Meulen, May 24, 1927, File 53686, Hungarian Loan, Box 302, Registry Files, 1919–1927, Section No. 10, LNA.
19 Royall Tyler to Harry Siepmann, May 25, 1927, OV 33/2, BoE.

there the mechanism for financial reconstruction appeared to have been discovered. As usual, when money needed to be found on the continent, Montagu Norman played the leading role. He was willing to help, however, only if an American would be appointed to head the Refugee Settlement Commission dealing with the problem. After this requirement was met, in November 1924, a loan of $60 million was issued, and the League demanded that Greece fulfill the same requirements as Austria and Hungary: a balanced budget, state reforms, etc.[20]

Although settlement of the Greek refugees was carried out with relative success, the promised balanced budget was nowhere in sight. By 1927 the financial situation was so desperate that the Greek government had to seek outside help again, and the League of Nations again seemed the only possible source. Because the Austrian and Hungarian examples served as precedent for future financial reconstruction, the League wanted to use Tyler's services in both a formal and informal ways. Tyler already planned to travel to Greece to replace John Hope Simpson as vice-chairman of the League of Nations Refugee Settlement Commission, and Geneva thought he might also spend some of his time there focusing on the Greek stabilization. So, instead of spending time with his family at Antigny, on July 19 Tyler left for Athens, Greece, and spent the rest of the summer in the Greek heat. It speaks volumes about his character and sense of duty—and also his belief in the League of Nations—that Tyler accepted the job offer without a second thought, and "couldn't resist the temptation of taking on this new job," that promised to be "very interesting."[21] He accepted despite giving up the possibility of spending three weeks with Elisina and William, although they were together for a week after the June Council meeting and another week when they joined him in Athens later. The assignment may have been very interesting, but he bumped into "the hottest summer that had been known in Greece for 31 years."[22] His short stint as vice chairman of the Refugee Settlement Commission had nothing

---

20 The paragraph was based upon Peterecz, *Jeremiah Smith, Jr. and Hungary*, 227–28.
21 Royall Tyler to Mildred Barnes Bliss, July 17, 1927, Budapest, "Bliss–Tyler Correspondence," https://www.doaks.org/resources/Bliss-Tyler-correspondence/letters/17jul1927, accessed December 11, 2015.
22 Royall Tyler to Mildred Barnes Bliss, September 25, 1927, Budapest, "Bliss–Tyler Correspondence," https://www.doaks.org/resources/Bliss-Tyler-correspondence/letters/25sep1927, accessed December 11, 2015.

in common with Greece's financial problems, and he was not supposed to force himself on the Greek authorities regarding the planned new bank of issue. Rather, he was to wait until he was approached by the Greeks.[23] The ongoing refugee crisis, "the biggest the world has ever seen," and the poor relationship between the Commission and the Greek government did not help the situation.[24] Greek politicians appeared obstinately resistant to persuasion, which was exasperating at times, and, as Tyler put it, "they would drive the most patient and philosophical-minded insane, if one didn't lose one's temper now and then and blow up and clear the atmosphere."[25] Despite the repeated political fluidity during the summer, soon an agreement was produced, and in exchange for financial help and knowhow, Greece undertook to pay its debts that were in arrears, and tackle currency stabilization, set up a new Bank of Issue, and maintain a balanced budget. For all of which it was provided with a £9 million ($39.6 million) loan in 1928. The League sent no Commissioner-General to practice outright control over the Greek finances, but did send a bank advisor to the new Greek central bank for a period of three years. H. C. F. Finlayson, the Briton chosen for this post, had to have his stay in Athens prolonged twice, and in the end he remained there until 1934.[26]

The refugee question kept Tyler busy, but it also gave him a good chance to take a closer look at Greece and its inhabitants. The characteristically open-minded American approached this South European nation with few Western stereotypes and let his experience on the ground dictate his observations. His impressions were generally positive, and it was inescapable that he contrasted Greece with Hungary. Although, knowing their self-consciousness, he never would have hurt the pride of his Hungarian hosts by being so outspoken, in the safe realm of his private correspondence he did not paint a flattering picture of the Hungarians—at least when compared

---

23 Royall Tyler to Jan van Waltré de Bordes, July 29, 1927, Athens, File 61897, Financial Situation of Greece, Box 321, Registry Files, 1919–1927, Section No. 10, LNA.
24 Royall Tyler to Mildred Barnes Bliss, September 25, 1927.
25 Ibid.
26 This paragraph was based upon League of Nations, *Reconstruction Schemes*, 61, 68, and, 73; Marx Winkler, *The Investor and the League Loans* (New York: Foreign Policy Association, Volume 4, June 1928, Supplement No.2), 21. The issue of the American tranche was dependent upon Greece concluding the debt settlement with the United States, which finally, although a little bit later, took place. FRUS: 1927, vol. 3: 1–19, and FRUS: 1928, vol. 3: 1–13.

Chapter 4

to the Greeks. He found the latter "frugal, sober, quick-witted, sensitive, mobile, prone to undervalue his own qualities though sometimes aggressive on the surface, not at all ostentatious," while finding the Hungarians "for good and for evil, the exact opposite."[27] Compared to Greece, salaries in Hungary were high and office buildings lavish, while the Greek ministerial buildings "in Hungary would be considered a disgrace to a fifth rate provincial town."[28] Coming from the Hungarian environment where "people usually imagine that the entire world has its eyes fixed upon their own particular little dump," it was little wonder that the Greek atmosphere and people struck Tyler as stimulating.[29] Naturally, the ancient Greek and Byzantine arts must also have proved refreshing to the scholar in Tyler, and perhaps that tainted his perspective. His friendship with the Blisses remained as fervent as ever, and so did his art reconnaissance on their behalf. He continued to advise them on available pieces that he considered worth purchasing, especially concerning Byzantine art.

Tyler arrived back in Hungary in the last days of August, where he found that the financial situation had improved rather than deteriorated in his absence, but the true overall picture was a more complicated issue. Harvest prospects were excellent—always a crucial factor for Hungary's well-being—and the Hungarian currency (the *pengő* since January 1, 1927) maintained stability, but there were also signs of a less promising future. Imports had increased considerably since the previous year, so the negative trend of Hungarian foreign trade showed no sign of improvement. Also, the budget surplus was obviously going to decrease, since much of what was paid from it and from the League Loan was not really investment but rather traditional expenditures. Government employees also were granted a relatively high salary, which—together with the reduced surplus—in part meant that reducing taxation was not a viable program.[30]

Tyler shed light on another problem regarding the mechanics of the Hungarian economy. Agriculture was traditionally the country's main revenue producer, and especially in good harvest years this meant that foreign

---

27 Royall Tyler to Mildred Barnes Bliss, September 25, 1927.
28 Royall Tyler to Jeremiah Smith, September 2, 1927, Budapest, OV 33/2, BoE.
29 Royall Tyler to Mildred Barnes Bliss, September 25, 1927.
30 Harry Siepmann to Royall Tyler, August 18, 1927, and Royall Tyler to Harry Siepmann, September 3, 1927, OV 33/2, BoE.

currency would flow into Hungary. However, heavy import duties levied on a score of necessary items hurt the projected outcome, since these expenses had to be added to the price at which the Hungarian products were offered on the foreign market. This meant that it was more difficult to find buyers in a tightly competitive international market. In other words, the Hungarian state took the money out of one pocket that it had put in the other one earlier.[31] Overall though, Tyler seemed to remain optimistic and believed that corrections could be made if needed down the road. As he informed Siepmann at the Bank of England, "I don't think there is anything to worry about just at present," and he informed the Financial Committee in the same vein at Geneva.[32]

The spring of 1927 also brought about the dissolution of the Inter-Allied Military Commission of Control in Hungary, another tangible remnant of the Trianon Treaty. After gaining their financial freedom the previous year, it is no wonder that the Hungarians were jubilant now that they were politically and militarily free from outside control as well. Such warnings that were, for instance, provoked by the Hungarian recruitment practices seemed a minor disturbance in light of the free hand Hungary had been given.[33] It was, after all, recognition of good and constructive work done over the past few years that Hungary was now accepted as a stable country and not a threat to the peace constructed in Paris after World War I.

Also parallel to the lifting of military control, Italy signed a Treaty of Friendship with Hungary. This was significant as it was the first time that a European power had elevated Hungary's importance in the field of diplomacy. For Hungary, this meant that there might be an important supporter for its Treaty revision claims down the road, for the Italian perspective was to hasten the dismemberment of Yugoslavia and thus dislodge French hegemony in Central Europe. Naturally, any weakening of the Little Entente automatically raised Hungary's hope of partial territorial revision.[34]

---

31 Extract from a Note officially presented to the League by Royall Tyler, September 1, 1927, ibid.
32 Royall Tyler to Harry Siepmann, September 3, 1927, ibid.
33 LNJ, 8th Year, no. 9 (September 1927), 1057–59.
34 For more detail about the Italian–Hungarian Treaty of friendship, see, Petra Hamerli, *Magyar-olasz diplomáciai kapcsolatok és regionális hatásaik (1927–1934)* [Hungarian–Italian Diplomatic Relations and Their Regional Effects] (Budapest: Fakultás Kiadó, 2018), 25–64.

Chapter 4

The year 1927 was important for other reasons with regard to the European peace and Hungary. The British press magnate Lord Rothermere wrote an article in the *Daily Mail* in which he favored giving back some of the territories lost to Hungary.[35] Although the article naturally "was received with the greatest enthusiasm throughout" Hungary, most European countries found it dangerous to an already precarious situation in which many dissatisfied voices vied for greater recognition.[36] After so much blood was shed and treasure lost, so much diplomatic wrangling conducted, and most of Europe compelled to live under a thin veneer of a workable system, no one wished to disturb the status quo, especially not for tiny Hungary. It is also questionable whether Rothermere's article helped Hungary's goal of a hoped-for revision. It is true, the article reached a large readership, but it did not necessarily receive responsive attention. As Siepmann chronicled the unfolding sentiment in the wake of the article, "Lord Rothermere's article did as much harm to Hungary as any other article which I have yet seen."[37] The Bethlen government realized this as well, and was quick to declare that not only did it have nothing to do with Rothermere's article it also did not think treaty revision was a realistic option.[38]

Tyler, as always, never touched such political questions and focused on his own work instead. In the fall he traveled with Peirce to Bulgaria by boat, starting from Budapest. He wished to take a look at the Refugee Settlement work in that country, since it was closely related to the Greek problem. Bulgaria was also an ex-enemy country and the only one aside from Germany that was burdened with heavy reparation payments in the Treaty of Neuilly in 1919—at an amount that the country could not meet. After the first two successful Central European financial reconstruction programs were started and had borne some fruit, Bulgaria, too, turned to the League

---

35   Harold Sydney Harmsworth (Viscount Rothermere), "Hungary's Place in the Sun," *The Daily Mail*, June 21, 1927. Also see, Ignác Romsics, "Hungary's Place in the Sun: A British Newspaper Article and its Hungarian Repercussions," in *British–Hungarian Relations since 1848*, László Péter and Martyn Rady, eds., (London: School of Slavonic and East European Studies, University College London, 2004), 193–204; Andrea Orzoff, *Battle for the Castle: The Myth of Czechoslovakia in Europe, 1914–1948* (Oxford: Oxford University Press, 2009), 154–57.
36   Joshua Butler Wright to Frank B. Kellogg, June 30, 1927, 864.00/703, Austria-Hungary and Hungary, 1912–1929, Roll 8, Microcopy No. 708, NARA.
37   Harry Siepmann to Béla Imrédy, August 18, 1927, MOL K 278, Béla Imrédy Papers, Bundle, 6, File 33. 1930–1934. (Imrédy's foreign correspondence, Bank of England, Siepmann), HNA.
38   *Magyarország*, August 6, 1927.

for help, and, after overcoming some obstacles, by 1926 the way was paved for a reconstruction plan there. Although Bulgaria's refugee crisis was on a much smaller scale than in Greece, the Bulgarian state was financially overextended. The League applied a two-step solution. First, in December 1926 a loan of a nominal amount of £3.3 million ($16 million) was raised for the refugee settlement. Second, two years later, a financial reconstruction scheme was launched with the help of a foreign loan of £5 million ($25 million). Similarly to the Austrian and Hungarian examples, certain revenues were set aside to meet the annual charges of the loan, while bank reforms and a decrease in state unemployment had to be carried out.[39]

The League's person in Sofia was René Charron, Tyler's old colleague and friend from Budapest, who was serving a six-year stint as Commissioner in Bulgaria. This was an obvious extra incentive for Tyler to travel to Sofia, which impressed him to the extent that he wrote that it was "not at all a bad little place."[40] Interestingly, another old colleague of his from Budapest formed a different view of the Balkan country and its populace based upon his own experience. Siepmann characterized Bulgarians as "the most absurdly incompetent people," although the people in Sofia—a capital city "with two passable hotels, pigs in the streets"—struck him as "amiable, simple, modest and attractively uncivilized."[41] Tyler, for his part, also wanted to investigate archeology and art on the ground. He liked Sofia, but it was the next stop on this small Balkan tour that really impressed him.

Tyler found Constantinople "a formidable experience." Especially Hagia Sophia exceeded his earlier expectations. He described it as "the grandest building man ever made; altogether unimaginable and incredible."[42] His anthropological observation of Turkey, however, was that the outer, tangible layer of modernization, mainly modern clothes and the pretense of becoming European, struck him as a negative development, and he realized that with this kind of Turk he had "less patience with his incredible ways than one had when he was openly an Oriental."[43]

---

39 All the information in this paragraph is from League of Nations, *Reconstruction Schemes*, 80–97.
40 Royall Tyler to Mildred Barnes Bliss, October 24, 1927, [1], Budapest, "Bliss–Tyler Correspondence," https://www.doaks.org/resources/Bliss-Tyler-correspondence/letters/24oct1927-1, accessed December 11, 2015.
41 Harry Siepmann to Montagu Norman, May 31, 1926, OV33/42, BoE.
42 Royall Tyler to Mildred Barnes Bliss, October 24, 1927, [1].
43 Ibid.

Chapter 4

The year 1927 was important for Tyler in the field of art history from other aspects as well. He contributed a chapter to a book on Spanish art, and also translated books on the same topic from Spanish to English. In addition to his long-running involvement with Spanish culture and art, his love affair with Byzantine art also flourished and bore results. The previous year he and Hayford Peirce had co-authored a book called simply *Byzantine Art*, which mainly focused on textiles and coins, representing the two authors' main areas of interest. It featured collotype images of many of the items described.[44] Also, appearing in print was the text of the talk on aspect of Byzantine scholarship that Tyler and Peirce gave at the earlier mentioned conference a Belgrade. As a sign of growing recognition of Tyler's expertise on Byzantine art, he was asked, together with Peirce, to contribute an article on the subject to the new edition of the *Encyclopaedia Britannica*, subsequently published in 1929.[45] In another art-related vein, in the mid 1920s the Tylers decided they wanted to create a research library, and with the Blisses' financial help, they installed a photograph library at Antigny to help professional and amateur students of art alike.[46]

In the meantime, Hungarian finances were still in good shape overall . Foreign borrowing continued, and that weakened the otherwise good data, but no obvious sign foreshadowed any fundamental problem with the system, despite the warnings and misgivings earlier mentioned. Agriculture was also pushed somewhat into the background "for the benefit of a recent and insufficiently equipped national industry, which cannot supply more than a small part of the internal demand, and produces at relatively high costs."[47] For instance, customs, tobacco, sugar, and salt, the four together providing insurance for the service of the loan, produced ever larger revenues.[48] The budgetary

---

44 Hayford Peirce and Royall Tyler, *Byzantine Art* (London: E. Benn, 1926).
45 "Byzantine Art," *The Encyclopaedia Britannica*, Fourteenth Edition, vol. 4 (London: The Encyclopaedia Britannica Company, Ltd., 1929), 488–92; Elisina Tyler to Mildred Barnes Bliss, November 20, 1927, Antigny-le-Château, "Bliss–Tyler Correspondence," https://www.doaks.org/resources/Bliss-Tyler-correspondence/letters/20nov1927, and Royall Tyler to Mildred Barnes Bliss, January 5, 1928, Antigny-le-Château, "Bliss–Tyler Correspondence," https://www.doaks.org/resources/Bliss-Tyler-correspondence/letters/05jan1928, both accessed December 11, 2015.
46 This paragraph was based on: James N. Carder, "Washington, D.C., and Stockholm (1920–1927)," in "Bliss–Tyler Correspondence," https://www.doaks.org/resources/Bliss-Tyler-correspondence/1920-1927, accessed June 14, 2015.
47 Royall Tyler to Arthur Salter, November 21, 1927, OV 33/74, BoE.
48 Royall Tyler to G. Bianchini, November 10, 1927, File 53687, Hungarian Loan, Box 302, Registry Files, 1919–1927, Section No. 10, LNA.

surplus was 97 million pengős ($17 million), a figure smaller than the preceding fiscal year, but still an impressive number.[49] Industrial unemployment basically disappeared, and an increase was detected in production, distribution, and consumption—another symptom of health, although the good results were thanks in part to the low base level the country started from in 1924.

Tyler thought that if a string of reforms were introduced, such as accounting, administrative measures, and registry—mainly in the Ministry of Finance—one could be optimistic as to Hungary's financial stability for years to come.[50] But whether the government would heed good and friendly advice and subsequently deliver on promises made was a question Tyler could not reassuringly answer in the affirmative. As he privately expressed his foreboding, "In this country perhaps more than elsewhere it is never safe to talk about a thing as assured until it has actually happened."[51] In light of all the good indicators, however, it was understandable that the Hungarian government wished to have access to the remaining sum of the Reconstruction Loan. The program the government prepared for submission to the Financial Committee was approved by Tyler toward the end of 1927.[52] The Committee and later the League Council both gave the green light for the approximately 33.9 million gold crowns or 39.3 million pengős ($7.8 million) to be spent according to the proposed Hungarian program.[53]

With its diplomatically motivated events, the year 1928 forced Tyler, if not to get involved in such dangerous territory as politics, then to reflect on larger issues concerning Hungary's place in Europe and the League of Nations. On various occasions he met with the American minister at Budapest, Joshua Butler Wright, and shared valuable information on either general conditions or finance-related subjects. About these meetings Wright noted, "One always gleans much information from him for he knows everyone here. Has been particularly helpful to me and comments have been most valuable."[54]

49　Eugene Havas, *Hungary's Finance and Trade 1928* (London: London General Press, 1929), 7.
50　Royall Tyler to Harry Siepmann, November 18, 1927, OV 33/3, BoE.
51　Royall Tyler to Harry Siepmann, February 17, 1928, ibid.
52　Balance of the Hungarian Reconstruction Loan, Report of the Financial Committee, December 5, 1927, OV 33/74, BoE.
53　LNJ, 9th Year, no. 2 (February 1928), Forty-eighth Session of the Council, 127.
54　Diary entry, February 22, 1928, Series 4: Diaries, Minister to Hungary, 1 Jan–6 Apr 1928, Box 2, Joshua Butler Wright Papers, 1909–1938, Seeley G. Mudd Manuscript Library, Princeton, USA. See also diary entries of February 14, and March 19, 1928.

Chapter 4

Cases regarding Hungary in that year were on the Council's agenda twice, and they proved that the country was sometimes a thorny case for that organization. It may very well not have been the only problematic member or issue in the second half of the 1920s as far as the League was concerned, but relatively close on the heels of successful financial reconstruction and despite the aid received from Geneva, at the end of the day, Hungary still felt disappointed with the League of Nations.

The question of optants posed a long-lasting and challenging issue for the League.[55] The Romanian government promulgated a law in 1921 in which it basically confiscated the lands there of those Hungarians who had opted for Hungarian citizenship after the peace treaty. Hungary claimed that this law violated certain aspects of the Treaty of Trianon, whereas the Romanians argued that their state's sovereignty took precedence over the protection of another treaty. In 1923, as a rightful member, Hungary turned to the League for help in establishing which party was right. That began a long and arduous but fruitless legal process that lasted for seven years. The League tried to mediate between the two countries, but that proved futile since the Romanian government disputed the jurisdiction of the Rumanian–Hungarian Mixed Arbitral Tribunal over the question. Romania wanted to connect the case of the optants with that of reparations. The issue was problematic from a domestic point of view in both countries, and the League did not wish to intervene on either party's behalf. An American diplomat well summarized the significance of the problem. Although he thought it was not "a transcendentally important question 'per se', but it is indisputable that it is a salient factor in the scrutiny and appraisal of the League by the smaller nations."[56] A solution was nowhere in sight.

---

55 On the optants question, see Francis Deák, *The Hungarian–Rumanian Land Dispute* (New York: Columbia University Press, 1928); Ferenc Matheovics, *A magyar–román birtokper* [The Hungarian–Romanian Optants Case] (Budapest, 1929); Elek Nagy, *Magyarország és a Népszövetség* [Hungary and the League of Nations] (Budapest: Franklin Társulat, 1930), 57–82; Gábor Aradi, "A San Remo-i tárgyalások magyarországi előkészülete" [The Hungarian Preparations for the San Remo Talks], *Levéltári Szemle* 52, no. 3 (2002): 24–38; Holly Case, *Between States: The Transylvanian Question and the European Idea during the Second World War* (Stanford: Stanford University Press, 2009), 27–30; Hamerli, *Magyar-olasz diplomáciai kapcsolatok*, 154–68. The latest scholarly work is Antal Berkes, "The League of Nations and the Optants' Dispute of the Hungarian Borderlands: Romania, Yugoslavia, and Czechoslovakia," In Remaking Central Europe. The League of Nations and the Former Habsburg Lands, edited by Peter Becker and Natasha Wheatley, Oxford, Oxford University Press, 2020, 283–314."

56 Joshua Butler Wright to Frank B. Kellogg, November 10, 1927, 864.00/709, Austria-Hungary and Hungary, 1912–1929, Roll 8, Microcopy No. 708, NARA.

The Szentgotthárd incident proved to be shorter in duration but more complex and awkward in its nature. In January 1928, at the western Hungarian border town of Szentgotthárd, Austrian customs officers stopped a train going from Italy allegedly to Poland. In five of the cars, weapons were found which were listed in the official customs documents as machine components. Soon it became clear that the shipment was destined for Hungary, a clear violation of the Treaty of Trianon, which forbade providing the Hungarian army with weapons. The shipment actually was a manifestation of the much improved and friendly relations between Italy and Hungary, which found embodiment in the treaty signed in 1927. Among other things, the new connection had a clearly avowed aim to carry out actions that would be to the detriment and at the expense of Yugoslavia.

Somewhat thanks to French backing, the Little Entente countries began a propaganda outcry against Hungary. The British Minister in Budapest opined to his American colleague that the French "rarely fail to improve an opportunity to counsel the members of the Little Entente to magnify small incidents."[57] (This comment also sheds some light on the "friendly" relationship between the leading powers in Europe.) At any rate, the League initiated an investigation and discussed the affair in the March Assembly.[58] The Hungarian government had auctioned off the now disabled weapons in February, hoping to defuse the scandal. They also knew that they had not much to fear, since a few days after the scandal surfaced, Benito Mussolini informed Bethlen that Italy was not worried about the French press attacks and his country would bear any blame if it was necessary, adding that in the future Italy would seek ways to help Hungary.[59] The League set up a Committee of Three, which suggested conducting a strictly technical investigation in Hungary. Based upon the report of a seven-member League delegation that carried out that investigation in April, in June the League Assembly deemed the affair closed without finding Hungary at fault.[60] The

---

57 Joshua Butler Wright to Frank B. Kellogg, March 9, 1928, 864.00 PR/4, Affairs of Austria-Hungary and Hungary, 1912–1929. Roll 10, Microcopy No. 708, NARA.
58 LNJ, 9th Year, no. 4 (April 1928), Forty-ninth Session of the Council, 387–397.
59 Benito Mussolini to Ercole Durini, January 6, 1928, quoted in Hamerli, *Magyar-olasz diplomáciai kapcsolatok*, 87.
60 LNJ, 9th Year, no. 7 (July 1928), Fiftieth Session of the Council, 905–18 and 1009–21. On the Szentgotthárd incident also see Tibor Zsiga, *A szentgotthárdi fegyverbotrány*, [The Szentgotthárd Arms Scandal] (Szombathely: Pannon Műhely Kft., 1990); Tibor Zsiga, "A szentgotthárdi fegyverbotrány" [The Szent-

news naturally "was received in this country with general expressions of satisfaction," the American minister in Budapest wrote.[61]

When the Council met in early March, the Hungarian optants and the Szentgotthárd affair were on the agenda. Tyler labeled the meeting "the most interesting I've ever attended there."[62] Although the Hungarians seemed to suffer no diplomatic defeat, being a sharp observer, Tyler noted that this was "due far more to the general conjunction of planets than to the exertions of the lone little Magyar star."[63] What he meant was that the French interpreted certain moves on the part of the Little Entente countries as steps against France's interests in the region, and so, as a warning, the French only half-heartedly supported the Romanian and Czech attacks on Hungary. But this almost unqualified Hungarian success may very well have been only a pause in the French–Romanian axis, so the Hungarians had to play it safe. Still, to put things in proper perspective, Tyler informed Mildred Barnes Bliss that the Hungarian questions were only a sideshow to the most significant issue of the year, since "really the Kellogg note over-shadowed everything else."[64]

The idea of renouncing war as an instrument of settling disputes, in fact trying to make war illegal, appealed to many at that time, and Tyler shared the enthusiasm. The Kellogg-Briand Pact was signed initially by the United States, France, and Germany in August 1928, but soon dozens of other countries joined, and it came into force in the summer of 1929. This idealistic moralistic-legalistic approach to international relations was questioned and outright ridiculed by many. American writer, reporter, and political commentator Walter Lippmann, for example, scathed the initiative with this skeptical, but realistic observation: "The renunciation of war and treaties of arbitration are...excellent devices for stopping wars that nobody intends to wage."[65]

---

gotthárd Arms Scandal], *Vasi honismereti és helytörténeti közlemények* 35, no. 1 (2008): 14–23; Ildikó Császár, "A szentgotthárdi fegyverszállítási botrány sajtóvisszhangja" [The Press Echo of the Szentgotthárd Arms Scandal], *Vasi Szemle* 68, no. 6 (2013): 579–91; Hamerli, *Magyar-olasz diplomáciai kapcsolatok*, 86–92.

61 Joshua Butler Wright to Frank B. Kellogg, April 2, 1928, 864.00 PR/5, Austria-Hungary and Hungary, 1912–1929, Roll 10, Microcopy No. 708, NARA.
62 Royall Tyler to Mildred Barnes Bliss, March 13, 1928, Budapest, "Bliss–Tyler Correspondence," https://www.doaks.org/resources/Bliss–Tyler-correspondence/letters/13mar1928, accessed December 12, 2015.
63 Ibid.
64 Ibid.
65 Quoted in Ronald Steel, *Walter Lippmann and the American Century* (Boston and Toronto: Little, Brown and Company, 1980), 254.

Hungary signed the Pact in 1929, but it was more of a gesture than a deeply shared idealism. A telling example was Albert Apponyi, who shared his opinion with a Reichstag committee in Berlin in November 1928. He attacked the otherwise "sympathetic" approach by pointing out its mistaken interpretation of international problems and particularly of war "with a dazzling, I am nearly inclined to say naïve, simplicity."[66] An editorial in one Hungarian newspaper made it clear in its conclusion that in Hungary, even this Pact was interpreted through the lens of revision: "The Kellogg Pact may be made a blessing to the world by one means only—the just revision of the peace treaties. By this Coolidge and Kellogg will become heroes of history. Without it the whole thing will turn into a Wilson program."[67] The Kellogg Pact was not part of the League of Nations' efforts, but it shared many of the same idealistic international hopes: maintaining the peace through disarmament and the diplomatic handling of any crisis. Unfortunately, there were too many have-nots around in the world. Hungary being one of them, it was, in fact, trying to beef up its armed forces to the maximum, partly because it was surrounded by much more powerful enemies, and partly because of the hoped-for revision someday.

When the League held its June meeting, however, the tables were turned, and the Hungarians walked away disappointed. Because Romania balked at accepting a mixed arbitral tribunal as competent in the case of the optants, the League of Nations exhibited hesitancy and dangerous incompetency at solving an issue of relatively minor significance. The whole idea of arbitration, an important element in the League's effort to settle possible international disputes, received a serious blow. Tyler well perceived the lurking difficulty. A man who believed in internationality and in the League as a proponent of it, he found it "shocking" that Romania could "paralyse the procedure contemplated by the Treaty by simply threatening to withdraw from the League if the Treaty is allowed to function against her."[68] People in England and France rightfully fretted over this, Tyler wrote, and asked themselves "what chances there are of ever getting a big power to submit to arbitration, if Rumania, on a question on which she pledged her-

---

66 *Budapesti Hírlap*, November 25, 1928.
67 *Pesti Hírlap*, Janaury 18, 1929.
68 Royall Tyler to Mildred Barnes Bliss, July 30, 1928 [2], Budapest, "Bliss–Tyler Correspondence," https://www.doaks.org/resources/Bliss–Tyler-correspondence/letters/30jul1928-2, accessed December 13, 2015.

Chapter 4

self, when she signed the Trianon Treaty, to accept arbitration, can buck the whole machinery because she thinks arbitration would go against her?"[69] Obviously when thinking about Germany, Japan, or Russia, the example Romania was setting was disquieting. And if one takes into consideration what happened, for example, in the Manchurian or the Abyssinian crises in the 1930s, this fear was reality-based.

In the end, a solution was achieved concerning the optants case, but it was a questionable success. In April 1930 the two governments at last agreed that Hungarian claimants were to receive 240 million gold crowns ($50 million), while Hungary agreed to pay an annual 13.5 million gold crowns from 1943 until 1966. This sum is often seen as a final act of reparations, but technically it was to liquidate other claims such as the costs of the Romanian occupying forces back in 1919 and of bringing home Hungarian POWs and internees after World War I, as well as Yugoslavia's claim for unshipped coal, compensation for Czechoslovakia for Hungarian Soviet troop movements on its territory, etc.

In light of such affairs, it is no wonder that Hungary did not really find what it had been looking for in the League of Nations; while it often seemed that Geneva provided a good platform for other countries, especially members of the Little Entente, to attack Hungary. A good example of how the official Hungarian political establishment viewed the League of Nations can be found in various government publications. One such is the *Külügyi Szemle* (Foreign Review), the Hungarian government's journal of semi-official foreign policy views. It is not surprising to read of a "stern, inflexible and one-sided League of Nations," which "in its composition and work as of today is the insurance company of the winners and their preys, which institution keeps at bay every rightful complaint, every reform attempt, and every attempt to change the peace decrees in a more just and reasonable way."[70] Although this opinion may have been too harsh and one-sided, another Hungarian example from the same year seemed more genuine, especially in light of the optants question: The League of Nations' "proceedings are hesitating, it dares to accept resolutions only rarely, it favors political aspects to

---

69 Ibid.
70 Alajos Paikert, "A Népszövetségi Ligák jelentősége" [The Significance of the League of Nations], *Külügyi Szemle* 6, no. 1 (1929): 67.

legal ones, which leads to a situation that the trust on part of the small states has been shaken... the issues that it deals with are stalled and, therefore, final act on them are belated. The large part of those feuds that are dealt with happens only in name but not in deed."[71]

These charges of belatedness and ineffectiveness document the Hungarian, and possibly other small countries', perception that the League's bureaucratic multilateralism was maladapted to the most pressing political challenges of the new order in Central Europe. The fragile small states that populated this region were the most sensitive to this problem, and therefore, it is understandable that to some of them internationalism—along issues and interests—was part of the problem and not the solution. Obviously the Hungarian political leadership and the public at large, as the above mentioned opinions attest, were dissatisfied with what the League might offer to Hungary.[72] On the other side of the equation, Hungary was helped immensely by the League in the financial sphere, and, even if in the background, Tyler was an everyday reminder of that help.

Despite these diplomatic tensions involving Hungary and the ambivalent Hungarian perspective on the League, Tyler did not have to worry too much about finances. After all, "unemployment has never been so low at this time of year, the traffic of the railways and the Post, Telegraphs and Telephones, and their receipts, continue to increase, bank deposits grow, very slowly but without interruption."[73] The one cause for concern was the increasingly obvious decline of the Hungarian credit situation. Closely related to this issue was the question of borrowing, against which trend Hungary had been warned time and again, through both official and private channels.[74] Tyler agreed that this was a dangerous symptom. Even if state finances overall were in good shape and consumption showed an increase, albeit a slow one, agriculture was in a precarious state, and without obtaining credit the outlook was bleak.

Concerning the mainly short-term borrowing that Hungary was carrying out to an ever greater extent, Tyler observed that "it would perhaps be

---

71   László Vince Weninger, "Népszövetség" [League of Nations], *Külügyi Szemle* 6, no. 1 (1929): 104.
72   This paragraph is taken from Peterecz, "Hungary and the League of Nations: A Forced Marriage," in Becker, *Remaking Central Europe*, 161–162.
73   Royall Tyler to Arthur Salter, May 19, 1928, OV 33/74, BoE.
74   Harry Siepmann to Béla Imrédy, March 6, 1928, OV 33/3, BoE.

Chapter 4

better if Hungary refrained from borrowing abroad at all for some time to come," but knowing his host country well, he added that no matter what, "borrow they will."[75] The Hungarian government did indeed prove to be obstinate on this point and chose the easy way out: seeking new money to repay old debt—a recipe for disaster if things took a turn for the worse. There was overall consensus among the financial decision makers—Sándor Popovics, the president of the National Bank of Hungary, Finance Minister János Bud, and Prime Minister Bethlen, though the latter halfheartedly—that since Hungary lacked capital, this type of borrowing should be put to productive uses, and that that would help the country in the long run.[76] This view involved taking a great deal of risk and assumed that all things would remain favorable to Hungary—which they did not. The characteristically sarcastic Siepmann opined that Hungary was "in a fair-weather-ship, which may or may not ride out the first real storm."[77]

Tyler's original tenure was supposed to last two years. Arthur Salter, Director of the Eocnomic and Financial Section of the League of Nations, became convinced, however, that financial supervision, even in the laxed form of Tyler's position, should be continued in order to keep check how things were going in Hungary. On the pretext, legally perfectly in order, that the remaining sum from the Reconstruction Loan required some close observation in order to be spent, the League of Nations proposed the extension of Tyler's contract for another year, starting from July 1, 1928.[78] This was not only good for the League because it had its man in Budapest to watch what the Hungarians were doing, but also there were plans for Tyler to visit Greece again in the summer. He was not against the idea, except that again it meant reduced family time.[79] He also did not mind carrying on in Hungary, if for no other reason than once he started a job he wanted to finish it. He believed in the League's agenda and honestly involved himself with Hungarian finances. His professional and straightforward attitude was

---

75 Royall Tyler to Harry Siepmann, March 24, 1928, OV 33/3, BoE.
76 William Goode to Harry Siepmann, March 29, 1928, ibid.
77 Harry Siepmann to Béla Imrédy, June 26, 1928, ibid.
78 Arthur Salter to István Bethlen, May 24, 1928, File 4994, Financial Situation of Hungary, Box 2935, Hungary, Section 10, Economic and Financial, League of Nations Archives, 1919–1927, LNA.
79 Royall Tyler to Mildred Barnes Bliss, May 10, 1928, Budapest, "Bliss–Tyler Correspondence," https://www.doaks.org/resources/Bliss–Tyler-correspondence/letters/10may1928, accessed December 13, 2015.

reflected in the fact that he did not invest in the Hungarian Reconstruction Loan, which would have been a wise investment at the beginning.[80]

Tyler found some precious time in the late spring of 1928 to travel and devote time to his passion for the arts. Step by step he managed to enlarge the photo collection at Antigny, which, by his own estimate, must have been the largest such collection in private hands. With its meticulous cataloguing and ease of access, it rivalled even famous public institutions, a fact that gave Tyler enormous pride.[81] He could spend time there mainly when he managed to get away from Budapest for longer periods, such as in August. The relative proximity of Antigny and Geneva continued to offer a way to divide his time between home and work. He returned to Hungary in early September, timing his reappearance with the fall assembly of the Financial Committee and the League Council.

A true upheaval in Tyler's life came during that summer in the form of a surprising job offer from the Hambros Bank in London, which had interests in various European countries. It wished to hire Tyler as its representative in Europe.[82] He would have an office in Paris, and his main duty would be to give advice regarding the political and financial conditions and situation in the various countries where the bank had interests: Spain, Portugal, Italy, and Germany being the main places. Since he was simultaneously offered a possible job as the League's adviser to the National Bank of Bulgaria for five years, the choice was not an easy one. A private letter in which Tyler wrote about the circumstances leading him to accept the Hambros offer allows some insight into Tyler's thoughts and personality. He felt "dreadfully torn" about giving up the job he had held for a number of years, a job that specially appealed to him since it gave him a chance to work "for a general, international purpose, and not to make money for oneself or any particular private interests."[83] Aside from his somewhat altruistic approach to life and work, there was a reality

---

80 Elisina Tyler to Mildred Barnes Bliss and Robert Woods Bliss, May 29, 1928, Paris, "Bliss–Tyler Correspondence," https://www.doaks.org/resources/Bliss–Tyler-correspondence/letters/29may1928, accessed December 13, 2015.
81 Royall Tyler to Mildred Barnes Bliss, May 10, 1928.
82 The Bank was founded in the nineteenth century. It assumed the name Hambros Bank in 1921 and expanded throughout the decade.
83 Royall Tyler to Mildred Barnes Bliss, September 6, 1928, Geneva, "Bliss–Tyler Correspondence," https://www.doaks.org/resources/Bliss–Tyler-correspondence/letters/06sep1928, accessed December 14, 2015. See also, Royall Tyler to Harry Siepmann, September 5, 1928, OV 33/4, BoE.

check that Tyler also had to take into consideration. Financial aspects did play an important role. At the age of forty-four, he knew that soon he would have to try looking for a job instead of being approached with one, since he had a very narrow field of expertise that could be of interest on the job market. Antigny's maintenance costs and his son's tuition imposed a heavy financial burden as well, and the job at Hambros Bank would in time offer the real possibility to secure a solid financial future, which he naturally craved "after a life time of uncertainty."[84] It also must have made him proud that the offer arrived not through strings pulled but unsolicited. This was proof that he had a wider reputation as a trustworthy and energetic worker with a broad range of experience and a talent for keen observations. That is why Hambros wanted him on its roster. The only possible obstacle was his present contract to stay in Hungary until June 30, 1929, but he hoped that from the beginning of the new year both the Financial Committee and the Hungarian government would let him leave Budapest. Actually, one of the reasons he did not mind plunging into the new job immediately was that in the remaining months before commencing a real full-time job he could concentrate on finishing the book on Byzantine art he co-authored with Peirce.[85]

The League and Hungary had no real reason to block Tyler's path to a new career, since the League loan was all spent, and the overall figures seemed reassuring, although the earlier mentioned complaints concerning weaknesses in Hungarian finances remained. As he summarized the May–July period for the Financial Committee,

> Hungary has now has a handsome budget surplus for four years running, which has contributed to the recognition of its state-financial position as a sound one. However, there are real drawbacks to the practice of budgeting for a large surplus. When it is public knowledge that the money is there waiting to be spent, it becomes exceedingly difficult to resist the claims of heads of departments, and it may happen that the money is spent not because a far-sighted programme of truly productive expenditure is awaiting execution, but simply because the money is available.[86]

---

84 Royall Tyler to Mildred Barnes Bliss, September 6, 1928.
85 Ibid. The first volume of *L'art byzantine* appeared in 1932.
86 Royall Tyler to Arthur Salter, August 4, 1928, OV 33/74, BoE.

In Tyler's estimate, this trend would continue as long as the status quo remained intact, and how the government would allocate future extra-budgetary expenditures, if it were able, "could be based on nothing but guesswork."[87] His summary assessment was, like almost all such opinions in this period, a mixed bag at best: "Most of the indications by which the general economic state of the country can be judged are favourable. But they do not point to as marked a rate of improvement as that which took place over the three years that followed stabilisation, and here and there the curve is no longer following an upward direction."[88] A few months later, in his regular summary of Hungarian finances over the past three months, he further tinted this picture. Foreign commerce had stopped increasing, exports hardly grew at all, and the deficit was substantial—all this at a time during which Hungary produced the best grain harvest since World War I. In addition, wages were low, prices generally high, and credit too expensive for agriculture or other small entrepreneurs to improve their lot or to begin a business.[89] This does not mean that Tyler was leaving a sinking ship; only that he saw signs that Hungary's financial situation was not as good as could have been hoped.

After he accepted the offer from Hambros, Tyler honestly kept up his work in Hungary, but at an almost mad pace he also tried to complete the book on Byzantine art. He knew that the job at Hambros would entail almost constant travel to various European countries and his free time would be much reduced. One reason he had to spend considerable time in Hungary in the fall, and perhaps beyond, was that a new Finance Minister took office, and he felt he could not "decently leave before I've had him under observation for a couple of months."[90] His first impressions of Sándor Wekerle, Jr. were positive, however, and he found him to be "full of sound sense and absolutely square."[91] This was welcome news, since it meant that Hungarian finances appeared to be in good hands, with Bethlen also seemingly secure in his position. Also, the good relations between Geneva and Budapest all but guaranteed that Tyler could join the Hambros Bank in 1929 and not need to worry about Hungary or spend much time there.

---

87 Ibid.
88 Ibid.
89 Royall Tyler to Arthur Salter, November 20, 1928, OV 33/74, BoE.
90 Royall Tyler to Mildred Barnes Bliss, September 6, 1928.
91 Royall Tyler to Harry Siepmann, October 19, 1928, OV 33/4, BoE.

Chapter 4

After a full month working at Antigny, mainly on the Byzantine art book, Tyler spent the next two months in Budapest, between the League Assemblies. He returned to Hungary in January 1929, and the following month Elisina joined him there to make a farewell tour among acquaintances. She heard nothing but genuine praise regarding her husband from all she met with. Hungarians, it seemed to her, had realized that Tyler had been "truly their friend, not only in discharging his official duties, but in his interpretation of them as a guide in his conduct of affairs."[92] In March, Tyler went on a warm-up road trip with Ronald Olaf Hambro, managing director of Hambros Bank since 1921. They spent an intense time in Milan, Turin, and Lisbon—typical centers of interest for Hambros Bank in Southern Europe—and later Tyler visited Warsaw, then spent a month in London preparing for his future work. He returned to Budapest in mid-May for his own farewell fortnight.

In 1929 Hungarian figures kept reassuring Tyler and the League regarding the overall state of Hungarian finances, though Siepmann expressed to Tyler "the uncomfortable impression that whenever you dig below the surface in Hungary, or whenever the crust breaks here and there of itself, you find that you are living over a morass."[93] In his last two reports, each covering three months, Tyler pictured Hungary as producing two almost diametrically opposing images of its financial and economic life. On the one hand, the surplus the government had gotten used to in the past four years had dried up, there was a significant negative trade balance that kept growing year by year, and there were the usual chronic problems: expensive credit, high tariffs, a consequence of which was high prices for manufactured goods, and narrowing export markets for Hungarian produce. The other side of the story showed an improving overall picture: the currency remained stable, there was a low unemployment rate, wages showed a slow increase, and bank deposits grew, although they still did not reach prewar levels.[94] Economist Iván Berend and others demonstrated that more than half of the loans to

---

92   Elisina Tyler to Mildred Barnes Bliss, March 29, 1929 [1], Hyères Var, "Bliss–Tyler Correspondence," https://www.doaks.org/resources/Bliss–Tyler-correspondence/letters/29mar1929-1, accessed December 15, 2015.
93   Harry Siepmann to Royall Tyler, Feburary 12, 1929, OV 33/4, BoE.
94   Royall Tyler to Arthur Salter, February 14, 1929, and May 25, 1929, OV 33/74, BoE; Royall Tyler to Harry Siepmann, May 30, 1929, OV 33/4, BoE.

Hungary after 1924 was short-term—typically with 10–12 percent interest, while 40 percent of the long-term loans was for debt payments and only 20 percent was for productive investments. Even if industrial output had grown by 70 percent between 1924 and 1929, and was 12 percent more than before the war, and the standard of living had also grown, the increasing amount of debts yet to be repaid foreshadowed financial hard times for Hungary.[95]

The tactful steering of Hungarian foreign policy also reassured Tyler that no foreseeable disturbances might arise. Bethlen showed pragmatism and restraint regarding the finances. He announced that Horthy would remain governor for life, thus pulling the sting out of the King question—a regular worry for the Little Entente countries. Hungary had improved its relations with Czechoslovakia, Romania, and especially with Yugoslavia, and informed them, and the rest of the world, that insofar as it was in his power, treaty revision would not be on Hungary's wish list. This was important for the country's stability, because only in a stable international environment and with normal working relations with its neighbors could Hungary expect its improved but still vulnerable economy and finances to improve. Tyler appreciated Bethlen's political acumen, and went so far as to call him "a great man."[96]

Royall Tyler's contract with the League of Nations expired on June 30, 1929. In light of the figures and opinion he had forwarded to Geneva, it is not surprising that he was enveloped in warm words of farewell. Eric Drummond, the League's Secretary-General, thanked him in the name of the League Secretariat for establishing relations with Hungary that had been "harmonious and have contributed much to the effective discharge of a common task."[97] In its official report regarding the cessation of Tyler's work in Hungary, the Financial Committee highlighted "the soundness of his judgment," "the range of his exceptional abilities," and the dedication he

---

95 T. Iván Berend and György Ránki, *Magyarország gazdasága az első világháború után, 1919–1929* [The Economy of Hungary after World War I, 1919–1929] (Budapest: Akadémiai Kiadó, 1966), 181–88; T. Iván Berend and Miklós Szuhay, *A tőkés gazdaság története Magyarországon, 1848–1944* [The History of Capitalism in Hungary] (Budapest: Kossuth Kiadó, 1973), 219–23.

96 Royall Tyler to Mildred Barnes Bliss, May 29, 1929, Budapest, "Bliss–Tyler Correspondence," https://www.doaks.org/resources/Bliss–Tyler-correspondence/letters/29may1929, accessed December 16, 2015.

97 Eric Drummond to Royall Tyler, June 27, 1929, File 4994, Financial Situation of Hungary, Box 2935, Hungary, Section 10, Economic and Financial, League of Nations Archives, 1919–1927, LNA.

Chapter 4

had "placed at the service of the League."[98] The Hungarian representative at Geneva, Pál Hevesy, thanked the American, in the name of his government, for "the distinguished manner in which he had fulfilled the task." He stated that "Hungary would remember him with feelings of gratitude and cordiality."[99] Hungarian newspapers also praised Tyler. Certainly, Hungary was happy to see the control leave, even if it had been practiced in a mild manner over the past three years as a consequence of the overall good results. But Hungarian sentiment also wanted to welcome helping hands from whatever corner of the world, but especially Anglo-Saxon ones, and Tyler was seen as a friend of Hungary—the highest accolade given to a foreigner in that period. The papers highlighted the facts that Tyler was a Puritan, a selfless person who had learned Hungarian, which latter fact had important emotional reverberations in Hungary.[100]

But he had no choice but to leave the country, and once again begin a new period in his life.

---

98 Extract from the Report of the Financial Committee to the Council of the League of Nation, LNJ, 10th Year, no. 7 (July 1929), Forty-fifth Session of the Council, 1181.
99 Ibid., 1016.
100 *Budapesti Hirlap*, June 2, 1929; *Az Est*, June 6, 1929.

CHAPTER 5

The League of Nations Years Part III: Out of and Back into the League of Nations

The years 1929 and 1930 were of immense importance for the financial landscape of Europe, indeed, of the world. Since September 1924, Germany and its reparations had been handled under the auspices of the Dawes Plan, named after the American banker, general, and diplomat Charles G. Dawes. The Dawes Plan, basically meant that mainly American incoming loans helped to keep Germany afloat, but it did not create a longtime solution, only an interim step toward solving the larger problem posed by the immense reparations burden on Germany. But the years under the Dawes Plan did help German's diplomatic re-integration. In 1925 the Locarno Treaties fixed Germany's western borders, the occupation forces on the Rhine began their withdrawal, and the next year Germany was admitted to the League of Nations. The Dawes Plan, however, worked only on the surface, and Germany's structural problems remained. The most devilish problem was that most of the loans raised for Germany went to municipalities and states, which did not necessarily use the money for productive purposes—eerily similar to the Hungarian example.

The German ambassador to the U.S. tried to stem the flow of American private loans to Germany by arguing to the American secretary of state that "money loaned to Germany is thrown away." The U.S. government nonetheless maintained a stance of official noninvolvement and assumed no responsibility.¹ In fact, once American capital dried up, Germany stopped paying even modest reparations. Therefore the Dawes Plan was succeeded by another initiative in which, once again, the Americans played the leading role. The Young Plan was agreed upon in late summer 1929, and it was finally adopted at The Hague Conference in January 1930. It reduced the annual payment expected from Germany, introduced a loosened form of Allied control over Germany's economy, and established the Bank for International Settlements (BIS) for handling reparation payments in the future.² However, the stock market crash in October 1929 and the growing insecurity on Wall Street had by 1930 already altered the financial outlook and possibilities, and the Young Plan remained more a plan than realizable action.

In this worsening situation, Royall Tyler started working officially for Hambros Bank in the summer of 1929, after he had finished his League liaison work in Hungary. The plan was that Tyler, relying on his deep international experience and his job in Hungary, would be made a director of certain of the Bank's allied institutions across Europe. On the list were the Nieder-Oesterreichische Escompte Bank, Vienna, the Banque Commerciale de Grèce, Athens, and the Union des Mines, the latter being a union of U.S. banks having the goal of American economic expansion in Europe, mainly in electricity. So, not surprisingly, Tyler enjoyed being in London for the time being, and found his new employers there "exceedingly nice and friendly."³

Once he started work in earnest, he crisscrossed the continent attending to his new responsibilities. For example, in November–December 1929, in a little over three weeks, he visited Vienna, Bucharest, Sofia, Budapest, Vienna again, and finally Prague. His trip coincided with the Wall Street crash in New York, but credit had already started to become less available prior to it, so he had a chance to size up the Central and Southeastern European Region under the already altered circumstances. These countries had all relied to a large extent on foreign loans and credit and now found themselves in an

---

1   Jacob Gould Schurman to Frank B. Kellogg, September 15, 1925, FRUS, 1925, 2, 174; see also his letters to the secretary of state, September 23 and 29, 1925, ibid., 174–76; Frank B. Kellogg to Jacob Gould Schurman, October 17, 1925, ibid., 177–78.
2   On the efforts to revise the Dawes Plan and about the creation of the Young Plan, see Frank Costigliola, *Awkward Dominion. American Political, Economic, and Cultural Relations with Europe, 1919–1933* (Ithaca, NY: Cornell University Press, 1984), 205–17.
3   Royall Tyler to Mildred Barnes Bliss, August 11, 1929, London, "Bliss–Tyler Correspondence," https://www.doaks.org/resources/bliss-tyler-correspondence/letters/11aug1929, accessed December 16, 2015.

uncomfortable situation. The only country that impressed Tyler as appearing to be able to weather the brewing storm was Czechoslovakia. But the overall outlook on the European scene, in light of what had recently taken place in the United States, seemed to portend harder days ahead.[4]

Tyler met with the most important people in the capitals he visited, political and financial alike, so he had firsthand information about the local situations. In Budapest, for instance, he met both Prime Minster Bethlen and Foreign Minister Lajos Walko, and there, the general opinion was rather sanguine—in the following weeks, it largely dissipated.[5] Tyler analyzed the unfolding situation in Europe, and maintained a perhaps unduly optimistic state of mind concerning both the political and financial possibilities. He maintained his optimism as he awaited the outcome of the The Hague Conference in January 1930. The results of that conference made him happy indeed. It gave not only Germany but also some of the countries to the east of it some breathing room, which made him "look forward to an appreciable improvement throughout Central and S. Eastern Europe – and it was about time."[6]

Tyler also gave a short course on reparations history for American readers in the columns of *Foreign Affairs*, in which he tried to explain some of the hitherto unknown intricacies of the issue at hand and the results of the Hague Conference.[7] As per Tyler's assessment, throughout the 1920s "the Danubian countries were tending to trade ever less with one another, and were striving, each and every one of them, to add economic self-sufficiency to political independence, indulging in a lively game of beggar-my-neighbor."[8] Herein lay a partial answer to the never really flourishing Eastern and Central European economic and financial picture.

In the following months, Tyler continued his job as roving financial ambassador for Hambros Bank, and traveled around the continent at a time when the financial and economic situations were becoming more and more precarious. Central Europe, Vienna, and Budapest in particular, featured

---

4 Royall Tyler to Mildred Barnes Bliss, December 26, 1929, Paris, "Bliss–Tyler Correspondence," https://www.doaks.org/resources/bliss-tyler-correspondence/letters/26dec1929, accessed December 16, 2015.
5 Royall Tyler to Harry Siepmann, December 29, 1929, Paris, OV 33/4, BoE.
6 Royall Tyler to Mildred Barnes Bliss, January 26, 1930, Paris, "Bliss–Tyler Correspondence," https://www.doaks.org/resources/bliss-tyler-correspondence/letters/26jan1930, accessed December 16, 2015.
7 Royall Tyler, "The Eastern Reparations Settlement," *Foreign Affairs* 9, no. 1 (October 1930): 106–17.
8 League of Nations, *Reconstruction Schemes*, 154.

Chapter 5

prominently on his itinerary. Two months of the summer were spent in the Hungarian capital—"the stiffest 2 months I've ever experienced," and it was not absolutely a success story either, but the ever optimistic Tyler put on a good face about it.[9] Niemeyer had earlier advised the Hungarians to follow certain guidelines. He thought it was essential to introduce "control and centralisation of Hungarian borrowing both at the Hungarian end and at the foreign end," and to come up with a detailed and well-devised plan. "It is hopeless," he added, "to live from hand to mouth (or rather from pawnshop to pawnshop)."[10] The plan was that Hungary would raise a 500-million-pengő ($88 million) loan pending the agreement of the Reparations Commission.[11] The Reparations Commission agreed with the argument that the loan was necessary and the flotation of it urgent, and the body gave its content that the first charge should be lifted according to the Paris Agreements in April of that year.[12] Under the circumstances, however, the hope of raising such a big loan was to be frustrated. It was annihilating when Norman declared that Hungarian "prospects of early long Loan are none too rosy!"[13] After a small part (87 million pegős) was still raised in November, a subsequent examination by Rothschild's Per Jacobsson and C. A. Gunston in early 1931 revealed that it was all spent on the budget deficit instead of for productive purposes. Obviously, there was no more money for Hungary in the City.[14]

Soon afterward, Tyler spent some time in Berlin, and gave a detailed description of the unfolding political and financial situation, as he saw it, to his faithful friend, Mildred Barnes Bliss. Tyler, of course, had already had contact with Germany and German culture. As a young man, he spent a long time there learning the language and getting to know the culture. He walked away with mixed feelings that would remain with him for his lifetime. During World War I and after its conclusion—thanks to his linguis-

---

9 Royall Tyler to Mildred Barnes Bliss, August 9, 1930, Budapest, "Bliss–Tyler Correspondence," https://www.doaks.org/resources/bliss-tyler-correspondence/letters/09aug1930, accessed December 16, 2015.
10 Niemeyer's memorandum, February 5, 1930, OV 33/5, BoE.
11 Villányi [sic] (Hungarian minister in France) to Sydney Armitage-Smith (Secretary General of the Reparation Commission), July 21, 1930, OV 33/5, BoE.
12 A. Antonucci's (Finance Section) Report to the Reparations Commission, July 23, 1930; Decision of the Reparations Commission, July 25, 1930, OV 33/5, BoE.
13 Bank of England memorandum, October 13, 1930, OV 33/5, BoE.
14 Katalin Ferber, "Lépéshátrányban: a magyar kormány kölcsönszerzési kísérlete 1930–1931-ben" [Handicapped: The Efforts of the Hungarian Government for a Loan in 1930–31], *Gazdaság* 22, no. 1 (1988): 89–108.

tic and other capabilities—he often interrogated Germans in order to learn hopefully vital information from them. With hindsight, he did not agree with the harsh peace terms forced on Germany. At some time while he was writing his unfinished Autobiography, one can only speculate, but probably in the very early 1940s, Tyler believed that a much more modest change and rupture should have taken place in Germany. The Western Powers ought perhaps to have preserved the ruling form of state, "with its traditional institutions, including its monarchies and its army, rather than drive into outlawry a class which had served the state for centuries."[15] But even at the war's conclusion he thought the Paris Peace Treaty too severe—and other such treaties with the defeated countries as well. From firsthand experience he could see the negative material and psychological consequences these treaties had caused in the various countries, and he proudly played a small role in Hungary to help them back on their feet. He did so not out of pity or altruism only but also from strategic considerations and belief in the League of Nations and its agenda in the international realm.

Tyler visited Berlin and Germany in the early fall of 1930, as the problems of the financial and economic world were starting to show their real claws. Seeing and interpreting the ongoing events there gave him a perfect opportunity to reflect on Germany, the Germans, and the possible future. He characterized September as "a very interesting time to be in Berlin," as Adolf Hitler's Nazi Party (officially the National Socialist German Workers' Party) had just become the second largest parliamentary force in Germany. In the recent federal elections it had gained a ninefold increase in the number of representatives it could send to the Reichstag, trailing only the Social Democrats, which had dominated elections since the end of World War I. This was a clear signal that the German population was not satisfied with the present situation and was looking for new solutions. Tyler agreed that the situation was "disquieting," but he believed that "the unnecessarily gloomy view of the international position" was not warranted. He compared the news in the foreign and the German press, and he saw that each concentrated on different points—the first on the Nazi voices raised against the Paris Peace Treaty and reparations, the latter on budget, insurance for the unemployed, and/or legislation.

---

15 Tyler, *One Name, Two Lives*, 88.

Chapter 5

Actually, Tyler's impression was that the success of the Nazi Party at the ballot box was due to the "dissatisfaction with the Government's orientation in internal affairs, and that external questions played a secondary part." He thought the devil lay in German welfare spending, which in the first place was made possible by foreign, mainly American, credits and loans. These meant that, somewhat consciously, yearly budgets were produced that were too large to live up to in the hopes of somehow convincing creditors to alleviate the reparations burden on Germany. In Tyler's view, most people, mainly of the bourgeois class, who had voted for Hitler's party were situated somewhere in the middle of the socialist-capitalist spectrum and had not voted before.

Tyler also showed signs of being overly optimistic, or just plainly wrong, concerning the future. He averred that it was "difficult to take seriously Hitler's confidence that his party is going to develop into an actual majority of the Reichstag." His prognosis was that a political leader who was the enemy of the Catholic Church, the bankers, the Jews, and the Communists, might not hold enough sway over the Germans to become their leaders. This view was—in hindsight—very idealist. In his final analysis, Germany was in September 1930 "far too weak and divided within itself, suffering still far too much from the effects of the war and the after war, for there to be any real international danger now or in the immediate future."[16]

Tyler's innocence concerning Germany future was not as foolish as one might think based upon the aforementioned letter. He also admitted that being optimistic "required something of an act of faith," which seems to suggest that it was not naiveté but rather embedded optimism that made him judge things in a positive light despite the many difficulties he was also well aware of.[17] He was of the opinion that no war would be imminent, since Germany was too weak and divided—and this was an accurate observation at that time. He also refused to believe in a concerted German–Italian effort to remake the European postwar order. Although in hindsight this view may be labeled naïve, in early 1931 an even beyond many shared similar views, and

---

16 All quotes in the last three paragraphs are from Royall Tyler to Mildred Barnes Bliss, October 4, 1930, Paris, "Bliss-Tyler Correspondence," https://www.doaks.org/resources/bliss-tyler-correspondence/letters/04oct1930, accessed December 17, 2015.

17 Royall Tyler to Mildred Barnes Bliss, March 7, 1931 [2], Paris, "Bliss–Tyler Correspondence," https://www.doaks.org/resources/bliss-tyler-correspondence/letters/07mar1931-2, accessed December 17, 2015.

under the circumstances, such an opinion must be accepted as quite realistic. What he feared instead was the internal danger to a stable Germany. If America and France were not willing to lend to the Germans, Tyler saw no chance of any real recovery there, which might pave the way even for communism.[18] These fears were also not unfounded—after all, the Communist Party had finished a not-so-distant third in the German elections in September.

Tyler was clearly touched by his generation's fear of the Bolshevists. This was not because of some general political view or religious fervor against the anti-democratic and anti-religious Soviet leadership. Instead, he saw an opportunity for the West to take advantage of the possible menace coming from the East, because he was not sure it was as serious as others made it out to be. In his view, the problem lay in the Western world's lack of any willingness to take a realistic measure of the Soviet Union and its political and economic system. "It is so much easier either to overrate or to underrate than it is to see clearly," he said. But he added it was "salutary, indeed essential for us, now and for a long time to come, to believe that the Soviets, unless we all get together and work hard to compose our difficulties, will wreck our capitalistic civilization and reduce us to slavery."[19] He thought the perceived danger might help the West in the longer run. More specifically, he was of the opinion that a failure of the Soviet economic plan (the 5-year plan) might lull the Western powers into bickering and selfishness. Therefore, he hoped that the Soviet model would keep the West together—"at any rate for years to come, until we have formed a generation believing in the reality of the Soviet menace as firmly as people of old used to believe in hell-fire. If, by misfortune, the Soviets were to fail, openly and patently, we would at once revert to our folly of 'defensive alliances'."[20]

Another element in Europe's ongoing crisis, to Tyler's mind, was that his home country was painfully absent. He clearly saw the need for touching on the war-debt issue, but a crucial condition for the United States to consider coming over was the cooperation of the European countries. His two trains of thought came together thus: given the fear of Soviet communism, the cooperation of the Western European powers (and others) was

---

18   Royall Tyler to Mildred Barnes Bliss, December 6, 1930, Paris, "Bliss–Tyler Correspondence," https://www.doaks.org/resources/bliss-tyler-correspondence/letters/06dec1930, accessed December 17, 2015.
19   Royall Tyler to Mildred Barnes Bliss, March 7, 1931 [2].
20   Ibid.

clearly desired, so instead of putting enormous effort into building up military capacities, a genuine sign of economic teamwork might lure America to Europe and pave the way for possible economic stability.

After a somewhat more relaxed interlude, in the spring of 1931 Tyler set out once more on a journey that included all the major Central and Eastern European capitals: Berlin, Warsaw, Bucharest, Athens, Budapest, and finally Vienna. Parallel to preparing for that stint, he was also busy co-organizing a Byzantine art exhibition, his real passion. His personal contacts and the high esteem he was held in paid off, since many objects had to be loaned from various institutions for the duration of the exhibition. For instance, he received everything he asked for from Hungary, and his requests were not very modest. The most conspicuous object that the Hungarian state was willing to lend was the eleventh century Crown of Constantine Monomachos, a venerated artifact that had never left the territory of Hungary. As an illustration of his good relations with the highest echelons in Hungarian political circles, he "had to mobilize Admiral Horthy and Count Bethlen to get [the crown]."[21] The exhibition, the first major show of Byzantine art, was held in Paris in the first half of the summer of 1931. In addition to Hungary and other countries—including Spain and Sweden, but with the notable exception of England—the Blisses were also important lenders.[22] After two years of organizing it, the success of the exhibition delighted Tyler, and he elatedly wrote that "it was the most enjoyable thing I've ever had anything to do with."[23]

From a financial point of view 1931 was perhaps the saddest of years, for Europe and large part of the world tumbled into the Great Depression. As one scholar put it, the "economic history of 1931 is an almost uninterrupted catalogue of disasters."[24] The calamity had already been brewing for almost two years, and since 1929, credit had been in short supply, which hurt any efforts for European recovery. Equally painful were the rising tariff walls, for instance the American Smoot-Hawley Tariff Act of 1930, which made

---

21 Royall Tyler to Mildred Barnes Bliss, March 7, 1931 [1], Paris, "Bliss–Tyler Correspondence," https://www.doaks.org/resources/bliss-tyler-correspondence/letters/07mar1931-1, accessed December 17, 2015.
22 Ibid.
23 Royall Tyler to Mildred Barnes Bliss, August 12, 1931, Antigny, "Bliss–Tyler Correspondence," https://www.doaks.org/resources/bliss-tyler-correspondence/letters/12aug1931, accessed December 18, 2015.
24 Gianni Toniolo, with the assistance of Piet Clement, *Central Bank Cooperation at the Bank for International Settlements, 1930–1973* (Cambridge: Cambridge University Press, 2005), 84.

healthy trade, and thus revenue from it, shrink further. Many countries only started to reach pre-World War I levels of economic output or wages by around the end of the 1920s. Without foreign capital, especially the Central, Eastern, and Southern European countries could not dream of maintaining the small gains they had achieved, let alone make any substantial progress.

And then, on May 11, 1931, the Creditanstalt Bank in Vienna, the largest Austrian bank, declared bankruptcy.[25] Despite the short-term loan secured by the Bank for International Settlements (facilitating central bank cooperation and managing German reparations transfers), Austria's financial woes did not cease; in fact, they became more serious. Capital flight, losing gold, runs on the banks, and the unavoidable political instability in the wake of all this were some of the frightening symptoms. The most detrimental effect, however, was the forces it set in motion—first in neighboring Hungary and Germany, then elsewhere as well—to which no one seemed to be able to offer any tangible and achievable solution. The gold standard—thought to be the main pillar of international financial stability—practically collapsed in a very short time.[26] The instinctive answer in most countries was heightened nationalism in politics together with autarchy and protectionism in economy. This all ran counter to the very idea of cooperation that Tyler thought could mean a solution for the ills of the international system.

No wonder these circumstances left their mark on Tyler's career as well. The overwhelming work pressure came from the international scene—both political and financial—in which Tyler had to make the most for Hambros Bank. Pressure also came, on a personal level, with the attempt to make sense of the ever-changing and more often than not seemingly unbalanced European affairs. In the middle of the ongoing financial crisis, when many people in Central Europe expected "the bottom to drop out altogether in a few weeks—or days," Tyler tried to cling to his unadulterated optimism and

---

[25] On the crisis, see, Aurel Schubert, *The Credit-Anstalt Crisis of 1931* (Cambridge: Cambridge University Press, 1991); Iago Gil Aguado, "The Creditanstalt Crisis of 1931 and the Failure of the Austro-German Customs Union Project," *The Historical Journal* 44, no. 1 (March 2001): 199–221. The latter work emphasizes that the customs union proposed between Germany and Austria two months prior to the Creditanstalt drama was abandoned—largely due to French pressure—in light of the unfolding financial crisis.

[26] On the financial crises in 1931, see Barry Eichengreen, *Golden Fetters: The Gold Standard and the Great Depression, 1919–1939* (Oxford: Oxford University Press, 1996), 259–87; Toniolo, *Central Bank Cooperation*, 90–100.

Chapter 5

went only so far as to admit that "the position certainly is the gravest that we have seen since the War."²⁷

The overall situation did not allow much room for optimism, however; only various shades of pessimism vied for position in public and political sentiment. In late June President Hoover proposed a one-year moratorium on payments on intergovernmental debts and reparations. This was clearly not the solution, and it barely even alleviated the problem. In order to avoid state bankruptcy, Hungary, similarly to many other countries, practically begged for credit and pulled all possible string to avoid having English and American short-term credits withdrawn.²⁸ The BIS tried to exercise some control over the situation and coughed up immediate credits and loans, but due to political bickering among the main powers, France being the most intransigent on account of German payments, the measures were not adequate to put out the fire—they merely bandaged a gaping wound. Germany proved one more time to be the hub on which the European wheels seemed to turn—or, this time, rather, to come to a screeching halt.

For Tyler, the German financial crisis signaled a possibility for the United States to get seriously involved in European affairs—on the level of official government participation. Of course, the Dawes Plan and the Young Plan clearly signaled that when it came to Germany, America looked at Europe differently, because the general American attitude was that if Germany was peacefully brought back to its economic capacity and into the continent's life, then the avenues of prosperity might once again be open to Europe, and perhaps to the United States as well. Also, as Tyler and almost every other observer saw clearly, "without the U.S.' participation nothing more than a stop gap can be hoped for."²⁹ Tyler maintained his assessment that Germany did not want deliberately "to frustrate the whole debt settlement by courting another bankruptcy. All she has done has been to follow the line of least resistance."³⁰

Naturally, the deluge of American private loans starting with the Dawes Plan in the fall of 1924, created the illusion that all was well, and so the rep-

---

27 Royall Tyler to Mildred Barnes Bliss, July 10, 1931, Paris, "Bliss–Tyler Correspondence," https://www.doaks.org/resources/bliss-tyler-correspondence/letters/10jul1931, accessed December 18, 2015.
28 István Bethlen to William Goode, June 23, 1931, Budapest, telegram, OV 33/6, BoE.
29 Royall Tyler to Mildred Barnes Bliss, July 18, 1931, Paris, "Bliss–Tyler Correspondence," https://www.doaks.org/resources/bliss-tyler-correspondence/letters/18jul1931, accessed December 18, 2015.
30 Ibid.

aration issue might be relegated to the sidelines. If anything, the 1931 financial crisis proved that it was the other way around: the whole system suffered from the demands of reparations and war debt settlements, and the intricate relationship between the two. The "brutal fact," Tyler felt, was that "the whole debt settlement, U.S. debts, interallied debts, reparation debts, is unworkable in conditions as they are now."[31] The United States simply had to stop "living in a fool's paradise," believing or pretending that it could collect debts but at the same time erecting high tariff walls and excluding the possibility for other countries to make money by trade.[32] And the repercussions of such a broken system were obvious. As Tyler acutely put it, the Austrian and Hungarian situation, and by extension the larger Central European region, would "be largely conditioned by the settlement or non-settlement of German problems."[33]

Despite the "nerve-wracking" days that Europe was going through that summer, including word of mobilizations here and there, Tyler did not believe that Europe was "going to destroy itself like that," and "going to commit suicide by permitting another war just yet."[34] Only in retrospect is it easy to say with confidence that the real price of the financial crisis lay in strengthening the National Socialist Party in Germany and, inevitably, ushering in Hitler's reign soon afterwards. In 1931 the outlook was certainly not rosy, but far from the tragedy that took place later on.

In the end, parallel to the BIS efforts to produce short-term credits and loans for the troubled countries in Europe, the League of Nations was the other obvious force for renewed efforts for reconstruction on the continent. On the one hand, this was the only forum where a more or less truly international body could talk, debate, argue, and perhaps take steps. Also, it was the League that initiated the string of successful reconstructions in the poorer half of Europe from 1922 onward. Now that certain countries found themselves even in deeper holes financially, their memory of previous days indicated that the League could show a way out of the present predicament, and it was only natural that they again applied to Geneva for help. That is how Royall Tyler, and thus Hungary, reentered the League of Nations family.

---

31 Royall Tyler to Mildred Barnes Bliss, August 12, 1931.
32 Ibid.
33 Royall Tyler to Mildred Barnes Bliss, July 18, 1931.
34 Royall Tyler to Mildred Barnes Bliss, July 18, 1931, and Royall Tyler to Mildred Barnes Bliss, August 12, 1931.

Chapter 5

Hungary was indeed in big trouble. The results of the financial reconstruction of the mid-1920s were fast fading by the end of that decade. Hungary always had to rely on foreign capital in order to get by, but in 1929 long-term loans, mainly British and American, became unavailable, and the country's debt service was met more and more by recourse to short-term loans and credits. This only made things worse. By 1931, Hungary's total indebtedness stood at 4.3 billion pengő ($860 million).[35] As an agricultural country, there was no alternative if that sector could not produce enough or its output could not be sold abroad at good rates. In the unfolding recession-turned-into depression years, foreign markets shrank, and Hungary suffered huge trade deficits. Not only agriculture but industry suffered as well, raw materials production and mining capacity both fell back. Scores of companies went bankrupt, unemployment grew, wages decreased, as did consumption. The latter point was important. Consumption of such staple items as sugar, milk, or meat was on average only 80–85 percent of the prewar years, and without a growing domestic consumption index, there was no chance of industrial growth either.[36]

In 1931 the bankruptcy of the Credit-Anstalt and the panic it caused spread to Hungary in just a matter of days, and there were runs on the major banks. Just when Hungary most needed loans, money was not available on the international market. It is true that between May and mid-August Hungary received about $30 million from the BIS and the Reichsbank, but this money was not enough to alleviate the problems.[37] In June the National Bank of Hungary also received a $10-million credit for three months, but that amount was spent almost immediately, and the government found no other measures to take but to raise interest rates and introduce exchange control.

Tyler visited Hungary in June, and in a dinner conversation with the American minister, Nicholas Roosevelt, he "talked about the extreme gravity of the situation," which information Roosevelt included in his report to the State Department.[38] In early July René Charron—another veteran of

---

35 Péter Gunst, *Magyarország gazdaságtörténete, 1914–1989* [The Economic History of Hungary, 1914–1918] (Budapest: Nemzeti Tankönyvkiadó, 1996), 48.
36 Ibid., 101–3.
37 See, Ágnes Pogány, "Válságok és választások" [Crises and Elections], *Aetas* 15, no. 4 (2000): 33, 35; Ferber, "Lépéshátrányban," 144.
38 Diary entry, June 28, 1931, Hungary 1930–1933, Box 19, Nicholas Roosevelt Papers.

the 1924–26 reconstruction of Hungary, now of the BIS—was in Budapest for a few days, and proposed a three-point program to address the difficult situation, with which Prime Minister Bethlen and Philip Weiss of the Commercial Bank of Pest agreed.[39] The agreement was strictly confidential, although Charron also informed Nicholas Roosevelt of the text of the agreement, which Roosevelt immediately wired to Washington.[40] A declared bank holiday only put off further unavoidable calamities: credit was unavailable, foreign deposits were frozen, the convertibility of the pengő came to a halt, and the gold reserves were depleted.[41] Although on August 14 Hungary received another shot in the arm in the form of 125 million pengő ($22 million), it evaporated within weeks.[42]

Bethlen resigned the premiership on August 24, 1931, after an unprecedented ten years in office. This was not surprising under the prevailing circumstances. As a fine point to illustrate how well informed the Bank of England's people were about Hungarian domestic affairs, and Bethlen's position amid them, it is worth quoting a memorandum from Siepmann concerning the new situation in the fall of 1930, almost a whole year before Bethlen's resignation:

> Bethlen on his return after a longish absence, finds a situation which he considers almost dangerous. Even if times were good, he might easily be regarded as having overstayed his leave after ten cotinuous years of Government. But times are bad, taxes are coming in very slowly, the price of wheat in Hungary is about 1/3 of what it was two years ago, and the peasants are discontented. There are also more particular reasons for anxiety. Otto von Habsburg comes of age on the 20th October. This is not likely to have any immediaste consequences... but the Legitimists, of course, are busy and, on the other hand, in the entourage of Admiral Horthy there is talk of Fascism and a Dictatorship ... The personal relations be-

---

39   Note of a telephone conversation with Dr. Popovics, July 2, 1931; "Hungary," Siepmann's confidential memorandum, July 4, 1931; Note of a telephone conversation with Monsieur Charron, July 4, 1931; Note of a telephone conversation with Monsieur Charron, July 8, 1931, OV 33/6, BoE.
40   Diary entry, July 4, 1931, Hungary 1930–1933, Box 19, Nicholas Roosevelt Papers.
41   See, Eichengreen, *Golden Fetters*, 271; Toniolo, *Central Bank Cooperation*, 97–99; Eichengreen, *Globalizing Capital. A History of the International Monetary System* (Princeton and Oxford: Princeton University Press, 2008), 77; Gunst, *Magyarország gazdaságtörténete*, 52.
42   Ferber, "Lépéshátrányban," 147.

tween Horthy and Bethlen are not all that they might be and the cohesion of the Government Party has been disturbed by the death of Joseph Vas [sic] who was Bethlen's second in command.⁴³

This was a quite accurate description. Bethlen was followed by Count Gyula Károlyi, minister for foreign affairs since the previous December. Despite his very short term as the counter revolutionary prime minister in the summer of 1919, Károlyi lacked much of his predecessor's talent. These were the immediate events preceding another request by the Hungarian government for the League's help. The request was made in early September, and the help received was in the shape of an advisor. This advisor, desired by the Hungarians for his past contact and good understanding of Hungary, was Royall Tyler.⁴⁴

Actually, at the end of August, Tyler had a week-long mission in Romania, then spent two days in Budapest, went via Ravenna back to Antigny, and within three days was summoned to London. His next stop would have been Berlin on behalf of his employer, but in London Tyler received a phone call from Alexander Loveday, recently named director of the Financial Section and Economic Intelligence Service of the League of Nations in Geneva. The urgent matter was Hungary, which, being in dire straits, had just again appealed for the League's help to "examine the financial situation of the country by means of any expert inquiry."⁴⁵ The League wanted Tyler to go there and prepare the ground for the soon-to-be-dispatched League delegation, of which he would also be a member. The other members who visited Budapest in October were: Charles Rist (French, former vice-governor of the National Bank of France and Technical Adviser to the National Bank of Romania), Vilem Pospíšil (Czechoslovak, governor of the Czechoslovak National Bank), Fulvio Suvich (Italian, current chairman of the Financial Committee), Hedding (president of the Regional Finance Office – Landesfinanzamt, Upper Silesia), and Sir Bertram Hornsby (British, former governor of the National Bank of Egypt). Loveday was accompanied by

---

43   "Hungary," Siepmann's memorandum to Norman, October 18, 1930, OV 33/5, BoE.
44   "Second Mission in Hungary," Hungary 1931, Thompson Todd Collection.
45   János Pelényi's letter to the Council, September 1931 ,5, LNJ, 12ᵗʰ Year, no. 11 (November 1931), Sixty-fourth Session of the Council, 2059. Also see, September 3–9, 1931, Item 42: Cases concerning the League of Nations, Bundle 48, K 64, HNA.

The League of Nations Years – Part III

Jan van Waltré de Bordes and Alfred von Suchan of the Financial Section and Economic Service. Hambros Bank was not enthusiastic about Tyler's departure, but the Bank of England convinced them to let him go, so he was granted a leave of absence for the period of the mission or for a longer period.[46] This extension was needed because Tyler was not going only as a member of the delegation but was to stay behind in Budapest in an advisory capacity to the Hungarian government. Similarly to the 1924 undertaking, Tyler "couldn't refuse to go."[47]

The new errand came at a bad time for Tyler concerning his work on the book that he had been co-writing with Hayford Peirce, since he would have needed a little calm and peace of mind in order to put the finishing touches on the work. Despite the renewed workload, the first volume did appear in Paris the following year.[48] So, in mid-September 1931, Tyler found himself in Hungary again. Little did he know that he would stay there for a considerably extended period of time: six years.

When Royall Tyler headed for Budapest again, Hungary was in the deepest throes of the Great Depression, and the country's financial conditions had been unstable for months. They had, as mentioned, the BIS and the League of Nations as a recourse, but when Tyler and later the other five members of the League delegation appeared in October, there was no room for optimism—a strikingly different scenario from when he arrived with Smith in 1924. Even before departing London, Tyler knew about the prospect that he might need to stay on in an advisory capacity, "in a particularly difficult situation" in which he could not formulate any idea regarding what might be achieved.[49]

Tyler's arrival coincided with the British government's decision to abandon the gold standard for the sterling exchange, a step which had quick and clearly negative repercussions all across the financial world. The Hungarian financial landscape also revealed unpleasant facts: "They have an unbalanced budget, a heavy short term position and a passive balance of payments which makes it well nigh impossible for them to procure foreign currency to pay service of

---

46 "Second Mission in Hungary," Hungary 1931; Royall Tyler to Mildred Barnes Bliss, September 26, 1931, Paris, "Bliss–Tyler Correspondence," https://www.doaks.org/resources/bliss-tyler-correspondence/letters/26sep1931, accessed March 20, 2019; Tyler to Niemeyer, September 28, 1931, OV 33/7, BoE.
47 Royall Tyler to Mildred Barnes Bliss, September 26, 1931.
48 Hayford Peirce and Royall Tyler, *L'art Byzantin* (Paris: Librairie de France, 1932).
49 Royall Tyler to Mildred Barnes Bliss, September 26, 1931.

their long-term loans."⁵⁰ The fact that there was no finance minister—since nobody wished to take on that onerous task—did not help the already serious situation.⁵¹ Wekerle, the last finance minister, had been accused by the British of negligence and of "lacking both in appreciation of the gravity of the situation and in the courage necessary to put the finances of the State in order."⁵² It was probably not Wekerle's qualifications alone that were to blame.

Tyler feared that the social peace would also be disturbed, in which case all hope of help might disappear into thin air. The reason for his apprehension came not only from the financial conditions prevailing at this time but also from the political shift that had taken place during the summer. After Count Bethlen resigned, having earned the nickname "permanent prime minister" after ten years at the helm, it turned out that his leaving the premiership did not mean he had also left politics. He remained the leader of the Unified Party and a confidant of Governor Horthy, so his influence was still significant. His successor, Count Károlyi, was also a veteran aristocratic politician. Károlyi immediately implemented austerity measures: state expenditures were heavily curbed—especially in the form of reduction of state officials' salaries, social entitlements, and pensions. In mid-September, after an act of domestic terrorism, martial law was introduced to stifle any possible dissent, mainly from the left. From its outset Károlyi's leadership was broadly resented both for the steps it took and for its lack of tangible results. Despite his efforts to economize, there was no discernable easing of the pressures on the Hungarian economy and finances, and, as a result, not only the traditionally poor classes but also agrarian interest groups and merchants turned against Károlyi.⁵³ His premiership was understood to be crisis management until better circumstances or leaders presented themselves.

Tyler's renewed presence in Budapest made waves. The papers welcomed the American back and highlighted his earlier work in Hungary, his good

---

50 Ibid.
51 Imre Vargha was appointed to take care of the administrative issues of the Finance Ministry from August 24 until December 16, 1931.
52 "Hungarian Situation," memorandum by R. H. Porters, August 17, 1931, OV 33/7, BoE.
53 On the times and problems of Károlyi's premiership in general, see, László Márkus, *A Károlyi Gyula kormány bel- és külpolitikája* [The Domestic and Foreign Policy of the Károlyi Government] (Budapest: Akadémiai Kiadó, 1968); Levente Püski, *A Horthy-korszak szürke eminenciása Károlyi Gyula (1871–1947)* [Gyula Károlyi, the Éminence Grise of the Horthy Era] (Pécs-Budapest: Kronosz Kiadó - Magyar Történelmi Társulat, 2016).

relations with the Hungarian government in the second half of the 1920s, and his always-ready-to-help style. Aside from the gratitude that Hungarians in general felt for Tyler, his fame was further elevated by the fact that he could speak Hungarian. The energy he had previously put into Hungary suddenly and despite himself was paying off. In the interwar years, when Hungary was interested mainly in revision, it was trying to find help far away from its immediate surroundings, where the successor states wanted to contain it and its revisionist aims. Hopes were pinned on Great Britain and the United States, and so, even if it was a grand illusion that the Anglo Saxon countries would help, when a citizen thereof made a friendly gesture toward Hungary, it was always interpreted as help with the intention to rectify the injustice committed against Hungary in Trianon in 1920. Said citizens, whether Harry Hill Bandholtz, Jeremiah Smith, Jr., Lord Rothermere, or Tyler, were without exception labeled "a friend of Hungary," which was more a psychological gratification than anything else, since the recipients had no power to offer Hungary concrete help regarding treaty revision. Neither did they want to, even if they admitted that the treaty might have been too harsh. Nonetheless, their kindness to Hungary was translated—mainly by revisionist propaganda—into an illusory hope that revision was coming closer. And since Tyler had learned the language, this was seen by many—because they wanted to see it in that light—as de facto American interest in Hungarian issues. Few looked at the situation realistically. Most of all, in the throes of this propaganda wave few seemed to note that Tyler, just like Jeremiah Smith, Jr. before him, was working for the League of Nations and not in any way for the American government. Nevertheless, the papers touted that "Mr. Tyler is the guarantee that in front of the League of Nations a true friend of ours will speak about our case."[54] The readers were informed that Tyler demanded that the staff of Hotel Hungaria speak to him only in Hungarian, and Hungarian was also the language in which he almost always handled his business there.[55]

Actually, as a roving ambassador for Hambro Bank, Tyler had visited Hungary on various occasions—without any fanfare—earlier in 1931 as well, in the spring. That April, when Tyler happened to be in Budapest, Nicholas Roosevelt, the American minister at Budapest, had turned to him for help.

---

54   *Ujság*, October 2, 1931.
55   *Pesti Napló*, October 2, 1931.

Chapter 5

Roosevelt was much interested in financial questions, and when asked Prime Minister Bethlen about the possible budget deficit and the dangers such a situation might incur and received no satisfying answer, he contacted Tyler. Roosevelt "begged him to use his influence with Bethlen to do something about it. Accordingly, on the 10th of April Tyler took the matter up with Bethlen and apparently raised the question of sending for Jeremiah Smith. Count Bethlen flatly rejected this suggestion."[56] If true, it seems to suggest that Bethlen did not wish to reveal the true shape of Hungary's financial condition, because he might have been afraid of outside control. It is hard to understand how, with his immense experience, he could not fathom that acting quickly might have alleviated, if not solved, the problem. In fact, the official numbers were hiding a gruesome budget deficit. Hungary was living on borrowed time.

Originally, the League of Nations seriously considered not taking up Hungary's case. Otto Niemeyer especially was against it: "The position of Hungary is more desperate even than that of Austria, and I do not at present see any hope of her avoiding complete bankruptcy in a very short time. But the proposal to send a delegation to see what can be done is right, and ought certainly to be undertaken, however hopeless the prospects seem."[57] Roosevelt also received information in this vein on his trip to Geneva: "the League had hesitated about helping Hungary, as many had thought it would be futile."[58] Tyler agreed that the current situation was almost impossible. He told Roosevelt that in his view, "the situation was hopeless and that there was no way out under present circumstances."[59] A few days later Tyler and Roosevelt had lunch together again. This time, he informed the American minister that he and his colleagues "had found things even worse than than had been feared; that the government debt was bigger; that more unreported items in the budget had been discovered; that the position of the National Bank was so serious that they dared not make it public; etc; and we talked about the curious unreality of these people and how hard it is for them to face facts."[60] Hungarian finances clearly faced an uphill battle.

---

56 *Hungary* (unpublished), Box 47, Nicholas Roosevelt Papers. In an official report to the State Department, he gave the date of this meeting as April 16. Nicholas Roosevelt to Henry L. Stimson, No. 408, February 6, 1933, Dispatches from Hungary 1930–1933, Box 59, Nicholas Roosevelt Papers.
57 Otto Niemeyer to Alex Cadogan, September 19, 1931, C 7422/2307/21, FO 371/15244, TNA.
58 Diary entry, September 21, 1931, Hungary 1930–1933, Box 19, Nicholas Roosevelt Papers.
59 Diary entry, October 1–6, 1931, ibid.
60 Diary entry, October 11, 1931, ibid.

Still, in light of the seriousness of the Hungarian situation and because of prestige, the League acted.[61] The Financial Committee met in Budapest between October 16 and 22, after the preliminary mission had completed its job. Their report a few days later emphasized that the roots of the problem were at least two-fold: on the one hand, the price of wheat had fallen back to one quarter of what it was in 1925, and Hungary, relying mainly on its agriculture to produce hard currency, found itself deprived of foreign currency and in a serious trade deficit (and in addition the 1931 harvest was a poor one). On the other hand, an older, ill-fated Hungarian policy had come back to haunt them, and had worsened the situation "by a scale of expenditure in recent years in excess of revenue, by excessive and often unproductive foreign borrowing and by insufficient credit control."[62] The solution was not further borrowing but to make sure that Hungary had recourse to credit again. Niemeyer emphasized that Hungary ought not to suspend its payments and must try to meet all immediate foreign obligations.

The Financial Committee's report created a mainly negative impression in Hungary. Everyone was aware of the problems, but many people did not agree with the League's advice. They criticized the high interest rates that were maintained and also the lack of concrete help, as opposed to good advice. Members of parliament also voiced their disappointment and criticism: Károly Wolff said that "throughout the report one can detect the rigid protection of the creditors. It is only about the severe vindication against the debtor."[63] Antal Székács, a member of the Upper House, also vice president of the Budapest Chamber of Commerce and Industry, did not mince words either. "What the Report states about the past is no news. What it has to say about the present is darker than what we have known so far. Regarding the future and reconstruction, it gives guidance and advice but offers no help."[64]

Tyler was of the opinion that Hungary did not have enough resources to meet such obligations and a moratorium would be unavoidable. He also felt that the Financial Committee's recommended policy "was in prac-

---

61 Diary entry, September 21, 1931, ibid.
62 "Report on the Financial Position of Hungary, Submitted to the Council on January 29th, 1932," LNJ, 13th Year, no. 3 (March 1932) (Part I), Sixty-sixth Session of the Council), 611.
63 Uj Nemzedék, October 29, 1931.
64 Ibid.

tice a dangerous one."⁶⁵ The League of Nations, however, decided to follow the ideas advocated in the official Report and left a two-person team—Tyler and British diplomat Henry James Bruce—in Hungary to try to help the Hungarians find their way back to more normal circumstances. Tyler became the Financial Committee's representative in Hungary and an advisor to the Hungarian government. As a good soldier, he accepted the new appointment and soon occupied an office in the Finance Ministry. Bruce was named advisor to the National Bank of Hungary.⁶⁶

The Committee's decision to leave two of their own behind met the official Hungarian request for a representative of the Financial Committee to reside in Budapest and help the government. The British minister in Budapest used an airplane metaphor to describe the situation:

> The Hungarian economic machine appears to me to be in the position of an aeroplane making an unpleasantly rapid forced landing owing to lack of petrol, this commodity being represented by foreign currency reserves, the pilot trying desperately to gain height or at least to keep the machine on a level. It is possible that the League of Nations aircraft might be able to fuel the Hungarian machine from the air and enable the flight to continue."⁶⁷

As was his custom, Tyler threw himself into the thick of the work and devoted all his energy to trying to help Hungary back on its feet again, which was a tall order, and was beyond the capacity of either him or the country at the time. In the given international situation, there was simply no magic pill for the financial and economic ills pervading every economy in Europe and North America. As Roosevelt noted in his diary, "More and more beggars

---

65 "Second Mission in Hungary," Hungary 1931, Thompson Todd Collection.
66 On Bruce's appointment, see Leon Fraser to Montagu Norman, October 24, 1931, and Montagu Norman to Leon Fraser, October 27, 1931, G1/306, BoE.
  Francis Rodd took care of an interim two weeks, after which he handed the tiller to Bruce. Originally, the BIS would have liked to see someone with expertise in Central Banking, however, Bruce's other skills and his personality still made him an ideal candidate. Ibid.
  Bruce was warned to be careful with Hungary. The National Bank was in need of certain reforms, and the country offered a "harassing" case of being "isolated in the Near East among doubts, suspicions and invertebracy." Otto Niemeyer to Henry James Bruce, December 29, 1931, OV 33/8, BoE.
67 Viscount Chilston to Rufus Isaacs, October 20, 1931, C 7820/2307/21, FO 371/15245, TNA.

are to be seen, and persons in rags. Starvation is round the corner for thousands, and the situation not only here but all through East Europe seems hopeless. The government and people here continue to live in world of make believe, and refuse to face facts. It is discouraging."[68]

Tyler met Károlyi several times and "called the attention of the Prime Minister and of the National Bank officials to the urgency of reinforcing foreign exchange control."[69] Tyler then traveled to Paris and conferred with a score of people on what should and could be done, then he returned to Budapest on November 13. After his return, he met with Károlyi again, together with Bruce, and tried to stress the urgency of implementing a program along the lines of the Financial Committee's recommendations, particularly concerning foreign exchange control.[70] The main points were that there would necessarily be additional austerity measures, mainly by further cutting back salaries and pensions; next year's budget should achieve equilibrium in state undertakings' budgets; and that monthly statements of the country's financial situation should be produced soon.[71] The advice resulted in some concrete steps being taken, but it hardly achieved the League's desired outcome, as expounded by Tyler.[72]

The reason why salaries and pensions were the primary target for slashing expenditure is easily understandable in light of the fact that these outgoing monies made up almost 50 percent of state expenditures. Of course, the government situation was far from secure, and Tyler thought that the only reason why it had not fallen yet was the simple fact that no one wanted to risk taking the helm under the unstable circumstances and facing the unpredictable near future.[73] When the budget situation improved to some degree, the government's position also strengthened somewhat, which was welcome news to Tyler and others, because a key element of any possibly successful achievement hinged on having stable political leadership.

68　Diary entry, October 29, 1931, Hungary 1930–1933, Box 19, Nicholas Roosevelt Papers.
69　First fortnightly letter from Mr. Tyler to Financial Committee, November 6, 1931, OV 33/8, BoE.
70　Royall Tyler to Julius Károlyi (Prime Minister), November 17, 1931, Folder 3. Notes addressed from Tyler to Károlyi on questions of budgets, Box 261, Royall Tyler Papers, 1920–1944, P. 32, LNA.
71　Ibid.
72　Royall Tyler to Otto Niemeyer, November 18, 1931, OV 33/8, BoE.
73　Royall Tyler to Alexander Loveday, November 20, 1931, Folder 1, Correspondence with A. Loveday, Royall Tyler Papers, 1920–1944, P. 32, Box 261, LNA.

Chapter 5

In mid-December 1931, Frigyes Korányi, whom Otto Niemeyer, the English member of the Financial Committee, described as "a straightforward and well-intentioned little man" was, at last, appointed minister of finance.[74] Nicholas Roosevelt wrote of him that he "was honest and efficient, and under his business competence sheltered the soul of an artist."[75] In the interim, the post had been filled by Károlyi himself, who was not really competent. Korányi's appointment was thus an "immense relief" for Tyler, because Károlyi "knew nothing about the matter, and I had to deal with the heads of departments who are hard-mouthed old official hacks."[76] Still, Tyler "liked Károlyi immensely and was always in accord with him."[77] He appreciated that the prime minster at least tried to initiate cutbacks and reforms, however mild and insufficient they turned out to be in the end. Bruce described Károlyi in similar terms: "The P. M. knows no fear, but also no finance."[78]

Despite the adverse trends, there were signs that not everything was lost, however. For example, revenue for the month of November exceeded expectations by more than 10 percent. As Tyler wryly commented, "a remarkable achievement in a way, but not altogether a matter for congratulation," the reason being that good numbers made it much harder to impress many politicians that further cuts were necessary.[79] With the value of Hungarian exports and trade in general shrinking, internal production and consumption falling heavily, foreign credit drying up, no loan being available, and having the highest debt burden per capita in Europe, it was only a matter of time before Hungary had to make drastic choices. Despite Tyler's prognosis that no general suspension of payments or moratorium should be expected, the Hungarian government issued a unilateral partial suspension of payments on foreign obligations shortly before Christmas.[80]

---

74 Otto Niemeyer to Henry James Bruce, December 29, 1931, OV 33/8, BoE.
75 *Hungary* (unpublished), Box 47, Nicholas Roosevelt Papers.
76 Royall Tyler to Mildred Barnes Bliss, January 29, 1932, Venice, "Bliss–Tyler Correspondence," https://www.doaks.org/resources/bliss-tyler-correspondence/letters/29jan1932, accessed March 20, 2019.
77 Royall Tyler to Mildred Barnes Bliss, October 1, 1932, Budapest, "Bliss–Tyler Correspondence," https://www.doaks.org/resources/bliss-tyler-correspondence/letters/01oct1932, accessed March 21, 2019. Roosevelt described him as "utterly unselfish and high-minded." *Hungary* (unpublished), Box 47, Nicholas Roosevelt Papers.
78 Henry James Bruce to Harry Siepmann, March 11, 1932, OV 33/9, BoE.
79 Royall Tyler to Francis Rodd, December 1, 1931, OV 33/8, BoE.
80 Royall Tyler to Alexander Loveday, December 2, 1931, Folder 1, Royall Tyler Papers, 1920–1944, P. 32, Box 261, LNA.

The measure was not wholly unexpected. The Hungarian minister at Washington, D.C., Count László Széchenyi, regularly called on Secretary of State Henry Lewis Stimson. While at the beginning of the recession in 1929, Széchényi only complained of low wheat prices, two years later he conveyed a very gloomy picture, because he had "found matters in Hungary very bad ... everybody was discouraged and blue."[81] Early in November 1931, Széchényi (accompanied by a prominent Hungarian banker) informed Stimson that due to the painful situation "a default as to amortization payments might become necessary."[82] The American minister at Budapest was also informed in early December "that a moratorium is now only a question of a few weeks."[83] The information was correct.

The Financial Committee basically accepted the transfer moratorium, since no other step really presented itself, and laid emphasis on closer trade relations with the neighboring countries.[84] Perhaps the critical but sympathetic reaction was due to the fact that the 1924 League loan and the BIS loan service were both exempt from the declared transfer suspension. Tyler, for his part, thought that the League "ought to have countenanced Hungary's declaring a partial transfer suspension 2 months before they did: if they had, we might have started in on the new régime with a little water under our keel."[85] Concerning the unilateral transfer moratorium, the Hungarian viewpoint was that "the government had to choose the lesser evil," that is, choose not to live up to the letter of the original bond agreement rather than face inflation and froze internal payments.[86]

Tyler was also pondering how to speed things up regarding the execution of the reform plans on the part of the Hungarian government. At first

---

81   Conversation with Count László Széchényi, October 31, 1929; Memorandum of conversation with the Hungarian Minister Count László Széchényi, October 29, 1931, Reel 163, Henry Lewis Stimson Papers, MS 465, Yale Archives.
82   Memorandum of conversation with the Hungarian Minister Count László Széchenyi and Dr. Oliver Jacobi, Lawyer and Banker from Budapest, November 11, 1931, ibid.
83   Diary entry, December 5, 1931, Hungary 1930–1933, Box 19, Nicholas Roosevelt Papers.
84   Work of the Financial Committee during its Forty-fourth Session, January 11th to 22nd, 1932, Report of the Committee, submitted to the Council on January 29th, 1932, LNJ, 13th Year, no. 3 (March 1932) (Part I), Sixty-sixth Session of the Council, 642–44.
85   Royall Tyler to Mildred Barnes Bliss, January 29, 1932, Venice, "Bliss–Tyler Correspondence," https://www.doaks.org/resources/bliss-tyler-correspondence/letters/29jan1932, accessed March 20, 2019.
86   János Teleszky's aide memoir, February 93–52. 1932, 3, Folder 6, Bundle 1, Papers of Frigyes Korányi, K 274, HNA.

he thought it might be a good idea to release to the press a letter of his to the League that underlined the slow progress in Hungary, because "these people are sensitive to what is said about them abroad."[87] But he also realized that with the good budget figures, for the moment this idea should be put on hold. All in all, he turned to the new year with characteristic optimism—based upon figures promising here and there—and informed his old-time friend, "I feel that the tiller is no longer as badly jammed as it was when I came."[88] For its part, the Hungarian government "was particularly grateful for the help of Mr. Tyler, the representative of the Financial Committee at Budapest, whose very judicious advice and whose competence were greatly facilitating the Hungarian Government's task."[89]

Despite Tyler's optimism, the outlook at the end of 1931 was grim. Even just meeting the amortization and interests on foreign loans amounted to 300 million pengős ($52 million), while foreign trade produced only 14 million pengős.[90] In his first Quarterly Report for October–December 1931, Tyler drew up his main observations and the available data regarding Hungary's finances. He stressed the necessity of a further decrease in government expenditure, which was to be implemented in the form of a further reduction of state employees' salaries from January 1, 1932. With the exception of the Post and Telegraph, state undertakings were in trouble, especially the railway company. Still, revenues were promising, and they at least covered the service of the 1924 guaranteed League loan. The silver lining was that Hungary possessed "great reserves of economic strength in its ability, given proper organisation, to feed its own people, with an exportable surplus to spare," but agriculture needed some overhaul in the changed circumstances and industrial protectionisms needed rethinking as well.[91] Commenting on this first report, a Hungarian newspaper observed: "His

---

87   Royall Tyler to Alexander Loveday, December 5, 1931, Folder 1, Royall Tyler Papers, 1920–1944, P. 32, Box 261, LNA.
88   Royall Tyler to Mildred Barnes Bliss, January 8, 1932, Budapest, "Bliss–Tyler Correspondence," https://www.doaks.org/resources/bliss-tyler-correspondence/letters/08jan1932, accessed March 20, 2019.
89   LNJ, 13th Year, no. 3 (March 1932) (Part I), Sixty-sixth Session of the Council, 486. Also see, János Pelényi to Foreign Ministry, January 5, 1932, no. 52–93, Bundle 1, Folder 6, 1932, (Private correspondence), K 274, Papers of Frigyes Korányi, HNA.
90   Pogány, "Válságok és választások," 33.
91   Financial Position of Hungary in the Last Quarter of 1931, First Quarterly Report by Mr. Royall Tyler, the Representative in Hungary of the Financial Committee, January 12, 1932, OV 33/9, BoE.

report is further proof that he understands not only our language but our difficulties as well."⁹²

Despite the mixed results that Tyler presented, and in light of the moratorium the Hungarian government had declared on transfers, it was obvious to all concerned that there was no quick and easy way out of the financial troubles. Tyler braced for the next difficult phase, which was to last until the end of the budget year (June 30, 1932), and he thought it would all come down to the price of wheat on the international market and the next harvest. "If wheat were to recover 20 or 30%, we'd breathe again; if it recovered 50% we'd be out of the wood."⁹³ Since Hungary was mainly an agricultural country, it earned its hard currency on wheat with which to pay the foreign debt after the loans. With wheat prices reduced to 25–30 percent of what they were a few years earlier, there was no possible way to meet those financial obligations in the near future. Tyler also thought, or rather hoped, that there would be no social disturbances in the immediate days ahead. But predicting what was going to happen was like looking into a crystal ball: "It's no good speculating now—too much depends on what happens outside."⁹⁴

As for the Hungarian point of view, Finance Minister Korányi was more apprehensive. In a private letter to Siepmann he complained that Hungary's "international situation is also extremely grave and I am rather dismayed at the thought, how will our people endure this period until the possibility of selling the next crop."⁹⁵ Bruce, who discussed everything with Tyler, was "not cheerful about anything at the moment" either, and thought Hungarians should get accustomed to "taking in their belts to the last hole, and then some."⁹⁶ And the situation as it stood in March also made Tyler wonder about future prospects. Things were "very difficult" in Budapest, and also because spring weather was late to arrive that year, "Hunkeydom looks grey and sad."⁹⁷

---

92 *Pesti Napló*, February 9, 1932.
93 Royall Tyler to Mildred Barnes Bliss, January 29, 1932.
94 Ibid.
95 Frigyes Korányi to Harry Siepmann, February 22, 1932, OV 33/9, BoE.
96 Henry James Bruce to Harry Siepmann, March 11, 1932, OV 33/9, and Henry James Bruce to Harry Siepmann, April 6, 1932, OV33/81, BoE.
97 Royall Tyler to Mildred Barnes Bliss, March 15, 1932, Geneva, "Bliss–Tyler Correspondence," https://www.doaks.org/resources/bliss-tyler-correspondence/letters/15mar1932, accessed March 20, 2019; Royall Tyler to Mildred Barnes Bliss, March 31, 1932, Budapest, "Bliss–Tyler Correspondence," https://www.doaks.org/resources/bliss-tyler-correspondence/letters/31mar1932, accessed March 20, 2019.

All these things were reflected in his second report Tyler submitted to the Financial Committee. Despite the "further notable progress" the Hungarian government had made regarding state expenditures, state undertakings presented an "urgent and unsolved" problem, trade was languishing and "continued to shrink," customs receipts had suffered a huge decrease, the value of Hungarian exports declined by 38 percent in the past twelve months, internal production by 14.5 percent, general consumption by 9.4 percent, and the unemployment rate increased.[98] The Financial Committee's report on Hungary was based primarily on the information received from Tyler. It warned the Hungarian government to make a greater effort to reach a balanced budget and, as a part of doing so, to resolve the harmful financial effect that the state undertakings (for instance ironworks and railways) were having on the state budget. The Committee was pessimistic, and it regretfully concluded that Hungary's position was "extremely grave and threatens to become increasingly difficult until the next harvest."[99]

On account of the bleak prospects and general frustration, voices of criticism unavoidably appeared in the Hungarian press. It was no surprise that, according to Bruce's observation, Tyler "puts on a lion skin when he gets to the Hungarian frontier."[100] Tyler's conclusion regarding the deficit resulting from the state undertakings was attacked in the press on the grounds that it was drawn based on one big company, but he had neglected to look at small state undertakings in Budapest that made some profit, and Tyler's generalization only hurt Hungary's possible credit.[101] Another newspaper pointed out that there was a contradiction between "smart capitalist" Tyler and "capitalist" Tyler, and that the problem regarding the state undertakings lay in incompetent leadership not inherently in state ownership as such. The paper, which specialized in the domestic economy, went as far as to call the report a page out of *Baron Munchausen' Fantastic Travels*.[102] Another piece

---

98 Financial Position of Hungary in the First Quarter of 1932, Second Quarterly Report, April 30, 1932, OV 33/9, BoE.
99 "Report on Hungary, April 12, 1932," LNJ, 13th Year, no. 5 (May 1932), Sixty-sixth Session of the Council, 1056.
100 Henry James Bruce to Francis Rodd, February 27, 1932, OV33/80, BoE.
101 *Magyarság*, May 3, 1932.
102 *Népszava*, May 3, 1932; *Honi Ipar*, May 15, 1932. The Hungarian title refers to Rudolf Erich Raspe's 1785 novel, *Baron Munchausen's Narrative of his Marvellous Travels and Campaigns in Russia*, which contained tall tales of adventures.

of criticism mentioned the lack of a comparison between Hungarian and foreign undertakings, which also produced deficits during the depression years. Therefore, the paper wrote, Tyler's other conclusions also "lack convincing power."[103]

Suddenly, Tyler was not being lauded as "a friend of Hungary." To make matters worse, when yet another paper asked the prime minister about Tyler's latest report, Károlyi gave a mixed opinion. On the one hand, he noted that what the report contained did not surprise the government, since they were aware of these trends. On the other hand, he articulated criticism concerning the narrowness of Tyler's examination. Károlyi objected to the strictly financial approach, although he understood that that was natural. However, the Hungarian government, he pointed out, must take into consideration economic and social points of view as well, which put things in a somewhat different light, and no solution could be produced from one day to the next.[104] Almost as if to counter or soften this criticism, in the first-ever radio broadcast from Hungary to the United States, Governor Horthy did not neglect to mention that in Hungary "everybody gratefully remembers the reconstruction work that was carried out in total selflessness by Jeremiah Smith and is being carried on today by Royall Tyler."[105]

The Hungarian National Assembly was not devoid of critical voices either. Perhaps surprisingly, and with an eye to his own long-time political agenda, none other than ex-Prime Minister Bethlen also spoke out. His focus was not so much against Tyler's latest report as against the League of Nations' action plan. His main argument was that the League was not needed to recommend that a budget with heavy deficit must be balanced by cutting expenditure and raise more revenues. By the same token, the suggestion that Hungary increase its exports while cutting back on imports was sound only if Austria did not receive the same suggestion. Since the two neighbors were each other's most important customers, the two trends extinguished the goal. Bethlen's main argument, however, was that, next to trade policy, the interest service on foreign debts was also crucial, and this latter should be decreased. Hungary looked to the League of Nations to solve both

---

103 *Városok Lapja*, May 15, 1932.
104 *8 Órai Ujság*, May 3, 1932.
105 *Uj Barázda*, May 5, 1932.

questions. "In my view, there is only one option," Bethlen said toward the end of his long speech, "the reduction of the interests of our foreign debt."[106]

Despite the strain of these weeks and months, Hungary's upper classes always found time for entertainment. Teas, dinners, and dances were frequent events in Budapest, and aside from during the summer, when almost nobody stayed in the capital, social life was busy. An ongoing economic and financial crisis did not dampen Hungarian aristocrats' and accredited foreigners' appetite for fun—principally meaning gossip and bridge. Tyler was a regular guest of honor at many of these gatherings, and in his private notes he sometimes meticulously recorded the composition of dinner parties, the main topics of conversation, and sometimes other features. The topics were wide ranging, from the present situation to World War I to Charles' aborted putsches and beyond. The roster of guests was a who's who of the Hungarian elite, and Tyler mentioned, among others: Governor Miklós Horthy and his wife, Sándor Vértessy, chief of the Governor's cabinet, and his wife, Melinda Károlyi, the prime minister's wife, Johanna Bissingegn-Nippenburg, alias Iska Teleki, the former and future prime minister's wife, foreign minister Lajos Walko and his wife, and many members of the diplomatic corps.[107] Antal (Tony) Sigray, one of Tyler's closest friends in Hungary, and his wife Harriet were also often present. But these fun moments were few and far between, and perhaps they really were needed to alleviate the stress that the situation was constantly placing on the participants. In addition, Tyler's art dealership for the Blisses went on uninterrupted and in addition to his usual workload. That he found the time and energy for such activity can only be explained by his never-ending passion for art and his friends.[108]

Things in Hungary continued to deteriorate, exacerbating the already serious situation. A good indicator of how deeply Tyler was immersed in Hungarian affairs and how much strain this put on him is his own formulation of the frustration he experienced in the spring of 1932. As he wrote in a letter to Mildred Barnes, "Having spent a very strenuous five weeks in

---

106 Bethlen's speech in the National Assembly, May 4, 1932, *National Assembly Diary – House of Representatives*, 1931, vol. 6 (Budapest: Athenaeum, 1932), 446–54. The quotation can be found on page 453.
107 "Second Mission in Hungary" Hungary 1931, Thompson Todd Collection.
108 See, Robert S. Nelson, "Argentina, Budapest, and Paris (1928–1933)," "Bliss–Tyler Correspondence," https://www.doaks.org/resources/bliss-tyler-correspondence/historical-introductions/argentina-budapest-and-paris, accessed May 10, 2019.

Hunkeydom, dearest Mildred, and feeling that if I stayed one day more, and saw one more Hunkey, I should scream."[109] It is little wonder that he desired to get away for at least for a short time, which he managed to do from May to early June—a well-deserved and much-needed break.

June saw the lowest point in the crisis of Hungarian finances. After having sold most of its remaining gold reserve, the country even defaulted on the Reconstruction Loan of 1924. At the time of the partial transfer moratorium of December 1931, this was almost the only obligation that Hungary loyally kept paying, but now the time had arrived when the country's capability reached the breaking point. The Hungarian government felt forced to declare a unilateral transfer moratorium on all of its short- and long-term debts. The Financial Committee, for its part, repeated its warnings and suggestions for financial and economic reconstruction, but it also admitted that as a country in which exports had fallen by almost 50 percent compared to the previous year and even more compared to 1930, Hungary could hardly possess the amount of foreign currency necessary to repay its existing obligations.[110] Perhaps there was a symbolic parallel between Hungary hitting the low point and Royall Tyler, contrary to his natural outlook, feeling pessimistic as well. He complained of "nothing concrete appearing to permit one to hope for alleviation."[111] He thought the agrarian forces were going to get the upper hand in domestic policy. He respected that Prime Minister Károlyi was putting up a fight, but he admitted "to being quite unable to see how things are going to develop."[112] Károlyi's position, which never was really strong, gradually weakened, and from the late spring he was attacked basically from all quarters, the governing party with Bethlen as its head included.[113]

Then some good news arrived. The unavoidable next step on the part of the Western powers took place in the summer. In June–July 1932, the

---

109 Royall Tyler to Mildred Barnes Bliss, May 11, 1932, Marseilles, "Bliss–Tyler Correspondence," https://www.doaks.org/resources/bliss-tyler-correspondence/letters/11may1932, accessed March 20, 2019.
110 Work of the Financial Committee during Its Forty-sixth Session (June 27–30, 1932) LNJ, 13th Year, no. 7 (July 1932), Sixty-seventh Session of the Council, 1275, 1453–54.
111 Royall Tyler to Mildred Barnes Bliss, June 3, 1932, Budapest, "Bliss–Tyler Correspondence," https://www.doaks.org/resources/bliss-tyler-correspondence/letters/03jun1932, accessed March 21, 2019.
112 Royall Tyler to Mildred Barnes Bliss, June 10, 1932, Budapest, "Bliss–Tyler Correspondence," https://www.doaks.org/resources/bliss-tyler-correspondence/letters/10jun1932, accessed March 21, 2019.
113 See, Márkus, *A Károlyi Gyula kormány*, 276–85; Püski, *A Horthy-korszak szürke eminenciása*, 73–80.

Chapter 5

Lausanne Conference reached a decision concerning reparations stemming from World War I. In the midst of the Great Depression, no one could harbor any illusions as to the capacity of the defeated countries to keep paying. All countries had their fair share of financial problems, and it was crystal clear that exacting reparations when most of these countries could not even meet amortization payments on foreign loans would be tantamount to shouting into the wind. The agreement finally reached said that 90 percent of the reparations would be waived, practically annulling them.[114] The protocols signed at Lausanne called on the League of Nations to convene an International Monetary Economic Conference.[115] There was hope that this might induce the United States to cancel war debts, but that was never going to happen. Although the cancelling of reparations payments was naturally a long-desired outcome sought by Hungary and the other defeated countries, in reality this changed the overall situation little, and just because the reparation payments were out of the picture, it did not mean that, for example, Hungary's woes disappeared overnight.

The rest of the summer of 1932 did not bring many changes, or any at all concerning Hungary's dismal economic and financial situation, which remained in place despite the sudden disappearance of the onus of reparations. The suspended payments played a preeminent role regarding how Hungary should resume the payments on the 1924 Reconstruction Loan, and on whether a new monetary policy ought to be introduced, an idea that the National Bank of Hungary opposed.[116] Tyler well summarized the state of affairs in layman's language in a letter to Mildred Barnes Bliss. One point he touched on was the wheat question. Up to the very last moment it seemed that the harvest would be bountiful, but a late heat wave killed almost a quarter of the harvest, and with it went the hoped-for exportable surplus. He also pointed out that Hungary's trade had further diminished, and the price disparity between Hungary and the international community basically thwarted selling anything abroad at a profit. What Hungary actu-

---

114 On the Lausanne Conference, the antecedents, the agreement it reached, and the reverberations, see, Jo-Anne Pemberton, *The Story of International Relations, Part Two: Cold-Blooded Idealists* (London: Palgrave Macmillan, 2019), 205–46.
115 Eichengreen, *Golden Fetters*, 320.
116 Royall Tyler to Arthur Salter, August 5, 1932, Folder 5, Royall Tyler Papers, 1920–1944, P. 32, Box 261, LNA.

ally suffered from was "a bad attack of price-inflation, which is closely allied with currency inflation," and all these meant that the country was "busted to the world."[117]

In the midst of the depression years the weaknesses in the postwar Central European picture became clear, especially in the economic dimension. The strategic considerations that laid down the region's foundations could survive only as long as these countries' economies more or less prospered. As soon as the wheels of an economy started to creak, it became more obvious that there were deep underlying problems with the structure. But a more important observation was Tyler's acute insight about the impossibility of the situation the peace accords had created and of the answers to the crisis that was raging in the former parts of the Monarchy. It is worth quoting his words at length:

> It's a question of holding the internal frame work together somehow until certain things happen—those certain things including the realisation by the outer world that the money lent to the Danubian countries in order to make each one of them self-sufficient economically (thus fulfilling the promises implied in the peace-treaties) is lost: and also the realization of the fact that, in some form or other, the customs frontiers put up in the former territory of the Habsburg Monarchy have got to go. But what will be left when these things have been understood? Something, certainly, and one's business is to see that it's as much as can possibly be preserved."[118]

Here one can see the reflection of the American thinking that was palpable until 1918, and gained strength again in the wake of the problems in Central Europe, namely, that the Austro-Hungarian Monarchy, with all its shortcomings, was still perhaps a more viable entity than the many antagonistic successor states that time and again had proven that they followed only narrow interests by failing to comprehend the larger picture, therefore producing a more unstable region in the end.

---

117 Royall Tyler to Mildred Barnes Bliss, August 15, 1932, Antigny-le-Château, "Bliss–Tyler Correspondence," https://www.doaks.org/resources/bliss-tyler-correspondence/letters/15aug1932, accessed March 21, 2019.
118 Ibid.

Chapter 5

When in early September Tyler informed Prime Minister Károlyi—who obviously was only a nominal prime minister by that time—about the country's financial position, he had only bad news to share. The budget was utterly unbalanced, mainly due to the state undertakings that kept draining the budget. Inflation was threatening to shatter the currency, and unless expenditure was cut back even more seriously, there was no escaping total financial ruin. He also scorned the Hungarians for cheating by misleadingly presenting the data, as if by masking the problem it would go away.[119] Trade suffered especially, because there was no commercial treaty in force with Austria and Czechoslovakia, Hungary's two most important foreign trading partners.[120]

Perhaps to further embitter the pill, Tyler experienced a significant measure of foreboding while in Geneva: "Pessimism, apathy, bad atmosphere generally. I don't believe the League is doomed, and I think it was bound, given the way the world wags, to go through a nearly-mortal illness, but it's not a pretty picture."[121] This mood reflected a larger pattern in the world. Naturally, in addition to the worldwide ongoing financial and economic crisis, additional troubles were giving the organization a headache, the most serious being the Manchurian crisis, which started in September 1931. Japan occupied the territory claimed by China and the next year created a quisling state named Manchukuo. The League of Nations, despite all its good intentions, did not address the situation adequately and did not offer a real and reassuring outcome when two member states were involved.[122] Instead of stabilizing the world situation and strengthening collective security, a pattern slowly emerged that would become the norm: the League of Nations proved to be a paper tiger and did not offered a real alternative or solution to the destabilizing forces emerging in Asia and later in Europe.

As for Tyler's narrower field of worries, Hungary went through yet another political change of some note when a new prime minister took office

---

[119] Notes on the Budget and Cash Position, September 7, 1932, (Handed to P.M. 7/9/32.) Folder 3. Notes addressed from Tyler to Károlyi on questions of budgets, Box 261, Royall Tyler Papers, 1920–1944, P. 32, LNA.

[120] Tyler's Fourth Quarterly Report, October 27, 1932, OV33/11, BoE.

[121] Royall Tyler to Mildred Barnes Bliss, October 1, 1932, Budapest, "Bliss–Tyler Correspondence," https://www.doaks.org/resources/bliss-tyler-correspondence/letters/01oct1932, accessed March 21, 2019.

[122] See, Lojkó Miklós, "Railways and Diplomats. The Failure of the League of Nations to Settle the Manchurian Crisis, 1931–1933," in Nóra Deák, ed., *At the Crossroads of Human Fate and History* (Budapest: Eötvös Loránd Tudományegyetem, Bölcsészettudományi Kar, Angol-Amerikai Intézet, 2019), 349–66.

in the first days of October. For the next four years Gyula Gömbös was the Hungarian premier, and Tyler, and the League of Nations, had to work with him to try to find the way out of dire straits.

CHAPTER 6

The League of Nations Years Part IV: Adviser to the Hungarian Governments

In the 1930s, with the Great Depression driving the agenda almost all over the world, the United States understandably concentrated on its own economic wounds. With the election of Franklin Delano Roosevelt to the presidency, a series of vigorous efforts began to fight the economic calamity under the aegis of the New Deal, which defined most of the 1930s, and Europe, especially Central Europe, got very far from outside the American political and financial radar. Not that the U.S. didn't follow events closely, but the unfolding political and diplomatic crises were not something it was directly involved in or indirectly wanted to be involved in. The country that had poured billions of dollars into Europe in the previous decade now cut its losses and focused mainly on the Western Hemisphere and the Pacific region.

Meanwhile, in Europe in general and in Hungary in particular, the efforts to rehabilitate finances went on under full steam. The League of Nations tried its best, and through Royall Tyler it was still trying to help Hungary, even if Hungarians sometimes complained. Tyler was not clearly the embodiment of control, since he was an adviser. Still, it was obvious that he carried almost as much weight as that of an official commissioner. From October 1, 1932, Tyler had to work with a new leading politician to find a way out, preferably together.

Gyula Gömbös had been a well-known figure on the Hungarian political scene since 1919, when he first appeared there as an ex-soldier and zealous counter revolutionary organizer. Gömbös was an almost fanatical nationalist,

Chapter 6

a staunch believer in revisionist aims, and he always held agriculture to be the backbone of the Hungarian economy, as opposed to heavy industry. In his political views he adopted some aspects from Benito Mussolini, but he could not and did not establish a fascist system in the political dimension when he became prime minster. However, highly concentrated power and an omnipotent government were central to his thinking. As a defender of race purity, Gömbös had been preparing himself for the premiership, and during his time as Hungary's political leader he put emphasis on and managed well the various layers of mass communication and the press. He took an active role in the conduct of foreign policy, and he was a realist. His main aim was to try to further Hungarian economic interests and lead the country out of the dire circumstances of the depression.[1] Beginning in the fall of 1932, this was the prime minister Royall Tyler had to cooperate with and find a way out of Hungary's crippled situation.

Actually, Tyler was toying with the idea of leaving Hungary behind—Hambros Bank was waiting for him to return, and the past year had also brought a lot of frustration. But both the League of Nations and Károlyi urged him to stay; and in this role he had a chance to play on an admittedly small national and international level, which appealed to him.[2] It was after an extended period of rest, mainly at Antigny, that Tyler returned to Budapest to face the change of government in which Károlyi was succeeded by Gömbös. Certain newspapers—according to their political views—accused Tyler of, or credited him with, Károlyi's ousting, a point that Tyler vehemently denied. Naturally, the financial picture of Hungary that he had presented in his reports did not strengthen Károlyi's position in any way, but that in itself was not and would not have been enough to initiate such changes. He rather thought that Károlyi was out because he "got no loyal support from Parliament, and the position had become ludicrous; a Govt. without support from Parlt., and that Parlt. having lost its hold on the country."[3]

---

1 On Gömbös's life and career see, Pál Pritz, *Magyarország külpolitikája Gömbös Gyula miniszterelnöksége idején, 1932–1936* [The Foreign Policy of Hungary During the Premiership of Gyula Gömbös, 1923–1936] (Budapest: Akadémiai Kiadó, 1982); Mária Ormos, *Magyarország a két világháború korában (1919–1945)* [Hungary in the Age of the World Wars] (Debrecen: Csokonai Kiadó, 1998), 147–68; Jenő Gergely, *Gömbös Gyula. Vázlat egy politikai életrajzhoz* [Gyula Gömbös. Sketches for a Political Biography] (Budapest: Elektra Kiadóház, 1999); and József Vonyó, *Gömbös Gyula* [Gyula Gömbös] (Budapest: Napvilág Kiadó, 2014).
2 Royall Tyler to Mildred Barnes Bliss, October 1, 1932.
3 Ibid.

As for the new prime minister, Tyler sized Gömbös up surprisingly accurately, despite knowing him only "casually." "As Min. of war for the last 3 years he has been competent and sober, though I don't suppose he has lost any of his sympathy for extra-parliamentary methods when circumstances seem to him to demand them."[4] Gömbös made a good impression on the other American permanently stationed in Budapest, Nicholas Roosevelt. The new prime minister "appealed to me," he wrote, "because of his directness, vitality and obvious simplicity. Count Bethlen and the aristocrats, by pose as well as by blood, gave an impression of fatigue, as if they lacked energy and virility. Goemboes [sic], in contrast, was immensely alive and refreshingly earthy." In addition, Gömbös "always spoke to me with great freedom—even about Hungarian political affairs—and I enjoyed his racy bluntness."[5] Initially, Henry James Bruce also reacted positively to a speech Gömbös gave in Parliament a few days after taking over the premiership: "There is a new feeling of optimism in the country," he wrote, "on the whole the general tendency is to hope much from the man's energy and readiness to learn and to admit where he has gone wrong."[6]

It also struck Tyler as a new feature that there were no nobles in the new cabinet—"the first time such a thing has happened, except during Bolshevism. Even the Hunk Republic had to be led by a Count."[7] Although he did not know what to expect from Gömbös, Tyler decided to "keep an entirely open mind, do what I can to help and form my opinion as things take shape."[8] Just a few days into his premiership, Gömbös received a memorandum from Tyler on Hungary's financial situation, which informed him especially about the serious budget deficit concerning the previous quarter, July–September, 1932.[9] In Tyler's view, Gömbös had "an opportunity, and if he understands that the budget must be balanced, and does what is

---

4 Ibid.
5 *Hungary* (unpublished manuscript), Box 47, Nicholas Roosevelt Papers.
6 Henry James Bruce to Harry Siepmann, October 12, 1932, OV33/11, BoE.
7 Royall Tyler to Mildred Barnes Bliss, October 1, 1932.
8 Ibid.
9 Memorandum on the Budget Position, October 6, 1932 (Handed to P.M. October 6, 1932.) Folder 3. Notes addressed from Tyler to Károlyi on questions of budgets, Box 261, Royall Tyler Papers, 1920–1944, P. 32, LNA. The name of the folder indicates material for Károlyi, but on October 6 Gömbös was already prime minister of Hungary.

necessary to that end, he'll deserve well of this country, where few people care to face 2 + 2."[10]

Tyler gave voice to his criticism concerning the "the protection of certain categories of agricultural debtors," which, as the Financial Committee stated, might "lead to the complete paralysation of those sources of agricultural credit on which the financing of future crops depends."[11] It was, of course, a open question what Gömbös would actually do as the leader of Hungary. "He is credited with the intention of democratising Hungary from the Right," wrote Tyler, "and unless he is to fall far below expectations he will have to produce a programme with thrills in it."[12]

As if on cue, Gömbös introduced his national plan to turn things around. The new government's program primarily focused on the economy, the main goal being to strengthen agriculture; the rest of the economy was to be subordinated to that goal. Also, he wanted to beef up the lower and middle classes, while the capitalists and their related trade, industrial, and financial interests were to be limited—this last point was a thinly veiled attack on the wealthy layer of Hungarian Jewry. In addition, nation-centered education received emphasis. All this envisioned a highly centralized and in many ways restrictive power.[13] Bruce dismissed the program as populist, too general, and containing many self-contradictory points. "One wonders," he wrote scathingly, "whether Gömbös, with his 103 points, knows Clémenceau's comment on Wilson's 14—'Le bon Dieu n'en avait que dix' [Even God was satisfied with ten]. I only hope that Gömbös will score a larger percentage of hits with his 103 than it has hitherto been possible to attain with the original ten."[14] Despite the fact that there were no nobles in the cabinet, Tyler nevertheless was not wholly pleased with the various appointments in Gömbös' new cabinet either.[15]

The Hungarian press gave a detailed account of Tyler's financial report regarding the third quarter of 1932. In it Tyler suggested that "drastic mea-

---

10 Royall Tyler to Mildred Barnes Bliss, October 1, 1932.
11 Report of the Financial Committee, October 13, 1932, LNJ, 13th Year, no. 12 (December 1932) (Part I), Sixty-ninth Session of the Council, 2009.
12 Royall Tyler to Mildred Barnes Bliss, October 1, 1932.
13 Vonyó, *Gömbös Gyula*, 172–79.
14 Henry James Bruce to Harry Siepmann, October 26, 1932, OV33/11, BoE.
15 Royall Tyler to Mildred Barnes Bliss, November 1, 1932, Geneva, "Bliss–Tyler Correspondence," https://www.doaks.org/resources/bliss-tyler-correspondence/letters/01nov1932, accessed March 21, 2019.

sures to restore equilibrium be taken" in order to avoid inflation.[16] One newspaper noted on reading it that Tyler "paints an even darker picture than heretofore," which was the general impression.[17] And the situation indeed allowed no room for much optimism. There was still no commercial treaty in force with either Austria or Czechoslovakia, which was highly detrimental to Hungary's financial status and equilibrium, since these two countries were responsible for roughly half of its foreign trade. Germany, a possible substitute to purchase some wheat, also suspended its agricultural imports. The budget deficit was way too big, efforts to have a higher yield from taxation did not produce the desired results, and "remedy can only be sought in drastic reductions in expenditure."[18] In his official report to the Financial Committee, Tyler also listed the country's ongoing ills: budget deficit, state undertakings losing money, further diminishing foreign trade with agricultural products basically impossible to sell, high price for industrial articles, and the population's decreasing savings deposits.[19]

Despite the initial good impressions, the official relationship with the new Hungarian leadership, mainly with Prime Minister Gömbös and Béla Imrédy, the new finance minister, was sometimes contentious. Very soon after Gömbös's inauguration, Tyler went over the main issues with him alone—later Imrédy was also included in such meetings, and sometimes Bruce joined the talks. Tyler pressed the idea that in order to achieve a manageable budget, a reduction must be made in salaries together with a parallel increase in the turnover tax, in addition to closing the state iron works and a quick overhaul of the railways. Gömbös and Imrédy argued that the deficit would not be as large as Tyler had forecast, and just a relatively small budget improvement was all that was necessary.[20] When they gathered again in December to talk after the latest numbers had come in, Tyler's prognosis was proven correct. However, Gömbös stalled, since such measures did not meet

---

16 Tyler's Fourth Quarterly Report, October 27, 1932, OV33/11, BoE.
17 *Ujság*, October 29, 1932.
18 Memorandum on the Budget Position, December 4, 1932, Folder 3. Notes addressed from Tyler to Károlyi on questions of budgets, Box 261, Royall Tyler Papers, 1920–1944, P. 32, LNA. The folder's title is wrong. As the handwritten note on it says, Tyler discussed these points with Gömbös, Imrédy, and Bruce.
19 Tyler's Fifth Quarterly Report, December 30, 1932, OV33/11, BoE.
20 Royall Tyler to Alexander Loveday, December 7, 1932, Folder 1, Correspondence with A. Loveday. Royall Tyler Papers, 1920–1944, P. 32, Box 261, LNA.

Chapter 6

his vision for Hungary. The prime minster wanted to cut personnel instead of salaries, the latter being already very low. Tyler countered that in that case, the pengő would be impossible to maintain at its current purchasing power, and that would lead to further disaster. In the end Gömbös agreed with Tyler, at least in principle, and promised to come up with some plans, together with Imrédy, that would follow Tyler's suggestions.[21] The weeks leading up to this meeting and the talk with Gömbös convinced Bruce that the prime minster was nothing else but a "Popularity Jack."[22]

When the discouraging summary of his latest report appeared in the Hungarian press, it "caused considerable comment and editorials appeared in the chief papers for a number of days tending in the main to lighten the sting of the report."[23] A legitimist and anti-liberal paper again criticized Tyler and his report, saying that he was hazy on how foreign exchange restriction and foreign trade could be harmonized, and the pet subject of that paper then surged to the fore: the sanctity of Hungarian state undertakings, which Tyler's reports attacked.[24] The government, through the press, also advocated its longstanding view that strictly financial considerations would not suffice and could not be the only considerations for Hungary.[25] In the British Foreign Office the opinion was also that it was a "very gloomy report. The absence of any effort to reform the country's finances is perhaps the most disquieting feature."[26]

After such a tough period, leaving Budapest a while would have brought Tyler some relief. But toward Christmas, when there was indeed a chance for a family reunion with Bill in Italy, Tyler had to decide against going. Only Elisina, who had been in Budapest for some time, went to see their son. The situation in Hungary was simply so unfavorable that it demanded all of Tyler's time and energy, and there was also the Financial Committee meeting coming up in January at Geneva. Still, the optimism seemed to have crept back into his system to a degree. At least he stated, "On the whole, I'm

---

21 Royall Tyler to Alexander Loveday, December 9, 1932, Folder 1, ibid.
22 Henry James Bruce to Harry Siepmann, December 6, 1932, OV33/11, BoE.
23 Nicholas Roosevelt to Henry L. Stimson, January 6, 1933, 864.00 P.R./61, Microfilm Publications, Records of the Department of State Relating to Internal Affairs of Hungary, 1930–1944, Roll 3, M1206, NARA.
24 *Magyarság*, December 25, 1932.
25 *Nemzeti Ujság*, December 28, 1932.
26 R. M. A. Hankey's Minute, January 12, 1933, C 184/29/21, TNA.

not dissatisfied, given general conditions—we in Hungary are worse off than many countries, and better than some, which is normal."²⁷ His only safety valve was, as always, Byzantine Art. The second volume of the work with Peirce on the subject was about to come out, and, as he confessed to Mildred Barnes Bliss, he had the feeling "I'd go crazy in this present economic and financial world if I hadn't that refuge."²⁸

On account of this volume, a singular article came out in one of the Budapest dailies that introduced Tyler to Hungarian readers as a Byzantine art expert. The author found it important to note that while the American played neither sports nor bridge, and also shunned social life, he devoted every minute of his free time to Byzantine art. A somewhat strange but heartwarming conclusion was drawn from this: "It can be reassuring to us, Hungarians, that the person conducting the financial issues holds dear beauty of a higher rank."²⁹ Regardless of his passion, he needed to focus mainly on finance, which could not be separated from political questions. And with the screw of the depression turning tighter, many in the defeated countries started clamoring more openly for treaty revision.

While among the political voices on the continent there was a growing chorus for some revision of the peace treaties, Tyler held a middle-of-the-road view—naturally, only in the private sphere. Although the song these countries were singing were not really new, the conditions were. And the depression years proved exactly how fragile the system created back in Paris in 1919 really was. Tyler, who, naturally, was exposed to revisionist propaganda in Hungary, maintained a somewhat distanced view of the issue. He did not think rewriting those treaties would in itself solve problems—political or financial. His take on the issue was the following: "I'm not very keen on revision, myself; I fear it would create as much trouble as it would settle, and I'd rather see progress on the economic plane—bigger units and lowering of barriers."³⁰ In other words, he also considered the Austro-Hungarian Monarchy to have been a much healthier economic unit, one that proved

---

27 Royall Tyler to Mildred Barnes Bliss, January 17, 1933, Paris, "Bliss–Tyler Correspondence," https://www.doaks.org/resources/bliss-tyler-correspondence/letters/17jan1933, accessed March 22, 2019.
28 Royall Tyler to Mildred Barnes Bliss, December 10, 1932, Budapest, "Bliss–Tyler Correspondence," https://www.doaks.org/resources/bliss-tyler-correspondence/letters/10dec1932, accessed March 21, 2019.
29 *Budapesti Hirlap*, December 25, 1932.
30 Royall Tyler to Mildred Barnes Bliss, January 17, 1933.

Chapter 6

to be more capable of functioning than the successor states, with their fair share of mutual hatred. This large-scale animosity among the countries of the Danube Valley stifled rational trade policies among neighbors, and economic hard times only made them turn even more inward, therefore economic cooperation was kept to a bare minimum, very far from what would have been needed to achieve a common comeback to earlier levels. Politically however, the genie was out of the bottle, and there was no way back to pre-1919 days, and the post-peace system created to replace it produced almost as many problems, especially in the economic sector. Tyler was not the only American with local knowledge who arrived at the same conclusion regarding the historical role of the Monarchy. The long-time American minister to Budapest, John Flournoy Montgomery, echoed the sentiment in writing to his State Department: "Personally, I am not of the opinion that the Austro-Hungarian Empire was a political monstrosity. Everything I have learned since I have been here convinces me to the contrary."[31] But one can add George Kennan to the list, who served in Prague in 1938-1939. He also "deplored the breakup of the Austro-Hungarian Empire."[32]

Tyler's private life was just as busy as his official life—insofar as the two could be separated. When Elisina was with him, they were neatly put up with Nicholas Roosevelt in Budapest. Tyler often discussed the prevailing financial situation with the American minister, who included some of these points in his reports to the State Department.[33] But whenever there was a chance, Tyler escaped to Antigny, where the Tylers had by now set up a mainly self-sufficient small farm. They produced a decent quantity of wine, various vegetables and fruits, chickens, duck, rabbits, fish from the pond, and honey from their own bees. The library had also grown, which was a reflection of the ongoing intellectual and financial investment Tyler made in his passion for Byzantine art. He was also planning to travel to Greece in the summer, as well as the United States. Greece was important mainly on account of the next volumes

---

31 John Flournoy Montgomery to Robert D. Coe, December 4, 1939, Folder 1, Box 3, John Flournoy Montgomery Papers, Yale Archives. On Montgomery's work in Hungary see, *Discussing Hitler. Advisers of U.S. Diplomacy in Central Europe, 1934–1941*. Edited and introduced by Tibor Frank, Budapest and New York: Central European University Press, 2003.
32 George F. Kennan, *Memoirs, 1925–1950* [1967] (New York: Bantam Books, 1969), 98.
33 See, Diary entries October 15, 1930, April 16, 1931, July 12, 1931, July 23, October 29, 1931, November 15, 1931, December 10, 1931, February 2, 1932, February 22, 1932, March 1, 1932, March 26, 1932, Hungary 1930–1933, Box 19, Nicholas Roosevelt Paper.

in the Byzantine art series with Peirce, but the League also wanted him to be there on site because of the Greek financial situation. And visiting his country of birth was essential partly for the future of his son, William Tyler, who had finished his education and was looking for a career. Thanks to his father's connections, he had a chance to try a life in banking. Tyler managed to have him enrolled in the banking school of the Guaranty Trust Co. of New York City, and was anxious that Bill should live in the Big Apple for a while. But first he had Guaranty Trust accept Bill for a crash course in central banking issues at Vienna, also thanks to his personal connections.[34]

Meanwhile, in Hungary the situation had not altered significantly by early 1933. The country's cash position remained weak and was expected to deteriorate further until the harvest, and there were also sporadic riots in suburbs.[35] Notwithstanding the negative tone of the past several months' reports and letters, there were small signs of possible improvement. The government, though reluctantly at times, at last had partially followed the advice of the League advisors. There had been "energetic measures taken by the Government in reducing personnel and other charges, and in increasing the rate of direct taxes."[36] New Standstill agreements—debts held in suspension for a period—were concluded with American, British, and Swiss creditors for one year, and Hungary's export values increased after three years of negative figures.[37] This alone did not give reason to rejoice, and until agriculture was back on its feet, there was no possibility to avoid or turn around the stagnation that had set in. But despite the very difficult position that Hungary was still in, there was at least a prospect of a smaller deficit

---

34 See the following letters: Royall Tyler to Mildred Barnes Bliss, February 11, 1933, Budapest, "Bliss–Tyler Correspondence," https://www.doaks.org/resources/bliss-tyler-correspondence/letters/11feb1933, Royall Tyler to Mildred Barnes Bliss, February 13, 1933, Budapest, "Bliss–Tyler Correspondence," https://www.doaks.org/resources/bliss-tyler-correspondence/letters/13feb1933, Elisina Tyler to Mildred Barnes Bliss, February 15, 1933 [1], Budapest, "Bliss–Tyler Correspondence," https://www.doaks.org/resources/bliss-tyler-correspondence/letters/15feb1933-1, Royall Tyler to Mildred Barnes Bliss, March 13, 1933, Budapest, "Bliss–Tyler Correspondence," https://www.doaks.org/resources/bliss-tyler-correspondence/letters/13mar1933, all accessed March 22, 2019; Royall Tyler, "Blind Turtle Swims the Sea," in *One Name, Two Lives*, 114.

35 Royall Tyler to Viscount Goschen, February 22, 1933, Folder 4. Various, Royall Tyler Papers, 1920–1944, P. 32, Box 261, LNA.

36 Work of the Financial Committee during Its Forty-ninth Session (April 24 to May 5, 1933), Report submitted to the Council on May 26, 1933, LNJ, 14th Year, no. 7 (July 1933), Seventy-third Session of the Council, (Part I), 906.

37 Tyler's Sixth Quarterly Report, April 22, 1933, OV33/12, BoE.

Chapter 6

in the current fiscal year—a very welcome sign.[38] As the Minister Roosevelt reported, Tyler's latest conclusions on Hungarian financial affairs "furnished a note of optimism which has been lacking for eighteen months."[39] And indeed, as the editorial of *Pesti Napló* wrote, Tyler's latest report "was the most refreshing reading for Hungary in a long time."[40] After Tyler spent some time at Geneva submitting his report and answering various questions from the Financial Committee and other actors, his short official excursion to Greece began.

As mentioned, Greece had been in dire straits for the better part of the postwar years, and the economic depression spreading across the globe had only made a bad situation worse. Similarly to in the mid-1920s, Athens had had no other recourse but to turn to the League of Nations for help in April 1932. Since Tyler was somewhat familiar with the country on account of his earlier stint there, and the situation resembled that of Hungary and other countries in trouble, it seemed logical for the Financial Committee to send him there. He was not against the idea, if for no other reason than that he hoped to do some field work for the next volumes of the Byzantine art project. He was to be a member of a League delegation to Greece commissioned to draw up a report on conditions there for the Financial Committee[41] and submit it to the Committee's next meeting, to be held in London just prior to the World Economic Monetary Conference, which was to begin in June 1933.

Tyler arrived in Greece ahead of the rest of the delegation and prepared the ground for the others. But despite the chance to work on Byzantine art there, he was "greatly dashed and disappointed," because this mission jeopardized his plans to sail to the United States, mainly in order to lay some groundwork for Bill's workplace at the Guaranty Trust Co. and to meet with Mildred Barnes Bliss.[42] His time in Greece took up most of May, and he traveled to London in early June for the Financial Committee meeting.

---

38 LNJ, 14th Year, no. 7 (July 1933), Seventy-third Session of the Council, (Part I), 829.
39 Nicholas Roosevelt to Cordell Hull, May 6, 1933, 864.00 P.R./65, Roll 3, M1206, NARA.
40 *Pesti Napló*, April 25, 1933, 1; Tyler's Sixth Quarterly Report, April 22, 1933, OV33/12, BoE.
41 The other members of the delegation were: Feliks Młynarski and Cesare Tumedei of the Financial Committee, a certain Laure representing Gabriel Dayras, Johan Ansgar Esaias Rosenborg, and Alfred von Suchan. Solon George Xenakis of the League Secretariat also accompanied the delegation.
42 Royall Tyler to Mildred Barnes Bliss, April 30, 1933, Geneva, "Bliss–Tyler Correspondence," https://www.doaks.org/resources/bliss-tyler-correspondence/letters/30apr1933, accessed March 22, 2019.

In Tyler's view, the work in Greece was "pretty heavy," while "the position [was] much obscurer than it was in Budapest in Oct. 31."[43] Still, cooperation between the Greek government and the League's experts created a favorable atmosphere: it was "very satisfactory indeed, and leaves a good taste in one's mouth after the very strenuous work one put in on it."[44]

The London Monetary and Economic Conference was basically a momentous League-orchestrated affair held in June–July 1933, with more than one thousand delegates from sixty-six nations attending. It "marked the first and only attempt to move international cooperation away from an obsession with debts onto wider terrain."[45] The central goal was to revive international trade and the gold standard, and also to ease tariffs in the midst of the Great Depression. However, due to political considerations, the question of the war debt was once again missing from the conference's agenda, although Neville Chamberlain brought it to the fore on the very first day. In doing so, he set acrimonious tone that would be witnessed. Three weeks in, currency stabilization started to take center stage, despite the League's best efforts. On account of Great Britain's gradual retreat from world affairs prior to the World War, the main actor was supposed to be the United States. Newly inaugurated Franklin D. Roosevelt, however, wanted to focus on his domestic arena and did not wish to tie up American interests with European problems, a clear sign of which that the U.S. had been taken off the gold standard in April. Therefore, the American delegation sent to London, headed by Cordell Hull, was against writing off the intergovernmental debts, which frustrated the Europeans for whom that was a major point. But when members of the American delegation agreed with the leading Europeans, that is, with British and French officials, on currency stabilization, Roosevelt dropped his "Bombshell Message," which had been an actual point in his inaugural address. He rejected the plan and choose to concentrate solely on the American economic and financial

---

43 Royall Tyler to Jan van Wlatré de Bordes, Athens, May 27, 1933, File 3485, Financial Situation of Greece, Box 4570, Section 10C, Finance, League of Nations Archives, 1933–46, LNA.

44 Royall Tyler to Mildred Barnes Bliss, June 15, 1933, London, "Bliss–Tyler Correspondence," https://www.doaks.org/resources/bliss-tyler-correspondence/letters/15jun1933, accessed March 22, 2019. In more detail on the Greek report, see, "Report to the Council on Greece," Financial Committee, Extraordinary Session held in London, June 6th to June 14th, 1933, File 3485, Financial Situation of Greece, Box 4570, Section 10C, Finance, League of Nations Archives, 1933–46, LNA; League of Nations, *League of Nations Reconstruction Schemes*, 72–76.

45 Clavin, *Securing the World Economy*, 84.

landscape.⁴⁶ With this move, Roosevelt practically scuttled the Conference. H. G. Wells's 1933 book *The Shape of Things to Come* gave a detailed description of the conference. True to the author's nature, he made fun of the various participants' incompetence but also expressed his poignant disappointment with their failure and the likely dire consequences to come in its wake. This was expressed in the title of the relevant chapter: "The London Conference: the Crowning Failure of the Old Governments; The Spread of Dictatorships and Fascisms."

As for Tyler, though the Greek business was done, as was his appearance in front of the Financial Committee, the stars were not aligned to free him to travel to the United States as planned. During the London meeting of the Financial Committee, just days before the Monetary and Economic Conference, "some serious Hunk questions have now blown up on the horizon," which meant Tyler would have to remain in Hungary for most of June and possibly some of July as well.⁴⁷ The issue he referred to was the question of the League Loan. When the Hungarians met with the League Loans committee in London, repayment was reduced to 50 percent, and for the service year 1933–1934, there was a reduction of 10 percent of the face value of the unpaid portion of the loan. This step on behalf of Hungary did not come out of the blue. Actually, the Hungarian government issued a communiqué on December 20, 1932, in which they already foreshadowed that they would not be able to uphold their end of the bargain for very long, especially after August 1933.⁴⁸

More importantly, however, the summer started to produce better results for Hungary. Yield in direct taxes grew somewhat, and this was also true for foreign trade.⁴⁹ This was thanks to two developments. One was the overall

---

46 On the Conference, see, Rodney J. Morrison, "The London Monetary and Economic Conference of 1933: A Public Goods Analysis," *The American Journal of Economics and Sociology* 52, no. 3 (July 1993): 310–13; George C. Herring, *From Colony to Superpower. U.S. Foreign Relations Since 1776* (Oxford: Oxford University Press, 2008), 494–95; William J. Barber, *Designs within Disorder: Franklin D. Roosevelt, the Economists, and the Shaping of American Economic Policy, 1933–1945* (Cambridge: Cambridge University Press, 2006), 34–35; for perhaps the most thorough summary of the conference with a special emphasis on the League of Nations' EFO's involvement during the preparation and the tensions that arose, see, Clavin, *Securing the World Economy*, 84–123. For Roosevelt's "bombshell message," see, FRUS: 1933. General, vol. 1: 673–74.
47 Royall Tyler to Mildred Barnes Bliss, June 15, 1933.
48 Royall Tyler to Viscount Goschen, February 22, 1933, OV33/93, BoE.
49 Tyler's Seventh Quarterly Report, August 10, 1933, OV33/13, BoE.

healthier trend that started to appear in international trading and, consequently, production. The other was the aggressive efforts on Gömbös's part to find new markets for Hungarian items, first and foremost agricultural exports. The three main countries where Hungarian wheat could be sold in larger quantities again were Italy, Austria, and Germany.[50] This was important from another point of view: Hungary had started to creep, slowly but surely, toward the fascist axis in the middle of Europe. Gömbös, although he did not copy either Hitler or Mussolini in his premiership, showed similar features in his style. No wonder, the British minister reported that Gömbös "can fairly be said to be of a Fascist temperament and an admirer and would-be disciple of Mussolini."[51] But as historian József Vonyó eloquently argued, this was not a slavish attraction to fascism per se on Gömbös's part, although his past would have determined him for such a course. Rather, the problems all three countries faced, and the similar solutions presented to them made it appear as if Gömbös had copied the Italian and German methods. He was also a rightwing radical and, consequently, his governing style shared many features with Mussolini and Hitler.[52] And there was no denying that by now, Germany, Italy, and Hungary were much closer to one another than previously. As a leading member of the British Foreign Office establishment noted, "It also goes to show how much we are drifting towards opposing camps composed of the 'haves' & the 'have-nots'."[53]

Despite noting some better indicators in his report for the second quarter of 1933, Tyler also drew up complaints. He particularly criticized the artificially high retail prices of certain staple items, which caused a decrease in consumption.[54] W.E. Houstoun-Boswell, the secretary of the British diplomatic mission at Budapest, described the report as an "able and particularly illuminating document," which "besides presenting a very accurate picture of Hungary's financial position to-day, its author has in unusually clear terms indicated a number of evils, which the Government have not yet seen their way to tackle."[55] The negative aspects highlighted in Tyler's report were out-

---

50 Gergely, *Gömbös Gyula*, 115; Vonyó, *Gömbös Gyula*, 182, 185.
51 Viscount Chilston to John Simon, March 18, 1933, C 2520/26/21, FO 371/16779, TNA.
52 See, Vonyó, *Gömbös Gyula*, 247–63.
53 R. M. A. Hankey's minute, March 21, 1933, C 2520/26/21, FO 371/16779, TNA.
54 Tyler's Seventh Quarterly Report, August 10, 1933, OV33/13, BoE.
55 W. E. Houstoun-Boswall to John Simon, August 15, 1933, C 7614/29/21, FO 371/16780, TNA.

right criticism of the government—though wrapped in diplomatic language. As he and Bruce expected, the report "has not been a popular document. Our Hunk can digest any amount of flattery," Bruce continued, "but a spoonful of criticism turns his stomach. The Socialist papers, however, are jubilant over [Tyler's] criticism of the cartels."[56] Indeed, the leading Socialist paper in Budapest sided with Tyler and attacked the government's financial policy.[57] The report did not create as much of a "particular stir" as Bruce and Tyler perhaps had anticipated, though quite a few editorials dealt with the report—according to their political point of view—and there was detailed reporting on it.

In any event, by the fall, the situation in Hungary was deemed to be on a modestly upward curve by both Tyler and Bruce. Certain signs of improvement could be detected, and this alone made room for optimism: the budgetary position was better (though far from reaching equilibrium), wheat sales picked up (even if at a reduced price), and agreements were again reached with American, British, and French short-term creditors.[58] Still, Tyler's next quarterly report did not contain much good news. The exceptional harvest in itself was not sufficient to turn things around. The newspapers wrote less copy than usual about the report. Houstoun-Boswell ascribed this lack of media interest, "despite certain apparently redeeming features," to the possible notion that "editors have reached the only sensible and indeed suitable conclusion that the Report affords them but little cause for satisfaction and, try as they might, they have found it difficult to escape the fundamental and distressing unpalatable accusation which it implies that Hungary is continuing to live beyond her means."[59] Be that as it may, Tyler summed up the previous five months and the improving situation to Mildred Barnes Bliss as follows: "The position here is a little better than it was: it stopped deteriorating about the end of June, and has improved a bit since. The same is true of most of Central Europe … I'm not without hope for the future."[60]

---

56 Henry James Bruce to Harry Siepmann, August 9, 1933, OV33/84, BoE.
57 *Népszava*, August 8, 1933.
58 Work of the Financial Committee during Its Fifty-first Session (September 18–26, 1933), Report submitted to the Council on October 12, 1933, LNJ, 14th Year, no. 12 (December 1933), Seventy-seventh Session of the Council, (Part II), 1614, 1663; Tyler to Viscount Goschen, November 23, 1933, Folder 4. Various, Royall Tyler Papers, 1920–1944, P. 32, Box 261, LNA.
59 W. E. Houstoun-Boswall to John Simon, November 27, 1933, C 10533/29/21, FO 371/16781, TNA.
60 Royall Tyler to Mildred Barnes Bliss, November 27, 1933, Pest, "Bliss–Tyler Correspondence," https://www.doaks.org/resources/bliss-tyler-correspondence/letters/27nov1933, accessed March 23, 2019.

Tyler used the better results as a partial excuse for a short getaway from Budapest. Also, the past few months' workload, the disappointment on missing out on the visit to the United States, the insufficient amount of time he managed to spend on his art history project all increased his desire to be somewhere else even if for a limited time only. The chance appeared in the shape of a request from the League's new Secretary General, Frenchman Joseph Avenol, that he attend the fourth Balkan Conference as an observer. It was held on November 5–12, 1933, in Thessaloniki, Greece. Afterwards he visited Mount Athos, the "Holy Mountain," so called because of the many Eastern Orthodox monasteries that can be found there.[61] Although from an art historian's point of view the place did not have much to offer, it still meant for Tyler "6 days of sunshine in such lovely natural surroundings."[62] He made an interesting cultural comparison between Hungarian customs regarding how one feeds guests and the monks' way of treating a visitor. He had dared to hike onto the mountain without taking food: "I found I fared quite tolerably well. In fact I've often fared worse in Hungary; for the Greek monks, at any rate, if they see one in difficulties, never press one to eat, whereas the hospitable provincial Hunk ladies, and sometimes even the Budapestians, make an awful fuss and are insulted unless one consumes large quantities of what they offer one."[63]

But business was awaiting Tyler back in Budapest. Although Hungary's financial situation was incrementally improving, it remained far from satisfactory. Since many traditional markets were closed to Hungarian wheat, the government needed to find countries farther afield to sell to and secure hard currency. However, greater distances caused higher shipping costs, therefore profits rarely were realized in the end. On the other hand, industrial goods were too expensive for the large majority of Hungarians to buy, and people in general cut back their consumption as much as possible, which in turn hurt the sales of products on the domestic market. Although receipts grew, state expenditures were still too high. The Hungarian government, now with Finance Minister Imrédy in the lead, wanted to effect changes in the coun-

---

61   Ibid.
62   Royall Tyler to Mildred Barnes Bliss, November 19, 1933, Thessaloniki, "Bliss–Tyler Correspondence," https://www.doaks.org/resources/bliss-tyler-correspondence/letters/19nov1933, accessed March 23, 2019.
63   Royall Tyler to Mildred Barnes Bliss, November 27, 1933.

try's monetary policy. Imrédy was of the opinion that devaluation of the pengő would create a more favorable budgetary situation. This was also an old preaching of Tyler's as well, a "bee in his bonnet."[64] Imrédy wished to make such a move once the country had some hard currency in reserve, and he thought a foreign loan might provide said financial basis. However, there was no prospect for such a loan.[65] At the Bank of England they spoke of Imrédy as someone who had "been infected with the hope of foreign money," who had "forlorn hope," and who was "letting his mind dwell upon such a mirage."[66] Another issue that created some tension was the question of transfer on the service of the League Loan and other state debts. Otto Niemeyer basically accused the Hungarian government of making only a half-hearted effort to pay more than a nominal amount on the League Loan service, while, for example, the Southern Railway Company's (Danube-Save-Adria Railway Co.) creditors had received increased payments, but Tyler pleaded not guilty on behalf of the Hungarian government.[67]

Prior to agreeing with Italy and Austria to buy more Hungarian wheat, Hungary also concluded an agreement with Germany concerning larger Hungarian contingents of wheat and live animals. The trade agreement of 1931 was supplemented in July 1933 and February 1934, but the German promise to buy 50,000 tons of Hungarian wheat a year was only one-sixth of what Austria and Italy together had promised in the Rome Protocols.[68] Strangely, this German gesture prompted Italy to have the Rome Protocols signed in early 1934, because they feared German domination in the

---

64 Henry James Bruce to Harry Siepmann, April 7, 1933, OV33/12, BoE.
65 Pogány, "Válságok és választások," 45–46.
66 Harry Siepmann to Henry James Bruce, February 20, 1934, ADM 25/9, BoE.
67 Otto Niemeyer to Royall Tyler, April 13, 1934, Royall Tyler to Otto Niemeyer, April 16, 1934, Otto Niemeyer to Royall Tyler, April 19, 1934, OV 33/67, BoE. The reorganization of the Danube-Save Railway was a direct result of the Rome Protocols signed on March 17, 1934, between Italy, Austria, and Hungary. The agreement had an economic emphasis, but it was clearly a regional pact against both Germany and Yugoslavia. The Germans and the Yugoslavs understandably were not happy with it, while basically all other countries welcomed it. The Protocols were popular in Hungary since, at least on paper, it made larger wheat sales (320,000 tons a year) to Austria and Italy and kindled the hope of a possible treaty revision with Italy's help. *League of Nations Treaty Series*, vol. 154, 282–303. See also, György Réti, "Gömbös és a Római Hármas Egyezmény, 1934" [Gömbös and the Rome Three Power Pact], *Történelmi Szemle* 36, no. 1–2 (1994): 159–65; Gergely, *Gömbös Gyula*, 125–26; Hamerli, *Magyar-olasz diplomáciai kapcsolatok*, 210–17; "Danube-Save-Adria Railway Bonds," OV33/95, BoE.
68 Iván Berend and György Ránki, "German–Hungarian Relations Following Hitler's Rise to Power (1933–34)," *Acts Historica* 8, no. 3–4, (1961): 313–46; Vonyó, *Gömbös Gyula*, 182.

Danube Basin.[69] However, the Rome Protocols did not provide the hoped-for results, namely, the substantial growth of Hungarian exports to these two countries, and Tyler spelled out this trend clearly in his reports.[70] As a result, Hungary would gravitate more and more toward Germany, both economically and politically.

In May 1934, Tyler finally managed to travel to the United States—the first such occasion since 1904. The main reason, again, may have been to meet with his long-time friend Mildred Barnes Bliss in person, but he also wanted to visit both public and private art collections.[71] The four week trip, which included Washington, D. C., New York City, and Boston, sometime proved hectic, especially toward the end, but overall it was satisfying to Tyler. Interestingly, he experienced very contradictory feelings toward America. Although it was his native country and the place where he spent the first fourteen years of his life, he was not patriotic in the traditional sense. He had, of course, a certain natural loyalty, which he had proved in World War I, and would again in World War II, but his decades in Europe had taught him to look at the United States and Americans with a critical and disapproving eye.

After his return to Europe, the summer heat produced two major developments—one personal and one that disturbed Europe. At the very end of July his son, William, married Bettine Mary Fisher-Rowe, known as Betsy. This was pure joy for the Tylers.[72] But the celebration had to be cut short so he could rush back to Budapest on account of the assassination of Engelbert Dollfuss, the Austrian chancellor since May 1932. Dollfuss dissolved Parliament and assumed dictatorial powers in 1933. He had both the Austrian National Socialists party (aligned with the German Nazis) and the communists outlawed, and tried to cement close ties with Mussolini's Italy in order to have protection against possible German moves regarding Austrian independence. He termed his own leadership style "Austrofascism."

---

69 Hamerli, *Magyar-olasz diplomáciai kapcsolatok*, 212.
70 See, Tyler's Thirteenth and Fourteenth Quarterly Reports, December 29, 1934, and April 18, 1935, OV33/15 and OV33/16, respectively, BoE.
71 Royall Tyler to Mildred Barnes Bliss, June 5, 1934, R.M.S. Empress of Britain, "Bliss–Tyler Correspondence," https://www.doaks.org/resources/bliss-tyler-correspondence/letters/05jun1934, accessed March 28, 2019.
72 Elisina Tyler to Mildred Barnes Bliss, August 18, 1934, "Bliss–Tyler Correspondence," https://www.doaks.org/resources/bliss-tyler-correspondence/letters/18aug1934, accessed March 28, 2019.

Chapter 6

The failed coup attempt by the Nazis—in which Hitler probably had a hand—that led to the murder of Dollfuss on July 25, 1934, understandably shook Europe, and had repercussions across the continent.[73] The effects of the assassination were felt sharply in Budapest as well, since the Gömbös government had been thinking of a regional pact with Italy and Austria, which ought to have served as a protective alliance in case of German aggression. While Hungary had to rely more and more on German markets, it was afraid of a possible German hegemony in Central Europe. And so, Tyler had to "rush back" to size up the situation on the ground.[74] The ruffles, however, soon were smoothed out, and afterwards Tyler wrote, "Everything is absolutely quiet here, and I hope the situation in general is now by way of quieting down." He then spent a too-brief but welcome month at Antigny.[75]

During those years of turmoil in Europe, it seemed that no sooner had one crisis disappeared than another took its place. Hungary was often involved in these, either directly or indirectly. Such was the case in October 1934 when the latest crisis, or scandal, arose with the assassination of King Alexander of Yugoslavia in Marseille. Louis Barthou, the French foreign minister, was also killed. Foreign policy considerations played a large role in the implication of Hungary in the aftermath of the murder, although not very seriously. The Hungarian government secretly helped Croatian separatists—the Ustasha, a revolutionary organization fighting for separation from the newly-christened Yugoslavia. The aid primarily came in the form of a small camp on Hungarian territory close to the Hungarian–Yugoslav border from which the separatists could strike at the central government of Yugoslavia in the early years of the 1930s. Under almost continuous pressure from Belgrade concerning the Ustasha enclave in Hungary, Budapest chose a diplomatic attack to muddy the waters, and complained at the League of Nations about Yugoslavia and its treatment of ethnic Hungarians in the border region. This political maneuver was only a short-lived success, because the accused in the

---

73 See, Gudula Walterskirchen, *Engelbert Dollfuß: Arbeitermörder oder Heldenkanzler* (Wien: Molden Verlag, 2004); Kurt Bauer, "Hitler und der Juliputsch 1934 in Österreich," *Vierteljahrshefte für Zeitgeschichte* 59, no. 2 (2011): 193–227.
74 Royall Tyler to Mildred Barnes Bliss, August 1, 1934, London, "Bliss–Tyler Correspondence," https://www.doaks.org/resources/bliss-tyler-correspondence/letters/01aug1934, accessed March 28, 2019.
75 Royall Tyler to Robert Woods Bliss, August 10, 1934, Budapest, "Bliss–Tyler Correspondence," https://www.doaks.org/resources/bliss-tyler-correspondence/letters/10aug1934, accessed March 28, 2019.

assassination all could be connected to Hungary in some form. As Siepmann put it, "from a diplomatic and political angle, the Jugoslav affair is extremely complicated and seriously threatening" for Hungary.[76]

Due to the great-power constellation in Europe at the time—endeavors to try to reach agreements about armament with Germany, the peaceful conduction of the Saar referendum, and the French-Italian rapprochement to balance the resurging Nazi Germany—Hungary was a comfortable scapegoat for many. On November 22, 1934, Yugoslavia officially filed a complaint in Geneva about Hungary's involvement in the assassination. As usual, a compromise was hammered out, mainly due to British and French influence, not to mention that of Italy—which country might really have been behind the assassination—and all parties accepted the Hungarian memorandum concerning the matter. In this the Hungarian government admitted only that some of its officers were negligent in issuing passports and supervising foreigners' activities in Hungary.[77] Once again, the League of Nations proved suitable only for soothing whipped-up emotions, and no real and progressive solution was found to the festering political instability that seemed to be growing with every session of the organization.

And it was not only the diplomatic situation alone that proved difficult. Despite some better results in the Hungarian economic and financial realm, the overall picture was still not rosy. True, the budget did become more balanced and the deficit shrank somewhat, while foreign trade also grew by modest numbers. The state undertakings had also seen some progress and rested on a firmer basis now, especially the railways, but they still represented a heavy burden and thwarted the otherwise unfolding economic revival. But Hungarian agriculture had still not found its way out of the woods. Changes were taking place at the National Bank of Hungary as well, namely the long-awaited retirement of Sándor Popovics, president since the institution opened its doors in 1924 but now growing sick and frail. The succession

---

76 Harry Siepmann, "The Jugoslav Affair," November 30, 1934, ADM22/21, BoE.
77 The most thorough book concerning the Marseilles assassination and its aftermath both in Hungary and Europe, is still Mária Ormos, *Merénylet Marseille-ben* [Assassination in Marseilles] (Budapest: Kossuth Könyvkiadó, 1984). Another academic writing, relying mainly on sources other than those of Ormos, reaches the same conclusion. See Bennett Kovrig, "Mediation by Obfuscation: The Resolution of the Marseille Crisis, October 1934 to May 1935," *The Historical Journal* 19, no. 1 (March 1976): 191–221. The newest summary, which relies heavily on Italian sources, is Hamerli, *Magyar-olasz diplomáciai kapcsolatok*, 123–28. See also, Nicholas Horthy, *Memoirs* (Safety Harbor, FL: Simon Publications, 2000), 166–68.

Chapter 6

was of great importance, perhaps especially to Montagu Norman and his Bank of England. The most logical man to follow Popovics was Béla Imrédy, the present finance minister, who also had been a director at the bank since 1928.[78] Imrédy was well respected in England and at the BIS due to his qualifications as a financial and monetary expert who also had the will to decide to act, although he sometimes proved too insistent on technicalities. After a meeting in Switzerland in 1934 among top financial figures on the continent, Siepmann, for instance, opined that Imrédy "made, as always, a good personal impression and managed, I think, to refurbish some friendships which were tending to become a little tarnished," and in addition, Imrédy also "had quite a good press."[79] Nicholas Roosevelt found him "a young man of real ability, with a clear, cold mind and a capacity for much work."[80] As finance minister, Imrédy's efforts were appreciated by the Anglo-Saxon advisers. When, toward the end of 1933, the position of the Hungarian budget had become somewhat better, Tyler and Bruce both agreed that Imrédy was "to be congratulated on a gallant and unostentatious effort."[81] Later events would change these opinions drastically.

With the anticipation that Popovics was about to retire and Imrédy would follow him as bank president, a lengthy report was drawn up concerning Hungary, in all possibility for the Bank of England's use. This was a sobering account of Hungary and Hungarian affairs, and well reflected the British view as to Hungary's contemporaneous financial, economic, and also societal situation. Siepmann, who drew up the points, had access to the latest reliable information in Hungary. The thesis of the lucid report was that "standards, habits, temperament, tradition combine to produce a state of affairs which does not pass muster," at least compared to Britain. As a consequence, "any remedy which may be prescribed for minor ills would have to operate in a system which is itself ailing," but it was questionable whether such an effort was commendable. The new breed of Hungarian politicians was not up to the good old standard shown by their predecessors—Bethlen in particular was praised in this sense. In Hungary a populist-nationalist mold was spitting out leaders that were as unreliable as much as they were

---

78 On Imrédy, see Ormos, *Magyarország a két világháború korában*, 186–201.
79 Harry Siepmann to Henry James Bruce, July 6, 1934, ADM 25/9, BoE.
80 *Hungary* (unpublished manuscript), Box 47, Nicholas Roosevelt Papers.
81 Henry James Bruce to Harry Siepmann, December 6, 1933, OV33/14, BoE.

demagogues. Gömbös, who was considered "capable of reckless and discreditable adventures both in home and in foreign politics," and his government were a living testament to this, at least in Siepmann's opinion, and only Imrédy was "a conspicuous exception." Imrédy, credited with "with soaring ambitions," was already seen as a possible successor to Gömbös, but he thought to bide his time for the present. As for the National Bank—so crucial for the Bank of England, and personally for Norman, who had always looked at it as his own "child"—the report emphasized that the key question was that of succession. Popovics was old and sick, and various possible successors were rumored to be in the wings: Lajos Walko, János Teleszky, Frigyes Korányi, and János Bud. All would eventually be dismissed as prospective appointees. The most likely candidate, according to the report, was Sándor Vértessy, vice president of the Bank and with good ties to Horthy. Béla Schober, the long-time general manager was thought to be, and hoped to be leaving together with Popovics, especially because he had lost the confidence of the president in addition to being "disgruntled and embittered, touchy, hypochondriac and disloyal."[82]

Finally, Imrédy was named the new president of the National Bank of Hungary, which was welcome news both in London and Geneva. He soon met with Tyler and laid out his planned program: "bank merger, consolidation of the B. I. S. loan to the National Bank, and afterwards, devalorisation of the Pengő by 25% or 30%, to ease internal prices, and favour trade, and an understanding with Hungary's foreign creditors."[83] As the bank's president, Imrédy paid a visit to Montagu Norman in London in the first days of June to discuss monetary policies. His vision was again to devalue the pengő, equalize exports and imports so as not to lose hard currency, and at the same time reduce the payments on short-term and long-term loans, including the League Loan, even if the latter was entitled to preference. Norman did not think this plan could possibly be realized in practice. There was the expected resentment on the part of the foreign creditors, short-term and long-term alike, and, Norman added, there was no likelihood for Hungary to secure any foreign credit, which would have been essential for the delivery

---

82 The quotes in this paragraph are all from Harry Siepmann, "Report on Hungary – November 1934," December 3, 1934, G1/306, BoE.
83 Diary entry, Budapest, February 10, 1935, Elisina Diary, Thompson Todd Collection.

of Imrédy's program in the first place.[84] In the end, although both Niemeyer and Tyler saw devaluation as a useful step, it did not come to fruition.[85]

In Tyler's life, the first months of 1935 were interesting in that his wife spent a longer time than was usual in Budapest. Elisina had been a frequent visitor to Hungary, but after Tyler's most recent Geneva stint, she made a protracted stay. Even more importantly, she kept a diary, in which she noted some of the events in which the couple participated, and her impressions of Hungarian social life in the upper and diplomatic circles. Through invitation to teas, dances, and dinners, she encountered a Who's Who of Hungary and of accredited foreign diplomats in early 1935, and it is of interest to learn her perspective. Being an independent and intelligent woman, she was not afraid to formulate her own opinion and stand by it. Since she had been to Hungary many times before, she knew many people well and was well acquainted with the traditions, rules, and customs of high society, but perhaps this only adds to the flavor of her diary notes. They are not first impressions based on a shallow understanding but rather are deeply pondered and carefully weighed thoughts and opinions.

Elisina Tyler found former prime minister Count Móric Esterházy, one of the leading legitimists, "handsome, intelligent, too sensitive, too nervous and morally not a very courageous man."[86] The American Legation was "a sad house," which the Tylers knew well, since they had lived there for many long weeks when Nicholas Roosevelt was the minister to Hungary.[87] She wrote of romantic rumors and of political intrigues, especially mentioning how ostracized the Little Entente ministers, the Yugoslav in particular, were, owing only to the political animosities between their home countries and Hungary. She was also a guest of the Horthys and liked them a lot, deeming the regent "a straightforward man."[88] Gömbös was usually not spoken of very affectionately in these circles, and Elisina also considered him "a demagogue."[89] The best quip she quoted on contemporaneous Hungarian politics came from Gyula Károlyi, the former prime minister. Regarding his relations with

---

84 Note of conversations between Dr. Imredy and the Governor, June 5 and June 7, 1935, G1/306, BoE.
85 Pogány, "Válságok és választások," 46.
86 Diary entry, Budapest, January 24, 1935, Elisina Diary, Thompson Todd Collection.
87 Diary entry, Budapest, January 27, 1935, ibid.
88 Diary entry, Budapest, April 21, 1935, ibid.
89 Diary entry, Budapest, February 6, 1935, ibid.

Parliament when in office, he opined: "They had me as Prime Minister for a year, and they didn't like my silence. They have had Gömbös since and they say he talks too much. I wonder what will please them."[90] Lily Hatvany, the popular author-journalist-playwright, came across to her as "intelligent, reckless, rich, handsome, in a rather sinister way."[91] Tibor Eckhardt, who at that time was the Hungarian envoy to the League of Nations, was "very intelligent, very ambitious" in addition to being talkative and somewhat overbearing, but altogether "sympathetic, but the impression is marred by something bitter and relentless in his manner."[92]

She clearly detected the "constant source of anger and disquiet" on the part of the Hungarians, especially because of the hardships placed on the ethnic Hungarians now living in foreign countries; but there was no apparent hope in sight.[93] This was, in her reading, a direct result of the botched peace treaties, and it was time "to admit that many wrongs were committed then and will have to be righted, or paid for heavily."[94] In summarizing the Hungarians, she chose to commit the following observation to her diary: "The Hungarians are a proud people, they have strong national pride. These days, they are humiliated and depressed. It is more tactful to withdraw a little, because they cannot bear to face the impression that foreigners must receive from the tale of events which it is beyond them not to discuss. Perhaps not with everyone, but with me, whom they honour with their confidence."[95]

Elisina also commented on the murder of King Alexander of Yugoslavia the previous fall. In a letter to Mildred Barnes Bliss, she wrote that the Marseille assassination was a tragedy that was not without some positive outcome. As she put it, "The disappearance of King Alexander, who was a grim soldier, and of Mons. Barthou, who had reached the stage of inconsequence, so dangerous when allied to power—are really two beneficial misfortunes!"[96] A few weeks after the Marseille event, Philippe Berthelot passed away. Back

---

90 Diary entry, Budapest, February 7, 1935, ibid.
91 Diary entry, Budapest, February 27, 1935, ibid.
92 Diary entry, Budapest, February 6, 1935, ibid.
93 Elisina Tyler to Mildred Barnes Bliss, March 27, 1935, Budapest, "Bliss–Tyler Correspondence," https://www.doaks.org/resources/bliss-tyler-correspondence/letters/27mar1935, accessed March 29, 2019.
94 Ibid.
95 Diary entry, Budapest, April 21, 1935, Elisina Diary, Thompson Todd Collection.
96 Elisina Tyler to Mildred Barnes Bliss, March 27, 1935.

in 1918 he had been instrumental in calling into being the Czechoslovak government in Washington. Elisina thought that Beneš had thus lost his strongest ally in France, but she felt that the unfolding "circumstances are just the wheels of God; the carrying of the logic of facts to their inevitable goal."[97]

Tyler, for his part, described early 1935 as a roller coaster period. He judged the European political landscape to be somewhat calmer after the Marseilles assassination, and hoped that the beneficial ripple effects might be felt in the economic and financial fields as well. As for Hungary specifically, he wrote of "having an exciting time here, things very difficult in many ways, and rather too interesting for comfort," while things in general had been "changing here so fast that it's difficult to start weaving a pattern."[98] His wife had a different reading on the intricate situation: "Peter's [Tyler's] presence here, the knowledge, shared by everyone who can read the papers, that he knows every movement of the economic life of the country, and that his quarterly reports are the faithful mirror of the situation, helps to prevent a sudden panic."[99] The latest of these reports, published in July, cautiously shared some good news: an agreement had been reached between the Hungarian side and the British and American banks concerning short-term credits for a period of one year; the Rome Protocols had been renewed, which was important for the wheat sales; the Treasury found itself in a stronger position; and after a hiatus of five years, a commercial treaty was again signed and in effect with Czechoslovakia on the basis of the most favored nation principle.[100]

Tyler had a different direction of travel in the summer, and he sought new horizons. This time he went east, since he was asked to make a report on Estonia. This gave him a chance to see some of the Soviet Union and Stockholm, to which he was looking forward. Kiev was at the top of his list of places to visit due to the city's eleventh-century Byzantine mosaics. He gave his trusted friend Mildred Barnes Bliss a thorough report of his experiences

---

97 Ibid.
98 Royall Tyler to Robert Woods Bliss, March 9, 1935, Budapest, "Bliss–Tyler Correspondence," https://www.doaks.org/resources/bliss-tyler-correspondence/letters/09mar1935; Royall Tyler to Mildred Barnes Bliss, March 15, 1935, Budapest, "Bliss–Tyler Correspondence," https://www.doaks.org/resources/bliss-tyler-correspondence/letters/15mar1935, both accessed March 29, 2019.
99 Diary entry, Budapest, February 23, 1935, Elisina Diary, Thompson Todd Collection. Peter was the nickname for Tyler used by his closest friends. Its origin is not known.
100 Tyler's Fifteenth Quarterly Report, July 13, 1935, OV33/16, BoE.

The League of Nations Years – Part IV

in Russia, which included, in addition to Kiev, Moscow and Leningrad. He had two main impressions. The first was that after the great famine of 1932 and 1933, things in general were improving, though the standard of living was frighteningly low. "At the very best," he noted, "it will be generations before they can attain anything which the masses in most European countries, let alone the USA, would at present call a tolerable standard of living, either as to housing, clothing or food."[101] The other point was that the communist regime had spawned a caste of officials and higher ranks of the military, who enjoyed much better circumstances compared to the masses, and the top leaders lived in luxury comparable only to European monarchs. The farther north Tyler moved, the worse off people seemed to be, at least as far as the clothing he could observe, but he admitted that the people were clean. The city landscape, however, especially in Leningrad and Moscow, was a saddening affair. While the Moscow subway was put on for show, housing conditions were atrocious, and most houses were in bad need of repair, as were the railways, but such steps were not taken, because there simply were no resources for it. Altogether, "there is a sort of smell of poverty, like the old familiar refugee smell with a peculiar Russian quality to it that I can't describe, all over the place; one never escapes it."[102]

As for the Russian people, Tyler's observations were on the mark. He found them "supremely indifferent, passive," and their miserable situation compared to that of the leaders was accepted as a fact of life: "They are far too fatalistic, too indolent and helpless and inept to face such a situation with any will to change it."[103] In Tyler's view, the basic characteristics of the Russian people had not changed with the change of regime that ruled over them. In his view, "what signifies about the Russians is, not that they had Czars and now are led by Communists, but that they were, are and will be Russians."[104] The Russian people were also afraid to make contact with foreigners, mainly because of the backlash they could suffer for it. Not surprisingly, "after that nightmare of the USSR," the experience in Tallinn, Estonia's capital, was in

---

101 Royall Tyler to Mildred Barnes Bliss, August 1, 1935, Tallinn, Estonia, "Bliss–Tyler Correspondence," https://www.doaks.org/resources/bliss-tyler-correspondence/letters/01aug1935, accessed March 30, 2019.
102 Ibid.
103 Ibid.
104 Ibid. A decade later, George Kennan had very similar observations about the Soviet Union. George F. Kennan, "The Sources of Soviet Conduct," *Foreign Affairs* 25, no. 4 (July 1947): 566–78, 580–82.

stark contrast, with "lots of agreeable buildings of all periods, and its cleanly, cheerful, honest, self-respecting people, few of them rich and hardly any of them destitute."[105]

The summer trip did Tyler good and he found a new dose of energy. Upon his return to Antigny, he and Hayford Peirce managed to finish their third volume on Byzantine art. At the end of August, he returned to Budapest in order to get ready for another round of talks about financial problems, "which promises to be pretty dramatic this time. I haven't the faintest idea what's going to happen."[106] Actually, and only painfully slowly, Hungary had started to show some signs of real recovery, and the low point of 1932–33 was evidently in the past. Despite the fact that the harvest of 1935 was a poor one and consumption showed no sign of recovering, the worst was clearly over.[107] This naturally did not mean that Hungary was out of the woods just yet, but at least there was a light at the end of the tunnel. With the Germans taking a substantial portion of Hungarian wheat, the country's all-important exports increased, through which a significant transformation took place: Germany became Hungary's number one trading partner.[108] Tyler spoke of "much anxiety and suspense" at Geneva toward the end of 1935, thanks to the Second Italo-Abyssinian War, which erupted in early October. That war proved once again that the League of Nations was helpless, and it proved absolutely ineffective in reigning in aggressors within its own ranks.[109] But to prove the point that as far as Hungary was concerned, the worst was over, he noted that his "own little affairs are going quite smoothly."[110]

Under these somewhat better financial circumstances, in February 1936 Tyler presented his memorandum on Hungary's budget situation to the prime minister. Although the cash position showed improvement, the country's financial position was still precarious. The danger lay not only in prices but also in the state's expenditures and receipts. The Hungarian price index

---

[105] Royall Tyler to Mildred Barnes Bliss, August 1, 1935.
[106] Royall Tyler to Robert Woods Bliss, August 20, 1935, Antigny-le-Château, "Bliss–Tyler Correspondence," https://www.doaks.org/resources/bliss-tyler-correspondence/letters/20aug1935, accessed March 30, 2019.
[107] Tyler's Sixteenth Quarterly Report, October 30, 1935, OV33/17, BoE.
[108] Tyler's Fifteenth Quarterly Report, July 13, 1935, ibid.
[109] Royall Tyler to Mildred Barnes Bliss, December 11, 1935, Geneva, "Bliss–Tyler Correspondence," https://www.doaks.org/resources/bliss-tyler-correspondence/letters/11dec1935, accessed March 30, 2019.
[110] Ibid.

in the previous two years had increased by a whopping 33 percent, compared to 10 percent in Great Britain and 13 percent in the United States, for example. The movement toward depreciation of the Hungarian currency, which Tyler had suggested for years now, was not a likely problem if it were held in check by the government. The public expenditure by state and local actors was still too high, however, and salaries and pensions made up a disproportionally large part of it, especially compared to other countries. And the taxpayers' capacity simply did not allow for this or for any increased expenditures—people were already overtaxed. So, Tyler's advice was to attain a limited increase in prices together with an increase in receipts in addition to lower expenditures. As he noted in his advisory capacity, "The remedy lies in the hands of the Government."[111]

The recovery that was tangible around the world had its positive effects on Hungary as well, and, despite the problems Tyler noted, the general picture showed a certain improvement.[112] As the report submitted to the Council on Hungarian Finances stated: "Industrial production has increased, but consumption shows little change. Imports of finished goods have decreased, while those of raw materials have risen. Foreign trade shows an increase in value, largely resulting from higher prices."[113] All in all, there was reason for cautious optimism.

And indeed, compared to the 1931–33 period, Hungary started to perform better. As Tyler pointed out to Gömbös, the situation was still far from satisfactory, but national income had started to grow, and the deficit shrank to the lowest point since the crisis began in 1931. Foreign trade had not changed markedly in volume, however, Hungary now conducted the largest volume of trade with Germany—more than with Italy and Austria combined.[114] Toward the second half of 1936, the various indices began to show favorable directions. The harvest was a good one, both production and consumption grew, State undertakings performed better, and the National Bank's foreign exchange position became stronger as well—all good indica-

---

111 Note on the Budget Position, February 17, 1936, Folder 3, Box 261, Royall Tyler Papers, 1920–1944, P. 32, LNA.
112 League of Nations, Financial Committee, Sixty-first Session. Verbatim Report of the Seventh Meeting, Geneva, May 4, 1936, Folder 6, Royall Tyler Papers, 1920–1944, P. 32, Box 261, LNA.
113 Report submitted to the Council on May 13, 1936, LNJ, 17th Year, no. 6 (June 1936), Ninety-second Session of the Council, (Part I), 672.
114 Tyler's Nineteenth Quarterly Report, July 29, 1936, OV33/18, BoE.

Chapter 6

tors that Hungary was climbing out of the Depression years and finding its way to more prosperous times.[115]

The various lengthy reports Tyler had to draw up, the change in personnel in Budapest, the meetings with bank groups negotiating various aspects of the Hungarian financial landscape and capability, or the Anglo-American Standstill Committee all made Tyler, according to his wife, "very tired indeed, and jaded."[116] On top of this, his son's health took an unexpected bad turn when doctors discovered a "very slight infection in the right lung," which forced him out of work for quite a while.[117] The only really good news was that Volume III of their Byzantine art series was nearing publication, although in the end, it did not come out.[118]

Tyler also played the role of intellectual ambassador on account on his art historian qualifications and League status. In the summer of 1936, Budapest played host to a gathering of the Arts and Letters Subcommittee of the League of Nations' Committee on Intellectual Cooperation.[119] While the organization was founded in 1922 and met at irregular intervals to discuss problems regarding Europe's spiritual questions, this subcommittee had been in existence only since 1932 and had held meetings every year since then. Its first gathering focused on Johann Wolfgang von Goethe, the next one, held in Madrid, on the future of culture, the Paris meeting in 1934 looked at the future of Europe's spirit, while the next year at Venice art stood in the spotlight. At Budapest in early June, the scientists, experts, artists, and authors invited from all across Europe and beyond put modern man and humanity as the focus of discussion. Since Tyler was staying in Budapest as a League official, and was known to be an expert on Byzantine art, he was included

---

115 Tyler's Twentieth Quarterly Report, October 20, 1936, OV33/19, BoE.
116 Elisina Tyler to Mildred Barnes Bliss, May 11, 1936, Sainte-Claire le Château, Hyères (Var), "Bliss–Tyler Correspondence," https://www.doaks.org/resources/bliss-tyler-correspondence/letters/11may1936, accessed March 30, 2019.
117 Royall Tyler to Mildred Barnes Bliss, April 6, 1936, Budapest, "Bliss–Tyler Correspondence," https://www.doaks.org/resources/bliss-tyler-correspondence/letters/06apr1936, accessed March 30, 2019.
118 Royall Tyler to Mildred Barnes Bliss, June 28, 1936, Antigny-le-Château, "Bliss–Tyler Correspondence," https://www.doaks.org/resources/bliss-tyler-correspondence/letters/28jun1936, accessed March 30, 2019.
119 On the topic of intellectual cooperation during the interwar years, see, Frederick Northedge, *International Intellectual Co-operation Within the League of Nations: Its Conceptual Basis and Lessons for the Present* (London: University of London, 1953); Daniel Laqua, "Transnational Intellectual Cooperation, the League of Nations, and the Problem of Order," *Journal of Global History* 6, no. 2, (July 2011): 223–47.

in the prestigious meeting, and via his presence, the United States was also represented—always a key goal for the League. Tyler presented a talk on the Byzantine era, which he represented as a bridge between the ancient and modern civilizations.[120] A few weeks later it was the Inter-Parliamentary Union's turn to come to the Hungarian capital for the second time, now for its thirty-second conference. Once more, Tyler was a convenient choice to represent the League officially at the meeting.

The summer and fall of 1936 brought another momentous change to Hungary. Gyula Gömbös had fallen ill in May 1936, and from then on he was basically incapable of fulfilling his duties until his death in early October. During the interim period, Minister of Agriculture Kálmán Darányi led the cabinet, and after Gömbös's death he became the prime minister on October 10. The cabinet remained almost intact, and though Darányi led a more conservative political agenda—for example, he rejected dictatorial powers—as far as financial and economic questions were concerned, he followed the path laid out.[121] These changes at the helm did not alter Tyler's relationship with Hungary, partly because the financial position started to get better. After a few months, Henry Bruce opined that Darányi was "evidently not strong and probably not imaginative."[122]

It did not happen by the touch of a magic wand, but gradually the accumulated efforts by the Hungarian government and the improving international economic, financial, and trade situation made their presence felt on the Hungarian situation: the data describing Hungary's economic and financial circumstances began to show positive progress. The harvest was a good one, receipts were higher than expenditures, the cash position was thus improved, although foreign trade volume was still roughly half of what it was back in 1929. Foreign exchange and the position of the National Bank also showed improvement. Production was growing, both heavy and light industry were doing well, consumption started to grow, though the cost of living sent signals urging caution. The State Undertakings also started to perform better and put less of a drag on the budget. Under such circumstances it was not the budget that caused headaches but the debt question: the transfer sus-

---

120 *Budapesti Hirlap*, June 10, 1936.
121 For more detail on Darányi's life and politics, see, Róbert Kerepeszki, *A „tépelődő gentleman": Darányi Kálmán (1886–1939)* [The "Pondering Gentleman": Kálmán Darányi] (Pécs: Kronosz Kiadó, 2014).
122 Henry James Bruce to Cameron F. Cobbold, February 4, 1937, OV33/19, BoE.

pension had been renewed for yet another year and had now been in force since December 1931.[123]

In the meantime, Tyler was discreetly asked whether he would be willing to undertake the job of League adviser to Austria, parallel to his task in Hungary. The former adviser the League had sent to Vienna, Rost van Tonningen, was showing signs of being converted to Nazism, and, without consulting the League, he had resigned his post in order to be active in Nazi politics in his home country, the Netherlands. Although Tyler's ambition would have urged him to take on the job, he realistically saw the various obstacles in the way. Most importantly, both governments would have needed to declare that they wanted Tyler's involvement, and especially the Hungarians ought to have had no objection to him looking after both posts. Plus, Tyler was well aware that in Austria the League advisers, starting with the Dutch Alfred Zimmerman in 1922, were not really welcome or well liked. But Tyler was pleased that the League, and the main power behind the idea, Great Britain, considered him unlikely to fall under the harmful influence of Franz von Papen, the German ambassador accredited to Vienna.[124] In the end, Tyler did not become a League adviser at Vienna and stayed in Hungary, while the Financial Committee observed the Austrian financial situation based upon the reports submitted by the National Bank of Austria and the Austrian Finance Ministry. Hungary, on the other hand, did not want to let go of Tyler, which thoroughly satisfied the American: "Arpad is a very decent fellow, when once he knows and trusts you."[125] And as an echo to this sentiment, Tyler's wife wrote, "We have good friends here, and a very pleasant and interesting circle, and Vienna just round the corner for great

---

123 League of Nations, Financial Committee, Sixty-second Session, Verbatim Report of the Second Meeting, Geneva, September 14, 1936, Folder 6, Royall Tyler Papers, 1920–1944, P. 32, Box 261; Tyler's Twenty-first Quarterly Report, January 16, 1937, OV33/19, BoE; Work of the Financial Committee during Its Sixty-second Session (September 14–19, 1936), Report submitted to the Council on September 25, 1936, LNJ, 17th Year, no. 11 (November 1936), Ninety-third Session of the Council, Ninety-fourth Session of the Council, 1341–42.
124 Royall Tyler to Mildred Barnes Bliss, September 8, 1936, Budapest, "Bliss–Tyler Correspondence," https://www.doaks.org/resources/bliss-tyler-correspondence/letters/08sep1936, accessed March 31, 2019.
125 Royall Tyler to Mildred Barnes Bliss, October 27, 1936, Geneva, "Bliss–Tyler Correspondence," https://www.doaks.org/resources/bliss-tyler-correspondence/letters/27oct1936, accessed March 31, 2019. "Árpád" was a term Tyler used in his private correspondence for Hungary and Hungarians. Árpád was a chieftain of Hungarian tribes when they took possession of some of the Carpathian Basin in the late ninth century.

music."¹²⁶ But, of course, nothing gave Tyler as much pleasure as the birth of his grandson in London in December. The child was named after him: Royall Tyler.¹²⁷

By the end of 1937, it started to become clear that the Hungarian economic and financial position, if not free of worries, showed a picture of recovery. Many of the indicators pointed in that direction, and Tyler informed the Financial Committee that the "position in Hungary shows some encouraging features."¹²⁸ Both the National Bank and the Hungarian Treasury had become stronger, the crop was good in 1936—this always being the most defining aspect of Hungarian economy—and employment and consumption had also increased. But that did not mean that all was well: the debt situation remained problematic, while the cost of living had risen. Overall production was close to its peak in 1928/29, but foreign trade had not really grown and was still only about 30 percent of the 1928/29 fiscal year.¹²⁹ Tyler's reports, or summaries of them, were regularly published in the Hungarian papers. The dry data rarely received much attention; it was usually noted with a collective nod. The latest report's numbers were, however, "well received, and even the Opposition papers agree that there was a gradual improvement in State finances and economic conditions during the last quarter of 1936. Some newspapers point out that since 1931 Hungary's foreign debt decreased from about 4.3 billion pengő to about 2.4 billion pengő as a result of currency depreciation and debt payments."¹³⁰

And in the course of the spring and early summer of 1937, there was at last a breakthrough on the external debt question as well. Agreement was reached with the creditors that Hungary would pay debt service in hard currency for three years, sometimes even interest. The League Loan was an exception in which case the Hungarian government "offered the bondholders a perma-

---

126 Elisina Tyler to Mildred Barnes Bliss and Robert Woods Bliss, December 11, 1936 [3], Budapest, "Bliss–Tyler Correspondence," https://www.doaks.org/resources/bliss-tyler-correspondence/letters/11dec1936-3, accessed March 31, 2019.
127 Ibid., and Royall Tyler to Mildred Barnes Bliss, December 21, 1936, Paris, "Bliss–Tyler Correspondence," https://www.doaks.org/resources/bliss-tyler-correspondence/letters/21dec1936, accessed March 31, 2019.
128 League of Nations, Financial Committee, Minutes of the meeting, December 7, 1936, Folder 6, Royall Tyler Papers, 1920–1944, P. 32, Box 261, LNA.
129 Ibid. See also, Tyler's Twenty-second Quarterly Report, April 19, 1937, OV33/19, BoE.
130 John F. Montgomery to Cordell Hull, February 9, 1937, 864.00 P.R./114, Roll 3, M1206, NARA.

nent settlement, interest to be paid in exchange at a higher rate than latterly, as from the service year beginning August 2nd, 1937, and, as from August 2nd, 1940, amortisation to proceed by repurchase on the market."[131] The League Loans Committee thought the offer was "fair and equitable" and should be accepted.[132] Payment agreements had started to take the place of the clearing agreements, another piece of good news. The only real data that did not work in Hungary's favor reflected the country's composition of active workers and retired people. As Tyler noted before the Financial Committee, "the total of pensioners is actually considerably higher than the total of actual officials. That is a very unsatisfactory position."[133]

Since the second half of 1937 engendered further good results, the time had really come for the League Advisor to leave Hungary. Accordingly, in his final report, Tyler drew up a balance sheet of the past six years and the achievements reached toward the end of that period. In it he profusely thanked the Hungarian governments for its cooperation and the sometimes brave and painful decisions that were necessary to reach the achieved results. The financial position had become satisfactory, the Treasury and the National Bank were strong, the budget was balanced for the third year in a row, inflation was avoided, the majority of the foreign bondholders had accepted the Hungarian government's offer for debt settlement, foreign indebtedness had shrunk from almost 5 billion to 1.274 billion gold pengő, after a long time foreign trade had produced high figures, and the largest export surplus since the World War had been registered. Naturally, a warning accompanied the good results: Hungary must be very cautious not to shrink the hard-won gains by irresponsible expenditure in the future.[134]

So, given the majority of good results, Tyler thought that, even if total financial stability had not been fully reached, the budget was balanced, and therefore his posting should be terminated at the end of the year. In his view, the Hungarians had "behaved very loyally to the Fin[ancial] C[ommi]tee, through a difficult series of years," and not only did they deserve termination of the control but they would also very much resent it if termination did

---

131 Tyler's Twenty-third Quarterly Report, July 15, 1937, OV33/20, BoE.
132 Ibid.
133 League of Nations, Financial Committee, Sixty-fourth Session, Verbatim Report of the Fifth Meeting, Geneva, April 28, 1937, Folder 6, Royall Tyler Papers, 1920–1944, P. 32, Box 261, LNA.
134 Tyler's Twenty-fifth and Final Report, February 26, 1938, OV33/20, BoE.

not take place.¹³⁵ The Hungarians would have raised the question of termination sooner rather than later, and Tyler was of the opinion that it was only fair for it to be initiated by the League. His opinion was shared by Alexander Loveday, director of the Financial Section of the League, and Vilém Pospíšil, current chairman of the Financial Committee, though the new British member, Frederick Phillips, was against it.¹³⁶ More importantly, so was Niemeyer, the former British member on the Financial Committee, who opposed lifting the control with all his influence, which was considerable.

Niemeyer had already warned Phillips in July that a move to terminate was afoot, and in quite clear terms he tried to persuade his compatriot to do something about it, since in Niemeyer's view Hungary's financial stability was far from assured.¹³⁷ He also managed to convince the British prime minister, Neville Chamberlain, to instruct Phillips to vote against the recommendation, and on the first vote the proposal indeed did not sail through the Financial Committee.¹³⁸ Only "after a long fight" and "two separate meetings of the F. C. to do it, and much labour in between" was the decision reached to terminate Tyler's functions in Hungary.¹³⁹ Bruce's position also played a role in Niemeyer's obstinacy; he wished to see Bruce's job terminated only when the credits had been repaid to the B.I.S. Accordingly, Bruce became the representative of the National Bank for three years. As Tyler summed up the uncomfortable episode concerning Niemeyer: "I'm sorry it couldn't be done without a conflict with Niemeyer, who has been of great usefulness where Hungary is concerned, always ready to help. But his political sense isn't always up to his technical ability, and this time I felt so sure of my ground that I couldn't yield to him. I felt absolutely certain that, in the circumstances, Jeremiah Smith would have wanted me to act as I did. I wonder whether N[iemeyer] will ever forgive me."¹⁴⁰

---

135 Royall Tyler to Mildred Barnes Bliss, September 4, 1937, Budapest, "Bliss–Tyler Correspondence," https://www.doaks.org/resources/bliss-tyler-correspondence/letters/04sep1937, accessed April 2, 2019; Memorandum by F. A. G., Geneva, September 17, 1937, OV33/20, BoE.
136 Frederick Phillips to Richard Hopkins, December 1, 1937, R 7982/534/21, FO 371/21151, TNA.
137 Otto Niemeyer to Frederick Phillips, July 26, 1937, OV115/7, BoE.
138 Note of Frank Ashton-Gwatkin of a conversation with H. J. Bruce, December 9, 1937, R 8288/534/21, FO 371/21151, TNA.
139 Royall Tyler to Mildred Barnes Bliss, December 19, 1937, Paris, "Bliss–Tyler Correspondence," https://www.doaks.org/resources/bliss-tyler-correspondence/letters/19dec1937, accessed April 3, 2019.
140 Ibid.

Chapter 6

In the end, the Financial Committee submitted its report to the League Council. In it the Committee emphasized a "steady improvement achieved," and decided, in light of the positive data and "in agreement with the Hungarian Government, to terminate as from March 31st next the office of Mr. Tyler at Budapest, and pays tribute to the exceptional merits of Mr. Tyler's services in the office held by him since October 1931."[141]

Echoing the termination of Jeremiah Smith's offices in Hungary back in 1926, a decade later both sides again lavishly praised each other. Tihamér Fabinyi, the current Hungarian Finance Minister, informed the Financial Committee of the Hungarian government's gratitude, "particularly to Mr. Royall Tyler and Mr. Henry James Bruce, for their self-sacrificing and invaluable collaboration which they have devoted, during the past six years, to the interests of Hungary, and which has largely contributed to the achievement of the favourable result of the past efforts and sacrifices made by Hungary for the sake of her financial and economic reconstruction."[142] At the Council meeting at the end of January, the end of the League's work in the stabilization effort concerning finances in Hungary was officially announced. Tyler's office would be terminated on March 31, 1938. In the future, reports based upon occasional visits from the Committee once or twice a year would suffice. The Hungarian representative to the League of Nations, László Velics, thanked, on behalf of his government, Tyler, Bruce, and the League for their work. The League, too, praised Tyler's work. It emphasized his "remarkable capability and vigilant and careful judgment in performing his duties... which he had rendered with untiring devotion, to be of exceptional value."[143] Tyler, for his part, thanked "the persevering efforts of the Hungarian Government over a long period of years," and said he was touched by the message that

---

141 Report submitted to the Council on January 28, 1938, Work of the Financial Committee during Its Sixty-fifth Session (November 29–December 4, 1937), LNJ, 19th Year, no. 2 (February 1938), One-hundredth Session of the Council, 162; Supplement to the Report of the Financial Committee on the work of its sixty-fifth session, Hungary, January 26, 1938, File 32491, Financial Situation of Hungary, Box 4565, Section 10C, Finance, League of Nations Archives, 1933–46, LNA.

142 Hungarian Finance Minister to the Chairman of the Financial Committee, around December 18, 1937, Folder 6, Royall Tyler Papers, 1920–1944, P. 32, Box 261, LNA. Also, Fabinyi's letter to the Chairman of the Financial Committee, January 7, 1938, LNJ, 19th Year, no. 2 (February 1938), One-hundredth Session of the Council, 129–30.

143 Second Meeting, January 27, 1938, LNJ, 19th Year, no. 2 (February 1938), One-hundredth Session of the Council, 78.

"Hungary regarded him as a friend."[144] Loveday also found it imperative to thank Hambros Bank for letting Tyler leave his job there in the first place so he could undertake the League mandate in Hungary.[145]

In Hungary the laudatory speeches began with Imrédy's words at the Annual General Meeting of the Hungarian National Bank praising the services of both Tyler and Bruce.[146] The British minister in Budapest also had a high opinion of the pair, especially of Tyler. He considered Tyler "one of the best brains that I know and [he] is a man of sober judgment."[147] He also informed the British Foreign Minister about "the excellent work which Mr. Tyler has performed in the interests of the League of Nations and of this country during his tenure of office."[148] He added that despite the difficulty of the task, Tyler had "accomplished it with remarkable efficiency and tact. The League has been fortunate to enjoy in Hungary the services of a representative of such high ability and of so wide a culture."[149] When Tyler received a letter of congratulations from the Hungarian National Industrial Art Association, he replied in very polite terms, saying, "I will always follow the destiny of Hungary with the greatest interest and honest sympathy."[150] He did not know how prophetic this statement would prove to be.

Now that the termination of foreign control had been announced, the Hungarian newspapers, which in the past had often showed only lukewarm interest in Tyler's quarterly reports, now devoted much more space to the good news that the League advisor was going to leave, and "held loud praise for Royall Tyler."[151] As the *Ujság* asserted, this was for Hungary "a memorable and happy event," and it hailed Tyler as a "distinguished expert" who "was *full of understanding for Hungary's position*, that he looked with sympathy on the measures taken to put our affairs in order, and that his conclusions, based on a thorough knowledge of the situation, contained many a valuable piece

---

144 Ibid., 79.
145 Alexander Loveday to Olaf Hambro, January 28, 1938, File 32491, Financial Situation of Hungary, Box 4565, Section 10C, Finance, League of Nations Archives, 1933–46, LNA.
146 Memorandum, February 11, 1938, in Geoffrey Knox to Anthony Eden, February 11, 1938, R 1451/221/21, FO 371/22378, TNA.
147 Geoffrey Knox to Orme Sargent, January 12, 1938, R 656/23/22, FO 371/22402, TNA.
148 Geoffrey Knox to Anthony Eden, February 11, 1938, R 1451/221/21, FO 371/22378, TNA.
149 Ibid.
150 *Magyar Iparművészet*, 1938, 44.
151 John F. Montgomery to Cordell Hull, February 10, 1938, 864.00 P.R./135, M1206, NARA.

of advice for those who managed our finances."[152] The paper also reflected the general pride and relief that Hungary had regained total independence regarding its financial destiny.[153] Béla Schober, former general manager of the National Bank of Hungary, praised Tyler's reports, "which were always thorough, wise, and comprehensive," and emphasized that the American had "rendered our country the greatest services in the most unobtrusive way."[154] He added that Tyler's part in the past six years had been "rather that of a wise and understanding observer and adviser than of a controlling agent," and said it was "to Mr. Tyler in the first place that we owe the fact that the conclusion of his duties here is regarded as a satisfactory and generally visible sign of the consolidation of Hungary's finances, and not as a great political occurrence."[155] Former finance minister János Teleszky also highlighted the personal aspect of Tyler's and Bruce's work in Hungary.[156] Another paper emphasized Tyler's personal relationship to Hungary: "In the course of long years we have got to like this tart Anglo-Saxon gentleman, who did not always say nice things to us, and who did not always go about it in a very agreeable way when he told us home truths, but who proved to be a true friend of ours, learned our language, and felt at home among us."[157] The economic periodical *Honi Ipar* stressed Hungary's role during the process of successfully fighting the Depression, but admitted that Tyler had "carried out the second task entrusted to him here in a way befitting a high-minded gentleman. We may give him the loftiest title which can ever be bestowed upon a foreign envoy who has worked here for us: 'Mr. Tyler, the friend of Hungary'."[158]

Bruce was similarly praised in all quarters, but unlike Tyler, he remained in Hungary. His post would be with the National Bank of Hungary in the capacity of maintaining contacts with foreign markets and organizations. Concerning the accolades they were receiving, Bruce's wry humor came to the fore once more: "It is a great disappointment to me that there does not appear to be any intention of putting up a statue to Tyler and me. We long

---

152 *Ujság*, January 28, 1938, emphasis in the original.
153 Ibid.
154 *Pester Lloyd*, January 28, 1938, in File 32491, Financial Situation of Hungary, Box 4565, Section 10C, Finance, League of Nations Archives, 1933–46, LNA.
155 *Pester Lloyd*, January 30, 1938, ibid.
156 *Pester Lloyd*, February 4, 1938, ibid.
157 *A Reggel*, January 31, 1938.
158 *Honi Ipar*, February 12, 1938.

The League of Nations Years – Part IV

ago chose a shady nook on the Margaret Island where we thought a little monument of us as the Babes in the Wood should be erected, but it seems it is not to be. Not even the bunch of primroses presented to the "Honest Broker" can console me for the absence of the statue."[159]

Tyler's modest fame caught some of his compatriots' eyes, too. In a book on Americans working across Europe, Africa, and Asia, one chapter was devoted to Tyler and his work in Hungary. This depiction highlighted the fact that since Tyler had the League of Nations behind him, his recommendations were seen in Budapest as coming from Geneva, and despite Hungarian stalling, were executed more or less over time. The author quoted from a conversation he had held in Budapest with an unidentified Hungarian who explained what Tyler and his role meant as follows: "One of the fine things Tyler did was to handle us so we retained our pride in our country. When a man, once rich, becomes poor and deep in debt he is likely to lose his self-respect. So it is with a nation. Tyler was like an athletic coach, encouraging us when we were far behind in the game. 'You are a great race,' he would say. 'You can't be licked.' And we came through, not ashamed because we practically were in rags, but proud that we had so cheerfully sacrificed our way to recovery."[160]

So, after more than six years, Royall Tyler was about to depart Hungary for the second time. Since May 1924, he had spent a cumulative total of eleven years in that country. Although he said he was "extremely sorry to leave Bpest.," it also must have been a relief in the sense that he could now turn his attention to new openings and new challenges.[161] Accordingly, the last weeks were bittersweet. He was "being killed with kindness these days— dinners every night, lunches every day, & between times the very painful task of clearing up the accumulated papers, books, etc. of 6 years, & deciding what to keep & where to send it."[162] Although he could not know whether he would ever return, it was a fair prediction that his connections to Hungary would not cease, and that the intellectual capital he had invested in learning about and getting to know Hungary and Hungarians might later be used to some extent and in whatever capacity.

---

159 Henry James Bruce to Cameron F. Cobbold, January 18, 1938, OV33/20, BoE.
160 Jerome Beatty, *Americans All Over* (New York: The John Day Company, 1938), 121–22.
161 Royall Tyler to Mildred Barnes Bliss, December 19, 1937.
162 Royall Tyler to Robert Woods Bliss, March 15, 1938, Paris, "Bliss–Tyler Correspondence," https://www.doaks.org/resources/bliss-tyler-correspondence/letters/15mar1938, accessed April 12, 2019.

CHAPTER 7

The League of Nations Years Part V: The Last Year of Peace

Tyler's departure from Hungary basically coincided with two momentous events. One concerned the domestic economy of Hungary, while the other concerned the whole political landscape of Europe. The Győr Program gave economic momentum to Hungary in the short run; the Anschluss foreshadowed that the days of Europe's political status quo were numbered.

On March 5, 1938, Prime Minister Darányi introduced the Győr Program, the town of Győr being an industrial center in northwest Hungary. The complex economic plan had a two-pronged approach: it wanted to revive the overall economy by various measures, mainly building infrastructure, but the larger part of the planned one-billion-pengő expenditure was to beef up the military. One part of that enormous amount was to be collected from a wealth tax, the other from a domestic loan. The latter was unrealistic, so the National Bank instead issued uncovered banknotes, which in turn led to inflation. Still, the program was completed in two years, contrary to the originally planned five.[1] It is not difficult to see a coincidence between the League's departure, the better economic and financial position of Hungary, and the launch of a military and economic plan when the general European peace was waning rapidly. However, this should by no means be simplified to such a view. At this point, despite the gathering clouds nobody was aware that the next world war would break out in one and a half years. To be sure, there were pessimists already, as always, but

---

1 On the Győr Progam, see, Gunst, *Magyarország gazdaságtörténete*, 104–5; Kerepeszki, *A „tépelődő gentleman"*, 102–8.

hope was still strong that agreements could be hammered out. Also, it had been a strategic goal for Hungary to reach at least a state of military equality with the various neighboring Little Entente countries. This reflected a hope that one day revision would come, in which case a stronger military force must be present. Also, the Anschluss happened just one week after the announcement of the economic program. Suddenly the plan made even more sense because an uncomfortable new German neighbor had unexpectedly appeared, and that heralded danger in the eyes of many leading conservative and liberal Hungarian politicians.

The Anschluss, Germany's occupation of Austria and the union of the two countries, took place on March 12, 1938, and it shook the European continent.[2] This possibility had been a vital issue over the past twenty years, but most of the time it had been swept under the rug. The peace treaty with Austria forbade such a union with Germany, but the forces behind unification never ceased to agitate for it. With Germany again becoming a considerable power, the question was on the table again. A forceful unification of the two countries did not only mean that one of the peace treaties was openly broken, but this move can be seen as the first nail in the coffin of the Versailles peace structure—indeed other nails followed in short succession. Tyler, for whom it was "sickening to think of Austria," saw in the event a mistaken policy of France and Great Britain.[3] "I've been gloomily reflecting on the fatal linking up of blunder after blunder after blunder that constituted the Western powers' policy in central Europe & particularly on the Danube, ever since the armistice," Tyler wrote at that time.[4] Assessing the past almost two decades, Tyler concluded that the problem was that Austria had been left on its own, and the Czechs, largely because of Beneš were—"able, clever, industrious, and with as much vision as a mole"—,

---

2   Some of the best books on the subject are: Jürgen Gehl, *Austria, Germany, and the Anschluss, 1931–1938* (London: Oxford University Press, 1963); Alfred D. Low, *The Anschluss Movement (1918–1938) and the Great Powers* (Boulder, CO.: East European Monographs; distributed by Columbia University Press, New York, 1985); William L. Shirer, *Rise and Fall of The Third Reich: A History of Nazi Germany* (New York: Simon & Schuster, 1998), 287–317; Rolf Steininger, "12 November 1918–12 March 1938: The Road to the Anschluss," in Rolf Steininger, Günter Bischof, and Michael Gehler, eds. *Austria in the Twentieth Century* (New Brunswick, NJ and London, UK: Transaction Publishers, 2009), 85–113.
3   Royall Tyler to Robert Woods Bliss, April 5, 1938, New York, "Bliss–Tyler Correspondence," https://www.doaks.org/resources/bliss-tyler-correspondence/letters/05apr1938, accessed April 20, 2019.
4   Ibid.

and the French, did not allow for Austria and Hungary to restore themselves to the full extent.[5] And while for most of Europe the Anschluss created a less stable continent, for Austria's neighboring countries, especially for Czechoslovakia and Hungary, it was often seen as a possible existential danger. The loss of Austria's independence was naturally a neuralgic question for Hungary. Although Hungary had slowly moved closer to Germany, especially during the Gömbös years, the basic political tone was to keep as much distance as possible from that ever-expanding country. From these strategic considerations Italy and Austria had meant a possible counterbalance, but the latter had now disappeared. Germany's sudden status as a neighbor on Hungary's west sent shock waves through Hungary's conservative and liberal circles alike. Only the German-speaking Schwabians and far right political groups welcomed the Germans proximity. It was a valid question whether the League of Nations, which with Tyler's departure was now only loosely linked with Hungary, could maintain its influence and could offer a real alternative for Hungarian aspirations. Or would Hungary be sucked into the German vortex in the middle of Europe?

Tyler well understood both this Hungarian predicament and his own inability to do anything about it, even in the most modest way. "Well, with all my affection for them," he noted, "the present juncture is one at which I don't think I could help them, and my presence would be more of an embarrassment to them than anything else. I'm glad I got out when I did."[6] He believed the League was to some extent the culprit for not having taken greater responsibility for the small Central European states. Decisions were too often too slow in coming, although making an effort to the contrary would have been useful. Then perhaps the fate of Austria might have been different, "instead of just waiting to be plucked like a ripe pear, which attitude has been the normal one for the padres of Western policy all these years."[7]

The future in the spring of 1938, then, promised to be anything but outright boredom for Tyler. Already in the early fall of 1937, when it seemed assured that Hungary would regain its financial independence and Tyler would be leaving, the League of Nations wanted to keep Tyler on its roster

---

5 Ibid.
6 Ibid.
7 Ibid.

and have him work for it. Tyler also found it important to secure an income, and he was eager to have some status at the League.[8] From April 1, 1938, he had a six-month contract working as an expert for the Financial Section and Economic Intelligence Service of the Secretariat, which contract was renewed on expiration, while from October 1, 1939, it was prolonged for a full year.[9] The exact capacity in which he would carry out further work was not clearly spelled out, but the plan was that he would travel once or twice a year to the United States and act as an unofficial liaison officer between Geneva and Washington. Although earlier there had been League attempts at establishing connections in America, those were mainly with pro-League people, and the U.S. government was not involved. Avenol and Loveday wanted Tyler for the job for the exact reason that he had no connection to such pro-League people in the United States, and his main task was to keep certain people in the American government informed, first and foremost, on financial and economic issues and decidedly not on political ones. Taking the latter approach would clearly have led to a dead end street. All this had to do with "getting an understanding, perhaps even parallel action, on this question or that, but without any sort of intention of trying to draw the USA into the League Ambit."[10]

Not everybody at the League was enthusiastic about such an endeavor. Niemeyer, perhaps as usual, opposed the plan especially on account of Tyler traveling to the United States once or twice a year instead of staying there. As he wrote to his successor on the Financial Committee, "I think if Tyler is going to do a liaison job with America (which I should imagine fairly useless in any case) he ought to reside in America. If he's not going to do that he might just conceivably do some good if he resided half the year in Buda. He can do no good at all—to Hungary—by residing in Geneva."[11]

---

8   Director of Financial Section and Economic Intelligence Service (Loveday) to Secretary General (Avenol), January 15, 1938, Tyler, Royall; Section Files, Personnel Files, Box S.896, File 3550, Financial Section and Economic Intelligence Service, LNA.
9   Contract of Engagement, Alexander Loveday to Secretary General, July 8, 1938, Seán Lester to Royall Tyler, July 18, 1938, G. Sampson to Director of Personnel and Internal Administration, November 3, 1938, Alexander Loveday to Director of Personnel and Internal Administration, February 7 and September 21, 1939, Joseph Avenol to Royall Tyler, December 21, 1939, Tyler, Royall; Section Files, Personnel Files, Box S.896, LNA.
10 Royall Tyler to Mildred Barnes Bliss, September 4, 1937, "Bliss–Tyler Correspondence," https://www.doaks.org/resources/bliss-tyler-correspondence/letters/04sep1937, accessed April 2, 2019.
11 Otto Niemeyer to Frederick Phillips, August 6, 1937, OV115/7, BoE.

The League of Nations Years – Part V

The idea of becoming a link between the two continents was to Tyler's liking, most likely not only because traveling to the United States raised the possibility of meeting with certain friends, but he could also feel useful in such a capacity, and his previous jobs and experience indeed predestined him for such work. Actually, it is hard to think of anybody else so well cut out for the planned liaison post. What also played a part in accepting this position was Tyler's anxiety to secure enough financial means to lead a life at Antigny. Although he was "aware of the difficulties of my little job," the "US Liaison idea is irresistibly attractive to me," he said, even if it was financially less accommodating.[12] However, since he was basically assured of some work in the League in the future, at the moment, he was not worried on the financial front.[13] He was to maintain relations with Hungary in addition to the United States, and perhaps also with other countries coming into his circle of responsibility. As he characterized his new job to a trusted friend, "The need has been felt for personal contact between G[eneva] & the US, supplementing & explaining the papers that are supplied on the work in hand, and that is what I'm wanted to do."[14] Naturally, the idea was to be a discreet presence overseas in order not to draw any unwelcome political attention in America.

Tyler therefore basically became what his previous twenty years predestined him to be: an intelligence officer. This is not surprising in light of his previous activities. First, during and right after World War I he had officially worked in such a capacity, and his relationship with the Blisses, for whom he acted as a private art reconnaissance expert and adviser made him well suited for such a job. Moreover, throughout his Budapest years, his main task had been to establish connections and gather information, to analyze and forward it—an intelligence officer's role. It is worth emphasizing that in the first half of the twentieth century, in "intelligence work" the lines were very blurry and unestablished between intelligence and diplomacy, just as between information gathering and spying. Also, the amateur and professional dimensions were not always easy to separate. In this sense and at this

---

12 Royall Tyler to Robert Woods Bliss, February 15, 1938, Paris, "Bliss–Tyler Correspondence," https://www.doaks.org/resources/bliss-tyler-correspondence/letters/15feb1938, accessed April 12, 2019.

13 Royall Tyler to Robert Woods Bliss, December 16, 1937, Paris, "Bliss–Tyler Correspondence," https://www.doaks.org/resources/bliss-tyler-correspondence/letters/16dec1937, accessed April 2, 2019.

14 Royall Tyler to Robert Woods Bliss, February 15, 1938.

Chapter 7

time, Tyler can be called an intelligence officer, although later he found himself in a more formal role concerning said activity. In any case, according to his new role, after two months in Geneva and Antigny, Tyler spent a month in the United States in the early summer of 1938.

Even before setting sail for his birth country, he submitted a memorandum on the Hungarian situation to Secretary of State Cordell Hull. Since he had spent eleven of the past thirteen years in Hungary, he was the best expert on this question in Western Europe. Not only was he absolutely familiar with the economic and financial side of the picture, but he also knew basically everybody who held an important position. He had an acquaintance with a cross section of the middle and upper middle classes, as well as the Hungarian aristocracy, that he could rely on and gain information from. Also, he had a deep knowledge and understanding of Hungarian culture and psychology. Given such familiarity with the country, it is understandable that he should have been asked to put together a comprehensive picture of Hungary. His report was also timely, because even as the country was finding its way out from under economic and financial stresses, it was also in the middle of a quickly changing Central European power structure due to the Anschluss as well as to Hungary's growing economic, financial, and political attachment to an ever more aggressive Germany. Tyler titled his report "Prospects for Hungary." It is not clear who prompted him to put down on paper how he saw the present situation in Hungary, but since he submitted it to the State Department, it is likely that the request came from there. This also indicates that in the United States there was a growing interest in Hungary, which was mainly due to its geographical situation. Now, as a neighbor to Germany, the country's strategic importance had suddenly grown in Washington's eyes.

The central focus of the eight-page memorandum was the repercussions of the Anschluss for Hungary. Tyler's tenet was that Hungary found itself in a serious predicament. On the one hand, the Anschluss, which arrived sooner than the Hungarian leaders had expected, "gave Hungary a profound shock" and the overwhelming sentiment was "dismay." Still, the German takeover of Austria foreshadowed that Czechoslovakia might be next, and it was obvious that the avenue for Hungary to regain some lost territories in the north would suddenly be open, and, as Tyler put it, "No Hungarian Government could survive one hour if it neglected an opportunity of recovering Slovakia." In his analysis, the sad reality was that Hungary was in an impossible situation. Its leaders clearly saw the German threat, which for the time being meant inferiority to Germany, and they worked to ensure as much independence for the country as possible. On the other hand, Hungary needed strong international support in order to realize its revisionist aims. However, since they sought this kind of help in Western Europe in vain, and especially in Great Britain, they had nowhere to turn but to Germany, or perhaps Italy. In this lay the clear Hungarian dilemma that would later turn into a national tragedy.

The Hungarian government's idea was, according to Tyler, that in case of recovering territories in Slovakia, there would be a Polish–Hungarian–Yugoslav belt arrayed against possible future German encroachment. To further complicate this line of possible movement in the foreign policy arena, the government faced domestic criticism from various sides: discontent grew not only because of the lack of recovered Hungarian territories and population, but also on account of the Jewish question. The government failed to take concrete steps in that direction owing to its fear for finance and industry, which were still largely in Jewish hands. The army leaders had been complaining of insufficient funds for national defense, while the question of how to provide some land to the poor peasantry had been a long unanswered one in Hungarian society. Partly because of all the above, the Nazi ideology was undoubtedly "gaining ground," despite the previous governments' efforts to alleviate the various complaints from different segments of society. And to round out the circle, the possible, if short-term, success of Austria under Nazi rule would only create further trouble for a responsible government in Hungary. And this was where the economy stepped in the picture. Hungarian trade in recent years had become ever more reliant on Germany, to such an extent that almost half of its foreign trade was conducted with Germany—more than six times the volume with Great Britain. In Tyler's view, the solution, or at least mitigation of the difficulty lay in Italy: "[W]ith some scheme for using credit to revive Italy's foreign trade, it could be arranged that Hungary's export surplus to Italy should be paid for in free exchange, a relatively small outlay might enable Hungary to avoid being drawn into the German economic system."[15]

---

15 For the quotations of the last two paragraphs, see, Royall Tyler, "Prospects for Hungary," May 10, 1938, R 4851/99/21, FO 371/22374, TNA.

Tyler thus believed, or at least hoped, that with outside financial help, mostly stemming from Great Britain, Hungary could be built up as a resistance point against Germany. In his view, there was a lot the British "could do financially to establish Hungary as a bulwark."[16] Incidentally, Bruce shared this line of thinking, and was wondering "whether there was not some more constructive attitude to adopt towards Hungary than merely to grouse with folded hands at German economic infiltration, leaving her the while to be perhaps gradually drawn, sorely against her will and looking longingly over her shoulder at England, towards the famous Axis."[17] A few weeks later he placed the emphasis on diplomatic help and symbolic action:

> Without some kind of visible assistance (e.g. trade encouragement) from the main source to which, in spite of everything, they still look for help—i.e. England—I'm afraid that sooner or later, and the accent is on the "sooner," Hungary will be all but swallowed economically, and, politically, that one of the last strongholds of Parliamentarism will disappear. Between the stout-hearted and the extremist elements there is the large mass of defeatists who think that there is nothing for Hungary to do but throw her hand in. It would be absurd to pretend that Hungary would be saved from the realization of these gloomy forebodings by England taking a few more truckloads of poultry and eggs. But a *visible* sign of England's readiness to help—flag-waving if you like—could not fail to react encouragingly here always supposing that we have an interest in at any rate slowing up the German damburst. I haven't really much hope of anything being done directly, so one must hope for such a favourable outcome of the present Anglo-Italian talks as would turn the lira into an Edeldevise—a more effective solution of Hungary's economic problems than the extra chickens, but still lacking the important element of flag-waving.[18]

---

16 Report of a conversation between Williamson of the U.S. Embassy and William Tyler (Royall Tyler's son), May 23, 1938, R 5089/99/21, ibid.
17 Henry James Bruce to Cameron F. Cobbold, February 2, 1938, OV33/20, BoE.
18 Henry James Bruce to Cameron F. Cobbold, March 28, 1938, ibid.

The response at the Foreign Office to such fancy, however, was laconic: "Hungary is completely at Germany's mercy economically and strategically."[19] The British minister at Budapest, Geoffrey Knox, examining the previous year, painted the picture in the following words: "Hungary's relations with Germany have been those of reserved friendship [while] Hungary's affection for Geneva is diminishing."[20]

Tyler's above memorandum was widely read in British Foreign Office circles. The conclusion of an FO Minute was to the point: "We cannot help Hungary economically either before or after she obtains Slovakia."[21] Probably hoping that the more channels he used, the more seriously his ideas might be taken, Tyler also had a long talk in Geneva with the head of the Southern Department of the Foreign Office, Maurice Ingram, who passed a copy of the memorandum on to the British minister in Budapest.[22] Knox, just a few months after profiling German–Hungarian relations as "reserved friendship," now provided a sobering judgment right from the horse's mouth. Lajos Reményi-Schneller, recently appointed Hungarian finance minister, and "a sober and balanced soul" in Knox's view, allegedly told the British diplomat that "Germany's economic and strategic domination of Hungary is complete."[23] Tyler's cry for help on Hungary's behalf fell on deaf ears in light of the international situation.

It was an irony that just four days after Tyler completed his memorandum on Hungary, Béla Imrédy became the new prime minister, and under his short reign of nine months a further shift to the right was to take place. Two weeks into Imrédy's premiership, the first Jewish Bill in Hungary was passed by the Parliament, strictly curtailing Jewry's rights: it restricted the ratio of Jews in the field of free intellectual occupations to 20 percent. This shows that despite his unquestionable knowledge of Hungary, Tyler missed or overlooked things, or perhaps his optimistic personal outlook blinded him to certain contingencies. A similar misjudgment on his part took place earlier concerning Hitler, just a few months before the future Führer assumed

---

19 David Stephens, "Notes of a conversation with Mr. H. J. Bruce on conditions in Hungary," October 17, 1938, and A. N. Noble's Minute, October 18, 1938, R 8335/99/21, ibid.
20 "Annual Report, 1937," in Geoffrey Knox to Anthony Eden, January 20, 1938, R 549/549/21, FO 371/22379, TNA.
21 Leith-Ross' Minute, May 17, 1938, R 4851/99/21, FO 371/22374, TNA.
22 Maurice Ingram to Geoffrey Knox, May 24, 1938, R 4351/99/21, ibid.
23 Geoffrey Knox to Philip B. B. Nichols, May 22, 1938, R 5128/99/21, ibid.

Chapter 7

power. "Hitler's day is past," Tyler wrote in the fall of 1932, "and I'm not sure that it's a bad thing that he should have been shown up by events to be the yellow warbler he is."[24] Naturally, Tyler was not the only one who did not properly recognize how far Hitler might go or who misread the tea leaves on other occasions. Still, it is clear evidence then on occasion his judgment and strategic thinking were not necessarily always reliable.

As planned, Tyler soon travelled to the United States and spent a month there. The explicit goal of his trip was to size up American sentiment concerning European political issues and to map the economic and financial questions in and out of government. This was important for the League of Nations, and the organization could not have found a better candidate for such a liaison job. Tyler, for his part, was eager to go to the States, not only because he could once again feel himself important in that capacity but also to have a chance to meet long-time friends, preeminent among them the Blisses. In the few weeks he spent there, Tyler met various officials in the current administration as well as people of importance outside Washington, both in politics and the world of academia. Although no names were mentioned in his concluding report, according to his own personal notes, among those in the current government he met with the president (this was a 15-minute conversation with Franklin D. Roosevelt on June 19, 1938), Secretary of State Cordell Hull, Under Secretary of State Sumner Welles, Assistant Secretary of State George C. Messersmith, Treasury Secretary Henry Morgenthau, Jr., and officials and advisers at the State Department such as Herbert Feis and Harry C. Hawkins. In addition, Tyler had talks with the chairman of the Federal Reserve Board, Marriner S. Eccles, and his numerous assistants, while the list of contacts also included congressmen and foreign diplomats serving in Washington. On the second part of his trip, in New York, Tyler had conversations with the chairman of the Federal Reserve Bank of New York, George Leslie Harrison, and many chief officers there as well as at the major private banks. His itinerary also contained foreign policy experts, soldiers, lawyers, journalists, and others.[25] He organized his experiences in a report submitted to the League of Nations soon after his return to Europe.

---

24   Royall Tyler to Mildred Barnes Bliss, October 1, 1932.
25   "Note of Royall Tyler," July, 1938, Thompson Todd Collection; Franklin D. Roosevelt, Day by Day, http://www.fdrlibrary.marist.edu/daybyday/daylog/june-19th-1939/, accessed June 17, 2015.

The 24-page report was sectioned into three distinct parts. The first explored the relationship between the United States and the League. Through his wide array of contacts in and out of the current administration, Tyler had learned that the League was in good standing and was seen favorably. That Americans were working on the League's various committees was a welcome sign in Washington because it provided first-hand channels to what was going on in Geneva. The League's work on economic and financial matters especially, and the high quality reports it produced were held in high regard in Washington and in American academic circles. Even unnamed persons in key positions in the American government viewed the League as valuable because of the "opportunities for contact and unostentatious consultation." This appreciation, however, did not mean that the United States believed that the League possessed the political wherewithal for shaping the world's financial and economic aspects to any significant degree. Of course, the main problem concerning the relationship between the United States and the League of Nations on any official level was political. There was the pervasive fear of getting involved in the growing European debacle—a point of view also shared by the majority of the American friends of the League as well. "The League issue still has dynamite in it," as Tyler put it. So, even if the League were to be reformed, it was not to be done in any way that might try to lure the United States into its ranks, but would be done only with the current member states in mind.[26]

The middle section dealt with American foreign policy. The main issue was, naturally, the European situation in general and Great Britain's attitude in particular, and the steps needed to maintain peace on the continent. Tyler detected a certain amount of fear in the United States that the British desire to negotiate with Hitler and allow him to get more each time only encouraged Germany "to believe it can get away with anything in Central and S. Eastern Europe." This was the majority view, although there was a small conservative element willing to give the benefit of the doubt to the German chancellor. Interestingly enough, Tyler found anti-Semitism also to be a prevalent U.S. sentiment. On the one hand, there were quite a few Jews in the administration, on the other hand, many people had become weary of listening to

---

26 All the quotations are from Tyler's report, in Alexander Loveday to F. Ashton-Gwatkin, July 12, 1938, A 5559/1202/45, FO 371/21546, TNA.

Chapter 7

Jewish complaints about Germany. Parallel to this there was a strong antipathy toward communism and totalitarianism in general. "Anti-Hitler and anti-Mussolini feelings run high," wrote Tyler, "but Soviet Russia is regarded as equally totalitarian, and Communism is credited by many with a mysterious power, an insidious capacity to undermine and to honeycomb, more sinister than the bare-faced piracy or detective-novel spy-methods commonly associated with the names of Hitler and Mussolini." The general pessimistic view of the European situation and the League's feeble role in the middle of it made Tyler conclude: "America still wants to steer clear of any European conflict." He also mentioned the clinical fear in Congress of doing anything that might even remotely signal American second thoughts about war debts and reparations. In Washington, the long-standing official line remained the same, and Tyler saw no chance of this changing any time soon.[27]

The report's closing pages focused on domestic issues in the United States. Here Tyler concentrated mainly on the financial and economic landscape, the result of which was that the "Administration and business disagree about most things, but agree that the economic position is bad." The civil service ought to be more competent, the president's expansive responsibilities should be curtailed, there was a lack of contact among department heads and Congress. All in all, he went away with the opinion that the lessons of the past decade should be adopted in the form of reforms to better "the mechanism of Government, in which the U.S. are as far behind many European countries as they are in advance in technical equipment." He rounded out the report with speculation on possible outcomes of the presidential election in 1940.[28] The report received a favorable review from those who read it. Loveday, director of the Financial Section and Economic Intelligence Service, found it "extraordinarily illuminating."[29] He also allowed that the paper should receive limited, if not exactly confidential, circulation at the British Foreign Office.[30] Voices at the Office called Tyler's report "a most instructive memo" and "a most interesting paper."[31]

---

27 For the quotations, see, ibid.
28 For the quotations, see, ibid.
29 Alexander Loveday to F. Ashton-Gwatkin, July 12, 1938, A 5559/1202/45, FO 371/21546, TNA. The Report is also attached to this letter.
30 Royall Tyler to F. Ashton-Gwatkin, July 27, 1938, A 6014/1202/45, ibid.
31 Unidentified person's and Ashton-Gwatkin's minute, n. d. A 5559/1202/45, ibid.

The League of Nations Years – Part V

Tyler's own personal impressions about America were mixed. It is not clear what expectations he had when returning to his homeland after a long hiatus, but in part due to his mission, he must have looked at the American political and financial-economic landscape with a critical and analytical eye. Not surprisingly, and maybe because he had not anticipated much, he was "not altogether displeased with what I've gathered."[32] One highlight that sheds light on some aspects of Tyler and his Anglo-Saxon peers was his remark concerning the heavyweight boxing match between the American Joe Louis and Max Schmeling of Germany. The fight was a rematch of the 1936 bout that Schmeling won by a knockout in round twelve. On the last day of Tyler's stay in the United States, the title match took place in Yankee Stadium in New York City in front of 70,000 spectators and a global radio audience. Even the first, but especially this second match had a serious political subcontext. Many saw the fight as a decider as to which regime, Nazi Germany or democratic America, was superior. The first-round technical knockout by Louis gave Americans still fighting the Depression an obviously proud moment.[33]

Tyler's private summing up of his interest in the match is indicative of the overwhelmingly racist worldview of the era's upper classes. "I was deeply interested in a prize-fight," he wrote to his friend on the way back to Europe, "and I really was pleased when the coon knocked the Boche's head off in the first round."[34] The racial slur he used was not a conscious act, and there are no other references to African Americans in his writings that would prove he looked down on them in any particular way. But as a representative of his generation and upper-class upbringing, he carried with him the seeds of a superior attitude toward racial minorities. This can sometimes also be observed concerning how he spoke of Jews. Although he never used racial stereotypes about Jewish people as he did when referring to Louis, still there was often a clearly negative tone on those occasion when he wrote about them.

While in New York, he was also invited to give a talk at the Council on Foreign Relations, an independent think tank on foreign policy founded in

---

32 Royall Tyler to Mildred Barnes Bliss, June 24, 1938, Cunard White Star – R.M.S. "Queen Mary," "Bliss-Tyler Correspondence," https://www.doaks.org/resources/bliss-tyler-correspondence/letters/24jun1938, accessed April 22, 2019.
33 On the match and its implications, see, Barbara J. Keys, *Globalizing Sport. National Rivalry an International Community in the 1930s* (Cambridge, MA: Harvard University Press, 2006), 116–21.
34 Royall Tyler to Mildred Barnes Bliss, June 24, 1938.

1921.³⁵ It had become an increasingly important voice concerning international affairs ever since. In addition to publishing its journal, *Foreign Affairs*, the organization regularly asked experts to give talks on certain topics, after which debates often ensued. Tyler was asked to summarize Hungary's position in the changing European political landscape and under the new circumstances of the Anschluss and its consequence that now Hungary and Germany were neighbors. The Council would have liked to hear Tyler outline what path Hungary now might take, but he argued that Hungary above all wished to remain independent, and that the Nazis that were to be found in Hungary were basically an anti-Jewish movement. His opinion was that there was no "imminent danger of Hungary's being absorbed by Germany." He also believed that the Imrédy government would take positive steps in finance and foreign policy. In the latter realm, he emphasized the Hungarian–Yugoslav rapprochement, but called attention to the inimical relations with Czechoslovakia. He thought that "the stability of Central Europe would be greatly enhanced if Germany seized Czechoslovakia and divided it among the Powers. Germany would keep Bohemia and Hungary might get Slovakia." This by now controversial view stemmed from the idea that in that case "Hungary would have an outlet to the Baltic by way of Poland," which could boost Hungary's trade possibilities and, therefore, its somewhat greater independence from Germany.³⁶ This was the same view that Tyler voiced concerning British economic help toward Hungary: if Hungary becomes more stable economically and financially, it would steer away from Germany. A more independent Hungary could naturally be no counterweight against Germany, but it might play an important role in strategic considerations.

After Tyler returned to Geneva, he was thrown into "a fearful amount of work."³⁷ He had to deal with various legal papers concerning loan contracts and do the seemingly impossible: harmonize the dissenting opinions and turn the whole into one clear draft report. In light of the overwhelming

---

35 On the history of the organization, see, Robert D. Schulzinger, *The Wise Men of Foreign Affairs: The History of the Council on Foreign Relations*, New York: Columbia University Press, 1984.
36 For the quotations, see, Royall Tyler, "Hungary's Position in the new European Alignment," June 14, 1938, Council on Foreign Relations Meetings Records, Box 438, Folder 3, Public Policy Papers, Subseries 4B: Records of Meetings, Council on Foreign Relations Meetings Records 1920–1995, Seeley G. Mudd Manuscript Library.
37 Royall Tyler to Mildred Barnes Bliss, July 2, 1938, Geneva, "Bliss–Tyler Correspondence," https://www.doaks.org/resources/bliss-tyler-correspondence/letters/02jul1938, accessed April 22, 2019.

The League of Nations Years – Part V

quantity of various papers, he confessed to a need to select them wisely and carefully. It did not help that Elisina's health suffered a blow just as he was crossing the ocean. She had an attack of "apoplexy," probably a mild stroke, and her doctors ordered months of rest and avoidance of all anxiety in order to reach full recovery.[38] The rest of the summer brought Tyler more work, sometimes in the form of American visitors, sometimes sifting through tons of official papers, reports, memoranda, financial data, etc.—all against the background of the worsening European political situation and the steady upheaval in the status quo that had been ongoing since 1919. Tyler had a good vantage point to study it all.

In his wry, characteristic style and customary references to nations using slang words of his own, Tyler predicted that at least in the summer of 1938 there would be no war, because, although "Mussbags would like to provoke one, no doubt, but Fritz isn't so keen. It will take him a long time to absorb Austria."[39] It is not absolutely clear which country Tyler meant by "Mussbags," but probably he referred to Italy, Mussolini's name being the root of the term. At other times he referred to Italians by the common racial slur "wop." He explicated his points in a more detailed and nuanced form to Henry Morgenthau, Jr., whom he had already met in Washington. The American treasury secretary was now visiting Central Europe and he met with Tyler in Geneva. Tyler drew up a long report on the present situation at the secretary's request—perhaps at President Roosevelt's order, as Roosevelt liked to have a wide range of people outside his close advisory circle reporting to him. So, while he had traveled to the United States to provide information on the situation there for the League of Nations, now back at Geneva, he did basically the opposite. And this became a regular activity on Tyler's part: to provide information about the European situation from within.

---

38 Royall Tyler to Mildred Barnes Bliss, June 18, 1938, New York, "Bliss–Tyler Correspondence," https://www.doaks.org/resources/bliss-tyler-correspondence/letters/18jun1938; Royall Tyler to Mildred Barnes Bliss, June 28, 1938, Bliss–Tyler Correspondence," https://www.doaks.org/resources/bliss-tyler-correspondence/letters/28jun1938; Royall Tyler to Mildred Barnes Bliss, July 10, 1938, Antigny-le-Château, "Bliss–Tyler Correspondence," https://www.doaks.org/resources/bliss-tyler-correspondence/letters/10jul1938; Royall Tyler to Mildred Barnes Bliss, July 13, 1938, Geneva, "Bliss–Tyler Correspondence," https://www.doaks.org/resources/bliss-tyler-correspondence/letters/13jul1938, all accessed April 22, 2019.

39 Royall Tyler to Mildred Barnes Bliss, August 10, 1938, Geneva, "Bliss–Tyler Correspondence," https://www.doaks.org/resources/bliss-tyler-correspondence/letters/10aug1938, accessed April 22, 2019.

Chapter 7

He divided the first long telegram to Morgenthau into three sections. The first dealt with the German financial situation, where—due to a number of factors—the Berlin Stock Exchange had suffered a setback and prices dropped 10–15 percent in just a couple of weeks. The main underlying cause was thought to be a shortage of cash and credit as a result of rearmament and nonproductive public works. Next, Tyler looked at the main continental countries related to the Czechoslovak crisis: Germany, Italy, Czechoslovakia, and France. He tried to assess what course these states would be likely to follow in the near future. He thought that because of the possible British and French mobilization, the Berlin–Rome Axis had a better chance at the moment, but with the passage of time, their hope of success might diminish. This latter point was more acute for Italy, where people in general were dissatisfied with the current economic situation, while in Germany many people were restless and, in the wake of the Anschluss, wanted more. Therefore, with the Czechoslovak crisis at hand, Tyler opined that it was "difficult to see how this problem is going to be steered out of the zone of immediate danger to world peace."

The last section of this report was titled "Peace or War?" His premise was that war would be avoided in 1938, and that that might just carry enough momentum for peace the following year. He based this optimistic view on the following factors: many of the high-ranking German military leaders were still sober and responsible men; Italy and Japan were still engaged in wars, while Germany needed the oilfields in Romania in order to ensure that the Luftwaffe could operate; there was clear tension among the Axis powers, which also worked against launching a war; the public statements of the American president and secretary of state might also have a sobering effect on Germany and Italy as to the possible consequences of American involvement. In his conclusion, Tyler stated clearly that although peace was far from guaranteed, "if a wager had to be made, however, peace still seems the better bet."[40]

Another report to Morgenthau followed one month later, just before the Munich Agreement was signed at the end of September. At Morgenthau's request, Tyler undertook a journey that included Austria, Germany, and Italy, in which countries he talked to a wide range of people: bankers, diplomats, members of the intelligentsia, etc. In Germany, the economic and

---

40 Royall Tyler to Henry Morgenthau, August 19, 1938, (sent on August 20), Thompson Todd Collection.

financial situation was not rosy, according to Tyler's sources, and as a result, in Berlin there was no real support for war. The general picture there showed a country in a worsening financial situation, and outside official circles people did not seem as hopeful as propaganda suggested. Munich struck Tyler as a great deal more normal: there were few Aryan signs in shops, people were more open and freely criticized the system. Despite this, there was great respect for Hitler everywhere and, interestingly, Tyler encountered "almost universal disapproval [of] anti-Semitic measures." Based upon his experiences in Milan, he characterized the Italian situation as having deteriorated in the past months: business was down, raw materials were in short supply, people were generally angry on account of the anti-Jewish measures.[41] Tyler's complete report was passed on to Roosevelt, so the president was also personally informed about his analysis of the European situation.[42]

Tyler was affected by the anti-Jewish laws in Italy for a personal reason, which serves as good evidence that he was not anti-Semitic at heart. One of his colleagues and friends, Doro Levi, a university professor and a renowned archeologist, was one of the many Italian Jews who suffered from the racial laws. He was deprived of his posts and salary. Tyler was annoyed not for the principle alone, but because Levi had volunteered to fight during World War I and was a fervent patriot, yet now the state was dispossessing him. More important perhaps for Tyler, his Italian colleague was a great archeologist of Greco-Roman history and was very good at picking digging sites, especially relating to the Mediterranean. Tyler saw the only way out for Levi would be for him to move to the United States and start to work at one of the universities specializing in his area. He urged the Blisses to help facilitate such an invitation for the Italian.[43] The

---

41 Royall Tyler to Henry Morgenthau, September 20, 1938, Thompson Todd Collection. Ten months earlier, after a trip to Italy, he already painted a very negative picture of Italy. Geoffrey Knox to Orme Sargent, January 12, 1938, R 656/23/22, FO 371/22402, TNA.
42 Henry Morgenthau to Franklin D. Roosevelt, September 22, 1938, Volume 142, September 21– September 26, 1938, Diaries of Henry Morgenthau, Jr., April 27, 1933–July 27, 1945, Henry Morgenthau, Jr. Papers, 1866–1953, Franklin D. Roosevelt Library and Museum Website; version date 2016.
43 Royall Tyler to Robert Woods Bliss, September 19, 1938, "Bliss–Tyler Correspondence," https://www.doaks.org/resources/bliss-tyler-correspondence/letters/19sep1938; Royall Tyler to Mildred Barnes Bliss and Robert Woods Bliss, October 8, 1938, Geneva, "Bliss–Tyler Correspondence," https://www.doaks.org/resources/bliss-tyler-correspondence/letters/08oct1938; Royall Tyler to Robert Woods Bliss, October 28, 1938, Geneva, "Bliss–Tyler Correspondence," https://www.doaks.org/resources/bliss-tyler-correspondence/letters/28oct1938; Royall Tyler to Robert Woods Bliss, December 11, 1938, Basel, "Bliss–

Chapter 7

Blisses' subsequently lent their support and Levi soon received a position at the Institute for Advanced Study in Princeton, New Jersey, where he remained for the next seven years. During the last phase of the war, he helped the American government prevent the destruction of various monuments in Italy. He returned to his home country only after World War II.[44]

The Munich Pact was signed on September 30, 1938.[45] By an agreement among Great Britain, France, Germany, and Italy, the Sudetenland—an area on the border of western, southern, and northern Czechoslovakia, with a disproportionally large German population—was annexed by Germany. This was the arrangement for leading European powers to defuse the rising tension that was caused by an ever more aggressive Nazi Germany. Czechoslovakia was left with no real choice but to accept losing a great chunk of its territory. This was perhaps the last time when optimistic people wanted to believe that war might be still avoided. Tyler, for his part, was not at all surprised at the outcome at Munich, since he had "expected a settlement." He was also of the opinion that the Czechs had themselves to blame given the obstinacy they had shown by not giving any meaningful concession to large ethnic minorities in their countries. Tyler realized that "these views aren't very acceptable" in Geneva, but he confessed to being "more hopeful about prospects for international collaboration now than I have been at any time in the last 7 years."[46] Basically, he repeated his earlier thesis about the flawed peace treaties, and he must have seen some vindication in the Munich Pact.

Others were more perceptive than Tyler about the situation. Beneš, for example, saw it much more clearly and presciently. As he told one of his close associates just a few weeks after the Pact, "They still perhaps think here (i.e. in the west) that Munich has saved the peace. But they will all understand soon that they are really at war. Munich made war inevitable. I don't know

---

Tyler Correspondence," https://www.doaks.org/resources/bliss-tyler-correspondence/letters/11dec1938; and Robert Woods Bliss to Royall Tyler, December 24, 1938 [2], "Bliss–Tyler Correspondence," https://www.doaks.org/resources/bliss-tyler-correspondence/letters/24dec1938-2, all accessed April 22, 2019. On September 2, 1938, Jews were expelled from universities in Italy. The comprehensive racial laws were passed on November 10, 1938, and they restricted Jew's rights in many aspects of life. See, Elizabeth Wiskemann, *Fascism in Italy: Its Development and Influence* (London: Palgrave Macmillan, 1970), 72.

44 "Doro Levi, Archeologist, 93," – Obituary, *New York Times*, July 6, 1991.
45 The most thorough account is Zara Steiner, *The Triumph of the Dark. European International History 1933–1939* (Oxford: Oxford University Press, 2011), 610–68.
46 Royall Tyler to Robert Woods Bliss, September 30, 1938, Geneva, "Bliss–Tyler Correspondence," https://www.doaks.org/resources/bliss-tyler-correspondence/letters/30sep1938, accessed April 22, 2019.

when it will break out, perhaps next year or perhaps in two or three years' time, but I myself think that it cannot be longer than a year."[47]

It is difficult to understand why Tyler did not fathom the looming danger in the situation. It is obvious that he did not much like Germany, and even if he might have had some bias toward Hungary, it was obvious that it would be next to impossible to stop Germany if it proved still unsatisfied, and that meant war. At any rate, the question naturally on everybody's mind was what came next. One tangible result was the First Vienna Award in which Hungary—by the decision of Germany and Italy—regained some of the lost territories in the north.[48] Clearly, Pandora's box had opened. Tyler thought the countries lying to the east and southeast of the suddenly swollen German territories would "gradually assume a defensive attitude towards" the new Central European behemoth, especially in the economic and financial fields, and this might open up a renewed trade avenue with Great Britain and France.[49] Tyler's somewhat naïve optimism may also have been boosted by his wife's slow but steady convalescence.

At the start of the new year, Tyler again completed a by now almost regular mission and report to Secretary Morgenthau. This time he analyzed the Italian situation based both upon the events of the previous few weeks and as he saw it from direct experience in the first two weeks of 1939. He mentioned the latest news first: the visit of the British prime minister and foreign secretary to Italy between January 11 and 14. Neville Chamberlain's and Lord Halifax's appearance in Rome was welcomed by the average Italian, and people hoped against hope that it might mean some forthcoming financial help, which was needed due to the downward trend of economic conditions in the country. The visit's real main aim for Chamberlain was to wield some Italian influence on Germany. The British thought that in the event they failed to

---

47 Richard Crampton, "Edvard Beneš," in Jonathan Wright and Steven Casey, eds. *Mental Maps in the Era of Two World Wars* (New York: Palgrave Macmillan, 2008), 137. Beneš added: "Poland will be the first to be hit ... Chamberlain will live to see the consequences of his appeasement ... Hitler will attack them all, the West and Russia as well, and finally America will come in." Ibid.

48 Hungary received about 4,600 square miles with almost a million ethnic Hungarians. For a comprehensive study on the First Vienna Award see, Gergely Sallai, *Az első bécsi döntés* [The First Vienna Award] (Budapest: Osiris, 2002).

49 Royall Tyler to Mildred Barnes Bliss, November 18, 1938, Geneva, "Bliss–Tyler Correspondence," https://www.doaks.org/resources/bliss-tyler-correspondence/letters/18nov1938, accessed April 23, 2019.

reach an agreement with Germany similar to Munich the previous year, Italy might play a moderating role on Hitler concerning issues of European security. But Mussolini was not willing to give any guarantee along those lines—aside from empty phrases.[50] One day after that visit, Tyler concluded that British optimism was misplaced, because it did "not give due weight to Germany's control of Italy and Fascism's impotence to get out of the economic mess and consequent tendency to be tempted to try more burglary."[51]

Concerning Italian opinion, Tyler noted that after Munich there was a short upward curve in popularity for Mussolini, which, however, soon evaporated. People in general were "pessimistic and resentful," and the reasons were plenty: they had not forgotten the Anschluss, which hurt Italian interests; the anti-Jewish laws were not widely popular; General Franco's successes in Spain had not translated into enthusiasm in Italy; even the expansion of Italian power to Corsica and Tunisia had not met with popular acclaim; while the anti-French propaganda was seen by many as a German plan to drive an irremovable wedge between the two countries. In addition, Tyler found more and more Italians who were willing to talk to English-speaking tourists or diplomats in particular and openly criticize the regime. He separately studied how Italians related to Fascism itself. In light of the above, it was hardly surprising that Tyler spoke about the decline of the once popular movement. He wrote that it was "rare to meet an Italian who does not speak ill of Mussolini." Tyler attributed this general feeling to the continuous loss of prestige in the shadow of Germany and the deteriorating economic situation that people were exposed to on a daily basis. He found a similar situation on the part of the Church regarding Mussolini's regime. Tyler closed his notes with a few observations about Hungary, Yugoslavia, and Greece.[52]

In a private letter written at the same time, Tyler stated that both Germany and Italy, the "two burglars," were experiencing a declining standard of living, and no deal with Britain and France could really alleviate the underlying economic problems there. Therefore, Hitler would keep pushing forward with his demands, which in the end would produce two alternatives: "either war,

---

50 Paul Stafford, "The Chamberlain-Halifax Visit to Rome: A Reappraisal," *The English Historical Review* 98, no. 386 (January 1983): 61–100.
51 "Notes on Italy, Jan. 1–15, 1939, and other matters," in Royall Tyler to Henry Morgenthau, January 26, 1939, Thompson Todd Collection.
52 Quotations are from ibid.

or a continuation of the armaments race and cut-throat economic warfare, with resulting impoverishment to all the chief actors."[53] And inevitably, with tensions rising to an ever higher pitch, it was impossible not to see that the League of Nations had proved absolutely inadequate as a conduit for peace making and upholder of collective security. As an employee of that organization, Tyler was clearly aware of this, and, together with many colleagues, could only watch helplessly as things always took a more ominous turn. But he and his colleagues also realized that the traditional Great Powers were just as much at fault in allowing the international situation to become so unstable. What remained for Tyler and his ilk was to watch and listen carefully, and analyze the situation as best and as intelligently as they could.

Tyler's analysis remained optimistic—though mistaken. Even half a year before World War II broke out, he proudly wrote that he had "never been a believer in the ineluctability of war."[54] In hindsight, this opinion can be dismissed as naïve, but it also shows his firm belief in the perfectibility of man even in the worst situation. This worldview must have come from his academic upbringing and deep understanding of medieval art: humanity standing at the center of the arts and the deep confidence of God's benevolent omnipotence that most of the artifacts Tyler dealt with exuded. Probably this belief made him hope that even in the extremely tense European situation war was not inevitable. In addition, even in the early spring he was still of the opinion that the international circumstances were becoming somewhat better. He understood that things were "going to be delicate and dangerous for some time to come," but the British military build-up, the election of "a good Pope," and mainly the attitude of the United States could, he believed, "hardly fail to act as a powerful deterrent to the gangsters"—the latter term referring to Germany and Italy.[55] And his mindset did not change throughout the spring of 1939. He still saw the German military leadership as reasonable, the Italians as morally low, and the Western powers—Great

---

53 Royall Tyler to Robert Woods Bliss, January 28, 1939, Geneva, "Bliss–Tyler Correspondence," https://www.doaks.org/resources/bliss-tyler-correspondence/letters/28jan1939, accessed April 24, 2019.

54 Royall Tyler to Mildred Barnes Bliss, March 2, 1939 [1], Geneva, "Bliss–Tyler Correspondence," https://www.doaks.org/resources/bliss-tyler-correspondence/letters/02mar1939-1, accessed April 24, 2019.

55 Royall Tyler to Robert Woods Bliss, March 9, 1939, Geneva, "Bliss–Tyler Correspondence," https://www.doaks.org/resources/bliss-tyler-correspondence/letters/09mar1939, accessed April 24, 2019. After the death of Pius XI, the papal conclave elected Cardinal Eugenio Pacelli as the next pope on March 2, 1939. He took the name Pius XII.

Chapter 7

Britain and France—stronger as compared to 1938, since he thought Poland was joining them. Although Hungary's and Yugoslavia's situations were also dangerous, Tyler still did not consider either of them lost to Germany. In fact, he hoped that despite the mess the French and British had caused in Central Europe, the situation might be rectified by the fear of an aggressive Germany. He was clearly aware, however, that his optimism was skating on thin ice. "I may be mad," he wrote in April 1939, "but I'm still inclined to think the crash may not take place."[56]

After a short visit to Hungary in late spring, at the behest of the new prime minister, Pál Teleki's,[57] Tyler once again traveled to his country of birth. His mission was the same as in the previous summer: to gather information in America concerning the League's standing there, to size up the domestic landscape, with an emphasis on the economic situation, and to evaluate American opinion regarding international questions. Due to the worsening crisis in Europe, this latter point in particular became a very important aspect of his work. His observations during his five-week stay were organized into yet another long report. The first two sections concentrated on the League, both from the American general public's point of view and that of the current administration. Almost all the issues in America were to be understood in light of the upcoming elections in November. As a consequence of both the international scene and the possibility of an unprecedented third term for Franklin Roosevelt, the campaigning started early. His opponents attacked Roosevelt on various points, a prominent one being that he wanted to steer the United States into a European war in order to help his reelection, basically accusing "him of wishing to light a world conflagration to roast his own chestnuts."

The general assumption was that war in Europe and the likely economic recovery in its wake would in all likelihood ensure his victory at the polls. This is where the League of Nations entered the picture. In Tyler's view, the president's political enemies, especially in Congress, would seize upon any small step Roosevelt made toward cooperation with the League "as further proof that he is plotting to rush the country into war and make him-

---

56 Royall Tyler to Robert Woods Bliss, April 15, 1939, Hyères (Var), "Bliss–Tyler Correspondence," https://www.doaks.org/resources/bliss-tyler-correspondence/letters/15apr1939, accessed April 24, 2019.
57 Teleki became prime minister on February 16, 1939.

self Dictator." This mindset endangered even modest collaboration between Washington and Geneva for the foreseeable future. In an non-election year, and with calmer public opinion, the issue might have been raised, but that moment was yet to come. And since the possibility of a Republican Party victory could not be dismissed, Tyler warned against any steps that would give the impression that the League conspicuously wished to achieve closer relations with the current American administration. Geneva and the League representatives must be careful, he advised, and they "had better keep buried in their bosoms any hopes they may entertain of the U.S.A., and in any case using the words 'American membership'. There is still dynamite in them."[58] The Roosevelt administration was nonetheless trying to achieve better contacts with the League, albeit very cautiously. Tyler saw evidence for this in the appointment of Harold Tittmann to head the American Consulate at Geneva. Tittmann, who Tyler had met in Washington, had a thorough knowledge of both Europe and the State Department. Also, the Roosevelt administration appreciated the useful things the League had done and kept doing in accumulating important data and acting as a conduit for contacts among democracies and states exposed to totalitarian pressures. But prudent domestic politics dictated no further moves.

As to general American public opinion regarding the League, Tyler detected a shift since the last summer and fall. He believed universal dislike of the Axis was palpable and blame for its advances was placed at the doorstep of the Western democracies: Germany's seemingly insatiable appetite had been made possible by a feeble Great Britain and France, whose job it should have been to keep Germany in check. However, that sentiment clearly did not mean that Americans wanted to get involved in actual fighting in Europe if it came to that. Despite the warnings of some foreign policy experts regarding the damage Germany may yet be able to cause, people generally believed that Germany might have missed the best time to attack, and that economically it was not in a comfortable situation.

Tyler closed his exhaustive report with a look at the economic outlook in the United States, upon which a possible war would naturally have con-

---

58   The quotations in the last two paragraphs are from "Notes on visit to U.S.A., by R. Tyler (Washington, New York, Baltimore, Boston, Cambridge and other places, 9 June to 13 July 1939)," July 20, 1939, Thompson Todd Collection.

Chapter 7

siderable impact. Tyler judged the present economic situation to be improving, but he was afraid the bitter antagonism between the administration and Wall Street might jeopardize and slow down any revival. He still thought that the New Deal effort to put money into consumers' pockets had succeeded, and despite the many mistakes along the way, a more centralized federal government was there to stay whether the Democrats were ousted or not. Another feature that he thought would be lasting was the unbalanced budget, this on account off the enormous scale of lending and spending programs throughout the country.[59] When it came to economic and financial issues, Tyler's observations were more spot on.

After returning to Europe, Tyler tried to spend more time in Antigny with Elisina, who still had not recovered completely. Like everybody else, his mind was occupied mainly with the shadow of a war that might start at any minute. Despite his earlier manifest optimism that war could be avoided, by the end of August he had finally realized that Hitler was about to launch his war. The last nail in the coffin for Tyler was the Molotov–Ribbentrop Pact of August 23, 1939. It was, he thought, "comparable to the movements of the earth's crust that threw up the Alps, separated Europe from Africa, ingulfed [*sic*] Atlantis."[60] The Non-Aggression Treaty left no doubt either as to Germany's aims or that the Soviet Union could be counted upon as a counterweight against Nazi Germany when the latter went to war.

On the one hand, Tyler scorned the British and the French as being "simpletons" for hoping for Soviet support in a possible showdown against Germany, and for having "made plans a prime condition of the success of which was Russia's sincerity!"[61] On the other hand, Germany's official pact with the unchallenged leader of the communistic sphere overthrew some of the basic tenets of the Anti-Comintern Pact, which had a clear anti-communist agenda that, although not specifically mentioning it by name, mainly had the Soviet Union in mind. Originally it was signed by Germany and Japan in 1936; a few more countries had joined later, for instance, Italy, Hungary,

---

59 Ibid.
60 Royall Tyler to Robert Woods Bliss, September 14, 1939, Geneva, "Bliss–Tyler Correspondence," https://www.doaks.org/resources/bliss-tyler-correspondence/letters/14sep1939, accessed April 25, 2019.
61 Royall Tyler to Mildred Barnes Bliss, August 24, 1939 [2], Geneva, "Bliss–Tyler Correspondence," https://www.doaks.org/resources/bliss-tyler-correspondence/letters/24aug1939-2, accessed April 24, 2019.

and Spain. The agreement between Molotov and Ribbentrop put the Anti-Comintern Pact's anti-communist agenda in a questionable light—at least on paper. Tyler wondered whether the other signatories would feel sufficiently cheated that they would express their dissatisfaction, or "will they all be so terrified by this conjunction that they dare think no thoughts of their own?"[62]

---

62 Ibid.

CHAPTER 8

World War II – An Intelligence Officer

"This is certainly a queer war, and I don't think we're at the end of our surprises."[1] This was Royall Tyler's first recorded thought about World War II, which erupted on September 1, 1939, with the German invasion of Poland. Aside from the terrible impending carnage—of which the previous world war could have offered a preview—the war just under way meant a reorganization of the world to a large degree. It was once and for all decided that appeasement had not worked, and any and all diplomatic efforts to restrain Hitler had not been enough to refrain him from trying to achieve as much domination as possible—for the time being in the eastern half of Europe. The war forced the democracies to make up their minds and try to stop the Nazi onslaught. The small countries on the sidelines began a watchful waiting as to the outcome and only then would they wish to declare their alliances or remaining neutral. The League of Nations was basically finished as an instrument of collective security. It had become almost insignificant in this role throughout the greater part of the 1930s. Though perhaps there were paths ahead contained in the theoretical work it had amassed, as a force to reckon with in international diplomacy, it had become a chapter of past history, even if on paper it lived to see the end of World War II. Tyler stayed on at Geneva after reporting to the League on his American trip, and after two weeks there, he summarized his vision of the future in a letter to Robert Woods Bliss: "When the great mountain ranges of world affairs have shifted as they have now, it may be expected that few of the features of the landscape as we have known it will remain unaltered."[2]

---

1 Royall Tyler to Robert Woods Bliss, September 14, 1939.
2 Ibid.

Chapter 8

Tyler believed from the beginning that in the end the Allies would prevail over Germany. His focus at this stage, perhaps also understandably in light if his past fifteen years of work, lay to the east and southeast of Europe. The major player there, in his estimation, was the Soviet Union, which could afford to play the waiting game and had already gained a lot by striking a deal with Hitler. However, in the long run Tyler judged the pact against Western democracies between Nazi Germany and the communist Soviet Union to be impractical. The Soviets, he thought, wished to wait to see both sides exhausted before moving in themselves. He saw the Hungarian situation particularly keenly, in that, with the Soviet Union suddenly becoming a neighbor, the staunchly anti-bolshevist Hungarians were made quite nervous. On the other hand, he believed that Hungarians would not fully open up their agriculture to German demands, and also hoped to sell their industrial products elsewhere.[3] Tyler actually thought the fighting might be ended within three years.[4] Since there was nothing solid to base this opinion on, one must surmise that this prediction stemmed from his optimistic nature. Also, at this point—less than two months into the hostilities—it was far from clear what direction the war would take, how many nations would be involved, what sacrifices in material and manpower would be made, and how long the conflict would last. So, Tyler's estimate of three years was not necessarily naïve at that point.

His work at Geneva consisted of economic intelligence gathering, which, under the circumstances of a large-scale war was a bigger challenge than he had faced earlier. He made short trips in the fall and winter to London, Paris, Brussels, and even to Budapest to facilitate this line of inquiry. Still, he would have liked to be doing something different, a perhaps more exciting job, but for the time being he was satisfied with what he had at hand. Parallel to his official job, he naturally worked on Byzantine art projects, together with his long-time collaborator, Hayford Peirce. At the time the project was the long-hoped-for third volume of their research on the history of Byzantine art. The first two volumes had appeared in 1932 and 1934,

---

3   Royall Tyler to Robert Woods Bliss, October 25, 1939, Geneva, "Bliss–Tyler Correspondence," https://www.doaks.org/resources/bliss-tyler-correspondence/letters/25oct1939, accessed April 25, 2019.
4   Royall Tyler to Mildred Barnes Bliss, October 27, 1939, Geneva, "Bliss–Tyler Correspondence," https://www.doaks.org/resources/bliss-tyler-correspondence/letters/27oct1939, accessed April 25, 2019.

respectively, and they were planning to publish the third one in 1940.⁵ But the war, especially the German occupation of Paris, made that impossible, and neither the third volume, nor a compilation of the three separate volumes ever appeared in print.

Meanwhile, he continued his now regular reports to Secretary Morgenthau. With the war going on, his long telegrams became increasingly important and valuable for the United States government, even if done in a private capacity. His latest back-channeling effort came just before Christmas 1939 in the wake of a week-long stay in Hungary and a few days in Italy. The material was sent in two separate telegrams, the first focusing on the Hungarian situation, while the second contained his impressions on Italy.⁶ However, the two telegrams contained only economic-related issues, and Tyler's original report was much longer. Luckily it has survived.

Concerning Hungary, the report focused on the financial and economic picture that was inseparable from the political one. Hungary planned to continue paying the American relief credits payments and League Loan service, but as to the other commitments concluded in the three-year arrangement, the Hungarian state could not undertake said financial burden beyond 1940. The problem was familiar: Hungary's imports and exports were too closely linked with Germany—roughly half of the total volume of Hungary's foreign trade—and since there was no free-exchange market to be reached, there was no real alternative but to turn to Germany. Also, German agents were busy buying up foreign assets belonging to Hungarians. This made further German penetration possible, which Hungary was trying to stave off as modestly as it could. Although a reality check revealed little space for freedom and opportunity, and this heavy-handed German influence was "unwelcome," it was still "regarded as lesser evil than invasion or forced customs union."⁷ Tyler's week in Hungary convinced him that the general attitude in Budapest was hatred toward both Germany and the Soviet Union on

---

5   Royall Tyler to Robert Woods Bliss, August 2, 1939, Geneva, "Bliss–Tyler Correspondence," https://www.doaks.org/resources/bliss-tyler-correspondence/letters/02aug1939, and "Annotation," https://www.doaks.org/resources/bliss-tyler-correspondence/annotations/lart-byzantin, both accessed April 24, 2019.
6   For Morgenthau from Tyler, in Harold Tittmann to Henry Morgenthau, December 22 and 23, 1939, Volume 232, December 22–December 31, 1939, Diaries of Henry Morgenthau, Jr., April 27, 1933–July 27, 1945, Henry Morgenthau, Jr. Papers, Franklin D. Roosevelt Library and Museum Website, version date 2016.
7   Tyler's Report to Morgenthau, December 21, 1939, Thompson Todd Collection.

account of the pact between them and the latter's attack on Finland.⁸ Based on his talks with upper-level officials he relayed two important observations: first, that Hungary would not get involved in any military adventure, and second, that "three Hungarians out of four expect and want German defeat and now seem to exaggerate German difficulties, though before the war they overestimated Germany's might."⁹

With regard to Italy, the original report contained at least four times more information than the one finally sent. Tyler's thesis was as follows: "In Italy confusion seems inextricable."¹⁰ According to the original text, the average standard of living was decreasing, and rumor was strong that next spring Italy might try its luck militarily. In the press, German news dominated while news of the Allies were either delayed or hidden. The feeling among average Italians was hatred toward Germany, and the government seemed to be waiting for a more certain course in the war before taking concrete steps. Tyler judged it doubtful that Italy was ready to fight, but he also was of the opinion that with Mussolini and Foreign Minister Galezzo Ciano at the helm of Italy's foreign policy, there would not be any collaboration with the Allies.¹¹

Tyler's intelligence reporting did not stop at Geneva and Washington. In addition to the Geneva-based economic intelligence gathering, which took up much of his time, he weaved in political intelligence he had gathered as well and informed not only the U.S. government through Morgenthau, but also the British, who were hungry for any information concerning the central part of the continent. This was voluntary on Tyler's part but not at his own initiative—he was sought out for advice, which he was very willing to give. It was essential, for example, for the British to know what they could expect in the Danubian Basin in terms of what might help and what might hinder German efforts there, and so a recent meeting between Tyler and Pál Teleki prompted Britain to ask for information about Hungary, mainly concerning the country's relationship with Germany. According to Tyler, the

---

8   On November 30, the Soviet Union attacked Finland. Despite initial difficulties and incurring heavy losses, after three months the Russians prevailed. In retaliation, the Soviet Union was expelled from the League of Nations.
9   Tyler's Report to Morgenthau, December 21, 1939.
10 Ibid.
11 Ibid.

Soviets had on two occasions signaled to the Hungarians that they would help reopen the Transylvanian question, but in both cases Teleki had shut down this avenue, actually threatening the Hungarian minority leaders of Transylvania that any such move on their part would be considered high treason. Tyler reported that the Teleki government was solid and the general mood of the country, both within and outside of government, was anti-German. Since more and more Hungarians, especially the leaders, had started to question the likelihood of a German victory, they desperately wanted to maintain contact with the West, which first and foremost meant Great Britain. This piece of information must have been pleasing to British ears, and equally so Tyler's closing remark, namely that His Majesty's minister, Sir Owen O'Malley, was spoken of in the highest regard by everybody that he, Tyler, had met during his stay in Hungary.[12]

Henry James Bruce, too, reiterated the Hungarians' anti-German feeling: "Two factors remain constant, namely the widespread anti-German feeling on the one side and on the other the necessity of acting in official relations and in the inspired Press as if the exact contrary were the case."[13] This observation remained a constant on the part of Anglo Saxons who knew Hungary well. As late as 1941, the last American minister, for example, wrote that most Hungarians "seem to dislike the Germans and hope for a German defeat ... and actually do as little as they can for Germany." In addition, "The American Legation is the center and inspiration of a great part of intelligence of Hungary which frankly fears Germany and hope for a British victory. They are, of course, frightened to death of Russia, and hope to see the Germans beat the Russians and then be bogged in themselves."[14]

Early February, 1940, in London, the British foreign secretary, Viscount Halifax, had a conversation with György Barcza, the Hungarian minister to Great Britain, who had just returned from Budapest. Among other things, the Hungarian diplomat asked for some encouragement from the British government concerning Hungary's wishes for territorial readjustment in Transylvania. He handed over an official note regarding this request, in

---

12 J. K. Robert's Minute, February 10, 1940, C 2326/529/21, FO 371/24427, TNA.
13 "Notes," by Bruce, March 27 – April 10, 1939, in Henry James Bruce to C. F. Cobbold, April 10, OV33/22, BoE. He basically strengthened this point later in "Notes," by Bruce, May 26, 1939, ibid.
14 Herbert C. Pell to William Bullitt, July 11, 1941, Box 65 Folder 1612 Pell, Herbert C. (1939–1941), William C. Bullitt Papers, Yale Archives.

Chapter 8

which the old Hungarian "bulwark of Christianity" thesis came forward, which now was presented as a defense against Bolshevism.[15] This may explain why Teleki was so set against the Soviet initiative regarding Transylvania. Aside from his staunch anti-communist outlook, he wanted to have stronger ties with Britain, and he may have thought that if Hungary acted according to British interests, even in a limited way, this might be rewarded by British backing concerning the Hungarian claim to Transylvania. The British foreign policy establishment's response, however, as much as it can be judged based upon the recorded minutes, was a resounding "no" to the Hungarian overture. Orme Sargent, deputy undersecretary at the Foreign Office, perhaps best summarized the prevailing opinion: "Since Hungary can render us no service in the war, it is not worth our while to make any sacrifices or run any risks on her behalf."[16] Since Britain recognized that Hungary fell within the German sphere, there was really nothing to expect from it or to give to it in any form.

Soon another of Tyler's confidential reports landed in the American State Department. The summary report on the Hungarian situation, completed in early March 1940, picked up where his December telegram to Morgenthau left off. It spelled out the economic woes of Hungary due to Germany's domination in the surrounding countries and the the lack of free-exchange markets, which it could partially reach only through Italy. But fear ran high that in case Italy entered the war, "Hungary would be cut off from the rest of the world." Also, Germany had been trying to link Hungarian prices to the German ones by various means, although so far Hungary had resisted such attempts, because it was clear that the German efforts were meant "to absorb Hungary into her economic system." This would be a stage along the road to almost complete domination of Hungary. Looking ahead, the purely Hungarian part of Transylvania, the Szekler lands, was the obvious collective desire of the Hungarians, and, according to Tyler, it was assumed that this territory would be regained. However, to achieve this with German help—similarly to the First Vienna Award in 1938—might mean the loss of Hungarian independence, while Soviet involvement was anathema to the Hungarians. Hungary, Tyler noted, did not believe in a Danubian federation

---

15   Note of Conversation with Barcza, February 9, 1940, C 2613/529/21, OV33/22, BoE.
16   Orme Sargent's Minute, February 22, 1940, ibid.

that might be dictated by the peace makers later on; it wanted to follow an organic development of such an idea.[17]

On May 10, 1940, the Germans launched their offensive on the Western Front, which really brought the war home for the Western Powers—and for the Tylers as well. In early May, Tyler was in Paris after returning from a mission to Finland, and he was trying to gather as much information as possible. In Paris he "saw daily the Ambassador," William C. Bullitt, Jr., and "the leading French Statesmen." [18] Although Switzerland maintained its traditional neutrality, Antigny lay in the path of the German invasion of France. Soon it became clear that the French would not be able to withstand the German juggernaut, and in early June, just a few days before the Germans occupied Paris, Elisina arrived at Geneva to stay with Tyler. Naturally, their home in France became a constant worry. Tyler could not leave Geneva for an extended period, so it was decided that Elisina, who had spent much more time there in the first place, would return and try to keep it intact and free from any harm.

The same day that Paris fell—June 14—Elisina secured a special permit to leave for France and go on to to Antigny, where she beat the advancing Germans by only a few days. Her presence there made a huge difference. She took steps to obtain the necessary official documents at the still open American embassy in Paris, and thus was able to provide a certificate that Antigny was U.S. property. As American neutrality was meticulously observed by the Germans at this stage, Elisina managed to save Antigny from certain looting and devastation. She quartered a few German officers and their men there, who had to follow her rules, and they indeed behaved properly.[19] This was crucial, since Antigny was home to vast troves of precious material Tyler had collected and written in the past. When he finished the first volume of the Byzantine art history book, he said, "If my name is to survive, it will be by reason of this work."[20] Therefore, it was essential that Elisina do all she could to preserve the treasures of Antigny.

---

17 Royall Tyler, "Hungary's Situation," March 11, 1940, 864.00/983, M1206, Roll 2, Microfilm Publications, Records of the Department of State Relating to Internal Affairs of Hungary, 1930–1944, NARA.
18 Diary entries, May 4–9, 1941, *Elisina Tyler's 1940–41 Diary*. Also, Royall Tyler to Mildred Barnes Bliss, September 1, 1940, Geneva, "Bliss–Tyler Correspondence," https://www.doaks.org/resources/bliss-tyler-correspondence/letters/01sep1940, accessed April 26, 2019.
19 Diary entries, June 19, 21, 29, July 15, 1940, *Elisina Tyler's 1940–41 Diary*; William R. Tyler, *The Castelvecchio Family*, 210–11.
20 Diary entry, March 23, 1941, *Elisina Tyler's 1940–41 Diary*.

Chapter 8

Tyler, in the company of Harold Tittmann, the American Consul General at Geneva, tried to get access into occupied France to visit Elisina, but the effort was unsuccessful.[21] In the middle of August, however, Elisina managed to secure a pass and cross the demarcation line to finally meet with his husband for four days.[22] Occasionally she managed to write him a card or a message came to her from Tyler, but Elisina was forced to manage to maintain order and security at Antigny alone for almost a year. Tyler, after failed attempts the previous year, succeeded in traveling to Vichy, but it was a long time before Elisina could join him. In the end, she managed to have Antigny and its precious contents sealed by the German authorities, and after long months of relentless effort she managed to secure a pass to Vichy to join Tyler.[23]

Tyler, for his part, tried to leave for the United States in May 1940 to resume his now regular reconnaissance missions, but due to a host of factors he had to abandon those plans. The main reason was that the future of the League of Nations hung in the balance. In the ongoing crisis, the leadership thought that at least a nucleus of the organization should be kept together in order to be able to start larger-scale work once again when the dust had settled. Avenol, the secretary general, wanted Tyler to be part of that smaller group and therefore to stay at Geneva. Tyler agreed that his doing so might mean he could do a more useful, if limited, service than if he spent a few weeks overseas. Reluctantly, then, he chose to stay, for, as he wrote, "I feel an obligation to do anything I can, at such a moment, for this outfit which has been my port of call for so many years."[24]

In the meantime, he did not forget the country in which he had spent the most time since 1924: Hungary. The current prime minister, Pál Teleki, on

---

21 Harold H. Tittmann, Jr. to Emma Roe Copelin Tittmann and Winifred Tittamnn, August 1940, Folder 59, Royall Tyler, 1940, Box 2, Tittmann, Harold H., Jr. Papers, Bulk, 1940–1945, Georgetown University Library Special Collections Research Center, Washington, D.C., USA.
22 Elisina Tyler to Mildred Barnes Bliss, August 26, 1940, Lyon, "Bliss–Tyler Correspondence," https://www.doaks.org/resources/bliss-tyler-correspondence/letters/26aug1940, accessed April 26, 2019.
23 Royall Tyler to Mildred Barnes Bliss, August 12, 1940, Geneva, "Bliss–Tyler Correspondence," https://www.doaks.org/resources/bliss-tyler-correspondence/letters/12aug1940, accessed April 25, 2019; Diary entries, August 15, September 2, 1940, April 2, June 16, 19, 27, 29, 1941, *Elisina Tyler's 1940–41 Diary*. Elisina spent the rest of the war with Tyler at Bern, but she still needed medical assistance during her long convalescence. Royal Tyler to Allen W. Dulles, July 19, 1943, File 477, NARA.
24 Royall Tyler to Mildred Barnes Bliss, May 18, 1940, Geneva, "Bliss–Tyler Correspondence," https://www.doaks.org/resources/bliss-tyler-correspondence/letters/18may1940, accessed April 25, 2019.

various occasions had sent notes saying that Tyler ought to visit Budapest. They had known each other for a long time, and in 1924, when Tyler began his work in Hungary as a League official, it was he who recommended Teleki to Secretary-General Eric Drummond for the post on the Mosul Committee, whose job was to draw the new border between Iraq and Turkey.[25] Now, the American tried to comply with Teleki's requests and traveled to Hungary in May 1940. The reason was, naturally, not to reminisce over past times but to face the realities brought on by the war. Teleki and people close to him in Hungary wanted to investigate every possibility that Hungary might face, and they were especially afraid of Germany. On the other hand, Hungarians almost as one believed in revision—partial or whole—and the First Vienna Award proved that without Hitler's good intensions this would not materialize. Teleki realized that further revision with German help would mean becoming a German vassal, while in the case of a German defeat, without Western help there was no real likelihood to get back any lost territories, particularly Transylvania. Also, there was the Russian bear in the east, a country with an ideology and political system that Hungarians in general loathed, and as already mentioned, Teleki had refused the Soviet proposal concerning Transylvania. So, to prepare for every possible contingency, Teleki forged a scheme to address a scenario in which Hungary was overrun by Germany and the country's independence was circumscribed or stolen. He wished to set up a fund of five million dollars in the United States in order to be able to finance a Hungarian immigrant government that would speak for the Hungarian nation and represent its true interests.[26]

Tyler had a role to play in this plan. First, he had talks with Lipót Baranyai, governor of the Hungarian National Bank in Trieste about the setup.[27] Since he knew the Hungarian elite, and particularly those in on the

---

25 Balázs Ablonczy, *Pál Teleki - The Life of a Controversial Hungarian Politician* (Wayne, NJ: Hungarian Studies Publications, 2007), 115–21.
26 For the history of the secret fund, see, Ministerial documents, 1939–1941, Pelenyi Papers, Rauner Special Collections Library, Dartmouth College (hereafter cited as Pelenyi Papers; John Pelényi, "The Secret Plan for a Hungarian Government in the West at the Outbreak of World War II," *Journal of Modern History* 36, no. 2 (June 1964): 170–77; Gyula Borbándi, "A Teleki-Pelényi terv nyugati magyar ellenkormány létesítésére" [The Teleki-Pelényi Plan to Establish a Western Hungarian Counter Government], *Új Látóhatár* 9, no. 2 (March–April 1966): 155–70.
27 Carlile Aylmer Macartney, *October Fifteenth: A History of Modern Hungary 1929–1945* (New York: Frederick A. Praeger, Inc. 1956–1957), 77.

plan, and he was an American citizen with good connections overseas, Tyler was asked to be the Hungarians' go-to man if the need arose. There was a short list of Hungarians who could get access to the proposed fund, and if only one of those could be present along with János Pelényi, the Hungarian minister in the United States, then Tyler, "a friend of our country, may be the third authorized for drawing on the fund."[28] In April, the fund was set up according to the plans, but in late May, Teleki changed his mind and had the money withdrawn.[29] Although the reasons are not absolutely clear as to the change in plan, probably the German victory in France convinced Teleki that the fund was not timely.

After Hungary joined the Tripartite Pact on November 20, 1940, Pelényi resigned his post in the United States and stayed there so he would be able to keep his contacts in America and through them provide any assistance for his country. When Tyler visited Budapest once again in late October, "after repeated requests from" Teleki, who knew of Pelényi's plan to resign, the Hungarian prime minister must have asked Tyler to help.[30] Tyler agreed again, and since he soon sailed overseas, he was physically on site to act on Pelényi's behalf as a contact person to the Hungarian government. For example, he sent Pelényi's message to Budapest in early 1941, which he received while he was in the United States. In it Pelényi asked whether he could be given money in order to be able to keep his contacts, which activity involved spending on clothing, lunches and dinners, otherwise he would have to take up some academic job, but in the latter case he would lose most of his now-still-active contacts.[31]

So, at the end of 1940 Tyler sailed to the United States for a two months stay. It seems from the available sources that this time one of his main activities there was to do Hungary a favor, and this must have been the reason he visited Budapest a few weeks earlier. Pelényi was just one part of his work

---

28 Pál Teleki to János Pelényi, March 17, 1940, in Pelényi, "The Secret Plan for a Hungarian Government," 176.
29 Pál Teleki to János Pelényi, May 21, 1940, and Lipót Baranyai to János Pelényi, May 21, 1940, Pelenyi Papers.
30 Royall Tyler to József Balogh, September 27, 1940, Balogh József Papers, Fond 1/3135, National Széchenyi Library, Budapest; Diary entry, November 9, 1940, *Elisina Tyler's 1940–41 Diary*.
31 János Pelényi to Royall Tyler, February 6, 1941, Royal [sic] Tyler after my resignation, Papers of John Pelényi, Hoover Institution Library and Archives (hereafter cited as Hoover Archives), Stanford University, Stanford, CA, USA.

there. From a private letter he sent right before he headed back to Europe, it is evident that a large amount of his time was taken up by trying to smooth out Hungarian financial problems. He worked on the standstill settlement between the two countries, a problem that went back to the mid-thirties. Most of his time, however, was taken up with working for the Hungarian National Bank, which had been sued by certain people who basically wanted to extract more money from the Bank than was due to them. This legal duel lasted three weeks. Tyler's side won in the end, but this intermezzo left him little time to take care of other things that preoccupied him. He did manage to squeeze in time to talk to government people in Washington, where he was reassured that the U.S. government understood the intricate problem Hungary faced.[32] This did not mean much perhaps, because America was far away from Europe and uninvolved in the ongoing war, but it must have been a psychological plus for Teleki and his circle, who planned to count on American help one way or another after the war was over.[33] From his later correspondence it is revealed that Tyler took with him certain papers with which Teleki entrusted him, and this must have been another request made in Budapest. Following Teleki's instruction, he left the papers in question in the custody of U.S. diplomat William C. Bullitt. However, a few years after the war, Bullitt denied possessing the papers and said he had given them back to Tyler before the latter embarked upon his journey back to Europe, a statement that Tyler repudiated. Unfortunately, regardless which of the two was negligent in the case, those papers are probably lost forever.[34]

With respect to the outcome of the war, Tyler remained optimistic. The passing of the Lend Lease Act in March 1941, just a few days after Tyler's sailing from the United States, signaled an American commitment to British victory, and Tyler thought Germany was "doomed" if Hitler could not suc-

---

32 He met, for example, with Adolf A. Berle and informed him about the situation in France and Hungary. Memorandum, January 31, 1941, Roll 2, Adolf A. Berle, Jr. Diary, 1937–1971, Franklin D. Roosevelt Presidential Library and Museum.
33 Royall Tyler to Mildred Barnes Bliss, March 2, 1941, New York, "Bliss–Tyler Correspondence," https://www.doaks.org/resources/bliss-tyler-correspondence/letters/02mar1941, accessed April 27, 2019; Memorandum, January 31, 1941, Roll 2, Adolf A. Berle, Jr. Diary, 1937–1971, Franklin D. Roosevelt Presidential Library and Museum, Hyde Park, USA.
34 See, Royall Tyler (Beirut, Lebanon) to William Bullitt, November 8, 1949, and April 4, 1950, and William Bullitt to Royall Tyler, March 29, 1950, Folder 2132, Tyler, Royall (1935–1950), Box 82, Series I. Correspondence, William C. Bullitt Papers, Yale Archives.

cessfully attack the British isles directly.³⁵ Such optimism was recorded by others as well. When he managed to spend a few days with his good friends the Blisses, Mildred Bliss wrote that she found him "at his very best—mentally, morally, physically."³⁶

In mid-March Tyler arrived in Portugal.³⁷ From there, through Spain and unoccupied France, he made his way to Geneva, and wanted to proceed from there to Budapest to meet with the Hungarian prime minister.³⁸ While en route to Geneva he learned that Pál Teleki had committed suicide. The Hungarian prime minister had been trying to steer his country's fate between forces beyond his control, although for some time he had been successful. On the one hand, with the Second Vienna Award on August 30, 1940, Hungary regained a significant part of Transylvania with many ethnic Hungarians, although a large number of Romanians came under its rule as well.³⁹ This, however, was achieved with the help of Germany and Italy, therefore Hungary had tied its fate to the Axis, which it joined in the fall of 1940. Teleki clearly understood the dilemma, but he fervently believed in revisionism, and that was what was expected of him from within Hungary as well. Still, Hungary had managed to remain neutral in the war, which was highly appreciated in Great Britain and in other Western countries.

The German's demand to cross Hungarian territory to press their offensive against Yugoslavia presented Hungary with an insoluble dilemma as just the previous December it had signed a treaty of friendship and non-aggression with its southern neighbor. With the German demand to use Hungary's territory against Yugoslavia, this fresh treaty had to be thrown out the window. This was too much for Teleki, who had been suffering from depression and illness in addition, and he committed suicide on the night of April 2,

---

35 Royall Tyler to Mildred Barnes Bliss, March 9, 1941, at sea, "Bliss–Tyler Correspondence," https://www.doaks.org/resources/bliss-tyler-correspondence/letters/09mar1941, accessed April 27, 2019.
36 Mildred Woods Bliss to Arthur Salter, April 17, 1941, Box 36, Series I: Personal Papers, 1878–1967 HUGFP 76.8, Papers of Robert Woods Bliss and Mildred Barnes Bliss, Harvard University Archives, USA.
37 Royall Tyler to János Pelényi, March 16, 1941, File: Royal [sic] Tyler after my resignation, Papers of John Pelényi.
38 Royall Tyler (Lisbon) to William Bullitt, March 18, 1941, Folder 2132, Box 82, William C. Bullitt Papers, Yale Archives.
39 On the antecedents, decision, and aftermath of the decision, see, Béni L. Balogh, *The Second Vienna Award and the Hungarian-Romanian Relations, 1940–1944* (New York: Columbia University Press, 2011).

1941.⁴⁰ It is true that Teleki's honor remained intact and he even became known as a martyr, but the trap that Hungary was in did not disappear, and Teleki's successor, László Bárdossy, was much more servile toward Germany.

The Tylers were shaken by Teleki's death. Elisina wrote in her diary upon hearing the news: Teleki was "a witty speaker, and a great gentleman," who "had the dignity and assurance that became his station." He possessed "a quick intelligence, a clear penetrating mind and easy grace. Nothing worth noting escaped him; without effort ideas fell into place in a delicately differentiated scale of values." She added: "He was a friend of ours, and the blow will affect Peter severely."⁴¹ Tyler, for his part, saw the loss of Teleki as "an exceedingly heavy blow."⁴² With Teleki gone, Tyler, and through him the Western world, lost a precious link in Central Europe, that much was clear. As mentioned, Teleki counted on Tyler as an important non-Hungarian to champion Hungary's cause in whatever capacity, as the story of the Teleki fund plainly showed. Also, as mentioned, Tyler conveyed some papers from Teleki to the United States, though it is not clear what that package contained. Tyler understood that Teleki had to choose between helping Germany or being invaded by it, and that left no room for a person of his temperament.

Tyler thought that "the irredentist education since 1919 bore its fruit. If a Govt. had tried to resist, it would have been swept away, and replaced by a Quisling."⁴³ He believed that taking a brave stand against Germany would have helped Hungary in Western eyes, but he of all people must have understood that it was easier said than done. And having also lost an important, confidential link in the highest office inside Hungary, that country now proved almost impossible to visit in person. When the U.S. entered the war in 1941 and Hungary declared war on the United States at the end of that year, the traveling there became completely impossible for Tyler.⁴⁴ Therefore, in order to learn about what was going on inside that country, he had to rely in the future on Hungarians visiting Switzerland.

---

40 The best biography of Teleki is Ablonczy, *Pál Teleki*.
41 Diary entry, April 3, 1941, *Elisina Tyler's 1940–41 Diary*.
42 Royall Tyler to Mildred Barnes Bliss, September 3, 1941, La Bourboule, "Bliss–Tyler Correspondence," https://www.doaks.org/resources/bliss-tyler-correspondence/letters/03sep1941, accessed April 28, 2019.
43 "Hungary," n.d., Hungary 1 Sept. 1931-, Thompson Todd Collection.
44 On the Hungarian declaration of war on the United States, see, Peterecz, "'A Certain Amount of Tactful Undermining.' Herbert C. Pell and Hungary in 1941," *Hungarian Quarterly* 52, no. 202-203 (Summer–Autumn 2011): 132–33.

Chapter 8

Actually, Tyler had been planning to visit Budapest in April after returning from the United States, possibly to inform Teleki and those in his close circle of his negotiations on the Hungarian government's behalf in America. With Teleki's suicide that plan came to naught. But he did not give up, and a month later he tried again to get to Budapest, this time through Italy. He managed to secure a visa for Italy, and got as far as Venice only to realize that there was no possibility to cross the border into Hungary or fly in by plane. He hoped to get a German visa and travel by rail, but in the meantime the U.S. consulate was withdrawn from Hungary, and finally he returned to Switzerland just before the American government issued an order stipulating that its citizens must not leave Switzerland.[45] Meanwhile, Germany attacked the Soviet Union on June 22, 1941, taking the war to the east.

All this took its toll on Tyler. When he finally was able to meet Elisina in Lyon in July after she had managed to secure a pass to unoccupied France, she wrote in her diary that he "was at a very low ebb, exhausted nervously and overcome by such a feeling of defeat as I've never experienced."[46] The couple spent the rest of the summer in an isolated hotel in south-central France. The extended rest was just what they needed, because by early September Tyler felt that he was back in his old psychological shape again and ready to resume work in Geneva and face the troublesome days ahead. Elisina, for her part, traveled to Hyères in southern France to take care of the villa that American novelist Edith Wharton had bequeathed to her.[47] And indeed, Tyler did restart his work in good health and with great enthusiasm, and was again doing what he had occupied him for the past decade: economic intelligence.[48]

After Tyler's three-month unpaid leave in the beginning of 1941, when he was in America, Charron pleaded with the League's new secretary general, Seán Lester, to retain Tyler at Geneva. As he saw it, the program that the remaining nucleus of the League's Economic Intellgience Section was able to provide, especially with an eye toward the postwar years, needed someone as thoroughly acquainted with as many countries and earlier reconstruc-

---

45 Royall Tyler to Mildred Barnes Bliss, September 3, 1941, La Bourboule, "Bliss–Tyler Correspondence," https://www.doaks.org/resources/bliss-tyler-correspondence/letters/03sep1941, accessed April 28, 2019. He had plans to visit Hungary later on as well, but it did not work out.
46 Ibid.; Diary entries, May 25, June 19, June 27, 1941, *Elisina Tyler's 1940–41 Diary*.
47 Royall Tyler to Mildred Barnes Bliss, September 3, 1941.
48 Royall Tyler to Mildred Barnes Bliss, October 13, 1941, Geneva, "Bliss–Tyler Correspondence," https://www.doaks.org/resources/bliss-tyler-correspondence/letters/13oct1941, accessed April 28, 2019.

tion efforts as Tyler. Although due to the prevailing circumstances no contract was obtainbable, provisional arrangements could be met for Tyler to go on working at Geneva.⁴⁹ After also having been on unpaid leave for most of the summer, in the fall Tyler was re-engaged with the League "as an expert attached to Department II for a period of three months," although at a reduced salary compared to what he had previously earned.⁵⁰ The agreement was regularly renewed, since it always ran for a short period. Tyler's job was to focus mainly on postwar settlement problems and economic data accumulation. After March 1943, he even received a substantial increase in his salary, at least compared to the 1,000 Swiss francs he was initially paid.⁵¹

The main product of Tyler's efforts during these years was *The League of Nations Reconstruction Schemes in the Inter-War Period*, officially published by the League of Nations in 1945.⁵² This book was clearly intended to serve the postwar efforts of economic and financial reconstructions. It wished to serve as a guidebook as to what should be repeated in the post-World War II reconstruction effort and what approaches ought to be neglected and substituted.

For the next twelve months, starting in the fall of 1941, there is little if any material available on Tyler's work but not on his insight. In all probability, he must have focused on his work at the League, while he was closely observing the ongoing war from the relative safety of Switzerland. In the summer of 1942, he managed to get away from the craziness of the world for some time, and in all likelihood, that was the time when he wrote his unfinished autobiography. A letter he wrote from a small hotel in the mountains appears to be the only surviving document in his hand that gives a clue to his state of mind in 1942. He wrote:

> By the time I came here [I] was able to take full advantage of my holiday—superb walks in this magnificent country, and a little, not too much work, and a bit of reading. I'm reading mainly Greek. I brought with me Aeschylus, and a volume of Herodotus, and Longus (Daphnis

---

49 René Charron to Seán Lester, May 16, 1941, Tyler, Royall; Section Files, Personnel Files, Box S. 896, File 3550, LNA.
50 Seán Lester to Royall Tyler, September 23, 1941, ibid.
51 Seán Lester to Royall Tyler, March 4, 1943, ibid.
52 Geneva: Economic, Financial and Transit Department, 1944.

and Chloe). Any other literature I require, I write for myself. Longus is a special pet of mine: I know him now almost as I used to know Izaac Walton when I was a boy, and I read him again and again with increased pleasure each time. Incomparable rhythm and music in that prose."[53]

What he wrote for himself and the notes he produced are interesting, because, although he made little effort to organize them, Tyler put down some of his thoughts on a wide range of topics based upon his experience in the past forty years. These notes are mostly sketches for a possible memoir, perhaps intended as elements of the later stages of the unfinished autobiography that suddenly ended in 1910. Among other subjects, he wrote about six countries in some detail: England, France, Germany, Italy, Hungary, and the United States. It was all the more important for him to record his thoughts because he realized that the living stereotypes of national traits were deeply flawed in many cases. Therefore, according to the accepted wisdom, the French "are witty; the Germans are thorough; the Br[itish] are phlegmatic; the It[alians] are talkative; the Sp[anish] are proud, etc."[54] He wanted to some extent to rectify these characterizations, and since he had spent most of his life among the people of various European nations, he had a good vantage point from which to view them.

Concerning the English, Tyler noted that they "don't believe in logic. They are suspicious of appeals to reason. What they recognize as supreme is that which is sensible… something which is in accordance with what one feels, as opposed to that which can be logically demonstrated."[55] He also made a comparison between the British and the French, the conclusion of which was that "each one regards as repulsive that which the other indulges."[56] He thought the present good relations between the two countries would be difficult to preserve, since one must not overlook "the underlying, bred-in-the-bone mistrust each country has for the other."[57] As for France, he highlighted its people's seemingly contradictory nature. Tyler believed that a very good argument

---

53 Royall Tyler to Mildred Barnes Bliss, August 28, 1942, Megève (Hte Savoie), "Bliss–Tyler Correspondence," https://www.doaks.org/resources/bliss-tyler-correspondence/letters/28aug1942, accessed April 28, 2019.
54 "Obiter," Hungary 1 Sept. 1931-, Thompson Todd Collection.
55 "England," ibid.
56 Ibid.
57 Ibid.

might be lost on a Frenchman, while an offhand expression might make a serious impression. But the French, and the Latin people in general, were "more adroit, tactful, graceful in the conduct of affairs than are the Anglo-Saxons."[58] Tyler never really liked Germany and the Germans, and the First World War but especially the Second obviously did not do anything to change it. He characterized Nazidom as "a socio-political South-Sea babble: collective madness of people frantic to make fortunes."[59] He also made an interesting comparison between the Anglo-Saxons and Germans with respect to conducting and concluding wars: "Fritz fancies himself as a warrior, the Anglo-Saxons fancy themselves as men of peace. Fritz loses wars, and then wins the peace, whilst the A.S., after having lost the peace, wins the war."[60] In his notes on Italy, he praised their diplomats for their humanity, which he saw as the main reason why Italian diplomats often succeeded where their other continental counterparts failed.[61] Regarding his home country, he mentioned the charm of New York together with the "monstrous regiment of women" and their "unrelenting dagger archness."[62] He also mentioned "professionalism and standardization," as well as the importance of the "slogan" and the "catch word."[63] The League of Nations was simply "the old Zoo," and Tyler observed that Wilson had "sold his League idea to Europe, which wrecked it. Will F.D.R. buy it back at scrap price, and make something of it again?"[64]

He also made a few notes about Jews, and not for the first time. When he had spent a longer time in Germany in 1905, he seemed to be impressed by the Jewish contribution within and to a host country that suppressed them. "Before I came to Germany I disliked Jews. Now I adore them. The way they are treated here, and the reading of Heine has brought this about. One very rarely hears of anyone doing anything in Germany that would suggest the possession of a Sense of Humour, but when one does, the man is a Jew. On the whole I think the way they take their treatment is admirable."[65] Now,

---

58 "France," ibid.
59 "Germany," ibid.
60 Ibid.
61 "Italy," ibid.
62 "USA," ibid.
63 Ibid.
64 "L. of N.," ibid.
65 Royall Tyler to Mildred Barnes, February 16, 1905, Cassel, "Bliss–Tyler Correspondence," https://www.doaks.org/resources/bliss-tyler-correspondence/1902-1908/16feb1905 accessed October 6, 2015.

Chapter 8

almost forty years later, he basically accused Hitler of delaying their absorption into Germany easily for centuries, and wrote that that was the German leader's "greatest crime" in his eyes.⁶⁶ Despite his young self having "adoring them," his latent anti-Semitism came out when he wrote that after the fall of Hitler the "Jews will be far more race-conscious, vindictive, dominating, than ever before, and will be supported by general consciousness among non-Jews of the monstrous injustice and inhumanity, meted out to them by Nazidom."⁶⁷ As in the case of his friend Levi, Tyler did not think twice about helping a Jew if he knew them well and that was what his humanity dictated. But he was also brought up in and infected with Anglo-Saxon anti-Semitism, which he could not rid himself of, nor did he make a particular effort to do so.

The longest of these notes concerned Hungary. This is understandable, since the greater part of his career, if his League years can be called that, was spent there, and even after he was no longer officially connected to that country, he maintained close relationships with its leading citizens. Also, Hungary must have represented something unique to Tyler. Almost all the other countries he had visited and especially lived in belonged to the West, whereas Hungary existed on an imaginary borderline between East and West. He thought he saw the reflection of ancient Hungarian history in the language, another striking difference to all other European languages. He theorized that words that repeated the same vowels in each syllable were a remnant and "the influence of the monotony of the great plains, the steppe, the *puszta*." He used the example of "*kereskedelem*," which means "trade" in English. This is a very original observation, but it is not surprising from a man who had mastered main tongues spoken in Europe and was well versed in European and Hungarian history. "Is there, in [the major European languages] a single word of 3 or more syllables each of which repeats the same vowel?", he wondered. Gender neutrality and the different use of conditional tenses were two other features that were strange to him.

He mentioned as well Hungary's conspicuous "Anglo-mania," meaning the sometimes meticulous imitation of the English upper classes among Hungarian nobles. Also, Hungarians reserved concept of "gentleman"

---

66 "Jews," Hungary 1 Sept. 1931-, Thompson Todd Collection.
67 Ibid.

for the British, and, Tyler believed, they knew it was a rare feature among Germans, and their looks when in conversation to Germans said as much. He had experience of listening to many Hungarians speaking among themselves in English, the result of which he deemed an "outlandish" Hunglish—English spoken with many Hungarian idiosyncrasies. In Tyler's mind the tragedy of modern Hungary was that it was in a state of being ripped apart by the opposing poles of Germany and Britain. The ongoing tension between the recovery of some of the lost territories with German help and the obvious fondness for the English could not be overcome, and when Hungary "had to choose between being invaded by G[ermany] and marching with G[ermany], that it decided to march." But it left a deep impression on Tyler that at a military ball at the best hotel in Budapest in February 1940, the event had started with the singing of "It's a Long Way to Tipperary."[68]

Tyler also put down pensive and philosophical notes as well. "We pay in the long run," he wrote. "We don't always pay precisely for what we've broken. It would be much simpler, if we did. It is vexatious to be naïve to pay for something one hasn't broken, and to have to remember the things one has broken, and not paid for."[69] Then he added that perhaps doing good for others sometimes would be repaid more bountifully.[70] But his deepest thoughts arose with the contemplation of what the world was going to be like after the war. He fancied these would become the book's foreword once all his notes could be woven into an overall narrative about the first four decades of the twentieth century:

> When the '39- war was brewing, people used to say that if it did break, it would be the end of civilisation, or, more cautiously, the end of civilization as we know it. Well, it has broken, and well might the whole globe is involved in it. It is perhaps not going to bring the end of the world, or even the end, literally, of civilisation, but it is certainly changing the face of the world. Our World: what was it? One set of things, one order of life, for those who knew it before 1914, another order of life for those who came upon it in the inter-war period. Now, yet another world is coming on.[71]

---

68 For the quotes in the last two paragraphs see, "Hungary," ibid.
69 "Obiter," ibid.
70 Ibid.
71 "Our World," ibid.

Chapter 8

He also outlined his thoughts on the coming of peace, and it is worth quoting them in full:

> The Allies supplied Hitler with the rank and file he needed to seize power. Ironically enough, they came largely from that very middle-class in order to make room for which the Empire had been swept away. But even now it does not appear to have dawned upon the Western countries that after 1918 it would have been safer from our own point of view to leave Germany with its traditional institutions, including its monarchies and its army, rather than drive into outlawry a class which had served the state for centuries, which possessed a great and relatively deserved prestige in the country, and to replace which Germany had no alternative ready. Our security, we apparently have yet to learn, depends upon our remaining strong and united ourselves, knowing what we want and willing to pay the price to obtain it, and not in attempting to keep Germany weak. If we again fail to agree among ourselves, as we did last time, the inducement to continue this Carthaginian-peace policy will fatally diminish, in the eyes of some of us, and the time will come when another inducement will become stronger: namely to utilise Germany towards the end which by then will have come to loom largest on our horizon. Thus ruthless settlement may give way to a competition to utilise the might of a resurgent Germany. In spite of the terrible punishment that country has taken, the race is still there, with its defects and its qualities, and is bound to become a prime factor once more. As to how to treat it, we had better guess again.[72]

With the United States joining the war after December 1941, that country found information-gathering in and about Europe to be even more crucial than before. Since Tyler counted as one of the best experts on Central and South-Eastern Europe, and his status in neutral Switzerland gave him some room to talk to various people, his services were required in the highest circles of the American government. When Tyler could no longer travel to Hungary in person, he became the channel through which information about Hungary arrived in the Anglo-Saxon world. Accordingly, in the fall of 1942 he submitted two reports pertaining to various dimensions of cur-

---

72   Royall Tyler, *One Name, Two Lives*, 88.

rent Hungarian affairs. This time his information was based not on his own experience, but on that of an unnamed Hungarian economist familiar with the highest circles, at least in finance and banking, but seemingly also to some extent in politics. Therefore, the information he relayed to Tyler—perhaps by mail, or perhaps the man traveled to Switzerland—could be seen as reliable.[73] At one point in these reports, Tyler noted intriguingly: "As already reported (Political Notes of September 9, 1942)." This can mean only one of two things. Either Tyler had full or at least partial access to the reports sent from Switzerland to the State Department, perhaps because he was a counselor on Hungarian matters, or he himself wrote that part of the report. In either case, he was deeply involved in the diplomatic reports sent to Washington.

In the beginning of August 1943, Tyler asked the League for an unpaid leave and termination of his salary due to the fact that he had accepted, with Lester's assent, "the post of representative of the U.S.A. Office of Foreign Relief and Rehabilitation, with the status of Special Assistant to the American Minister, Berne."[74] Although between 1943 and 1949, Tyler officially served as the Swiss representative of the United Nations Relief and Rehabilitation Administration (UNRRA) and, in 1944, as the special attaché to the U.S. Legation in Bern, in reality under his new title he also became an intelligence officer for the American government, and he finished out World War II in that capacity. His expertise in Central Europe in general, and in Hungary in particular, which country became strategically important from mid-1943 on, made him the number one expert at a time when the question of whether Hungary would leave Germany became urgent. During the next phase of his work for the USA, under the leadership of Allen Dulles, Tyler became involved in real spy work and played a prominent role in Hungary's efforts to leave the Axis alliance.

Certain figures in the Hungarian government—led by Miklós Kállay since March 1942—and persons close to them realized by 1943 that Germany was going to lose the war. This opinion was not new. As a matter of fact, before his death Teleki sent a memorandum to his ministers in London and Washington, respectively, warning that "the outcome of the war

---

73 "Hungary," Tyler's Reports, September 19 and 23, 1942, in Leland Harrison (Bern) to Cordell Hull, September 30, 1942, 864.00/1045, Roll 2, M1206, NARA.
74 Royall Tyler to Seán Lester, October 20, 1943. Tyler, Royall; Section Files, Personnel Files, Box S.896, File 3550, LNA.

is doubtful."⁷⁵ From 1942, especially after the German defeat at Stalingrad in early 1943, it became clear that the Soviet Union would not only drive out the Germans but might soon push them westward, which would result in a Russian presence on Hungary's borders, if not on Hungarian territory itself. Since it had declared war on the Soviet Union on June 26, 1941, a mere four days after the German attack, Hungary had irrevocably jumped on the German bandwagon. Also, because it sent fighting units to Russia, it had Soviet revenge to fear if the Red Army reached Hungary's territory first. It therefore became increasingly important to find a way out of the German grasp and into the Allied camp. This was a paramount goal in view of the possibility of a German invasion. Also, Hungary had regained some of the lost territories with Axis help, and if it did not switch sides in time, it would surely once again lose those territories, which were inhabited by almost two million ethnic Hungarians. In addition, there was a historical Hungarian antagonism toward Russia and then the Soviet Union, so the anti-Bolshevist Hungarian elite wanted to tie their fate to the Allies in the West.

The American-Hungarian relationship was friendly—although not really close—throughout the interwar years, but then the Hungarians took part in the German offensive against the Soviet Union, and declared war on the United States on December 13, 1941. The degree to which this last action was taken under German pressure is clearly shown by the fact that László Bárdossy, then the Hungarian prime minister, was "almost in tears" when he conveyed the declaration of war to the U.S. minister in Hungary, Herbert C. Pell.[76] The United Sates and especially the president did not take Hungary's case as crucial, and maintained that its war declaration, together with those of Romania and Bulgaria, had been made under duress, and only several months later, on June 5, 1942, did the United States Congress formally declare war on these countries.[77]

---

75 Prime Minister Pál Teleki's memorandum to the ambassadors in London and Washington about the future foreign policy of Hungary, 3 March 1941, quoted in László Zsigmond, ed., *Magyarország és a második világháború: Titkos diplomáciai okmányok a háború előzményeihez és történetéhez* [Hungary and the Second World War: Secret Diplomatic Papers to the Antecedents and History of the War] (Budapest: Kossuth Könyvkiadó, 1966), 288.

76 Herbert C. Pell, *Memoirs*, Folder: Herbert Pell, Trip to Hungary, Container 20, Herbert Claiborne Papers, Franklin D. Roosevelt Library, United States. Also see, Leonard Baker, *Brahmin in Revolt. A Biography of Herbert C. Pell* (New York: Doubleday & Co. 1972), 235, and György Barcza, "My Memoirs as a Diplomat 1911–1945 (Excerpts)," *Hungarian Quarterly* 36, no. 140 (1995): 95–96.

77 FRUS:1942, Europe, vol. 2: 833–42.

World War II – An Intelligence Officer

The long process to achieve the Hungarian goal began in 1943. The first important step toward this was taken earlier: it was imperative to change prime ministers. Miklós Horthy, the Regent, appointed Miklós Kállay to replace the clearly pro-German Bárdossy as premier in March 1942. Kállay was known as a moderate and an anti-Nazi politician, therefore reliable in trying to carry out an exit from the Axis camp. Since these Hungarian efforts are well known in the relevant historiography, the following section is going to focus mainly on Tyler's role in the negotiations and execution of the relevant plans—the Hungarian peace feelers.[78]

Allen Dulles arrived in Bern, Switzerland, at the end of 1942 as the main representative of William J. Donovan's Office of Strategic Services (OSS).[79] The OSS was called into being in the summer of 1942 as the successor to the Office of the Coordinator of Information (OCI). Its explicit aim was

---

78 The most significant contributions in English concerning Hungarian efforts to leave the Axis and then the German occupation are: Macartney, *October Fifteenth*; Florimond Duke and Charles M. Sawyer, *Name, Rank, and Serial Number* (New York: Meredith Press, 1969); Nicholas Kállay, *Hungarian Premier. A Personal Account of a Nation's Struggle in the Second World War* (New York: Columbia University Press, 1954); Elisabeth Barker, *British Policy in South-East Europe in the Second World War* (London: Palgrave Macmillan, 1976), 244–59; Wilhelm Höttl, *The Secret Front. Nazi Political Espionage 1938–1945* (New York: Enigma Books, 2003); László Borhi, *Dealing with Dictators. The United States, Hungary, and East Central Europe, 1942–1989* (Bloomington & Indianapolis, IN: Indiana University Press, 2016), 12–49. Some of the most relevant Hungarian sources are the following: Gyula Juhász, ed., *Magyar-Brit titkos tárgyalások 1943-ban* [Secret Hungarian–British Negotiations in 1943] (Budapest: Kossuth Kiadó 1978); Gyula Kádár, *A Ludovikától Sopronkőhidáig* [From the Ludovica to Sopronkőhida], vols. 1–2. (Budapest: Magvető 1978); György Barcza, *Diplomata emlékeim, 1911–1945* [My Diplomatic Memoir], vols. 1–2. (Budapest: Európa História, 1994); István G. Vass, "Bakach-Bessenyey György tárgyalásai az Egyesült Államok megbízottaival Bernben, 1943. augusztus 28. és 1944. március 19. között: A Kállay-kormány béketapogatózásainak újabb dokumentumai" [The Negotiations of György Bakach-Bessenyey with the Emissaries of the United States in Bern, between August 28, 1943, and March 19, 1944: New Documents of the Peace Feelers of the Kállay Government], *Levéltári Közlemények* 65, nos. 1–2 (1994): 153–205; Antal, Czettler, *A mi kis élethalál kérdéseink – A magyar külpolitika a hadbalépéstől a német megszállásig* [Our Little Life and Death Questions. Hungarian Foreign Policy from Entering the War until German Occupation] (Budapest: Magvető, 2000); Zoltán András Kovács, "A Janus-arcú tábornok. Adalékok Ujszászy István vezérőrnagy pályaképéhez" [The Janus-faced General. Additions to the Career of Major General István Ujszászy], in Haraszti György (ed.), *Vallomások a holtak házából. Ujszászy István vezérőrnagynak, a 2. vkf. Osztály és az Államvédelmi Központ vezetőjének az ÁVH fogságában írott feljegyzései* [Testimonies from the House of the Dead. The Notes of Major General István Ujszászy, Head of Department 2 of Intelligence and Counterintelligence and State Security Center, during in his Captivity by ÁVH] (Budapest: Corvina, 2007), 72–153; András Joó, *Kállay Miklós külpolitikája. Magyarország és a háborús diplomácia 1942–1944* [The Foreign Policy of Miklós Kállay. Hungary and Wartime Diplomacy 1942–1944] (Budapest: Napvilág Kiadó, 2008).

79 Allen Dulles, "European Affairs as Viewed from Berne," September 26, 1944, Council on Foreign Relations Meetings Records, Box 440, Folder 3, Subseries 4B: Records of Meetings, Council on Foreign Relations Meetings Records 1920-1995, Seely G. Mudd Manuscript Library, Princeton.

Chapter 8

to analyze strategic information required by the Joint Chiefs of Staff (JCS) and conduct special operations as necessary. Other functions included propaganda, espionage, subversion, and even post-war planning. Its director, General William J. Donovan, a competent executive and a friend of Franklin D. Roosevelt, also had the privilege of reporting personally to the president. JCS, however, of which the OSS was an "agency," gave it perfunctory treatment and often stymied its work. This poor relationship between the military and the new intelligence organization constrained OSS operations throughout the war, and sometimes discouraged effective intelligence gathering and dissemination. Although the OSS was active in every theater of the war, its far-flung outposts never worked together harmoniously. An example is the well-known OSS Research and Analysis Branch in London. Despite great potential and high hopes, it spent its time during World War II, as historian Nelson MacPherson put it, "in a desperate, if largely futile, struggle to secure a meaningful role."[80] The mutual distrust among the different branches of the OSS, and between the OSS and the larger military establishment, did not bode well for success in clandestine operations and intelligence collection aimed at neutralizing the enemy and ensuring Allied dominance, or in guerilla warfare operations designed to disrupt Axis power and communications lines. The two great prizes in Europe were, naturally, Germany and Italy, but the smaller satellite countries also received considerable attention. Hungary constituted a leading example.[81]

Although militarily insignificant, Hungary derived its importance from its geographical situation, its food production, and such raw materials as

---

[80] Nelson MacPherson, "Reductio Ad Absurdum: The R&A Branch of OSS/London," *International Journal of Intelligence and Counter Intelligence* 15, no. 3 (2002): 390.

[81] This paragraph was based largely on works in the vast field dealing with the history of the OSS: Allen Dulles, *The Secret Surrender* (New York: Harper & Row, 1966); Richard Harris Smith, *OSS: The Secret History of America's First Central Intelligence Agency* (Berkeley, CA: University of California Press, 1972); Kermit Roosevelt, ed., *War Report of the OSS* (New York: Walker & Co., 1976); Anthony Cave Brown, *The Last Hero: Wild Bill Donovan* (New York: Times Books, 1982); Bradley F. Smith, *The Shadow Warriors: O.S.S. and the Origins of the C.I.A.* (New York: Basic Books, 1983); Barry M. Katz, *Foreign Intelligence: Research and Analysis in the Office of Strategic Services, 1942-1945* (Cambridge, MA: Harvard University Press, 1989); Neal H. Petersen, ed., *From Hitler's Doorstep: The Wartime Intelligence Reports of Allen Dulles, 1942-1945* (University Park, PA: Pennsylvania State University Press 1996); Robert Louis Benson, *A History of US Communications Intelligence during World War II: Policy and Administration* (Fort Meade, MD: National Security Agency Center for Cryptologic History, 1997); Christof Mauch and Jeremiah Riemer, *The Shadow War Against Hitler: The Covert Operations of America's Wartime Secret Intelligence Service* (New York: Columbia University Press, 2003).

bauxite and crude oil. An early 1943 OSS report estimated that Hungary produced enough crude petroleum, of a quality nearly equal to America's best, to fill about 200 tank cars per day.[82] The Hungarian political elite was rightly considered to be the most independent among the German satellite countries: legal opposition survived there, and the government had managed to protect the Jewish population despite the various anti-Jewish laws passed earlier. The new premier, Kállay, faced the enormous task of establishing contact with the Anglo-Saxon powers and securing a mutual understanding that would allow Hungary to withdraw from the war. At first, Hungarians were in negotiations primarily with the British, mainly in Istanbul and Stockholm, and they achieved some tentative success. In early September 1943, a preliminary armistice based on the formula of unconditional surrender was signed by the representatives of Hungary and HMG at Istanbul, and there were plans for secret British missions to be sent to Hungary.[83] Prime Minister Churchill informed President Roosevelt of this development a few days before the Second Quebec Conference, but the news had no discernible effect on the latter, who found it only "interesting."[84] Talks were also going on between American and Hungarian representatives. Despite endeavors for contacts to continue in Turkey as well, the main arena for such activity was Switzerland.[85]

Once in Switzerland, Dulles built up a wide web of contacts from the Axis countries and other places, since neutral Switzerland was a perfect location for such activities.[86] His main focus was obviously Germany and Italy, but from the spring of 1943, Hungary gradually started to assume a more important place on the list of places where useful work could be done. This was where Tyler, who was in many ways Dulles's right-hand man, entered the picture. When the Hungarian government decided to send out peace feelers to such places as Istanbul, Stockholm, Lisbon, and Bern, in Switzerland, there

---

82 Telegram, January 5, 1943, Series 15 Reports, 1939–1977, Subseries 15A English, 1943–1977, Allen W. Dulles Papers, Digital Files (hereafter cited as ADP-DF).
83 Juhász, *Magyar-Brit titkos tárgyalások 1943-ban*, 63–65. For the British secret missions, see, Peterecz, "SOE Operations in Hungary during the Second World War," in *Contemporary Perspectives on Language, Culture and Identity in Anglo-American Contexts*, Éva Antal, Csaba Czeglédi, Eszter Krakkó, eds. (Cambridge: Cambridge Scholars Publishing, 2019), 216–30.
84 Quoted in Juhász, *Magyar-brit titkos tárgyalások 1943-ban*, 235.
85 As for different Hungarian peace feelers in Europe in 1943, see FRUS, 1943, 1, 484–93, 497–501.
86 For Dulles' activities during his war years in Switzerland, see, Petersen, *From Hitler's Doorstep*.

was no doubt that the go-to-man in the latter would by Tyler. Now effectively working for the OSS, he coordinated, to a large degree, the Hungarian contacts he met, the memoranda he forwarded to Dulles, and how he informed the secret Hungarian emissaries about the relevant possibilities and requirements. This was a delicate job. Both sides had to try to carry out this activity in the strictest confidence and secrecy, because if Germany got wind of it, it might decide to occupy Hungary.

Tyler was already having informal meetings with György Ottlik in the fall of 1942. Ottlik was general editor of the Hungarian daily *Pester Lloyd*, and a long-time acquaintance of Tyler, and their meetings were the first contact of this nature between Hungary and the United States. The first noteworthy Hungarian contact with the Americans in Bern, however, was made in early March of 1943. The Hungarian side at this time sought only "non-committal conversations," and it approached the American side through Tyler.[87] Most probably it was Antal Radvánszky of the National Bank of Hungary who carried out the talks on behalf of Lipót Baranyai, the president of the same institution. Baranyai had resigned in early February in protest against the ongoing financial pressure from Germany.[88] The letters back and forth between Budapest and Bern were carried in the Swiss diplomatic pouch every two weeks, and were addressed to Aladár Szegedy-Maszák, *head of the political section of* the Foreign Ministry.[89] By return pouch, Tyler regularly received the Hungarian dailies, which he read with an eye to detecting the general sentiment in Hungary and reporting on it.[90] Evidently, there were more Hungarian emissaries sent separately by Kállay, for instance Istanbul or Stockholm. This struck the Americans as strange, because they believed a concentrated effort in one location would be more useful but Tyler was of the opinion that "Hungary is fairy-land, and everything is possible there."[91] Dulles, who considered Tyler his "mentor on Hungarian (not to speak of other) affairs," thought that Tyler's "unique possibilities" in this field "should be utilized," and with the special

---

87 Telegram 193-C out, March 3, 1943, Series 15 Reports, 1939–1977, Subseries 15A English, 1943–1977, ADP-DF. According to Macartney, it was Tyler who first suggested establishing some informal liaison between the two countries. See, Macartney, *October Fifteenth*, 122–23.
88 Royall Tyler to Allen W. Dulles, February 9, 1943, Lipót Baranyai to Royall Tyler, March 9, 1943, File 477, 1943, 190/38/24/5, Box 12, RG 226, NARA.
89 Anthony Radavansky to Royall Tyler, March 24, 1943, ibid.
90 Royall Tyler to Allen W. Dulles, March 29, 1943, ibid.
91 Royall Tyler to Allen W. Dulles, April 1, 1943, ibid.

sense of a pragmatic manager he gave Tyler almost total freedom in dealing with the Hungarian contacts.[92] This was a good decision because, in addition to understanding the present European situation, Tyler also enjoyed the unqualified confidence of the Hungarian political elite.

Dulles, for his part, also knew Hungary comparatively well because of his years in Switzerland at the end of World War I and his participation in the Paris Peace Conference, and he understood Hungarian issues. He believed that Hungary, together with Romania and Bulgaria, was "in a position to put sprags in the wheel of various kinds of economic and military cooperation."[93] In Dulles's view, "the Hungarians are past masters in quiet obstructionism and in tactics of passive resistance which might be converted to our military advantage."[94] Both Tyler and Dulles were "convinced [of the] good faith of this [Hungarian] approach," and the latter asked the State Department for instructions on to how to proceed.[95] At the time, the State Department considered it too early to deal with Hungarian peace feelers in earnest and cautioned "extreme reserve" in accepting Hungarian propositions.[96] However, a green light was given to unofficial action, and the Americans—meaning first and foremost Tyler—started long discussions with the Hungarians, especially with Baranyai, the former bank president and Tyler's personal friend.

Tyler met both Baranyai and Antal Radvánszky several times in June and July. For months, their supposedly secret talks centered on what Hungary wanted to achieve. However, the Germans obviously knew about Baranyai's trip to Switzerland, and, in all likelihood, they also guessed correctly the goal of the trip. This was in a large part thanks to the almost 2,000 German agents planted in Hungary, some of them in influential political and military positions.[97] But the German counterespionage was busy and effective as

---

92   Allen W. Dulles to Royall Tyler, March 25, 1943, ibid.; Telegram 193-C out, 3 March 1943, Series 15 Reports, 1939–1977, Subseries 15A English, 1943–1977, ADP-DF. Tyler regularly sent memos and notes on his conversations with various Hungarian contacts, and sometimes he sent his own translations of leading politicians' speeches, most typically those of Kállay, and other newspaper articles from Hungary. He was also instrumental for Dulles concerning Bulgarian, Italian, Spanish, and French issues as well.

93   Telegram 1529, March 6, 1943, quoted in Petersen, *From Hitler's Doorstep*, 48.

94   Telegram 4158, Section Two, July 14, 1943, quoted in Ibid., 82.

95   Telegram 193-C out, 3 March 1943, Series 15 Reports, 1939–1977, Subseries 15A English, 1943–1977, ADP-DF.

96   The Department of State to the British Embassy, April 28, 1943, FRUS, 1943, vol. 1, 492.

97   Igor-Philip Matić, *Edmund Veesenmayer: Agent und Diplomat der nationalsozialistischen Expansionspolitik* (Munich: De Gruyter Oldenbourg, 2002), 206.

well. László Veress, after escaping to Italy in the summer of 1944, informed his Allied interrogators that the Germans "made no secret of having decoded a long report by Mr. Royall Tyler on his conversation with Mr. Bede in Switzerland in January."[98]

Hungary's main points were that it would be willing to antagonize Germany only with concrete backing from the Anglo-Saxon powers. Hungary required guarantees not only against possible German reprisals but also against the approaching Soviet Red Army. Such a scenario was possible only if the British and Americans decided to make a Balkan landing and then proceed north toward Budapest and Vienna. The anti-Bolshevist Hungarian leaders hoped that their stance would bind the Americans and British to their aims. Since the Soviet Union was formally allied with the United States and Great Britain, however, there was no realistic prospect for such an outcome. In a war of such scale, military strategy overrode any secondary political aims. As Tyler tried to explain to one of his Hungarian contacts, "the Russians [a]re our allies, and we would certainly be loyal to them. It [i]s equally vain to hope we would discuss the future organisation of Europe with the Hunks while they [a]re in the field against our allies."[99] Thus, the Americans clearly declared that there could be no meaningful talks as long as Hungarians were fighting the Soviets, together with the Germans. Although the Hungarian political leadership had been trying to order their troops home for some time, the Germans would not allow that. The Hungarians did not truly grasp the situation and so come to the correct conclusion that for the United States, the main goal was to defeat Hitler's Germany and keep the shaky Allied alliance together at all costs. The American government regularly informed both the British and the Soviets about its clandestine plans concerning the enemy. Hungarian whims did not and could not merit serious consideration in comparison with the gigantic task of defeating the Germans.

Also, for a long time the Hungarians clung to the almost blind belief that there would be an Allied landing in the Balkans, and, as a consequence, Hungary might fall into the Anglo-Saxon sphere of interest.[100] This myth

---

98 Report on László Veress' Interrogation, July 13, 1944, Folder 1741, Box 61, RG 226 Entry 119A, NARA.
99 Royall Tyler to Allen W. Dulles, 1 April 1943, File 477, NARA.
100 See, Joó, *Kállay Miklós külpolitikája*, 136–46; Rudolf Andorka, *A madridi követségtől Mauthausenig* [From the Madrid Legation to Mauthausen] (Budapest: Kossuth, 1978), 295–96, 304, 310; Horthy, *Memoirs*, 249.

was again based on a mistaken interpretation of Allied policies and British initiatives, and, of course, on Hungarian hopes.[101] Due to the realities of the war, a Balkan landing was never a very seriously considered option.[102] It must be noted, however, that in the first half of 1943, when the first round of negotiations began with the aim of Hungary perhaps leaving the war, even some British Foreign Office officials thought there was a chance and need for an Allied landing in the Balkans.[103] What is more, in the spring of 1943 it was also accepted in the U.S. State Department that it was "pretty plain that the second front will be in the Balkans."[104] In the summer of 1943, during the First Quebec Conference (August 17–24) the question was seemingly put to rest for good, however, when the Balkan area was excluded as a possible candidate from any Allied military landing. Only special operations, supplying local partisans and engaging in bombing campaigns, were on the docket.[105] Nonetheless, the Americans informed the Hungarians as late as mid-September that "their plan was to arrive in Central Europe before the Russians, nor did they wish to see Russian influence in the Balkans."[106] As late as mid-November, Eisenhower supposedly had recommended a Balkan move if it were led by a British commander.[107]

---

101 See, Miklós Lojkó, "The Failed Handshake over the Danube. The Story of Anglo-American Involvement in the Liberation of Central Europe at the End of the Second World War," *Hungarian Studies* 13, no. 1 (1998/99): 126. On British plans concerning post-war Central and Eastern Europe see András D. Bán, *Pax Britannica. Brit külügyi iratok a második világháború utáni Kelet-Közép-Európáról, 1942–1943* [Pax Britannica. British Foreign Policy Papers about Post-War Central and Eastern Europe, 1942–1943] (Budapest: Osiris, 1996).

102 On the Allied strategy and the role of the Balkans in it, see, Michael Howard, ed. *Grand Strategy*, vol. IV, August 1942–September 1943 (London: Her Majesty's Stationery Office, 1972); John Ehrman, ed. *Grand Strategy*, vol. V, August 1943–September 1944 (London: Her Majesty's Stationery Office, 1956); *Foreign Relations of the United States, Conferences at Washington and Quebec, 1943*, and *The Conferences at Cairo and Tehran, 1943*, (U.S. Government Printing Office, 1943).

103 Elisabeth Barker, "Problems of the Alliance: Misconceptions and Misunderstanding," in William Deakin, Elisabeth Barker, and Jonathan Chadwick, eds. *British Political and Military Strategy in Central, Eastern and Southern Europe in 1944* (London: Macmillan Press, 1988), 43.

104 Memorandum, May 12, 1943, Roll 4, Adolf A. Berle, Jr. Diary, 1937–1971, Franklin D. Roosevelt Presidential Library and Museum.

105 See, "Memorandum by the United States Chiefs of Staff," August 9, 1943, as a preparatory paper to the First Quebec Conference, August 17–24, 1943, in FRUS:1943, Conferences at Washington and Quebec: 475. The proposal became official Allied policy at the Cairo and Teheran Conferences toward the end of the year.

106 Lisbon, September 18, 1943, Folders 19–20, Budapest/Lisbon, Wodianer Reports, August 1943–March 1944, Roll 1, MF 53671, György Bakach-Bessenyei Papers, P 2066, HNA.

107 Harry C. Butcher, *My Three Years with Eisenhower. The Personal Diary of Captain Harry C. Butcher, USNR. Naval Aid to General Eisenhower, 1942 to 1945* (New York: Simon and Schuster, 1946), 440–41.

Chapter 8

When the Hungarians received the information that there would be no Anglo-Saxon landing in the Balkans, they refused to consider it as reliable intelligence.[108] So, there was confusion married to hope in Hungarian minds as to the real significance of the Balkans in the Allied strategy. The Hungarians concluded that there would be no Allied landing in the Balkans only after the Teheran Conference at the end of 1943, by which time their room for possible maneuvering was very narrow.[109] The Allies naturally knew that the Hungarians hoped for a landing in South-East Europe. British Permanent Under-Secretary Alexander Cadogan well summarized the Allied stance on this issue when he minuted the following after an official in Cairo, Christopher Steel, raised the issue in early March: "Mr. Steel seems to share the delusion of some of the satellites that we can stage a 'Balkan expedition.' We can't. We could tell Mr. Steel this. We can't tell the satellites, but while they remain in ignorance of the truth we can discount ... the value of their 'peace feelers'."[110]

This issue is important, because it was largely the uncertainty about the location of the second front that helped the Americans demand specific and sometimes vigorous steps on the part of Hungary. These included, among others things, to prevent the transit of German troops across Hungarian territory by road or rail; to keep the Germans from using Hungarian airfields; and, above all, to break with Germany.[111] Since these demands went farther than anything the Hungarians were prepared to do, they instead suggested largely naïve contributions to the Allied war effort, especially in connection with a landing in the Balkans. In the spring and summer of 1943, Hungarian leaders still imagined that they could define the outcome in some way. Dulles grew exasperated with them at times. He noted in July:

> It is appreciated that there is on the part of these people a tantalizing tendency to consider that they deserve special treatment because their table manners happen to be better than their neighbors, to say nothing of their

---

108 Antal Ullein-Reviczky, *German War—Russian Peace. The Hungarian Tragedy* [1947] trans. Lovice Mária Ullein-Reviczky (Saint Helena, CA: Helena History Press, LLC, 2014), 134, 187.
109 Even later, however, there is evidence that they hoped against hope that there would after all be an Allied landing in the southeast of Europe. Royall Tyler to Allen W. Dulles, January 24, 1944, File 477, NARA.
110 Cadogan's minute March 11, 1944, quoted in Barker, *British Political and Military Strategy*, 49.
111 Telegram 387 out, 3 July 1943; Telegram 443 out, 15 July 1943, Telegram 193-C out, 3 March 1943, Series 15 Reports, 1939–1977, Subseries 15A English, 1943–1977, ADP-DF.

irritating insistence on some deserved heritage from their history of one thousand years. It is my belief that these ideas should be knocked out of their heads if possible, and they be brought down to cold realities of the military necessities of the situation."¹¹²

The State Department and the Joint Chiefs of Staff were in no hurry to decide how much they wanted to exploit the Hungarian connection. This behavior did not satisfy Dulles either. The American leadership wanted to avoid any political complications, and there was disagreement between the JCS and the State Department as to how and when to proceed. Unsurprisingly, in late August 1943 Dulles complained that "to date it has not been possible to obtain any commitments or opinion on matter from State [Department] notwithstanding [the] fact that we are in constant personal contact with the Hungarians."¹¹³ Almost half a year after establishing contact, the parties had achieved only a tentative proposal without official American support and approved by the Hungarians only in principle.

It was not until mid-September that the JCS issued directives favoring clandestine activity in Hungary.¹¹⁴ By then, events on the battlefield had heightened that country's strategic significance. Assistant Secretary of State Adolf A. Berle expressed his interest in it and wrote to Secretary of State Cordell Hull that "Hungary is probably the most important factor in the Balkan situation since her army is reasonably good, reasonably intact, and capable of rendering some assistance against the Germans in due time were the Hungarian Government disposed to do this."¹¹⁵ Meanwhile, in the early fall, Baron György Bakach-Bessenyey, formerly Hungarian minister at Vichy, arrived as the new Hungarian minister in Switzerland and became the chief negotiating partner for Dulles and Tyler. In fact, when Bakach-Bessenyey was already on his way to present his letter of recall at Vichy he met Tyler and started the urgent negotiations about Hungary's future.¹¹⁶ The

---

112 Telegram 4158, Section Two, July 14, 1943, quoted in Petersen, *From Hitler's Doorstep*, 82.
113 Telegram 479 in, August 29, 1943, Telegram 193-C out, March 3, 1943, Series 15 Reports, 1939–1977, Subseries 15A English, 1943–1977, ADP-DF.
114 Memo on the Sparrow Mission, January 1, 1945, ibid.
115 A. A. Berle, Jr. to the Secretary of State (Cordell Hull), September 18, 1943, Decimal File, 1940–1944, from 740.00119 EW1939/1635 to /1949, Box 2956, RG 59, NARA. In American minds, Hungary was sometimes included in the Balkan region.
116 Royall Tyler to Allen W. Dulles, August 28, 1943, August 29, 1943, File 477, NARA.

Chapter 8

two Americans saw him as the "only person endowed with authority from headquarters in this country," and believed that through him there was a "possibility of bolstering resistance to Axis in his country."[117] The State Department was slow to respond, perhaps, as one historian put it, because of its "reluctance to acknowledge and accept the legitimacy of independently produced intelligence [which] stemmed from its own lack of experience and knowledge in this area," and because it "placed little priority on, nor saw much need for, intelligence collection and evaluation."[118] In the meantime, Dulles and Tyler tried to make the Hungarian envoy understand that his country's unrealistic attitude was unacceptable. Tyler tried to convince Bakach-Bessenyey that, despite the risks of a German occupation, the greatest risk of all for Hungary was to do nothing.[119]

When Italy jumped out of the war in September 1943, Tyler warned the Hungarians that this was the last chance to leave Germany, but the Hungarian side responded that "complete domination of Italy by the Germans is held to be a harbinger of what the Hungarians could expect if they were to withdraw at this time from their connection with the Germans."[120] Kállay first wanted to cleanse his general staff of pro-German elements. This obviously sound approach, however, certainly gave the Americans the impression that "Kállay meant to do nothing more than give us a hopeful line of talks, so as to get himself recorded as wanting to help, but that when it came to doing something, he would always find an excuse to defer."[121] Tyler had earlier gone so far as to characterize Kállay as "a sly politician, lazy and not over-scrupulous. He regards Parliament, even with the four-fifths majority he has in it, as an all-round nuisance. At the same time, he thinks the Totalitarians are going to lose the war, and he is anxious to preserve for Hungary (and himself) whatever good will may attach, on the winning side, to the country's

---

117 Telegram 407 out, 8 July 1943, Series 15 Reports, 1939–1977, Subseries 15A English, 1943–1977, ADP-DF. It is interesting to note that Bakach-Bessenyey provided Dulles with petrol for months. Memorandum from Allen W. Dulles to Royall Tyler, November 12, 1943, File 477, NARA; Dulles's notes on various matters related to his work in Switzerland during World War II, 23 March 1965, Series 15 Reports, 1939–1977, Subseries 15A English, 1943–1977, ADP-DF.
118 Betty Abrahamsen Dessants, "Ambivalent Allies: OSS' USSR Division, the State Department, and the Bureaucracy of Intelligence Analysis, 1941–1945," *Intelligence and National Security* 11, no. 4 (1996): 725, 727.
119 Royall Tyler to Allen W. Dulles, August 29, 1943, File 477, NARA.
120 Telegram 5876, September 21, 1943, quoted in Petersen, *From Hitler's Doorstep*, 129.
121 Royall Tyler to Allen W. Dulles, October 25, 1943, File 477, NARA.

traditional representative institutions."[122] The Americans looked with suspicion at Kállay's stalling.

In addition, there were also misunderstandings and sometimes outright animosity among the various OSS centers, and voices from Lisbon, Algiers, or Istanbul argued against the planned mission for Hungary.[123] Other OSS people sent a suggestion to Bern that Hungary lie low. This was in opposition to Tyler's efforts in Switzerland. He informed Dulles that, via Bakach-Bessenyey, he had the following message sent to the Hungarian prime minister:

> Kállay was free to make up his mind as to the value of "advice" given to him, but that his attitude reminded me of the behavior of a sick man who, when the doctor advises something unpleasant, looks around for a healer or quack who is willing to tell him about a pleasanter way to get well. It had not been suggested that Kállay should defy the Germans, or do anything spectacular. He had merely been given an opportunity of showing that he was willing to help in a modest way, and it was discouraging to find him invoking arguments which would no doubt apply if he had been asked to make some public reversal of Hungary's war policy, but had no real bearing on the little matter under discussion.[124]

This was, of course, the American point of view, and from Bern it was easy to criticize Kállay, who was in a tight situation. On the other hand, the American side could not understand the Hungarian hesitancy. Kállay, from his point of view, wanted to avoid both German and Russian occupation. In this intricate situation he felt, "There is therefore no other way, no other possibility, than to take the most difficult decision: *not to take a jump in the dark, in either direction* ... Hungary must therefore gain time, for with time things will improve for us."[125]

To make things worse, German counterintelligence knew what was in the offing.[126] They were able to read some of the American cables going in

---

122 "Talk with a Hungarian Diplomatist," Memorandum by Tyler, May 9, 1943, ibid.
123 Peterecz, "Sparrow Mission: A US Intelligence Failure during World War II," *Intelligence and National Security* 27, no. 2 (2012): 251–52.
124 Royall Tyler to Allen W. Dulles, October 25, 1943, File 477, NARA.
125 Miklós Kállay to Antal Ullein-Reviczky, March 1, 1944, in Ullein-Reviczky, *German War—Russian Peace*, 109–10. Emphasis in the original.
126 Borhi, *Dealing with Dictators*, 40.

Chapter 8

and out of Bern and were well informed about the goals of their disloyal satellite.[127] Ironically, the Germans were able to read some of the American messages partially thanks to their Hungarian colleagues, who were a small but effective group and had been in close cooperation with German signals intelligence since 1922.[128] In early November an important telegram arrived from the State Department to Dulles: "JCS have approved specifically effort to detach H[ungary] and other satellites from Axis immediately. Adolf aware of this decision and informing his boys. JCS directive should govern your attitude."[129] "Adolf" in all possibility meant Adolf Berle, whose name might have been mentioned to let Dulles know that the State Department, too, was aware of the JCS directive.[130] Dulles, for his part, was skeptical of the plan under the present circumstances. He showed considerable insight into the Hungarian character when he noted, "Hungarians are easy going unheroic people [and] they are unlikely [to] take course which involves immediate risks."[131] He may well have formed this opinion after World War I, but he may also have derived it from a passage in the Hungarian foreign minister's message to Switzerland: "I very much hope that the relations will not break off, but we would have to bow to this, because, at the moment, our efficiency is very limited and as perhaps Mr. T. [Tyler] knows as well, we do not possess a special tendency for conspiracy."[132]

Tyler also took on passing former prime minister Bethlen's memorandum to Washington. Bethlen was still seen by some as the possible future leader of Hungary, and he enjoyed prestige in Western political circles largely due to the fact that he had managed to govern with stability for a long period

---

127 "Hungary," July 13, 1944, Folder 1741, Box 61, Entry 119A, RG 226, NARA; Interview with Dr. Hottl [*sic*], February 19, 1966, Series 1, Correspondence, Box 32, Folder 11, Hungary, 1918–1968, Allen W. Dulles Papers, Seeley G. Mudd Manuscript Library, Princeton (hereafter cited as ADP); Höttl, *The Secret Front*, 183, 268.
128 David Alvarez, "No Immunity: Signals Intelligence and the European Neutrals, 1939–45," *Intelligence and National Security* 12, no. 2 (1997): 22–43. According to Anthony Brown, it was the Soviet intelligence service that leaked the details of the Sparrow Mission to the Germans. Anthony Cave Brown, *The Secret War Report of the OSS* (New York: Berkley Publishing Corporation, 1976), 300.
129 Telegram, No. 2699, November 3, 1943, Subseries 4K Telegrams d'etat, 1942–1945, ADP-DF.
130 Berle's first name much earlier in the war was used by various people as a codename for Hitler. See, Memorandum for the President, May 31, 1940, Roll 2, Adolf A. Berle, Jr. Diary, 1937–1971, Franklin D. Roosevelt Presidential Library and Museum.
131 Telegram, No. 2699, November 3, 1943, Subseries 4K Telegrams d'etat, 1942–1945, ADP-DF.
132 Jenő Ghyczy to György Bakach-Bessenyey, November 16, 1943, in Vass, "The Negotiations of György Bakach-Bessenyey," 187.

in the 1920s and was considered to have some democratic leanings compared to the Hungarian prime ministers following him. This memorandum was basically his last substantive political memorandum, so it is worth looking at the main ideas it contained. The main argument was that Hungary and the neighboring countries found themselves between Germany and the Soviet Union, and they wished to belong to neither sphere. According to Bethlen, the solution lay in a federation, but in order to achieve this, some of the Paris treaties had to be superseded in light of their—in his view—artificial outcomes. He mainly attacked the founding of Czechoslovakia and Yugoslavia as not natural entities: "There is no such thing as a Czechoslovak people. There are Czechs, and Slovaks, and Ruthenians ... There is no Yugoslav people. There are Serbs, and Croats, and Slovenes." Although history vindicated this perspective, since once the artificial glue was gone, these nations created their own respective states, other tenets of Bethlen's memorandum were very far off the historical track. He professed that a federation should be contrived with all the major independent nations in the area joining a monarchy in Austria and Hungary, with an autonomous Transylvania.[133] It is hard to understand how, with his rich experience, Bethlen could have thought such a scheme possible in light of the interwar years.

Perhaps Bethlen understood that he had gone overboard, because he specifically warned Tyler that his memorandum and the ideas it contained must not reach Beneš and other leaders of the neighboring countries. This shows, however, that he well understood that the Czechoslovaks would never agree to such a scheme and probably neither would the Yugoslavs. Bethlen perhaps hoped that the United States would play the most defining role in the postwar Danube Basin and would force Bethlen's ideas on the implicated countries in order to create a more stable region. The memorandum was drawn up in Hungarian and handed over to Tyler by Bakach-Bessenyey sometime in late January 1944. Tyler undertook to translate the original Hungarian into English (another sign of how proficient he had become in the Hungarian language) and made sure it was forwarded to the State Department. He shortened the original to some degree so as to make it more favorable to Hungarians, in his view, but he also thought that the text

---

133 Abstract of a memorandum on a Danubian Federation, by Count Stephen Bethlen, n. d. Miscellaneous, Thompson Todd Collection.

was too optimistic, despite the fact "some of the ideas contained in it really deserve consideration."[134] In a private letter Bethlen profusely thanked Tyler for his help, both past and present.[135]

In the end, the Hungarian side, after much hesitation and prodding from Tyler, approved of a plan to parachute an American unit into Hungary to establish direct contact with the prime minister's close associates. Tyler regularly told the various Hungarian contacts that fence sitting would end disastrously for Hungary, and he posed a question to one of them: Hungary "out of a desire to play safe, might be incurring the gravest danger of all. Even a brief German occupation would be bad, no doubt, but wouldn't it be worse to be treated as an impenitent ally of Germany by a victorious Russia?"[136] Dulles attributed the Hungarian willingness to go ahead with the plan largely to the "extraordinary personal influence of" Tyler.[137] Donovan himself sent a cable that ended this way: "It seems well worth doing."[138] The plan that had gone through many changes over the months until it was finally executed in mid-March 1944. It bore the name Sparrow.[139] The three-man team, led by Florimund Duke, was dropped into Hungary on March 16, 1944, and was in the initial phases of contacting high level officials in the Hungarian government when the German occupation took place on March 19, sealing Hungary's fate.

The Sparrow Mission, and its failure, cannot be separated from the German occupation of Hungary, if for no other reason than their almost identical timing. Nazi intelligence officer Wilhelm Höttl, testifying many years later, answered a question concerning the influence the Sparrow Mission on the German occupation of Hungary:

---

134 György Bakach-Bessenyey to Andor Szentmiklóssy, February 10 and February 21, 1944, Folder 6, Bethlen memorandum, Roll 1, Bakach-Bessenyey Papers, P 2066, HNA; Royall Tyler to Allen Dulles, February 9, 1944, File 477, NARA.
135 István Bethlen to Royall Tyler, February 23, 1944, Miscellaneous, Thompson Todd Collection.
136 Royall Tyler to Allen W. Dulles, January 24, 1944, File, 477, NARA.
137 Telegram, January 11, 1944, Subseries 4K Telegrams d'etat, 1942–1945, ADP-DF.
138 Telegram, No. 3106, December 14, 1943, and Telegram, No. 2436, 17 January 1944. Ibid.
139 For more detail about the Sparrow Mission, see, Duke, *Name, Rank, and Serial Number*; Kádár, *A Ludovikától Sopronkőhidáig*; Kállay, *Hungarian Premier*; Vass, Bakach-Bessenyey György tárgyalásai; Aladár Szegedy-Maszák, *Az ember ősszel visszanéz... Egy volt magyar diplomata emlékirataiból* [One Looks back in the Fall ... From the Memoirs of a Hungarian Diplomat] (Budapest: 1996); Petersen, *From Hitler's Doorstep*; Czettler, *A mi kis élethalál kérdéseink*; András Zoltán Kovács, "A Janus-arcú tábornok,"; Charles Fenyvesi, *Három összeesküvés* [Three Conspiracies] (Budapest: Európa Könyvkiadó, 2007); Peterecz: "Sparrow Mission,"; Borhi, *Dealing with Dictators*, 36–46. The mission was even the subject of a novel: Richard B. Beal, *Sparrow: Sparrow Mission* (New York: Writers Club Press, 2002).

This mission had vital influence on it ... Sure, there was the possibility of other events which also could have unleashed it ... Duke's arrival and arrest set the machinery in motion. Hitler considered his arrival as the Fait Accompli, as Hungary's betraying him ... Kaltenbrunner later on personally told me that Hitler, in front of Himmler and Ribbentrop, had shouted upon hearing of Duke's arrival: "I always told you that the Hungarians ultimately will try to stab us in the back. And this is what's happening right now."[140]

Although Höttl's testimony must be viewed with caution, there was an undeniable link between American clandestine activities and the German occupation of Hungary. In fact, the Germans had started to consider the occupation of Hungary as early as September 1943, precisely because of intelligence reports about contacts between the Hungarians and the Western Allies. The plan, named *Unternehmen Margarethe*, went through several phases without any clearly projected date of execution. Hitler and his close collaborators had little respect for Kállay and did not trust Hungary, either militarily or politically.[141] The Hungarian side, always afraid of German occupation, realized only in February that such a move was imminent, but it was too late for the hesitant Kállay to make up his mind as to any active steps. Also, it is hard to see what he actually could have done to forestall the German occupation of his country. With the Soviet Red Army approaching from the east, Hungary's territory became vital for German defenses, so Hitler would not have let Hungary leave his sphere at any rate.

---

140 Interview with Dr Hottl, February 19, 1966, in Duke to Dulles, March 31, 1966, Series 1, Correspondence, Box 32, Folder 11, Hungary, 1918–1968, ADP. In 1939 Höttl became leader of the Viennese Department VI station, patterned on the Reich Security Administration's Department VI. Later he was posted for a time as an advisor to the German ambassador to Hungary, then returned to Vienna. He was considered an expert on Hungary. On his career see, "Introduction" by David Kahn, in Höttl, *The Secret Front*, ii–ix. Florimond Duke was the leader of the Sparrow Mission. Ernst Kaltenbrunner was chief of the RSHA (Reichssicherheitshauptamt – Reich Main Security Office) from 1943.

141 For the German plans about occupying Hungary, see, Helmut Greiner, *Kriegstagebuch des Oberkommandos der Wehrmacht, 1940–1945* [War Diaries of the Wehrmacht High Command] (Frankfurt: Erster Helbband, 1961–1965); József Kun, "Magyarország német katonai megszállásának előkészítése és lefolyása, 1943 szeptember–1944 március," [The Preparation and Execution of the German Occupation of Hungary, September 1943–March 1944], *Hadtörténelmi Közlemények* 10, no. 1 (1963): 37–84; Gyula Juhász, "A német-magyar viszony néhány kérdése a második világháború alatt" [Some Questions of the German–Hungarian Relationship during World War II], *Történelmi Szemle* 22, no. 1–2 (1984): 269–78.

Chapter 8

With the Sparrow Mission on its way to Hungary and with the German occupation still a few days away and something of which the Americans were unaware, Tyler was finishing up an intelligence report outlining how Hungary got into the war and what were then the relations with the surrounding countries. This report was probably ordered by the State Department, wishing to explain the contours of Hungary to Americans. No one else on the American side at the time could have provided such a thorough examination of the Hungarian situation. Tyler must have started the account in February and possibly was putting on the finishing touches at the time the Sparrow Mission was on its way to Hungary. The long report had two sections of 23 and 14 typed pages, respectively. In the first, titled "How Hungary Got into the Second World War," Tyler meticulously summarized Hungarian history from 1918 up to the present, with an emphasis on how Hungary became involved in the war on Germany's side. He started with an anecdote, and it is worth quoting it in full, because after the conclusion of World War II the anecdote gained some prominence in a slightly different version. This appears to be the earliest version:

> Shortly after Pearl Harbor, a story went the rounds of the Budapest cafés: Mr. Hull calls up Mr. Roosevelt and tells him a declaration of war on the U.S.A. has been received from the Kingdom of Hungary.
> Mr. Roosevelt: "Kingdom of Hungary? Who's the King?"
> Mr. Hull: "The throne is vacant. There is a Regent, Admiral Horthy."
> Mr. Roosevelt: "An Admiral! So now we'll have to fight the Hungarian navy?"
> Mr. Hull: "No, Hungary has no navy."
> Mr. Roosevelt: "Well, what's Hungary's grievance?"
> Mr. Hull: "Territories it lost by the Treaty of Trianon."
> Mr. Roosevelt: "Whom have the Hungarians been fighting, so far?"
> Mr. Hull: "Russia."
> Mr. Roosevelt: "So Russia took part of former Hungary?"
> Mr. Hull: "No."
> Mr. Roosevelt: "What countries are holding any ex-Hungarian territories?"
> Mr. Hull: "Slovakia, Roumania, Croatia, Italy and Germany."
> Mr. Roosevelt: "So Hungary is fighting all those countries, as well as Russia?"

World War II – An Intelligence Officer

Mr. Hull: "No, Hungary is fighting alongside of all those countries, against Russia."

Mr. Roosevelt: "Say, old man, you must have had a long day! You want some sleep. We'll try and straighten all this out to-morrow."[142]

"Indeed," Tyler appended, "Alice never met anything more wonderful in Wonderland than this Hungary, a kingdom without a king, headed by an admiral without a fleet, declaring war on the U.S.A. because of territories annexed or occupied by the U.S.A.'s enemies, in association with whom Hungary had just joined in a crusade against the Soviet Union, which power had nothing to do with the case."[143]

Tyler's report gave a detailed account of Hungary's road to the World War II—not just mentioning the facts but also blaming the military leadership for all the missteps along the way. Tyler identified the unresolved troubles of the interwar years in Hungary as the reason for the disproportionate influence these high-ranking soldiers wielded. The immediate postwar upheavals had created a layer in society that tended toward conspiracy and adventure, and the League-orchestrated financial reconstruction managed only to put on a veneer of lasting success, which was wiped out by the approaching Great Depression. All this, of course, was saturated with the "Nem, nem, soha!" slogan of interwar Hungary, that is, revision of the Trianon Treaty. Under Gömbös the situation worsened further, although on the surface the old generation still played a prominent role. "Gömbös's vanity, love of pomp, uniforms, and medals served to divert attention from the method and pertinacity with which he pursued his deeper designs," which were "a gradual, systematic packing of the higher posts in the army with men who set loyalty to Gömbös's person above all else."[144] Gömbös filled the General Staff with German- or Austrian-born men, or Hungarians who looked to the German army as the example to follow. Under Imrédy the last chance of trying to follow the West was lost, but, as Tyler pointed out, when Great Britain and France allowed Germany to get away with the Czechoslovak adventure, that greatly influenced Imrédy to bet more and more on Germany. Teleki tried a

---

142 Royall Tyler, "Hungary's Predicament and the Chances for an Enduring Peace," March 17, 1944, Miscellaneous, Thompson Todd Collection.
143 Ibid.
144 Ibid.

delicate dance between two worlds, but reaching a solution was beyond his, or any one's, abilities, and the General Staff basically betrayed him. In February 1944, at the time he was writing this part of the report, Tyler thought it was part of Hungary's tragedy that the overarching rhetoric was still the same, namely that Hungary was fighting the Soviet Union for self-defense.

The second section of the report was titled "Hungary and Its Neighbors," and it was finished on March 17, two days before the German occupation of Hungary. Here, Tyler focused on the postwar possibilities of the Danubian states. His thesis was that first the borders should be rectified—thereby implying that the peace treaties were in large part responsible for the present situation—while, on the other hand, the Great Powers rivalry must cease if people wanted to live in a peaceful world. Such rivalry would only lead to competing factions among the Danubian states, in effect sowing the seeds of future conflict. The crux of the problem was, as Tyler explained, the overarching French policy of containing Germany in the East, for which they needed Czechoslovakia, a country which contained too large blocks of other ethnic minorities. When the French withdrew from the area in the 1930s, Czechoslovakia sought possible protection against a more aggressive Germany in the form of the Soviet Union. The repercussions of the Treaty of Trianon made this situation even worse and led an isolated Hungary to want to break out and regain some territories. For this it needed a Great Power as an ally, and since neither Great Britain nor France was willing to consider such a step, it was perhaps inevitable that Hungary tied its fate to a resurgent Germany.

In light of this, Tyler argued, in the postwar settlement "any attempt to impose upon this region an order that is not recognized as substantially just by all the peoples inhabiting it would be as ill-fated as Trianon." What he suggested was a moderate change in the frontiers with more conscientious acknowledgement of Hungarian minorities in the successor countries, but only after the two Vienna Awards had been disregarded. In the case of Transylvania, only autonomy might work as a solution. In order to create stability, even Hungary's war guilt should be treated in a mild way otherwise further trouble lay ahead. He wanted the various nationalities in the region to choose freely the country they wanted to live in. He envisioned the Czech Republic and Slovakia as two separate countries, and also an independent Croatia. "But if any great power or powers attempt to force [these nations] into a pattern devised to serve the ends of the constellation that happens to prevail when this war ceases," Tyler warned, "the prospects for Europe's future will not be good."[145] Tyler's vision can be characterized as both naïve and farsighted. He did not see the approaching Soviet Army posing any danger to a peaceful settlement in the Danubian region, but the situation after the Cold War proved his vision to have been correct.

It is an irony of history that two days after Tyler completed his report, Germany occupied Hungary, causing all the secret negotiations aiming to detach Hungary from Germany to come to naught. This was not such a big a problem for the Allies. In fact, it was useful in the sense that German forces had to be deployed in the Eastern theater, somewhat weakening German forces in the West, where the Allied landing at Normandy was only two and a half months away. Whether this was conscious strategy on the part of the Allies, as László Borhi states, or it was a comfortable coincidence is an intriguing question.[146] It is certain that there is some indication in Anglo-Saxon planning that a German invasion of Hungary would be useful for the Allied military strategy regarding the Normandy landing. For example, as early as February 1942, the last point in a four-point scheme outlined in a British draft policy paper argued that one of the aims should be "eventually to compel Germany to divert a certain number of troops to Hungary, either as a safeguard against disorders and sabotage, or as an occupying force."[147]

After its occupation, Tyler's job changed regarding Hungary. Obviously, the contacts who had carried letters, newspapers, and messages back and forth no longer did so. This did not mean that he stopped dealing with Hungary or the Danubian region, and his efforts yielded two tangible results. One, he kept up his working relations with Hungarian diplomats who refused to recognize the new government in Hungary, arguing that it was inaugurated under German pressure and therefore was illegitimate. These diplomats organized a committee to try to represent pre-occupation Hungary in the West. Two, Tyler kept working on explaining the situation in Hungary, past and present, as he saw it. With his immense experience he wished both to inform the American government about what he considered one of the

---

145 The quotations in the paragraph are from ibid.
146 Borhi, *Dealing with Dictators*, 31–36.
147 "Plan of Political Warfare for Hungary," February 3, 1942. Draft. C1330, FO 371/30965, TNA. Also quoted in Juhász, *Magyarország nemzetközi helyzete és a magyar szellemi élet 1938–1944* [The International Situation of Hungary and Hungarian Intellectual Life] (Budapest: Akadémiai Kiadó, 1987), 39.

most critical regions in Europe, and also, in all likelihood, he wanted to summarize for himself what Hungary meant to him.

Accordingly, in the summer of 1944 Tyler wrote another text that enlarged upon his earlier comprehensive reports concerning the history of Hungary's involvement in the war and the hoped-for postwar situation in the Danubian region. "Feudalism in Hungary" was written in the late spring or perhaps sometime in June 1944.[148] In it Tyler was endeavoring to put Hungary's past into perspective, especially the oft-repeated accusation that Hungary was a feudal country and its anachronistic stance did not make it a possible candidate for a new and democratic Europe. These allegations naturally were proclaimed most loudly in the Little Entente countries, but the Western democracies held a similar view as well. In fact, many Americans echoed the indictment. The notion that Hungary remained a "feudal" country and therefore represented backwardness, was a recurring charge against interwar Hungary. George A. Gordon, a career diplomat serving at the American Legation at Budapest, after two years of service, expressed his idea that especially the legitimists in general were "not only Orientals at bottom, but also still thoroughly mediaeval and feudalistic; as corollary to this I do not hesitate to register my opinion that the Magnate class here—which of course, generally speaking, is synonymous with Legitimism—is arrogant, egotistical, narrow and subjective minded to a high degree."[149] Former American minister to Hungary Nicholas Roosevelt, for example, wrote of the Hungarian aristocracy in 1925 that they lived "politically in the Middle Ages. They were, and many of them still are, completely impervious to modern ideas of democracy and liberalism."[150] The years he spent in Hungary did not change this view; if anything, they strengthened it. In his memoirs Roosevelt charged that the "extent to which peasants and servants derived prestige and satisfaction from 'belonging' to one of the great families was repeatedly borne in on me during my two and one-half years in Budapest. It was, of course, a survival of feudalism."[151] An American political commentator analyzing the election results of 1927 stated that Bethlen, despite his outstanding victory, would have to steer his ship between "the remnants of the old feudal aristocracy of

---

148 Royall Tyler to Allen W. Dulles, June 30, 1944, File 477, NARA.
149 George A. Gordon to Frank B. Kellogg, June 3, 1927, 864.00/702, Roll 8, Microcopy No. 708, NARA.
150 Nicholas Roosevelt, "Count Karolyi Begins His Memoirs", *New York Times*, March 29, 1925.
151 Nicholas Roosevelt, *A Front Row Seat* (Norman, OK: University of Oklahoma Press, 1953), 190.

Hungary in power" and "the pressure of the lower classes."[152] Voices like these are another proof that Hungary was labelled as a "feudal" country.

As far as Tyler was concerned, it was historically and technically wrong to speak of feudalism in Hungary in the twentieth century. It was undeniable however that large estates often thrived on the cheap labor of the large mass of landless people living in their proximity. In this paper Tyler tried, with the help of statistics and argument, to introduce the outlines of the land question in Hungary. The various measures of land reform in the interwar years were, in his opinion, trending in the right direction. But the high density of the agrarian population in post-Trianon Hungary, together with too many dwarf holdings (created where the allotted land too small to cultivate for the market), the lack of capital with which to equip agriculture in general, and the conservative cultivation techniques practiced by most of the Hungarian peasantry all together created an environment that gave some basis to the accusations of feudalism. Tyler blamed the creation of a huge rural population with a very low standard of living on the forced industrialization of Hungary in the interwar years, together with other elements such as loss of two thirds of the country's territory, new customs frontiers in the Danubian region, old trade channels being clogged up, and the lack of the safety valve of immigration, which had worked before World War I. In this sense, Tyler opined, one could speak of a new "feudalism" in Hungary.[153] Tyler sent a copy not only to Dulles but also to Leland Harrison, who was the long-serving American minister to Switzerland at that time.[154] He probably wanted to ensure a larger readership in American governmental circles for his opinions.

In December 1944, Tyler completed yet another long report, which contained the finalized version of his earlier reports of that year. It bore the title "Hungary Explained." He added to the earlier reports a long section titled "The Wrong Horse" and a substantial conclusion. "Hungary Explained" was probably sent on to the State Department or/and JCS.[155] In the "Wrong Horse" section Tyler picked up the story of Hungary where he had left off in March, that is, from Teleki's suicide in April 1941. Here he mainly focused

---

152 Malbone W. Graham, Jr., "The Elections to the New Hungarian Parliament," *American Political Science Review* 21, no. 2 (May, 1927): 388.
153 Royall Tyler, "Feudalism in Hungary," File 477, NARA.
154 Royall Tyler to Allen W. Dulles, June 30, 1944, ibid.
155 Royall Tyler to Allen W. Dulles, March 8, 1945, ibid.

Chapter 8

on and analyzed Kállay's years as prime minister and his activity concerning the possible detachment of Hungary from the Axis Powers. Kállay was, in Tyler's view, an "opportunist with no great experience of the outer world but a goodish guesser" who never really believed in a German victory over Britain or the United States, and who "showed willingness to live dangerously when he undertook to reverse" Hungary's earlier course. Also, the Hungarian premier was "[h]alf country-gentleman, half horse-dealer, with a touch of the gypsy thrown in, this Szabolcsi Svihák [crook] is rather like some Irish squire than anything Herr Professor Haushofer ever dreamt of," therefore far from a reliable politician for Germany.[156] Kállay dexterously managed the careful steps toward leaving Germany and established contacts with the Anglo-Saxon powers for this reason. However, the goals of the two sides were different to such an extent that it made it difficult to reach common ground. From Tyler's account it is clear that he sent a personal letter to Kállay, also to be shown to Horthy, containing the American argument as to what Hungary should do. In the end, of course, the German occupation in March 1944 put an end to all these efforts. After that event, the warnings that the Jews would be in danger were realized. Most of them were deported to death camps, during which campaign "the Hungarian Gendarmerie displaying such zeal in its desire to make up for lost time that even SS-men were sickened by the spectacle." Tyler also concisely told the story of October 15, when Horthy tried to jump out of the war but so belatedly and hesitantly, that it was easy for the Germans to put a stop to it—when the "last ray of hope flickered out." With Ferenc Szálasi's Arrow Cross Party taking power, an already tragic situation became even worse. Tyler's somewhat prophetically closed his account at the point when the Soviet Army reached Budapest and put it under siege: the "Russian invasion and the destruction of Budapest close a chapter of Hungarian history."[157]

In the concluding section of the long memorandum, Tyler once again examined the possibilities of a long-term solution for the countries of the Danubian Basin. In a region where, partly due to Great-Power meddling, the nations' fortunes were "turning in a vicious circle of foreign meddling

---

156 Karl Haushofer was a German officer and intellectual whose theories of German geopolitics influenced the thinking of the Nazi regime. He was especially closely connected to Rudolf Hess.
157 The quotes are from Royall Tyler, "Hungary Explained," December 1944, File 477, NARA.

and local vendetta," a new approach was needed for a permanent and peaceful settlement. Tyler saw the solution in much fairer borderlines that would leave as few minorities as possible under foreign rule, with the borders to be as "permeable" and "imperceptible" as possible. While the drawing of the border lines would involve the Great Powers, the second part of his solution, the relatively free penetrability of the new frontiers, should be worked out by the countries involved in the region without Great-Power influence. And the borders should allow people and goods to cross as freely as possible. Tyler argued that despite the fact that spheres of influence had already seemingly been established for a postwar Europe, the Great Powers would only profit by refraining "from using smaller states as pawns;" and he saw the United States as possibly playing the role of power broker "thus wielding a moderating influence, the lack of which was sorely felt throughout the inter-war period." He firmly believed that shaping the region's new—and hopefully lasting—frontiers must be done by experts representing neutral countries. He mentioned the successful Mosul region under the auspices of the League of Nations as a good example. He naturally highlighted Hungary's case in the final passages of the memorandum. He was professing a sentiment that was as pro-Hungarian as perhaps any American had ever expressed before or ever would. His main line of argument was that despite certain and sometimes egregious mistakes by Hungary in the decades before and after World War I, in hope of a better future "the right line for us to take towards Hungary is to secure practical recognition of its right to order its internal existence as it sees fit." Only with such an approach might America "contribute towards creating conditions in which Hungary, as well as its neighbors, will also take the right line, and good-neighborliness may at last prevail on the Danube."[158]

After the German occupation of Hungary, Tyler did not cease gathering and passing on information about Hungary, mainly through Bakach-Bessenyey. He remained closely connected to the Hungarian minister, who was soon stripped of his citizenship as punishment for breaking with the new regime in Hungary, which was set up under duress and was very friendly to the Germans. The Hungarian diplomats in the West who refused to recognize the Döme Sztójay-led German puppet government organized a Dissident Ministers' committee (Committee of Hungarian Ministers),

---

158 Ibid. The memo was sent to Allen Dulles, Leland Harrison, and Isiah Bowman in early March 1945.

Chapter 8

which they saw as a preliminary step toward establishing a government-in-exile similar to the Czechoslovak and Polish examples.

Tyler watched the birth and early phase of the dissident diplomats' committee closely. It is interesting to note that Kállay, like Teleki a few years earlier, had also created a fund for future contingencies. Since the German occupation had been a constant threat and the Hungarian government was looking for a way to detach itself from the Third Reich, Kállay wanted to make sure that either a government-in-exile or the Hungarian diplomats who could not return to Hungary would have access to some money and could work to promote Hungary's interests. Just five weeks prior to March 19 Kállay sent a letter legally creating the circumstances for the fund to function as planned. It held about 6 million Swiss francs (about $12 million), and when, soon after the German occupation, most of the dissident diplomats were stripped of their citizenship, the fund started to provide them with regular financial aid. In April 1947, partly due to American pressure through Tyler, the remaining sum in the fund, by then a little more than 1 million Swiss francs, was returned to the Hungarian government. Due to various difficulties, however, it was not delivered until two years later. After handing the money over to Hungary, Tyler requested both a "strictly confidential" memorandum in which one could read about the circumstances of the transfer and a receipt signed by the then current Hungarian prime minister, Ferenc Nagy.[159]

In addition, through Tyler, Dulles and the American State Department was more or less able to follow the events in now-occupied Hungary, and also in Yugoslavia or France, for example. He was at one point shown Kállay's letter to Bakach-Bessenyey of July 14, 1944, in which the former prime minister, who at the time had found temporary refuge at the Turkish Embassy in Budapest, told in his own words the story of the German occupation and the events leading up to it. Kállay's recounting tallied with the information Tyler had had during that period.[160] Tyler was often shown letters that Kállay sent to other Hungarian diplomats in Western Europe, sometimes with the help of the Americans.

But official Hungary was "lost," so Tyler needed to focus his main energies on other subjects. He remained busy giving his opinion about the pos-

---

159 On the Kállay Fund, see, András Joó, "A 'Kállay Alap' története – tények és kérdőjelek" ['National Treasure.' The Story of the Kállay Fund: Facts and Questions], *Századok* 154, no. 2, (2020): 327–62; Royall Tyler to Allen Dulles, November 7, 1944, File 477, NARA.

160 "Abstract of letter, dated July 14, 1944, from Premier Kállay to Bessenyey," File 477, NARA.

sible future. Creating all the memoranda that he was asked for about issues that he was deeply interested in made him write, "I'm well and enjoying my work, which indeed becomes more interesting all the time."[161] Accordingly, in December 1944, at the request of Isaiah Bowman, an advisor to the U.S. State Department, Tyler also put on paper his notes concerning the Dumbarton Oaks resolutions (the foundations of the Charter of the United Nations, signed at San Francisco on June 26, 1945) .[162] He mainly focused on the differences between the League of Nations and the United Nations. He argued that two main differences were the centralization in the form of the Security Council responsible for maintaining collective security, and that the weaker nations could have access to fewer safeguards in the United Nations. Compared to the League Covenant, Tyler noted, "the Dumbarton Oaks Charter will look to many like international oligarchy, rather than democracy."[163]

Tyler also wrote a follow-up on this report half a year later, right after the UN Charter was signed. It ran to 25 typed pages and he produced it on his own initiative, without it being requested. Since he received no feedback on his first paper concerning the Dumbarton Oaks resolutions, he concluded that his ideas probably "didn't go down any too well."[164] In this new long thesis he tried to outline the possible shortcomings of the freshly created United Nations, which observations he based upon his understanding of the systemic problems of the international system in the League of Nations years. He was not sure that the new setup with the Security Council and the General Assembly would be able to cope with the problems that had created the crisis in the interwar years. And he thought that economic issues should

---

161 Royall Tyler to Mildred Barnes Bliss, November 14, 1944, and December 12, 1944, Geneva, "Bliss–Tyler Correspondence," https://www.doaks.org/resources/bliss-tyler-correspondence/letters/14nov1944, and https://www.doaks.org/resources/bliss-tyler-correspondence/letters/12dec1944, both accessed April 28, 2019. This was also the first time since May 1940, that he had been back to Paris for a day and a half, where he could meet his son once again. He had traveled to the French capital with Dulles, and on the way back David Bruce joined the party.

162 Isaiah Bowman to Royall Tyler, October 16, 1944, and November 28, 1944, Thompson Todd Collection. On Bowman's life and wartime activities, see, Geoffrey J. Martin, *The Life and Thought of Isaiah Bowman* (Hamden, CT: Archon Books, 1980), and Neil Smith, *American Empire. Roosevelt's Geographer and the Prelude to Globalization* (Berkeley, CA: University of California Press, 2003).

163 "Notes on the Dumbarton Oaks Proposals," December 1944, in Royall Tyler to Dulles, April 26, 1945, File 477, NARA.

164 Royall Tyler to Allen W. Dulles, April 26, 1945, ibid.

lie at the heart of a stable peace. "In order to secure peace, be it repeated, the first requisite is growing prosperity, which can only result from an increasing flow of international trade ... Our most dangerous enemies will now be not the Axis but poverty and the sense of frustration: hard times, in a word."

The possible solution, Tyler argued, lay in the hands of the Great Powers. If they could agree and prevent a gathering crisis by wise action, there was hope.

> There is no great mystery about what ought to be done. The question is how Authority can be induced to do it: whether the Powers in whose hands the world's destinies [sic] now lie will intervene at the pre-fever stage, while action in peace is still possible; whether they can agree on practical measures, and particularly whether they will make the requisite sacrifices themselves. The mightier a nation, the greater its responsibility, and the line our own USA takes may be decisive. It would be well to impress this upon our people, rather than let them expect that if the United Nations stamp out Nazism and agree on an anti-aggression pact to-day, we shall live happily ever after.

He thought that the making the same mistake of imposing punishing reparations must be avoided, so economy across the board could start with international cooperation, and ex-enemy countries must be allowed to take their place in a free flow of trade. In the final analysis, he saw that it was raw power that would decide whether there would be peace or not, and from this perspective Tyler criticized the UN Charter. "The controversy over voting procedure on proposals involving sanctions in the Security Council loomed large at San Francisco, but that issue may soon be forgotten, for either the Great Powers continue to set agreement among themselves above all other considerations, in which case there will be no aggression, or they cease to do so, and there will be no Security Council." And the wonderful economic analyses are not enough if they are not put into practice and carried out by everyone. On this aspect Tyler was not very confident.

> Nothing in the United Nations Charter seems to offer any serious reason for hope that things are going to be different from now on ... But the proof of the pudding is in the eating, and only time will show whether the Security Council, i.e., the Great Powers, are going to make it their

business to right an economic situation out of which prospects for international trade have been fading ever since the first World War.

Therefore, it was all the more crucial to have a Great-Powers understanding and cooperation. The UN would be seen by many as the promise of a peaceful new epoch, but as Tyler saw it, "When the wheels begin to creak, as creak they will, the adversaries of international co-operation are likely to raise their heads once more." That is why he thought that not too much should be expected from the new organization, and only slow and patient work might result in true international cooperation.[165]

Although Tyler had no way of knowing it, he was to have a very modest role to play in the new world order, but that new order proved a far cry from the promised and hoped-for Great-Powers cooperation and understanding. Soon the Cold War engulfed much of the globe, and the world Tyler was so familiar with was divided into two camps.

---

165 The quotations for the last five paragraphs are from Royall Tyler, "The Outlook for the Economic Issue, after San Francisco," Geneva, June 28, 1945, Enclosure in Leland Harrison to Royall Tyler, Bern, July 9, 1945, Thompson Todd Collection.

CHAPTER 9

Tyler in the Early Cold War

With the conclusion of the war and the total victory of the Allies, it was beyond the slightest doubt that a new epoch would begin. Many thought and hoped that a more peaceful era would be ushered in. Understandably, the first and foremost problem was that of formalizing the peace in the form of consensual treaties among victors and defeated states. On the other hand, the reconstruction of a devastated Europe—both in life and treasure—had to take priority, and based upon the experience of the first decade after World War I, clearly a better recipe was needed. Since the League of Nations could not fulfill its hoped-for role in maintaining the peace and stifling possible aggression, it was a given that a new international organization had to take its place. This time, however, the United States was the prime mover of the postwar world order, and it wanted to create an organization that would provide collective security in which peaceful free trade could thrive and American values and interests might lead the way. This decision to meet internationalism head on marked a big turnaround in American foreign policy.

The first big step was already taken by the American leadership in 1943 when, in agreement with Great Britain and the Soviet Union, it joined in the founding of the United Nations Relief and Rehabilitation Administration (UNRRA). Altogether some forty countries signed the founding document in November 1943, with the idea that once the war was over a relief agency could help the millions of refugees. With the birth of the United Nations in 1945, UNRRA became its official agency. It functioned until 1947, then this type of work was taken over by the Marshall Plan, which had a sharper focus on Western

Chapter 9

Europe as the Cold War unfolded.[1] At the Bretton Woods Conference in New Hampshire in 1944 (officially the United Nations Monetary and Financial Conference), the International Bank for Reconstruction and Development (IBRD, or World Bank) and the International Monetary Fund (IMF) were established. Both became operational in 1946 with the goal of financing the efforts to reconstruct Europe, which were largely assumed by the Marshall Plan from 1948. Much of this new-found internationalism on the part of the Americans had to do with majority opinion in and out of government, which saw that after World War I a golden opportunity to assume leadership in the world with an aim to maintaining peace and prosperity had been squandered. Also, many in key positions recognized that the Soviet Union would, in one way or another, pose a challenge to American aims, and it was much better, the argument went, to bring the Russians into an international organization and thus have indirect influence on them than to leave them outside the forum for international cooperation.

Tyler had been working for the UNRRA from its inception back in 1943, with a detour for intelligence gathering, mainly on Hungary but on other European countries as well. Reflecting on the second half of World War II, he wrote to Allen Dulles, "The three years will remain as not only the most exciting I've lived, but as the fullest of satisfaction."[2] Dulles could also look back on his own years with the OSS in Switzerland with satisfaction, but he tried to stay modest and, at least privately, gave credit where it was due. He wrote to Tyler that "whatever success I may have had is in a very major degree due to your constant help."[3]

A tragedy occurred in Tyler's private life soon after the war ended. In February 1946, Hayford Peirce, his long-time collaborator on Byzantine art, suffered a stroke. When the news reached Tyler, he felt "as if my own future had been jeopardized, and measure the emptiness of my illusions about recreating any part of one's own plans."[4] When Peirce died within two weeks,

---

1 On the founding, the internationalism, and the tensions within the UNRRA, see Jessica Reinisch, "Internationalism in Relief: The Birth (and Death) of UNRRA," *Past and Present*. Vol. 210, Supplement 6, (2011): 258–89.
2 Royall Tyler to Allen W. Dulles, January 16, 1946, Box 55, Folder 19, Tyler, Royall, 1945–1953, Series 1: Correspondence, 1891–1969, ADP.
3 Allen W. Dulles to Royall Tyler, November 28, 1945, ibid.
4 Royall Tyler to Mildred Barnes Bliss, February 22, 1946, Geneva, "Bliss–Tyler Correspondence," https://www.doaks.org/resources/bliss-tyler-correspondence/letters/22feb1946 accessed May 15, 2019.

Tyler often was observed just gazing at a huge map on the wall showing the Balkans and Thrace, where together the two men had investigated so many valuable pieces of Byzantine art history.[5]

With the conclusion of the war, the options were both open and limited for a man of Tyler's skills and expertise. One the one hand, after two decades of League work and being immersed in international problems of finance and its unavoidable political nuances, Tyler had immense knowledge about Europe inside and out. On the other hand, however, with the demise of the League of Nations, and the headquarters of the new United Nations being in the United States, it was no longer physically possible for him to both work for the organization and be close to home at Antigny. Also, in addition to his on-going love of and energy for Byzantine art history, Tyler still wanted to be useful in the world, and he needed a salary to boot. As a compromise of sorts, he found an ideal job opportunity: head of the Paris field office of the International Bank for Reconstruction and Development, where he worked for the next three years. This change of career was not surprising. After all, his expertise lay in implementing financial loans and the negotiations pertaining to them. In the previous two plus decades, most of his official time had been taken up by such activity, mainly regarding Hungary. Now, of course, only other regions could come into view.

Unfortunately, not much is known about Tyler's work during this period, except that he was kept busy. After UNRRA closed down its activities in 1947, Tyler soon found himself on the roster of the World Bank, now under the presidency of John McCloy, until the fall of 1949. Despite the heavy workload, he wanted to serve while in France, and kept asking Allen Dulles throughout 1946 to pull strings if possible.[6] It is not known whether Dulles did so or not call, but the next year he was entrusted with serious work. Since France had been the first major recipient of a large loan, $500 million in 1947, and Tyler lived in and near Paris, he was chosen to lead the young organization's effort. This mainly meant monitoring the French loan. He had to reside in Basel, Switzerland, but that was close enough to Paris. Indeed, he

---

5   Royall Tyler to Mildred Barnes Bliss, March 12, 1946, Geneva, "Bliss–Tyler Correspondence," https://www.doaks.org/resources/bliss-tyler-correspondence/letters/12mar1946, accessed May 15, 2019.
6   Royall Tyler to Allen W. Dulles, June 11, 1946, September 20, 1946, and December 30, 1946, Box 55, Folder 19, Allen W. Dulles Papers.

Chapter 9

played an important role in the French reconstruction project loan when he became the head of the operation on French soil.

This overseas monitoring activity was no easy task under the prevailing circumstances. There were numerous strikes in Paris, telephone services and electricity were not reliable, and there were also problems caused by inadequate equipment of all sorts. In addition, life was much more expensive in Western Europe than in Washington in those days, and, owing to a tight budget, additional pecuniary tensions reared their ugly heads. Naturally, all of this caused some tension between the World Bank headquarters and its overseas offices, such as in Paris.[7] Actually, until the French government provided an office, Tyler had often travelled between Basel and Paris.[8] But with his undying optimism and unceasing efforts to be useful, Tyler did not allow desperation to creep into his workdays, and tried to look on the bright side even under the unfavorable circumstances. As another participant remembered the days of the end-use mission prior to granting the French loan, Tyler "was a chevalier de tate-vin and always seeking and giving information about new dishes, wines or restaurants. For him, the discovery of a new restaurant or the enjoyment of a particularly good bottle or dish was a moving experience to be shared with friends and fully discussed."[9] Also, Tyler's position made it possible for him to travel to the United States on rare occasions, which was always a high point in Tyler's later years.

Although it was understood that he would regularly travel to the United States on behalf of the Bank, on more than one occasion his employer actually prevented him from embarking upon such a journey. Once, in the spring of 1948, he already had secured a reservation on an ocean liner, when the Bank chose him to attend a meeting of the Economic Commission for Europe in Geneva.[10] However, once that conference was concluded, he did manage to travel to the United States in mid-May 1948. Whenever he had a little spare time, Tyler focused again on more scholarly activities. He returned to editing the Spanish Calendar of State Papers, a work he had been doing just at the

---

7 Jim Huttlinger, "The First Field Offices," *Bank's World* 14, no. 7 (July 1995): 18–19.
8 Ibid., 18.
9 Gordon M. Street, "Memories of a Mission to Paris," *International Bank Notes* 15, no. 7 (July 1961): 5.
10 Royall Tyler to Robert Woods Bliss, March 20, 1948, Geneva, "Bliss–Tyler Correspondence," https://www.doaks.org/resources/bliss-tyler-correspondence/letters/20mar1948, accessed May 17, 2019, and Royall Tyler to Allen W. Dulles, March 22, 1948, Box 55, Folder 19, Allen W. Dulles Papers.

start of World War I. Now he set out to complete three more volumes, and found that "working on them has rekindled all my passion for the subject, and I now spend every moment I can spare at the" Bibliothèque Nationale in Paris.[11] This ambitious project did not, however, come to fruition. Volume twelve did appear in 1949, but the next volume was published posthumously, in 1954.

Tyler retired from the World Bank as its treasurer in Europe on September 28, 1949. The Bank expressed "its appreciation of the valuable services performed by" Tyler for the past three years.[12] Actually, Tyler left the bank because he had reached the mandatory retirement age of sixty-five. It was not, however, the end of his work for the organization, and on the same day his resignation went into effect, another job was already awaiting.

His last assignment for the World Bank was the Clapp Mission, officially the United Nations Economic Survey Mission for the Middle East. Gordon Clapp, former director of the Tennessee Valley Authority, was its chairman. The mission's main aim was to establish the circumstances concerning the economic possibilities in the Middle East. With the founding of Israel in 1948, the Middle East suddenly became a hotbed of possible and real outbursts of violence. Israel's Arab neighbors refused to accept the existence of the Jewish state, and right after it had declared its independence, a coalition of Arab countries attacked it in the first of many wars between Israel and its Arab neighbors. The volatile situation was not helped by the existence of a large number of Palestinian refugees, and the fact that the economies of these countries were considered too weak to maintain long-term, or any, prosperity.

The Clapp Mission was sent to make a survey of Palestine and craft proposals for the future.[13] Tyler traveled there on behalf of the World Bank but as "an individual and not as a representative of the Bank." This distinction was made for two reasons.[14] One, officially he was no longer an employee

---

11 Royall Tyler to Mildred Barnes Bliss, undated, before April 4, 1949, Paris, "Bliss–Tyler Correspondence," https://www.doaks.org/resources/bliss-tyler-correspondence/letters/undated-10, accessed May 18, 2019.
12 International Bank for Reconstruction and Development, *Fifth Annual Report, 1949–1950*, Washington, D.C. 1950, 42.
13 For the Clapp Mission, see, FRUS, 1949, vol. 6, (1977), 60–71, 165–67, 178–9, 1327, 1350–54, 1357–58, 1374, 1389–90, 1392–93, 1399–1404, 1407–09, 1413–17, 1422–26, 1442–44, 1450–53, 1459–60, 1463–65, 1469–81, 1493–94, 1505–06, 1548–51, 1563–64.
14 R. L. Garner to Royall Tyler, September 29, 1949, Thompson Todd Collection.

Chapter 9

of the organization; two, the Bank was afraid that the UN and the State Department would drag it into making impractical loans. The vice president of the IRBD specifically warned Tyler that the Bank did not "wish any report and recommendations of the mission to commit the Bank in any sense of financing projects which might arise out of it," and, therefore, Tyler's good advice should "prevent the report from proposing financial arrangements which are impractical whether the financing eventually comes from governmental grants or loans or from other sources."[15] Although Tyler was asked to join the mission just a week before its departure, and with the above caveats, he made the right decision.[16] The work was intense, but he still found time during those two months to get acquainted with places he had never visited earlier. The Arab countries in the Near East were uncharted territory for him and he found "the experience prodigiously interesting."[17] At that time, the Near East was not only a possible place for Tyler to conduct his work for the Bank but his art historian interests was also quite piqued by the possibility of staying there for more months granted by the mandate.

Tyler committed himself to the job at hand and gave the usual hundred percent. The results, as in the past, were to the liking of his superior. As Clapp noted concerning a memo Tyler submitted on Lebanon, it was "precisely the kind of analysis & observation needed for each country we are commissioned to study. These analyses will be an important source of ideas & comment for our final report."[18] The mission's final report was completed on December 18, 1949, and was issued ten days later.[19] Appendix II, an 83-page financial survey, was mainly written by Tyler.[20]

It was earlier recommended that a permanent UN agency be set up in the Middle East region, and Tyler would have liked to secure a job under an American director. He asked Dulles and Robert Woods Bliss to use their connections to help him secure either the post or an assistant post. Both Dulles and Bliss recommended Tyler for the Middle East mission to

---

15 Ibid.
16 Royall Tyler to Mildred Barnes Bliss, October 7, 1949, Paris, "Bliss–Tyler Correspondence," https://www.doaks.org/resources/bliss-tyler-correspondence/letters/07oct1949, accessed May 18, 2019.
17 Royall Tyler to Mildred Barnes Bliss, October 21, 1949, Beyrouth, "Bliss–Tyler Correspondence," https://www.doaks.org/resources/bliss-tyler-correspondence/letters/21oct1949, accessed May 18, 2019.
18 Gordon R. Clapp to Royall Tyler, November 4, 1949, Thompson Todd Collection.
19 For the text of the report, see, FRUS, 1949, vol. 6, 1548–51.
20 Royall Tyler to Allen W. Dulles, December 21, 1949, Box 55, Folder 19, Allen W. Dulles Papers.

Secretary of State Dean Acheson, but the State Department already had other ideas as to personnel, though Acheson promised to keep Tyler's name in mind.[21] Simply put, there were other candidates with very good connections, and Tyler failed to secure the nomination.[22] As had happened so often earlier, soon enough circumstances and previous experience landed Tyler his next and final job. When the Clapp Mission was over, and he found himself out of Near East job possibilities, he became involved in the National Committee for a Free Europe (NCFE).

As mentioned in the previous chapter, Tyler had paid close attention to the birth and first phase of the Hungarian dissident diplomats' committee, and he stayed in contact with various persons in exile and émigrés of Hungarian origin after World War II. Now this took place under the changed circumstances of the Cold War, which was slowly but inevitably setting in, and as it did so, the various Central and Eastern European exile groups became increasingly important to the United States government. The American leadership, at least on a rhetorical level, never gave up on the countries that now found themselves in the Soviet sphere. Accordingly, if and when the desired change came, the reliable persons in exile could assume a leading role in the new democratic states presently behind the "Iron Curtain." The countries in questions—Poland, Czechoslovakia, Hungary, Romania, Bulgaria, and the Baltic states—all had organized groups in the West, mainly in the United States, Great Britain, and France. These were often fragmented groups that also appealed to the State Department for help in any way they could. They regularly organized events and tried to hold their political-cultural communities together, which was no easy task owing to the various points of views of their respective members. These national committees could, however, provide sometimes vital information about what was going on in the

---

21 Allen W. Dulles to Dean Acheson, February 10, 1950, and Dean Acheson to Allen W. Dulles, March 7, 1950, Box 1 Folder 4, Acheson, Dean, 1940–1964, Allen W. Dulles Papers; Royall Tyler to Robert Woods Bliss, December 29, 1949, Paris, "Bliss–Tyler Correspondence," https://www.doaks.org/resources/bliss-tyler-correspondence/letters/29dec1949 accessed May 19, 2019.

22 Raymond A. Hare to Allen W. Dulles, March 15, 1950, Box 55, Folder 19, Allen W. Dulles Papers; Royall Tyler to Robert Woods Bliss, December 19, 1949, Paris, "Bliss–Tyler Correspondence," https://www.doaks.org/resources/bliss-tyler-correspondence/letters/19dec1949; Royall Tyler to Robert Woods Bliss, February 27, 1950, Paris, "Bliss–Tyler Correspondence," https://www.doaks.org/resources/bliss-tyler-correspondence/letters/27feb1950, both accessed May 20, 2019. Finally, John B. Blandford was nominated by the White House.

Soviet sphere, so it was in the interest of the American leadership to take some responsibility for them.

This trend well reflected the public–private relations that were typical in trying to implement American foreign policy goals during the Cold War.[23] (During the interwar years similar steps were taken by various American governments.) In order to coordinate these sometimes loosely organized groups, the State Department tried to synchronize their activities. This coordinating effort—with substantial help from the nascent CIA—bloomed into the National Committee for a Free Europe, Inc. (NCFE), which was established in June 1949. Later, in 1954, it was renamed and today perhaps is best remembered as the Free Europe Committee (FEC). Many members of the Hungarian exile community took part, in one form or another, in the aforementioned activities, and Tyler soon became a link between them and the NCFE, especially after he became involved in that organization as well.[24]

George Kennan, the architect of the policy of containment of Soviet expansion, argued for launching a secretly funded private organization with the overt aim, implemented by covert means, of making whatever inroads were possible into the Soviets' newly acquired satellite countries in Eastern and Central Europe, thus to undermine the Soviet regime and its influence within these countries.[25] The most high profile branches of the NCFE were the well-known Radio Free Europe (RFE) from 1949, and the Assembly of Captive European Nations (ACEN) founded in 1954. The NCFE comprised such household names as Adolf A. Berle, Jr., Dwight D. Eisenhower, Joseph C. Grew, Henry R. Luce, and Darryl Zanuck, together with the ubiquitous Allen Dulles. It was Dulles, in fact, who recommended Tyler to represent NCFE in Europe. As historian Giles Scott-Smith pointed out, the organization teemed with ex-OSS men as well as leading persons from media, advertising, and public relations.[26]

---

23 See, Helen Laville and Hugh Wilford, eds., *The US Government, Citizen Groups and the Cold War: The State-Private Network* (London and New York: Routledge, 2006).
24 On the history and various aspects of the NCFE, see, Hugh Wilford, *The Mighty Wurlitzer* (Cambridge MA: Harvard University Press, 2008), 29–40; Katalin Kádár-Lynn, ed. *The Inauguration of "Organized Political Warfare": The Cold War Organizations Sponsored by the National Committee for a Free Europe/Free Europe Committee* (Saint Helena, CA: Helena History Press, 2013).
25 Kádár-Lynn, *The Inauguration of "Organized Political Warfare,"* 17–20.
26 Giles Scott-Smith, "The Free Europe University in Strasbourg: U.S. State–Private Networks and Academic 'Rollback'," *Journal of Cold War Studies*, 16, no. 2 (Spring 2014): 82.

In the second half of May 1950, Tyler spent about two weeks in the United States, in New York and Washington mostly. He met with Dulles, and they talked about the possibility of Tyler making himself useful in Europe in a new capacity. Dulles knew very well the deep contacts Tyler had mainly among Hungarian emigrants and some other nationalities as well. Also, he was keenly aware of Tyler's desire to find something useful to do, and here was a golden opportunity. Not surprisingly, Tyler was offered the opportunity to become European representative of the NCFE. Dulles's involvement was a welcome prospect for Tyler. At last, he felt, it was "such a relief to have a human being to deal with, instead of Bureaucracy."[27] Naturally, Tyler accepted the offer. On June 1, 1950, in a small Paris office with a secretary and a stenographer, Tyler officially started his work for the Cold War organization.[28] The new position called for trips to New York for NCFE meetings, always a welcome opportunity for Tyler to meet old friends, primarily the Blisses. Admittedly, in Hungarian emigrant circles Tyler's posting to Paris as a representative of NCFE created the rumor that he would take $2 million with him for welfare purposes and for organizing more robust political activity.[29] This, of course, was not true, but Tyler did indeed meet regularly with the representatives of the Hungarian immigrants in Europe such as György Apponyi, but especially Pál Auer.[30]

Tyler also conveyed criticism of refugees from Central and Eastern Europe regarding how Radio Free Europe functioned. These critical complaints mainly referred to the length of the news items and the uninspiring speeches of immigrant politicians that were aired. The latter were tailored too much to American taste, and the BBC and Voice of American broadcasts met their needs more. The Polish newsmen of the London-based International Federation of Free Journalists asked Tyler to relay their views

---

27 Royall Tyler to Mildred Barnes Bliss, May 29, 1950 [1], New York, "Bliss–Tyler Correspondence," https://www.doaks.org/resources/bliss-tyler-correspondence/letters/29may1950-1, accessed May 20, 2019.
28 Royall Tyler to Robert Woods Bliss, May 30, 1950, New York, "Bliss–Tyler Correspondence," https://www.doaks.org/resources/bliss-tyler-correspondence/letters/30may1950, accessed May 20, 2019.
29 James G. McCargar. "Memorandum – Political Aspects of the Hungarian Emigration in France," in Charles E. Bohlen to Dean Acheson, December 28, 1950, 864.00/12-2850, Roll 1, Internal Affairs of Hungary 1950–1954, NARA.
30 Royall Tyler to DeWitt C. Poole, September 30 and December 23, 1950, Royall Tyler to C. D. Jackson, March 31 and June 12, 1951, Royall Tyler to Frederic R. Dolbeare, May 14 and November 24, 1951, Royall Tyler to John W. Cutler, June 19, 1951, Folder 1, Auer Paul, Box 150, RFE/RL Corporate Records" Collection, Hoover Institution Archives, Stanford, USA.

according to which the programs were ineffective as propaganda, the content and skills of the speakers were questionable, while the choice of music was unfortunate. They also objected to the overblown optimism concerning the future of the captive nations. Tyler expressed his opinion toward NCFE that Eastern European political refugees living in Western Europe should be used in to a larger extent concerning both the contents of the programs and propaganda effects. Only this way was it possible to ensure a more solid and larger audience in the target countries. Tyler also challenged the situation that the various National Committees had too much influence in these radio programs, and the solution would have been an American editor-in-chief working in Europe. Therefore he welcomed the idea that the center should be moved to Europe, which indeed took place in the late spring of 1951.[31]

In the August 1950 meeting of NCFE, Tyler's services were assigned a further role. This was another small chapter in the long saga of psychological warfare during the Cold War. The idea was to prepare as many young immigrants from Eastern Europe as possible for a hoped for return to their native countries. As A.A. Berle, a former member of Roosevelt's "Brain Trust," put it at the official launch of the Free Europe University in Exile, Inc., the goal was "to assist in maintaining the great intellectual traditions and cultural heritage of the Iron Curtain countries by giving exiled scholars from those countries a place to coordinate their work."[32] Or, in other words, "to provide 'the raw material for democratic leadership'."[33] Such preparation was to be provided in the framework of the Free Europe University, an institution funded by NCFE, and located in Strasbourg, France. The FEU's goals were clearly established in terms similar to Berle's, as NFCE president, C. D. Jackson, put it:

> When liberated, those countries will have urgent need of their own young men, well-educated and equipped for leadership in a free world. My of these young men are at present exiles in Europe. The Free Europe

---

[31] Priscilla Roberts, *Frank Altschul, 1887–1981: A Political and Intellectual Biography*, unpublished manuscript, 42–44, 62–64.

[32] "Scholars Prepare for a Free Europe," *New York Times*, June 2, 1950.

[33] "Memorandum on Conversation between A. A. Berle, Jr., Edgar A. Mowrer, Spencer Phenix, Alan Valentine, and Richard Sears," September 22, 1950, quoted in Veronika Durin-Hornyik, "The Free Europe University in Exile, Inc. and the Collège de l' Europe libre (1951–1958)," in Kádár-Lynn, ed. *The Inauguration of "Organized Political Warfare,"* 457.

University can offer them education and equipment for the part they can play in rebuilding a peaceful world and in maintaining their own national culture and traditions.[34]

The association responsible for working out the details on the ground needed a reliable president, and this was the role for which Tyler was nominated.[35] He was the most senior member on location in France, and his French connections and understanding of the French culture made him an ideal choice for the job.[36] The first academic year commenced in November 1951, with 97 students chosen out of 900 applicants.[37]

In the summer before the grand opening, Tyler formulated his opinions concerning the feasibility of any possible unity among the peoples of the Danubian region that could point to further democratic evolution. What prompted his thoughts were thoughts on how the exiled immigrant groups in the United States imagined the future once their respective countries were no longer under Soviet rule. In Tyler's view, until political unity existed, there could be no talk of any customs and monetary union either, but that first component had always been so elusive as to leave no doubt in his mind as to its impracticality. It is worth quoting his letter to NCFE President Jackson in detail, because it gets to the core of the problem.

> The Satellite countries are pretty primitive, for the most part. Primitive people are apt to be highly suspicious of one another, and crudely cunning. They will talk 'union' as long as they think they can obtain our money by so doing. But the chances of their practicing it, I believe, are nil. There was once an economic customs and monetary unit of 50 million souls, in the old Austro-Hungarian monarchy. We thought it would serve the ends of "democracy" to destroy it. But when it comes to putting Humpty-Dumpty together again, we can guess, and guess, and guess. I believe it would be more profitable, or less mischievous,

---

34 "College for Iron Curtain Exiles set up in Europe by Charter Here," *New York Times*, July 23, 1951.
35 On the establishing and launching of the Free Europe University, see, Durin-Hornyik, "The Free Europe University in Exile," in Kádár-Lynn, ed. *The Inauguration of "Organized Political Warfare*," 439–78.
36 Scott-Smith, "The Free Europe University in Strasbourg," 93–94.
37 "Exiles Preparing Role in Liberation," *New York Times*, March 13, 1952; Royall Tyler to Robert Woods Bliss, June 27, 1951, Paris, "Bliss–Tyler Correspondence," https://www.doaks.org/resources/bliss-tyler-correspondence/letters/27jun1951, accessed May 20, 2019.

Chapter 9

to recognise the unpromising nature of the task, and devote our energies to aims that might conceivably be achieved. If Belgium and Holland cannot get together, is it likely that our Danubian and Balkan pets can?[38]

Rarely had he spoken in such raw terms, which must have reflected his frustration with the process of possibly bringing freedom to people who were not able to live peacefully with one another in the first place. In many ways he was right on the money, because neither in his lifetime nor afterwards was seeking to unify the Danubian region's countries a realistic approach. After the Soviet Union withdrew from the region at the end of the 1980s, none of the countries toyed with the idea of union with its neighbors, and as the 1990s showed, the return of fervent nationalism produced breakups—mild and quick in the case of Czechoslovakia but sadly violent and protracted in Yugoslavia. And the relations between Hungary and Romania, for example, are often strained on account of the Hungarian minority living in Transylvania. So, history has borne witness to Tyler's earlier observation. With entry into the European Union in the twenty-first century, some of the customs union aims have been achieved, but politically serious antagonism can still be seen emanating in part from the more than one hundred years old Trianon treaty.

Tyler kept a diary in which he loyally kept entries concerning daily affairs. Unfortunately, this little book, which was still in Antigny in the early 2010s, has since seemingly been lost. Giles Scott-Smith was apparently the only historian who had access to it before the family sold Antigny.[39] Regrettably he focused only on the FEU, so it remains a matter of conjecture what valuable information might have been hidden in that diary. At any rate, Tyler's private notes concerning the FEU offer a grim picture of decisions made without adequate planning or preparation for the possible results. In addition, there were personal conflicts among the participants that bred mistrust, which Tyler felt keenly.[40] As he complained to himself, "The trouble is that

---

38 Royall Tyler to C. D. Jackson, July 9, 1951, Folder 9, European Movement, Box 184, RFE/RL Corporate Records" Collection, Hoover Institution Archive.
39 I reached out to the family a few years ago and asked them to try to trace it, but they could not.
40 See, for example, Berle's diary entry, April 14, 1953, Roll 6, Adolf A. Berle, Jr. Diary, 1937–1971, FDR Library, Hyde Park.

the New York Trustees have no real understanding of the Strasbourg operation, and Tyson doesn't understand its inner problems well enough to make the Trustees see them."[41] Levering Tyson replaced DeWitt Poole as president of the FEU in May 1952. His tenure was not a success, and he was replaced by John Pelényi in the fall of 1954.

The visible results proved Tyler's observations right. The opening of the institution was a rushed affair, with a confused student and teacher body, unclear guiding principles, and vexing linguistic inadequacies, all of which contributed to the basic problem.[42] The second academic year was afflicted by personnel problems, and there was some jockeying for power between New York and the European centers, Paris and Strasbourg. Tyler's very last diary entry, a mere week before his death, painted an unsatisfactory picture: "The Strasbourg Affair is an awkward one. Not cleared up yet; at best it will take time."[43] In addition to these problems, the FEU was not immune to the changing international political landscape, and after some changes in functions for a short time, the college courses came to a halt in 1958, although summer programs continued to run for years.

On March 2, 1953, Royall Tyler committed suicide. He was found by his son, who wrote the following to C.D. Jackson four days later:

> He spent the last day of his life with us. He and I drove up to see young Royall at his school in Normandy, (it was Sunday, March 1) and walked in the woods together in the afternoon. We returned to Paris, he and I, and we dined quietly at home with Betsy and our daughter Eve. We drove him home afterwards and he was a little tired—that's all. The next morning he was found dead in his bed.[44]

This account, for obvious reasons, left out the nature of Tyler's death. Many years later his grandson also remembered the event vividly.

---

41 Tyler's Diary entry, September 21, 1952, quoted in Scott-Smith, "The Free Europe University in Strasbourg," 95.
42 Durin-Hornyik, "The Free Europe University in Exile, Inc.," 478–85.
43 Tyler's Diary entry, February 23, 1953, quoted in Scott-Smith, "The Free Europe University in Strasbourg," 95.
44 William R. Tyler to C. D. Jackson, March 6, 1953, Folder, Tyler, William R., Box 106, Jackson, C. D. Papers, Eisenhower Library, USA.

"I think that the housekeeper telephoned my father when she found RT's bedroom door locked, and that it was really my father who was the first to see what had happened—the blood everywhere. ... [T]he method he chose (at the age of 69), as well as the context of the act (his son & family there in Paris with him), conveys not only violently self-destructive anger and despair, but also a conviction of irremediable isolation. Apparently he lived only to finish *Charles V*. Beside that, all for him seems to have been darkness.[45]

According to Tyler's granddaughter, in his last years he found office work too demanding and missed physical exercise and Antigny a lot. Also, Elisina's health had taken another turn for the worse in 1952, and Tyler had to take care of everything at times.[46] Another relative, his great-granddaughter, conveyed the story of his death—probably from her mother, Tyler's granddaughter—as follows: "RT was suffering from depression and had been on antibiotics that had made him feel really ill. The maid called after she found him in the bathtub, having slit his wrists. My grandfather had to go and take care of it."[47] It is difficult to know what really took place, or why Royall Tyler chose to end his life in the fashion he chose. The now-living relatives also allude to the strong possibility that Elisina had cheated on Tyler, in particular with Hayford Peirce, which would have been a painful sting for Tyler. In all the material, especially in the private letters, there is no trace of this whatsoever, but if true, it might have played a role in Tyler's deteriorating condition.[48]

A friend of his wrote an obituary for the *Times* saying, "Good fairies brought manifold gifts to his cradle and dowered him with a mind of first rate quality ... The privilege of his friendship was an enrichment of life to those who came close to that admirable mind, and in our sorrow we must be grateful for all he revealed to us of existence at its highest level of intellec-

---

45 Royall Tyler, "Royall Tyler (1884–1953)", essay by Royall Tyler' grandson on his grandfather, dated October 28, 2009, in possession of the author. A shortened version of this essay appeared in Tyler, *One Name, Two Lives*, 153–57.
46 Email message from Eve Thompson to Gwenyth Huxtable, February 12, 2015.
47 Email message from Gwenyth Todd to Zoltán Peterecz, September 21, 2016.
48 Royall Tyler, "Blind Turtle Swims the Sea," in *One Name, Two Lives* (Charley's Forest: NSW, Australia: Blue-Tongue Books, 2017), 157; email message from Royall Tyler to Zoltán Peterecz, October 18, 2009; email message from Gwenyth Todd to Zoltán Peterecz, September 21, 2016.

tual excellence."⁴⁹ His long-time friend and fellow spy during World War II, Allen Dulles, wrote that Tyler's "death was for me a cruel loss. There was no one to whom I felt closer and whose friendship I had treasured more."⁵⁰

It is somewhat ironic, if not outright tragic, that due to the changed political atmosphere in the Cold War setting, Tyler's death did not even make the news in the country where he served the longest, Hungary. At that time the West was the enemy and Westerners, but especially Americans, were collectively seen as trying to uproot socialism. Personalities from the interwar years who collaborated with the Horthy regime in any way were anathema to the state and often persecuted if still living in Hungary—evicted, stripped from their titles, jobs, livelihood, and often put in prison. If they had immigrated or if they were foreigners, then they were totally ignored and/or lied about. Tyler felt no love for communist Hungary, and seemingly liked the former regime much more. This was not only due to the many years he had spent in Hungary, it was also his ideological stance. As an art historian and cold warrior, for example, he was vehemently against the idea that the sacred crown of St. Stephen, Hungary's first king, could be the subject of political blackmail between Hungary and the United States. When the American Robert Vogeler, the deputy director of IT&T in Hungary, was arrested on the charge of spying, the Hungarian government wanted to exchange him for the crown and the regalia—without success.⁵¹ The succinct opinion on this affair that Tyler confided to Dulles speaks volume on how he saw the crown and the relationship between East and West in the early Cold War: "I hope our people realize that, if we were to hand over the Crown to the communists, our name would be mud with all Hungarians for ever more, communists and non-communists, without distinction ... Don't think this is just the fancy of an impertinent Byzantimologist [sic]. It's the plain truth."⁵² It was a small but important consolation for the family that at least in the United States the Hungarian community did remember him with fondness. The Hungarian National Council organized a requiem mass for him

---

49 Violet Markham, "Mr. Royall Tyler," *Times* (London), March 9, 1953, 10.
50 Allen W. Dulles to William R. Tyler, May 9, 1953, Box 55 Folder 18, Tyler, William R, 1954–1969, Allen W. Dulles Papers
51 See, Robert A. Vogeler, with Leigh White, *I Was Stalin's Prisoner* (New York: Harcourt, Brace and Company, 1951); Borhi, *Dealing with Dictators*, 81–82.
52 Royall Tyler to Allen W. Dulles, June 21, 1950, Box 55 Folder 19, Allen W. Dulles Papers.

Chapter 9

in Washington.[53] It was C. D. Jackson who asked Monseigneur Béla Varga, a Catholic priest and chairman of the Hungarian National Council, to come to the capital and celebrate the mass.[54] Varga's words touched Elisina and William Royall Tyler deeply, and they felt it was fitting that this religious service was performed by somebody from Hungary, the country "which he loved and for which he worked so splendidly."[55] In a limited way at least, the Hungarians bade him farewell.

His legacy remains largely to be explored. His passion, perhaps a calling, was clearly Byzantine art history. To this subject he devoted immense energy, and grew from a lay person into a trusted professional, and later a renowned expert in the field. He was devoted to the beauty of these old masterpieces, and tirelessly worked on various means to get them introduced to the larger public. He published both smaller and larger works on the subject, often together with Hayford Peirce. His last work, concerning Charles V, was not completed at the time of his suicide but was published posthumously with the help of his son three years later.[56]

As far as the League of Nations years are concerned, this period can be clearly evaluated as something like a career, although it lasted no longer than twenty years. This was, however, almost the whole lifetime of the organization, and Tyler joined at a crucial moment when the financial reconstruction efforts were beginning in Central Europe. It may be of interest to note with respect to financial and economic affairs that Tyler was not at all good at arithmetic and mathematics. His success was not due to expertise of that sort but rather to being able to grasp the more essential features beyond the numbers.[57] Also, he had a very keen memory for the places he had visited, and could recall the tiniest of details. In addition, he was a great food and wine connoisseur.[58]

---

53   James N. Carder, "Paris, Strasbourg, and Washington, D.C. (1950–1953)," "Bliss–Tyler Correspondence," https://www.doaks.org/resources/bliss-tyler-correspondence/historical-introductions/paris-strasbourg-and-washington-dc, accessed May 20, 2019. He incorrectly gives the name of the organization as National Hungarian Committee.
54   William R. Tyler to C. D. Jackson, April 19, 1953, Folder, Tyler, William R., Box 106, Jackson, C. D. Papers.
55   William Royall Tyler to György Bakach-Bessenyey, April 26, 1953, File 76, Roll 4, P 2066, György Bakach-Bessenyei Papers, P 2066, HNA.
56   Royall Tyler, *The Emperor Charles the Fifth* (London: George Allen and Unwin, 1956).
57   Royall Tyler, "Royall Tyler (1884–1953)."
58   Tyler, *One Name, Two Lives*, 158–59.

Royall Tyler seems to have enjoyed a well-deserved renaissance in the past decade. Earlier, he was seen only a character in a supporting role to other, more well-known persons and events. It is true that he was rarely in a situation to decide about momentous things and was a real team player. His name appeared ubiquitously in historical works, but most of the time as a background person, as a reference, or as a footnote. In the twenty-first century a belated recognition appears to have arrived, and it is both understandable and due. He was one of many people who observed decades of historical significance for Europe and the United States. He experienced the pre-World War I peace in Europe, World War I, the Paris Peace Conference, the birth, heyday, and demise of the League of Nations, World War II, and the early Cold War—and all this not only as a close observer but more often than not as an active participant. But it was his undying thirst for knowledge in various fields, together with his innate capability of synthetizing and understanding the various subjects at hand that made him unique. Mastering all the major European tongues, and some lesser, unique ones, also meant that he possessed an exceptional expertise that could be and was used by various organizations and governments in his lifetime. His deep understanding of Europe's past and its contemporaneous politics, his familiarity with and inside and out knowledge of the League of Nations, his oversight of the continent's financial problems and ability to blend in to European culture—all this as an American citizen—made him indispensable in times of crises, of which there was an almost unceasing supply. In light of all this, it is not surprising that scholars are now turning to him and gaining precious perspective on history through an investigation of his activities. What is somewhat astonishing is that he was never taken out of the mold of the historical sideshow he was relegated to in the twentieth century. I hope this book is not too late an attempt to place him more in the center of European history in the first half of that century.

For all these reasons it is now perhaps important to introduce Royall Tyler as a man of history, and to show what he thought about that subject. Because of his enduring passion, from his teenage years, for art history, especially Byzantine art, his life was already, at least on one level, inseparable from studying some of the roots of European history and civilization. He could excel at this not only on account of his interest in the subject but also his open mind and devotion to learning languages. He crisscrossed Europe

Chapter 9

countless times and he was always on the lookout for cultural roots as he studied humanity. Actually, his faith in humanity defined him as a human being and shaped his personality. His first official job started with studying and writing about history, when he was commissioned by the British Public Record Office to edit the Calendars of State Papers. He did an outstanding job, and that, to a certain degree, launched his multifaceted career.

In his younger years, he approached the question of history somewhat philosophically, perhaps because he was in the habit of writing about it to his mentor and friend, the Spanish philosopher Miguel de Unamuno. Prior to the outbreak of World War I, he was weighing in his mind what significance and what value history possessed. In a letter to Unamuno in 1913, he wrote that he refused to worry about the value of history and suggested instead that one should "confess that what attracts us to it is something similar to what drives us to study art--let's not lie to ourselves and admit that he who studies art does not produce it."[59] In other words, at that stage in his life and career, Tyler understandably belittled his own possible role, both concerning history and art history. In 1913, the last year of peace on the continent, the study of history mostly represented satisfaction for his curious mind. Its main value lay in expanding one's imagination and helping one to understand earlier times. He also saw it as a synonym for travelling. Although he clearly characterized himself as "someone who occupies himself with the past," he was also clearly afraid of the responsibility inherent in writing about it, especially art history, because of the possible distortion between thought and the written text.[60]

World War I reshaped his perception. Most importantly, with his keen sense of understanding and analysis, he grew well aware that he was going through historic times and he was a tiny, imperceptible part of them. After he started to work in the American Army in 1917, his reflections sounded much more self-assured and ambitious. "I am a historian and a man of history, of the past ... and I dare to say that as I live I will prove it."[61] He outlined as his goal "describing the overlapping influences during the medieval

---

59 Royall Tyler to Miguel de Unamuno, May 27, 1913, in William Royall Tyler, "A Young American Friend of Miguel de Unamuno," 731. I want to thank Isaiah Romo for the translation of Tyler's letters to Unamuno.
60 Ibid.
61 Royall Tyler to Miguel de Unamuno, February 21, 1918, ibid., 732.

period of the major European forces," and he clearly dedicated a large part of the next thirty-five years of his life to realizing that goal.[62] But he attributed it to Unamuno's influence that "when the time came to choose, I chose service over never-ending whimsical pursuits, and since then the sky has cleared up at times and I think I know where the north lies."[63]

---

62 Ibid.
63 Royall Tyler to Miguel de Unamuno, February 22, 1924, in William Royall Tyler, "A Young American Friend of Miguel de Unamuno," 733. I want to thank Isaiah Romo for the translation of the letter.

Appendix

Royall Tyler to Henry Morgenthau, December 21, 1939.

I have just returned from one week in Budapest and few days in Milan, Venice, Rome paragraph

Hungary now has definite assurance Italy will accept clearing liras for maritime freights of Hungarian exports and imports returning Hungary where Italy is bound by contract to demand payment in the currencies stop

Hungary intends continuing American relief credits payments and League Loan service as at present stop

For other foreign debts covered by three year arrangement concluded summer 1937 Hungary fears she cannot renew on same terms after summer 1940 and it contemplating asking creditors agree to suspension of amortisation meaning reduction of about 15 million gold pengö yearly from present 40 stop Hungarian gold and the exchange losses now not as heavy as in first weeks of war but governor expects these losses to average round three to four million gold pengö monthly at which rate Hungary might rock along for about two years supplying her industry with essential raw materials avoiding unmanageable unemployment and resisting German attempts to reduce her agrarian colony status stop German attempts now taking form of increases up to 60% in Reichsmark prices of German goods needed by Hungarian industry like dyestuffs and some chemicals while prices of finished goods remain unchanged although the choice of goods available is narrowing and total value of imports from Germany decreasing stop Germany still filling Hungarian orders of automobiles and trucks whole motor truck in German hands affording opportunities for penetration propaganda and espionage stop Hungary endeavoring to reach free exchange markets but constrained by lack of other markets to sell some 50% of total exports to Germany stop Hungary's Reichsmark holdings now round 45 million having been up to 100 million and likely to rise somewhat again accumulation Reichsmark holdings unwelcome but regarded as lesser evil than invasion or forced customs union stop Germany trying to link Hungarian food prices to German so that any rise in Germany may take Hungarian prices along thus making sales on free markets increasingly difficult stop Director General of National Bank has been in London for six weeks trying to settle blockade problems I have today heard by telephone from Budapest that he is returning tomorrow with an agreement considered as satisfactory by Hungary stop So far Hungarian food prices fairly steady but manufactures and imported goods are rising these increases being prevented from affecting official cost of living index by excluding articles like coffee as no longer of current consumption stop German agents making frantic efforts to buy up any foreign assets belonging to Hungarians paragraph Hungarian Government has situation well in hand Nazi factions losing ground and government ready to outlaw them if they get off the reservation stop Hatred of Germany increased by Nazi and Soviet collusion and Soviet attack on Finland stop Regent in fine shape despite his 72 years Stories about impending appointment of Teleki as vice-Regent apparently baseless although if anything happened to Regent now Teleki would probably succeed him Minister of Finance Keresztes Fischer becoming premier latter a good man stop General belief in Hungary that German leaders can't make up their minds what to do their calculations being thrown out by British French intention to fight which Ribbentrop promised Hitler they never would do stop Three Hungarians out of four expect and want German defeat and now seem to exaggerate German difficulties though before the war they overestimated Germany's might stop Pathetic individual appeals from Germans for food gifts however small pouring in past censorship by thousands supported by harrowing stories such gifts at one time reaching six tons daily until Hungarian authorities limited amounts any individual could send present daily average still round three tons stop Hungarian authorities planning food rationing and two meatless days weekly though unnecessary so that visiting Germans may not think Hungary land of inexhaustible plenty stop Germany now makes entry for Hungarian nationals exceedingly difficult Hungarians believe this is because Germany does not want Hungarians to witness conditions especially in Austria where young Austrian SS men swagger around while older native Austrians are sent to the front this causing resentment which might blaze out despite ferocious repression stop Responsible Hungarians are apprehensive lest Germany decide to end odious comparisons by walking in stop At times German has appeared to encourage Hungary to seize Transylvania but Csaky told me Dec. 13 that Germany was promising Rumania deliveries of Polish war material and even guarantee of Rumania's present frontier against Hungary and that German promises of Czech war material to Hungary were never kept stop Mussolini assured Hungary he will intervene if she is attacked from whatever quarter stop Hungary properly grateful but not altogether reassured stop Hungarian Government knows about Italian plans for founding a Danubian monarchy under an Italian prince perhaps Aosta grouping several countries in a personal union stop Gratitude for past Italian help and hope of more to come counsel extreme tact but it is inconceivable that Hungarian opinion would ever accept an Italian king and there are suspicions that Germany may be behind the plan meaning to use it for a new peace offensive including stream reestablishment of Czech Austrian Polish independence or at any rate to forestall Habsburg restoration stop Ciano's speech Dec 16 soft pedalling talk of a Danubian Balkan bloc under Italy's aegis sounds as if above plan were dropped or put on ice for the present stop Hungarians friendly to Germany talk mysteriously of forthcoming reversal of European lineup Germany resuming enmity towards Soviets and deriving through Ukraine to Black Sea stop This may be devised to counteract disastrous effect on Hungarians of German Soviet association or perhaps further evidence of German irresolution stop Others think Soviet will reoccupy Bessarabia and that Rumania will then break up enabling Hungary to regain Transylvania stop Present Premier may be trusted not to try any adventurous course stop Though he cannot say so publicly I believe he devoutly prays that nothing will happen paragraph

In Italy confusion seems inextricable stop True that Mussolini after making Italians' flesh creep with war talk is now blessed for keeping out of war and telling Italians their duty is to profiteer stop But the standard of living is still worsening except for a privileged few comma prices are rising in spite of rigorous treatment of boosters comma the State is scandalously in arrears with its trills even for small sums comma unemployment increasing comma German Soviet deal is odious comma no one sees a way out stop Government appears not to rely exclusively on profiteering to right situation and the word goes around that spring will bring Italy's turn to tear off something big stop A few months back this was to be at Britain's or France's expense then it was to be South East Europe hegemony erecting a barrier against Soviets now after Ciano's quote peace unquote speech there is again talk of making the Allies pay through the nose for Italy's forbearance stop It is reported all military leave and suspensions of call to colors are cancelled beginning March and arrangements made for having school and after roomy buildings empty by then stop The Italian Press after displaying a certain objectivity in October and November has swung round again giving prominence to German news and delaying Allied news or putting it where it escapes notice stop German Gestapo agents and others planted before war started in public departments and industrial works are still there stop Capping the tall German stories carried by the Italian papers rumours are circulated about the real Hitler invincible weapon a torpedo which can be propelled and directed from shore according to information wirelessed from observation planes straight to British fleet wherever it may be comma the requisite material being manufactured in underground works near Leipzig all set for spring when Britain will be destroyed etc etc stop Italy is now manufacturing war material for France and trading or rather talking trade with Britain but British businessmen say that can get nothing done without bribery right up to the top their assertions tallying with accounts heard for years past from Italian business sources stop Nonofficial Italian opinion hates Germans and would like to see them beaten without however desiring Allied victory stop What the official view may be is a mystery colon perhaps it is simply determination to sit on the fence till the outcome is certain This fitting in with Ciano's efforts to establish a reputation for moderation Mussolini's bellicosity stop The changing of the guard that ousted Farinacci Altieri etc apparently had no international color but was a sop to opinion that had come dangerously to hate the party at the same time putting in key positions new men personally devoted to Ciano who is now reputed stronger than ever though cordially untested stop Farinacci and Altieri though Nazi enthusiasts were not sacrificed as such stop Ciano's deferent if shifty attitude towards Germany perhaps obeys more tangible reasons than ideological sympathies or even belief in German invincibility stop Much of this is felt by opinion which is torn between relief at not having had to fight on Germany's side comma fear of being dragged in as a result of some desperate gamble by leaders who see no sane way out of the mess comma fear that Germany if balked of other prey will come down on Trieste and a thickening apprehension that Italy will finally have to pay for the folly of those who make her risk fighting out of her class stop as time passes without German threats to destroy Britain materializing signs show that some even among the leaders would like to change their bets but Ciano seems committed to Germany and as Ciano's internal position waxes stronger the vicious circle seems complete Fascism fearing that if the king kin goes they will all go with him stop whether it would be possible to drag Italy in the war on Germany's side now or indeed to make Italians fight anyone for anything seems doubtful stop But although Italy may doublecross Germany on the Danube she cannot be expected under present leadership to collaborate sincerely with the Allies unless and until Germany is patently beaten stop No serious indication seen that the Royal house is gaining control End message

Thompson Todd Collection

Appendix

Royall Tyler, "Treatment of War-Criminals and Propaganda for Axis Countries," Geneva, April 12, 1943,

A war-story from Rome tells of a passage between a Nazi diplomat and a Monsignore. teh diplomat expresses wonderment at the vitality shown by the Church. "Two thousand years old, and still going strong," says he, "while our movement is already showing signs of wear, after only twenty years of existence. How did you ever get such a hold on the hearts of men?" The ecclesiastic, softly rubbing his hands, answers in unctuous tones: "Have you thought of having your Founder crucified?"

Have we, the United Nations, now got to render Nazidom and Fascism this supreme service, and lift the appeal they make onto a higher plane than they unaided could ever reach, by judging and executing their war-criminals? To start with, are we sure that the war-record of all the United Nations will be clear of any action calling for retribution, given equitable treatment? Well, let us assume for the sake of argument that we should be willing and able to punish the guilty on our side, if there were any, or that war-crimes are only committed in the Axis camp. There would still be difficulties. To proceed against the Axis small fry and not to bring the two big leaders to book would be ludicrous. To punish Führer and Duce would be fatal. Before taking such a leap in the dark, let us pause and consider where it may lead us. What Hitler and Mussolini may deserve is of little interest compared with the world's future: the way to cultivate all our chances of developing in the nations a will to live together in peace, and to avoid sowing dragons' teeth. If we execute Axis leaders, some of the blood we shed will be regarded by many in the Axis countries as the blood of martyrs, and martyrs' blood is worse than the teeth of any dragon. Whatever enormities the men we prosecute may have bene guilty of, and whatever care we may take to give them a fair trial and only execute those whose crimes have been proved up to the hilt, the procedure will stir opinion in their countries to its depths. Some people there may hail our action as the beginning of a world-tribunal destined to make such piracy as Hitler's forever impossible. But we shall certainly not succeed in persuading everyone that we are moved by love of justice and not by thirst for vengeance. It would suffice that there should be some trait in the personality of a single one of those convicted and executed that appealed to his fellow-countrymen, something pathetic or brave about his end, to make him look a victim in the public eye. One would be enough. The crimes of all the rest would fade out of the popular memory, giving place to hatred of the foreigner for putting a patriot to death.

We believe we are going to won this war. Defeat, for the Axis countries, will crown years of privation and suffering. Their present leaders may well be called to account by their own nationals. It is not suggested that we should protect them. But let us beware of punishing them ourselves if they fall into our hands, or of forcing any neutral country to extradite such of them as may take refuge within its borders, or of trying to have it both ways by bringing pressure to bear on the defeated Germans and Italians to try them, without our appearing in the proceedings. It would be better for us that Hitler should end his life in comfort and obloquy on the shores of a Swiss lake than that we should dignify him with a trial, which would be a world-sensation and would stir up whirlwinds of passion, for and against, on an issue which is not worth it. Realisation of the dangers lurking in this question has already shown here and there on our side; there have been warnings that Hitler dead might prove more dangerous than Hitler alive. May they be heeded! Even today there are Frenchmen whose souls revolt when they remember Napoleon's captivity at St. Helena; Napoleonic legend long remained factor in European politics. What would it have been if the British had hanged him? Can anyone believe that his fate would gave deterred Hitler or Mussolini? We shall have enough on our hands, when this war is over, to start life going again, without wasting our time on them or their associates, let alone that dangers that would loom up for the future, including possible revulsions of feeling in our own countries when the war-fever has abated, if we actually did justice on any of them.

In this connexion, it may be asked whether there is anything to be gained by attempting, as Allied propaganda frequently does, to drive a wedge between Axis internal opinion and its leaders? Germans and Italians no doubt often respond differently to our propaganda, but their reactions are sometimes much the same. They all know we want to sow them in mistrust of Hitler and Mussolini, and the more we try to do it, holding out hopes of better treatment the sooner they get rid of their present masters, the more Germans and Italians ask themselves whether, if it is our game to divide them, it should not be their game to be united. Good war-news are the best propaganda, of course, but we cannot count on a succession of victories and no set-backs form now on, and it may be worth to take stock of the propaganda lines we have been following and the results achieved. These are hardly such as to justify in going on as heretofore.

Why not try another approach, which although indirect might prove more effective, and proceed on the assumption that the peoples of Germany and Italy are as solidly behind their leaders as Hitler and Mussolini assert? Our prospects of victory are improving; there is news we can hand out, while betraying no military secrets, about production, indications of our increasing might in relation to that of the Axis and of revolt and sabotage in the occupied countries. If we concentrate on such points, and leave Axis opinion to scratch its head, without repeating hackneyed couplets about not confusing good peoples and wicked leaders, we may get sections of opinion in those countries alarmed about their future and determined to do something about it themselves, lest when the day of reckoning comes they be lumped together with the goats. Observant persons who have lived the war in Italy and minor Axist [sic] countries are aware of a belief, fortified by pattings [sic] on the back by the BBC (and now by General Giraud), that they will get off lightly, whatever happens. In Germany the atmosphere is different, but there also it is clear that no broadcast assurances of our sympathy will succeed in fomenting effective opposition against the régime, and that the result of this line of talk, so long continued, is rather to rouse suspicions of our candour.

If we carry out any plans for punishing war-criminals, opinion in the Axist [sic] countries will assume that those scape-goats have bene laden to our satisfaction with all the sins of the nation, will remember the nice things we have said about their masses, and will then be outraged if some of the post-war measures we may think necessary are not to their taste, and if we are not prepared at once to let by-gones be by-gones, and to treat them as we treat our Allies. After the last war, the hang-the-Kaiser talk, and the encouragement which Germans found in it to consider themselves as innocent victims, greatly contributed, when conditions weighed heavily upon them, to help Hitler spread the conviction that they had not been defeated in battle, but tricked into laying down their arms. It would be well to make Germans and Italians realise that we regard them as responsible for their leaders, instead of assuring them of our pity, poor lambs that they are, for having fallen into the hands of bad shepherds. If we go on telling them that it is all Hitler's and Mussolini's fault, they will conclude that we are not dealing squarely by them, when the war is over, and in the meantime will feel relieved of any obligation to overthrow their present régimes. It would of course not be wise, nor it is necessary, to drive them to despair by telling them that we consider them all equally guilty. But it might by well to allow them to reflect on the probable consequences of having followed Hitler and Mussolini, without any prompting from us, rather than assure them that we quite understand how they must hate it all. It would also be honest not to dwell on the treatment the German and Italian peoples are going to get after the war, for we do not yet know ourselves what is going to happen to them, or even what line we ourselves are going to take where they are concerned, assuming that we one day have that responsibility.

Thompson Todd Collection

Appendix

Royal Tyler, "Feudalism in Hungary," December 1944.

If the term is used in its proper sense: i.e., a system of land-tenure based on the relation of vassal and overlord arising from the holding of land in feud, feudalism does not exist in Hungary. Indeed, even in the middle ages, feudal institutions were less prevalent there than in most European countries. If we mean fiscal and other privileges possessed by the nobility, then all such rights were abolished in Hungary about a century ago, together with serfdom.

But those who speak of Hungary as feudal often have in mind its landless agrarian proletariat and large estates. Other Danubian countries, successors of the late Dual Monarchy, have carried out land-reform measures resulting in the sitting-up of latifundia, which are generally believed to have survived undiminished in Hungary. This notion subsists, mistaken as it is, thanks largely to the difficulty of obtaining any clear account of what has happened. Not to speak of Hungarian and other polemical writings and propaganda, which are usually beside the point, even statistical publications, while giving a mass of detail on secondary issues, fail to answer the main questions that anyone interested in the subject is likely to put. It takes much labor to discover the actual changes in land-tenure that have occurred over the last quarter of a century. An attempt is made here to throw a little light on the matter.

Trianon-Hungary's area is 16 million cadastral hold (1 hold = 0.575 hectare). Of this total, arable land amounts to 9.7 million hold. Forests account for just short of 2 million, pasturage for 1.7 million, meadows for 1.1 million. Over 900,000 hold, exempted from land-tax, are valueless for agriculture. The rest is vineyards, gardens, orchards, etc. For the present purpose, arable land alone counts. Important changes in its ownership have resulted from the land-reform law passed in 1920/1921 and from subsequent measures still in course of execution. Voluntary sale has also resulted in the breaking-up of big holdings.

Under the 1920/1921 law, about one million hold, expropriated from large estates, were allotted to small owners. It will not be attempted to show how this total splits up into the various descriptions of land. But a comparison of figures showing the distribution A) of the whole national area, and B) of the arable land, first when the 1921 law was about to be applied and then, in 1935, just before a further measure was adopted, may be of interest. It will be

Appendix

remembered that the differences between these two sets of figures represent all changes of ownership, whether through land-reform or by other processes.

A. Hungary's total area, classified according to the size of holdings (in million hold).

	April 30, 1921	December 31, 1935
a, Dwarf holdings (under 5 hold)		1.4
b, Small estates (5 to 100 hold)	a+ b 7.5	7.4 a+b 8.8
c, Medium estates (100-1000 hold)	2.7	3.1
d, Big estates (over 1000 hold)	5.8	4.1

B. Hungary's arable land, similarly classified.

	April 30, 1921	December 31, 1935
a, Dwarf holdings (under 5 hold)		1.0
b, Small estates (5 to 100 hold)	a+ b 5.6	5.7 a+b 6.7
c, Medium estates (100-1000 hold)	1.4	1.5
d, Big estates (over 1000 hold)	2.7	1.5

Over the fifteen years, the big estates' share in Hungary's total area decreased by 30%, and in its arable land by 44%. Practically the whole difference benefited dwarf and small owners. The medium estates very slightly increased their arable land, and a bit more their total holdings of all kinds of land (including forests). In absolute figures, the big estates owned 16.9% of the arable land in 1921 and 9.3% in 1935. If medium and big estates are grouped together, then 25.6% of Hungary's arable land was in estates of over 100 hold in 1921. By 1935 the percentage had decreased to 18.7%

In 1936 a new land-reform measure was enacted, providing for the expropriation and distribution of a part, varying with the size of the estate, of properties exceeding 3000 hold, the owners being compensated two-thirds in cash and one-third by instalments over 30 years. Restrictions were imposed upon the right of entail.

This measure did not work rapidly enough for public opinion, especially from 1938 on, when Hungary began to reoccupy parts of the provinces lost by the Treaty of Trianon, in which regions drastic land-reform laws had been applied in the early twenties. In 1940 further legislation reduced from 3000 to 500 hold the lower limit of estates subject to expropriation, the part to be expropriated rising from 20% to 80% (estates over 10,000 hold). Moreover, compensation was to be effected one-third in cash and two-thirds in instalments, over 30 years. The act also layed [sic] it down that distribution was to proceed at a rate not to fall below 100,000 hold in any one year.

Statistics are not yet available to show the effect of the recent measures on small holdings. But it has been calculated that the 1935 law resulted in the expropriation of about half-a-million hold, and that the 1940 law will distribute 1.7 million. It cannot be stated how much of this will be arable land. The figures given above, it will be remembered, are based on ownership, and take no account of whether the land is being actually worked by or for a big owner or by a small farmer who pays a rent for it. In many cases, the farmer hiring the land he cultivates is better off for equipment, buildings and stock than the small owner. A certain amount of land belonging to small owners is indeed rented by them to big proprietors who exploit it together with their own. These considerations should be borne in mind when drawing conclusions about this intricate problem.

What the social and economic effects of the measure now being carried out will be, no one can venture to predict. Also, further legislation may be introduced before the 1940 law has been executed. The 1920/21 law showed that land-reform is an expensive business. If an enforced distribution is to be of general benefit to a country, the new owners must have money to provide themselves with buildings, implements, stock and everything else needed to farm the land. In the early twenties, Hungary was struggling with the economic consequences of the Peace and in no position to equip the new owners. Neither could it compensate the old, although the case for giving them equitable treatment was strengthened by the fact that they had already had taken away from them, in most cases without equitable compensation, the land they owned in the 60% of old Hungary's territory annexed to the Successor States. Many new owners, unable to farm the land they had received, sold it, rented it back to the former proprietor, or even abandoned it. Generally speaking, the 1920 law did little to satisfy the agrarian proletariat's land-hunger. On the other hand, it tended to reduce the production of marketable crops and the fiscal capacity of the rural population at large, without appreciably bettering the lot of the peasantry.

Another important point is that land-reform is apt to take land away from competent and incompetent big owners alike, and to distribute it irrespectively of beneficiaries' capacity as farmers. There would be much to be said for a system of devolution so devised as to limit as far as possible the danger of reducing production. The 1920/21 law was open to criticism from this point of view, and the way it worked out could hardly fail to make a Government reluctant to proceed further on the same lines.

Hungary depends in large measure upon export-crops for its supply of foreign means of payment. Its industry has only recently developed on a scale permitting it to sell abroad. Indeed, even in the last years before the present war, Hungarian industrial exports were often marketed at an accounting loss, and were objected to in some quarters (e.g. in the U.S.A.) as exchange-dumping. Thus there were and are limits set to what could be done in the way of land-reform without prejudicing the country's economic position as a whole. The problem was more difficult for Hungary than for any of its immediate neighbors. Austria and Czechoslovakia were already industrialized. In Yugoslavia small farms had been the rule; its large holdings consisted mainly of forests. Roumania, whose circumstances were more like Hungary's, had its petroleum exports to fall back upon as a source of foreign exchange.

Further, there is the demographic problem. The density of agrarian population excessive throughout South-Eastern Europe, is greater in Hungary than in any of the surrounding countries. It is claimed that even if all the farm land in the country, big estates included, were cut up into farms averaging 10 hold each (which is regarded as the minimum form which a family can draw a livelihood), less than one-half of the present dwarf-owners, farm laborers and employees could be provided, and that as the remaining landless peasants would then be unable to earn a living by working on big estates, their plight would be worse than before. Industry could not take up the slack, for a long time to come. This line of reasoning may of course be pressed too far. It cannot constitute a valid case for leaving the land-problem to take care of itself, true though it is that land-reform alone is incapable of ensuring subsistence for all, or nearly all, the country's rural population. Much can be done by intensive cultivation and specialization to attenuate present hardships and to take advantage of Hungary's soil and climate for the production of valuable crops. But for that, money, education, and time are necessary. The peasant does not take readily to new ways. As emigration possibilities are unlikely to be opened up again on an appreciable scale, recourse must be had to other remedies, including a degree of industrialization. In the meantime, it would be dangerous to push through a rapid and drastic reform. The 1940 act, if it is executed as provided, perhaps goes as fast as would be wise, having regard to all the circumstances, even if it does spare some traces of Hungary's feudal past.

It has been widely asserted, in and out of print, that in the parts of pre-Trianon Hungary reoccupied by the Magyars from 1938 on land-reform allotments from big estates distributed to small holders a quarter of a century ago were returned to the former owners. As Hungary is now being ejected once more from the said territories, the question now lacks practical interest. Still, as such stories contribute to Hungary's reactionary reputation, it is perhaps worthwhile to inquire into what really happened. No statistics are as yet available on this point, but the following indications are believed to be roughly right.

After reoccupation, the Hungarian authorities took steps in two directions:
a) In territories given by Trianon to Czechoslovakia and Yugoslavia and afterwards reoccupied by Hungary, allotments in regions mainly inhabited by Magyars had been made in some cases by the Successor State to non-Magyar settlers from other regions. Such settlers were evicted, after reoccupation, from holdings estimated not to exceed a total of 50,000 hold (for the Slovak and Yugoslav territories together), which represents an infinitesimal fraction of the land-reform allotments that had been distributed by these two Successor States in the regions which Hungary reoccupied. Moreover, in the case of Slovakia, a convention was concluded between that country and Hungary providing that settlers so dispossessed were to be compensated by means of land belonging to Hungarian proprietors in (Tiso-) Slovakia.
b) Decrees were issued under which former owners from whom land had been taken in reoccupied regions might sue the beneficiaries (and in circumstances the Hungarian State) for additional compensation. Some suits were started under these decrees, but it appears that in no individual case has any additional compensation been awarded, let alone the question whether any such additional compensation could be collected from land-reform beneficiaries, even were the courts to allow it.

No general measure reversing land-reform procedure in the reoccupied regions has been enacted or even planned in Hungary.

The Hungarian rural population's standard of living is very low. But not solely or mainly because about 15% of the country's arable land belongs, or belonged until recently, to estates of over one thousand hold, or 30% of it to estates of over 100 hold (126 USA acres). If that were all, the remedy would not be far to seek. There are other and less tractable reasons, from which noisy attacks on the landowners divert attention. The old proverb: "Give a dog a bad name and hang him" certainly applies where they are concerned.

In the first place, Hungary's exportable food surplus, which before the 1919 frontiers were drawn was marketed in other parts of the old Dual Monarchy, has since then had to contend with former customers' attempts to attain agrarian self-sufficiency. Where the neighbors still went on buying food from Hungary, they now bought it in the cheapest form possible: e.g. wheat instead of flour. Prices of food-stuffs on the domestic market sank during the thirties to absurdly low levels. The Government, in order to permit the farmer to earn a bare livelihood, had no choice but to accept clearing arrangements by which Germany took the food which could not be sold elsewhere. Hungary saw her "favorable balance" on clearing account soar, but could not use it to obtain from Germany goods she needed, to anything like a corresponding value, the Hungarian farmer being paid by the National Bank of Hungary in the form of "advances" which were never compensated or refunded by Germany. This swindle was suffered by the Hungarian government, not for any foreign political motive but solely because there was no alternative way of taking surplus produce of the farmers' hands.

To make matters worse, as the already industrialised regions of the Danube Valley strove for autarky by forcing agriculture, often in branches which were not remunerative given their climate and soil, so Hungary struggled to attain the same fools' paradise by means of a hasty and ill-considered process of industrialisation under the shelter of prohibitive tariffs. To enquire whether the agrarian countries or the industrial started this ruinous competition would be like trying to discover which came first, the hen or the egg. Suffice it to say that the Hungarian masses were obliged to pay, for the manufactured articles they required, prices greatly in excess of what the same goods might have been sold for if imported, even including a sizeable duty. This system, iniquitous because it made current-consumption goods dear, while luxury-articles not produced in Hungary could be imported and sold relatively cheap, weighed heavier on the agricultural community than on the urban. Industry was booming, and factory workers' earnings, scanty though they were in comparison with wages ruling in other countries, put them in a relatively favorable position. There was no industrial unemployment.

The disparity between what the Hungarian farmer received for his produce and what he had to pay for textiles, tools, fertilisers and other necessities, sugar included although it is produced in and exported by Hungary, came to be known as the agrarian shears. The whole rural community suffered increasingly from it during the inter-war period. In presence of the obstacles that kept Hungarian food-exports from reaching the markets that had formerly absorbed them, the advocates of industrialisation could plausibly argue that Hungary must now develop its industry still further or see a considerable part of its population reduced to unemployment and destitution. It is a fact that in the last decade before the present war Hungary's supply of sound exchange proceeded more and more from the export of manufactured goods. But it must be added that in many cases these goods could only be sold, for the sake of the foreign exchange, on the distant markets willing to take them, at prices which involved an accounting loss, compensated however by the broad margin of profit maintained on the domestic market.

The maladjustment following the tracing of many thousands of new customs frontiers in the Danube Valley, the duplication of industry, the clogging up of time-honored trade-channels and the stoppage of emigration, coming on the top of the loss of two-thirds of the former national territory and the destruction of savings caused by the ruin of the currency, inflicted great hardship, particularly on the rural community. Landowners who managed to keep their heads above water could only do so by making a whole-time job of farming. Monte-Carlo saw them no more. Meanwhile, new fortunes were piled up in industry, by selling dear to the consumer and by paying the worker wages which, thanks to excessively depressed food prices, kept down production costs, in spite of the fact that most of the plant was new and had to be amortised. Thus there arose a new "feudalism", taking the word in a pejorative sense as meaning the exploitation of defenseless labor for less than equitable hire. If a profiteer must be denounced in the economic tragedy of inter-war Hungary, industry is the region where he may be found.

File 477, Box 12, RG 226, NARA

Appendix

Royal Tyler, "The Outlook for the Economic Issue, after San Francisco," Geneva, June 28, 1945,

The United Nations Charter just signed, now submitted to the governments for ratification, provides for the creation of an Economic and Social Council consisting of eighteen members, which is to be a principal organ of the world security organisation. Member states are to undertake to act singly and collectively in co-operation with the organisation in order to solve world-wide economic, social and cultural problems. Inter-governmental agencies dealing with these matters are to be brought into relationship with the organisation through agreements negotiated by the Economic Council, which will act under the authority of and may make recommendations and submit conventions to the General Assembly. The Economic Council may also call conferences and create whatever subsidiary commissions it considers necessary. "For the first time in history," to quote a release given to the press on completion of the Charter (June 22) "there will be an international institution to prevent economic causes of war from arising." What are the Economic Council's chances of discharging this responsibility?

The Charter distinguishes between:
a) the prevention of aggression, reserved to the Security Council; and
b) the removal of political, economic and social causes of war, to which end recommendations may be made to the Security Council by the General Assembly.

If actual aggression is prevented by the Great Powers (i.e. the Security Council, practically speaking), the argument would seem to run, or may be left to the General Assembly, assisted by the Economic Council, to deal with potential causes of discord. But however grave a view the Economic Council may take of a problem arising in its proper sphere, and which it cannot solve by the means at its disposal, it can make no recommendation to the Security Council. It can only appeal to the General Assembly.

There will clearly be no aggression as long as the will prevails as between the Big Five, or indeed the Big Three, to adjust all disputes. For close on four years of the European war which has just ended, the Big Three were held together by a common determination to defeat Germany.

It is apparently assumed that in future an equally effective binding force is to be supplied by the will to prevent Germany from ever again becoming a menace. But Germany has been crushed. Many other things will happen before it becomes a military factor again, and some of them may severely test the Big Three's will to remain united. Certain political questions have already caused anxiety. At the present stage, such issues will probably not cause the attempt to work together for security to be abandoned. Indeed, it is hardly conceivable that mankind should do so, just after the most terrible war it has ever experienced. But the goal is not reached, simply because the victorious Powers agree on a world-charter, or on a peace-settlement. Later, unsound positions will be revealed, and those originating in the economic field will not be easily recognisable to start with for the dire perils they will eventually show up to be, if neglected: perils so subtle indeed that by the time it is generally realised how grave they are, they may already have eaten the substance out of the Chief Powers' will to act together, and have left nothing but a fragile outer shell of what was once a firm intention. It is precisely these economic questions which the new Charter leaves the Economic Council to deal with, under the authority of the General Assembly.

The degree of confidence felt in any international organisation's ability lastingly to secure its objectives by concentrating against aggression must depend on one's views as to what causes wars. If one is content to explain them by the wickedness of Hitlers and Mussolinis or the predatory instincts of the Germans, one may believe in their prevention by punishing those guilty of war-crimes by re-education of the peoples they led astray, by destroying their heavy industry and by holding in readiness sufficient force collectively to overawe or overpower would-be aggressors in the future. But, however many wars lust for conquest had caused in the past, there is a strong case for suspecting that Hitlers and Mussolinis, common enough phenomena in themselves, alas, even in other than Axis lands, only rise to the surface and become menaces to security when much preparatory mischief has been done by economic restrictive policies, maladjustment and stagnation. The authors of the new Charter recognise this, in principle. Mr. Stettinius himself uttered a timely warning in his radio-address on May 28: "The most important task in the next decade is not likely to be the enforcement of peace, but to prepare the economic and social basis for peace.

Will the new organisation find it easier than the League of Nations did to secure the necessary action? Certain happenings during the inter-war period show the kind of difficulty that is likely to arise. The League of Nations sponsored reconstruction schemes for several countries, in the Danube Basin and elsewhere; and the schemes were successful, in themselves. Budgets were balanced, exchange-transactions were set free. Financial stability seemed assured. Some recovery followed in the economic situation, from the depths reached after the war, but it did not keep pace with what was happening on the financial plane. Along the new frontiers, tariff barriers rose ever higher. The industries that flourished, apart from the armament boom from 1933 on, often duplicated an older industry across a border, which declined as the newer creation throve. The Danubian countries traded less and less with each other and spent more and more of their substance on trying to make themselves self-sufficient. This process was advocated not only on national defence grounds but also by the more reputable argument that a region which had always been over-populated in relation to local possibilities of gainful occupation was no longer allowed to export surplus labor to Western Hemisphere at anything like the rate which, before the First World War, had proved an essential safety-valve. Indeed, even the seasonal movements of workers that formerly had taken place inside what was then a single customs area were now for the most part out of the question. There was a dangerous degree of unemployment, in Austria and Hungary. After a dozen or fifteen years of vain waiting for business to pick up again, many people at last looked for a break in the only direction in which they, unable as they were to emigrate, thought they could find it: i.e. National Socialism. Meanwhile, in some of the neighbor countries, there was a shortage of educated personnel.

It had been expected that if the financial affairs of the new Danubian States could be ordered, common sense would prevail in politico-economic questions. Also, the authors of the schemes realised that if they made a frontal attack on such matters as tariffs and other hindrances to the movement of goods or of persons, the schemes would probably never gain the assent of all the interested States, without which they could not be applied. The League and its representatives did not fail to point out, again and again, in the texts of the schemes themselves, in reports and resolutions of Committees and Conferences and whenever occasion offered that unless tariffs were reduced and frontiers became permeable the region would not lastingly benefit from its financial successes. But the advocates of protection and similar restrictive policies, in the various countries concerned, soon realised that they had nothing worse than advice to fear from the only effective international authority, i.e. the League Council. Thus the consultative bodies preached to deaf ears. The channels in which trade had once flowed freely and persons had moved at will throughout a customs area comprising fifty million consumers dried up one after the other. Confidence in the Democracies' ability to make their peace-settlement work suffered an eclipse.

After the present war there will again be situations, especially where former customs-units have been cut up by new frontiers, in which the individual states will probably, if left to their own devices, prove incapable of escaping from the vicious circle of excessive protection, high costs, low standards of living and economic policies aiming rather at beggaring a neighbor than at increasing the volume of international trade. Will the Economic Council agree on a diagnosis of ills that are bound, if ignored, to become international dangers? If governments fail to take timely action on the Economic Council's initiative, will the General Assembly be moved to ask the Security Council to intervene? And will the Security Council regard the matter as coming within its scope? The abandonment of restrictive practices and the removal of obstacles to trade across frontiers are matters upon which everyone agrees in the abstract. But when it comes to action, remedial measures are found to call for sacrifices. Each government is apt to regard those required of it as more difficult than those demanded of other states, and finally to adopt the position that, sincerely as it would deplore a failure of the negotiations, its concern for its own people's safety and welfare forbid it to make—or to ask its legislative bodies to make—concessions at the very points upon which agreement depends. So principles are re-affirmed, resolutions which governments fail to act on are passed, hopes are voiced that further progress may be made next time, and things continue to take their course, with the aggravation that once a negotiation or an economic conference had failed, statesmen and governments are not easily persuaded again to expose themselves to the risk of another set-back, and the advocates of autarky take new heart.

When such a situation arises, one may be tempted to say that it would be justifiable to have recourse to concerted action to compel a state or several states to abandon an obdurate attitude. But if this were admitted, it would scarcely be possible to draw a line at which coercion would cause to be legitimate. The discussions at San Francisco have revealed a consensus of opinion where national sovereignty is concerned. At the present stage of international co-operation and until we have moved much further towards union, we must reconcile ourselves to the necessity of finding a common denominator in economic affairs between the views and aims of many sovereign states by the process of give and take, with all the delays and hazards involved.

In order that there should be a prospect of success in this task of creating sufficiently sound and progressive economic conditions to give peoples reasons for building their hopes on peace instead of gambling in courses that may lead to war, the world over and more especially in certain regions which have proved most fruitful of trouble in a recent past, it is clear that the Powers wielding the greatest influence would have to set an example and to possess a common doctrine, making the matter a prime concern of each one of them. Even so, it would require all the prestige and energy possessed by the very top men in these countries, supported by an enlightened public opinion, to overcome obstacles that have so far defied all attempts.

Once more, will the leaders (i.e. the Security Council) recognise their direct responsibility for obtaining a sustained increase in the volume of international trade and in employment, and act up to it? Are they prepared to devote themselves to this cause, facing labors which will be never-ending, arduous, politically ungrateful and disheartening, at the best? Is it realised that there is no serious hope of preserving peace for long if economic questions are left to secondary bodies and are only taken in hand by the highest authority when they have reached a stage at which they involve a direct threat of war? That by that time the damage will have been done, and any chance of concerted action will have been fatally prejudiced?

If the future answers the above questions in the affirmative, prospects for peace under the aegis of the new world-organisation will be encouraging. What may arouse misgivings is that pride of place in accorded to the quelling of aggression, a negative task which will probably never have to be faced at all unless the Big Five fall out, in which case the Security Council will be unable to act, whilst the study of means to secure "the removal of political, economic and social causes of war" is relegated to organs which can take no action themselves. In these circumstances, can we expect that the underlying problem will be attacked with the necessary authority while they are still sufficiently ductile? Or will protracted delays, with half-successes veiling disagreement or essential points, once more gradually turn a great part of Europe into the slough of despond it became during the interwar period, the great Powers meanwhile being pulled apart by divergent interests and varying degrees of concern, until it is an open secret that there is no prospect of their acting of one accord to repress international brigandage, and the stage is set for another reign of violence? The Security Council's role tends to be envisaged in terms of the German problem, as that problem existed yesterday. German armaments may very well become an anxiety again some day, but long before then we shall have other worries. Indeed, the more we concentrate on holding Germany down, the more surely will Germany find opportunities for working her way back to a position in which she can again defy us, either alone or connivance with other malcontents, some of whom may have been on our side in this last war. In order to secure peace, be it repeated, the first requisite is growing prosperity, which can only result from an increasing flow of international trade. If we set this aim first, and do not allow ourselves to by hypnotised into imagining that we can solve our problem by negative means, we shall recognise that our organisation needs members, not primarily in order that they may agree to permit the passage of troops carrying out sanctions, but to collaborate in creating conditions in which there will be no aggression. Among the European states most capable of helping us to that end, there are some whose record as friends of peace is second to none, and which may be expected to decline to abandon a traditional policy of neutrality. It is greatly to be hoped that every effort will at least be made secure the collaboration of neutrals on the less political level represented by the Economic Council. For years, when the USA was not a member of the League, it did belong to the International Labor Office, and Americans, some of the US officials, sat on the League's consultative bodies. It would be a handicap to make the new organisation less supple than the old one was, in this respect.

Our most dangerous enemies will now be not the Axis but poverty and the sense of frustration: hard times, in a word. It will not be easy to disarm such foes. One has only to glance at the discussions that took place after the first World War – the proceedings of the 1920 Brussels Conferences, for instance – to measure how far we have fallen from the state of economic grace that prevailed for generations prior to 1914. In 1920, the world's leading experts could enumerate the three fundamental freedoms thanks to which a remarkable rate of expansion had long been kept up. They were:

Freedom of movement across frontiers for persons;
Freedom of movement across frontiers for goods;
Freedom of movement across frontiers for capital.

In 1920, it was possible not only to hope that these freedoms would be restored, but indeed to make plans for the future based upon that confident assumption. The Brussels Conference, with a straight face, could unanimously pass resolutions pointing out the futility and ultimate mischievousness of attempts to regulate dealings in exchange or to determine the respective values of currencies otherwise than by leaving them to find their own levels. They could seriously talk of reducing the tariffs and other restrictions on trade that then existed, and of permitting the unimpeded movement of persons in response to ever-changing economic opportunities and of capital in search of employment.

That was twenty-five years ago. We know what ground we have covered since then. By whose fault, it would be idle to enquire. We all have our shares of responsibility, and of attenuating circumstances. New situations have had to be faced, new threats have had to be fought off. The belief has spread that, given the failure of concerted international action, the free play of the Economic Freedom, in our world of to-day, would involve risks on the social plane which no government has proved willing to run. We have all found ourselves impelled to do things which we would have preferred to leave undone. The economic planning we have become so good at these last decades has usually, at least when it has produced any practical results at all, been in the direction of restriction, of monopoly, and we now discover that it is much easier to start interfering with economic processes than it is to return, afterwards, to free competition. The blessed state of liberty that existed up to 1914 was the result not of planning but of a thousand unrelated trends. Now, we can only look back at it with a sigh of regret, as at an age of innocence.

To-day, we are undertaking to re-create, deliberately and consciously, conditions which had then come about no one knew quite when or why, but certainly not as a result of concerted international action, which indeed we have not yet begun to learn how to enlist in this cause. The experience gathered in the inter-war years should demonstrate to everyone's satisfaction that it will not suffice to instruct bodies without executive powers to think up ideas for removing political, economic and social causes of war. There is no great mystery about what ought to be done. The question is how Authority can be induced to do it: whether the Powers in whose hands the world's destinities [sic] now lie will intervene at the pre-fever stage, while action in peace is still possible; whether they can agree on practical measures, and particularly whether they will make the requisite sacrifices themselves. The mightier a nation, the greater its responsibility, and the line our own USA takes may be decisive. It would be well to impress this upon our people, rather than let them expect that if the United Nations stamp out Nazism and agree on an anti-aggression pact to-day, we shall live happily ever after.

Among the issues which will determine whether our future course is to lead towards security or not, that of reparations may have to be faced first. After the last war, the Reparation Commission had a prior lien on all the assets of the ex-enemy countries. The League of Nations loans for reconstruction purposes to ex-enemy states in difficulties, involving service-transfers abroad from the assisted country, needed the Reparation Commission's consent, and long delays intervened before it could be secured. The 1920 Brussels Conference's commercial credits plan, known as the ter Meulen scheme, broke down over this difficulty. A round dozen years elapsed, after the signature of peace, before the reparation tangle ceased to clutter up the economic track. By then the Great Depression was upon us, with its motto: "Each country for itself, and the Devil take the hindermost!" The problem will be more difficult this time. Destruction is on a larger scale. Also, whereas the 1918 Armistice found Germany with its manufacturing plant, its railways and cities intact, the only devastated sector being that of finance, we are now faced by a heap of ruins in the very country which is being called upon to make good similar ravages in other lands, both East and West. We are told that security will depend on agreement with our allies on the treatment of Germany. But it will not depend on that factor alone. It will also depend on our ability to restore prosperity, which cannot be lastingly distributed according to merits acquired in war, but demands the participation of all contributing factors. And among these the ex-Axis countries loom large. Unless the new International Organisation has a voice in determining priorities as between reparation claims and reconstruction, understood in the broadest sense, there will be little reality in the mission, solemnly entrusted to it, consisting in "the removal of political, economic and social causes of war".

Another question of prime importance will be how soon ex-enemy countries are allowed to trade freely between the various zones of military occupation into which German and other territories are divided. The rate at which Europe can recover economically will depend in large measure on the answer. We all agree that Germany has merited severe punishment. How much more punishment can we impose upon her, over and above what she has already taken, without thereby harming ourselves? We know by experience what German aggression means. We have yet to see what landslides may be released by attempting to leave a vacuum where Germany's economic structure once stood.

xxx

The chief lesson the present generation discerns in the events culminating in the second World War appears to be that where effective power lies, there responsibility must also rest; and that inadequate recognition of this principle condemned the 1919 League of Nations to failure. Hence the dominant position now given to the Security Council.

This view is correct, as far as it goes. But it does not follow that our security organisation will stand or fall by its power to quell aggression. Ills, economic and demographic, from which the international body has long suffered will have to be overcome, or the basis of agreement among the Great Powers, the only lasting guarantee of peace, will not endure. This being the case, one may doubt whether the creation of the Economic Council offers any guarantee that these problems will be taken in hand by the authority exercising supreme power. When the Covenant is criticised for leaving power without responsibility, it may be answered that the Charter looks like leaving responsibility without power. Things went wrong last time, not because the Covenant did not vest responsibility in those who held effective power, not even because the USA did not remain a League member, but because an unhealthy condition arising from politico-economic and demographic causes developed in Central and South Eastern Europe, that region and others wearied of attempts to cure disorders by such palliatives as could be applied internationally at the time, and it was notorious by 1938 that opinion in the democratic countries was divided on the necessity or even the desirability of maintaining a much-decried settlement. Hitler then assumed that there were no limits to the outrages which Great Britain and France would put up with, and Europe had to endure nearly six years of war in order to impress the error of their ways upon the aggressors. We must reverse the trend towards economic nationalism, or there will be another conflagration, eventually, to whatever undertakings all the Powers may have not their hands and seals.

With war in Europe only just ended, the technique of dealing with aggressors naturally absorbs attention. But the face of things is apt to change. To-day's problem pushes yesterday's aside. After the first World War, the "hang the Kaiser and squeeze Germany till the pips squeak" frame of mind hardly survived ratification of the peace treaties. In no time, we were set on reconstruction, which we realised could not be achieved without permitting, indeed helping our ex-enemies to prosper. By 1925, a new dawn seemed to be breaking behind Locarno. When the Great Depression of the early thirties began to lift, we had become highly conscious of defects in the settlement and of the difficulty of improving economic prospects without altering it. We had begun to pin our hopes upon the peaceful change of international obligations. Mr. Chamberlain's appeasement policy would not have been supported by opinion, there would not have been a public subscription in France to offer him an estate as an expression of a nation's gratitude, had countless people not felt that Munich was not just a case of yielding to a threat, but that steady refusal to consider revision had plugged up the safety-valve until the mechanism burst. Now, history does not repeat itself exactly, but like causes do produce like effects, other things being equal. It is probable that before long force of circumstances will compel us to view the essential problem of security in a different light from that in which we see them at the present moment. The controversy over voting procedure on proposals involving sanctions in the Security Council loomed large at San Francisco, but that issue may soon be forgotten, for either the Great Powers continue to set agreement among themselves above all other considerations, in which case there will be no aggression, or they cease to do so, and there will be no Security Council.

The crucial test of the new organisation is likely to be carried out on other ground, and indeed on its ability to secure an increase of international trade. This comes within the purview of the Economic Council, but there is no indication as to how it is proposed to escape from the dilemma that defeated the old League: Prosperity demands security, and security demands the respect of treaties. But the respect of treaties, when coupled with economic nationalism, makes for rigidity, which in the long run is inconsistent with security, and indeed destroys that which it seeks to protect. Such are the thesis and the antithesis. Will the new Organisation find a synthesis?

The central problem will not be the multiplication of councils and commissions and the appointment to them of the most eminent experts. The old League also obtained the best possible advice. From the Brussels Conference on, its consultants supplied Assembly and Council with reports giving clear and penetrating analyses of the questions they were set to study, and proposing remedies which might well have been efficacious if they had ever been applied. As we have seen above, the trouble was that the remedies cut across certain policies of individual states, and that even in 1927, in the palmiest days of Geneva internationalism, the problem of gaining acceptance for an Economic Conference's resolutions was so forbidding as to scare off the Great Powers, determined advocacy on whose part, together with convincing evidence that they themselves meant to practice what they preached, would have been necessary to turn back the drift towards self-sufficiency and restriction.

Nothing in the United Nations Charter seems to offer any serious reason for hope that things are going to be different from now on. We are told that the Economic Council is to study how to raise standards of living, obtain full employment, promote economic and social progress and international co-operation in the domains of intellectual activity and education, and secure respect for the rights of man and the fundamental freedoms, regardless of race, language, religion or sex. These words perhaps carry more emotional appeal than the prosaic terms used in Article 23 of the old Covenant, by which Members of the League stated agreement on a few fundamental economic and social principles, although one would not have been sorry to find, in the Charter, a mention of "freedom of communications and of transit and equitable treatment for the commerce of all Members", such as occurs in paragraph (e) of that Article. But the proof of the pudding is in the eating, and only time will show whether the Security Council, i.e. the Great Powers, are going to make it their business to right an economic situation out of which prospects for international trade have been fading ever since the first World War.

If it is hoped that the Economic Council will manage to intervene so adroitly, or plead an old cause in a new manner so persuasively that states which heretofore have been pursuing self-sufficiency will see the light and act accordingly without being led, there may be disappointments in store.

When it is remembered that progress in the desired direction will certainly require the modification of many international conventions, it is not encouraging to note that, just before the announcement appeared setting forth the increased dignity and far-flung aims of the Economic Council, Committee Two of Commission Two quietly voted, by 37 to 1, that there should be no specific grant of authority to the General Assembly for making recommendations to revise treaties.

It would be unreasonable to critcise the San Francisco Conference for wishing to work out a perfected mechanism, or because orators, or even drafters, found in the statement of aims opportunities for lyrical outbursts. From the moment on when it was decided to draw up a new charter, there was bound to be a tendency to exaggerate the value of formulas and their expectation of life. A more realistic approach might have been made if the United Nations had contended themselves with amending the old Covenant. Had they done so, they would have been reminded that, when the hangover left by the first World War had passed off, public opinion realised that the weakest point in the League's performance was failure to revise the Covenant or any of the treaties into which it had been written, although these instruments patently wanted overhauling. Once recognition of the principle of revision had been achieved, it would have been easier to obtain further peaceful changes, as need arose.

But now that the world has presented to it a new organisation, claimed to be a marked improvement over the old one, people will expect smooth working from it and from the treaties revision of which the General Assembly now has no specific authority to recommend. When the wheels begin to creak, as creak they will, the adversaries of international co-operation are likely to raise their heads once more.

xxx

A sober commentary on the prospects may yet admit a note of optimism. Some think the Charter represents the last chance for our civilization. This, happily, is by no means certain. The same was said of the ill-stared 1919 Covenant. And yet we are still there to try again. We must do our best to help the new organisation to succeed. But to give up work for peace on the international plane as a bad job, if the Charter does not altogether answer our purpose, would be taking our generation too seriously. We have probably not been singled out by fate for the honor either of inaugurating a millennium or of assisting at the last act of a tragi-comedy, true though it may be yet another failure would dishearten many of us, especially those who are now keying their hopes highest. Perhaps we shall have to experience many setbacks yet before we succeed in discovering how to handle the essential problems on whose solution by international agreement security depends. But even so we need not utterly despair. Humanity has so far managed not to succumb to the forces of darkness, and the chances are perhaps not so bad that it will continue to worry along, somehow. The old Covenant will not have lived in vain, if the experience acquired under it serves to light some tricky turns on the way.

Vast numbers of people now realise as never before that faulty as our techniques of international consultation may be, it is better to use and develop them than to rely for peace on trimming a balance of power. That is a gain, although a balance of power that helps keep the peace is not to be despised. Clearly, a perfect international system should be universal. It is right for us to devote our best energies to making it so. But we of the Western world may have to recognise that the theory and practice of democracy obtaining in the USSR, for instance, are too unlike our own for it to be possible to achieve the ideal at the present time. The Soviet Union has its problems some of which we may not understand, as the Russians may not understand all of ours. We should not presume to dictate how theirs are to be handled. But we have conceptions, common to most of the rest of us, which we hold sacred. We cannot sacrifice them for the sake of a theoretical unanimity. We may have to consider whether it is worth while to maintain an international organisation among the chief members of which fundamental differences of principle and practice subsist.

Our answer should be that it is highly worth while. One of the drawbacks of hoping too much of a new Charter is precisely that failure to obtain the maximum may so dispirit us that we neglect to reap advantages lying within our reach: limited advantages, no doubt, but substantial and precious. We know the road that has got to be travelled; if we turn back now we shall only make the start harder for another generation.

Our chances of working out a *modus vivendi* might improve if, rather than trust to question-begging shibboleths like "democratic" and "peace-loving", we made up our minds to it that if we want international co-operation we must seek it by a patient, point-to-point process of adjustment on a modest level of expediency. If we face facts where Russia is concerned, we may be more prepared to admit them in the case of others also, and thus divest ourselves of the double delusion that, because certain Powers found themselves fighting on our side to down Hitler, an identity of higher purpose and ideal must exist between them and us, and that because certain other states did not break with Hitler, or practiced with or even deified him, they had better be excluded from the fellowship of nations. We need them all, because membership involves duties rather than privileges.

We should be wise to content ourselves with agreements that are as elastic and flexible as we can make them, and not tempt fate by claiming permanency for what is by nature ephemeral. If the Soviet Union is unable to go the whole way with us to-day, we need not conclude that there will have to be another world-war to decide whether their ideas of ours are to prevail. We may give the Russians credit for wanting peace, too. They want it on their own terms, no doubt, which cannot be altogether harmonised with ours, but we shall probably discover common ground here and there on which we can work with them, especially if we let sleeping dogs lie. As for the lines beyond which we on our own side and they on theirs cannot go, we may remember that there are cases where tacit understandings are more profitable than contracts. If we Westerners, meaning more or less the same thing, do our best to loosen up the economic deadlock that paralysed us on the eve of the recent war, Russia may before long be more anxious to collaborate on the economic plane, as we understand collaboration, aiming towards freedom, than she is now, after much talk about bedrock need for universality may well have made her believe that no price is too high to set on her full contribution.

Let us not force the pace towards the desired goal: i.e. a universal system so perfect that all nations may unreservedly submit to it without fear of giving away more than they are gaining. It has taken long ages for the modern state to evolve its mechanism for adjusting matters which formerly were settled by force. Now, it is a question of doing something similar as between states. We had better feel our way cautiously on ground about which we still know very little.

As for the likeliest approach to our economic problems, we might consider, in the light of what happened between the two wars, whether it would not be better to shun publicity rather than to court it. World conferences and the meetings of a body possessing such exalted status as the Economic and Social Council is endowed with carry a heavy handicap in that that they make for oratory and statements of utopistic aims, thus warning the forces of autarky and giving them time to mobilise: as if a fisherman were to approach his trout-stream accompanied by a brass-band. This is one reason why full-dress international meetings on economic questions have so seldom produced concrete results. If we want progress towards greater freedom in trade and exchanges, we had better work towards our objective as unobtrusively as we know how. Consultative bodies convened by an international organisation can certainly help, but they can help the more effectively the less attention they attract. The practical problem is how to make their exploratory efforts lead up to the actual inter-state agreements which, if they are to be worth anything, it will require the biggest man in the biggest countries to impose. At this point, there has so far been a hiatus. Poor Richard's advice: "If you want a thing well done, do it yourself", should be pondered by governments in this connexion.

The Economic and Social Council would do well to reduce its plenary sessions, attended by the public, to a minimum, and to set up committees which would work at private meetings, held quietly at regular intervals, so as to accustom the public to see them convene without expecting sensational achievements. The trouble is the long flight of steps that has to be climbed, from their level to that of responsibility, in cases where governments need to have their elbows jogged. Resolutions will have to be laid before the Economic Council, which then reports to the General Assembly, which in its turn, if the requisite majority is attained, may address recommendations to the Security Council.

It may be hoped that the Economic Council will possess such prestige and wield such influence that its findings will move governments to agree on appropriate action without there being any need to take economic problems onto the highest political plane, which can only be reached in the Security Council. Past experience affords no encouragement for such expectations. If they are built upon, the United Nations' economic meetings are likely to become side-tracks such as those onto which major economic issues have been shunted, ever since the world became aware of the necessity of approaching them internationally: the Brussels Conference of 1920, the Geneva Conference of 1927 and the London Conference of 1933. Fortunately, there are other alternatives, and to them we shall sooner or later turn.

Thompson Todd Collection

Bibliography

Primary sources

Thompson Todd Collection, Tharwa, Australia.
Hungarian National Archives, Budapest, Hungary.
National Széchenyi Library, Budapest, Hungary.
Bank of England Archive. London, UK.
The National Archives, London, UK.
League of Nations Archives, Geneva, Switzerland.
Allen W. Dulles Papers, Digital Files.
Dwight D. Eisenhower Presidential Library, Abilene, KS, USA.
Franklin D. Roosevelt Presidential Library and Museum, Hyde Park, NY, USA.
Franklin D. Roosevelt Library and Museum Website.
Harvard University Archives, Cambridge, MA, USA.
Hoover Institution Library and Archives, Stanford University, Stanford, CA, USA.
National Archives and Records Administration (NARA). Washington, D. C., USA.
Manuscript and Archives, Yale University Library, New Haven, USA.
Massachusetts Historical Society, Boston, MA, USA.
Rauner Special Collections Library, Dartmouth College, Hanover, NH, USA.
Seeley G. Mudd Manuscript Library, Princeton, NJ, USA.
Tittmann, Harold H., Jr. Papers, Georgetown University Library Special Collections Research Center, Washington, D.C., USA.
Special Collections Research Center at Syracuse University Libraries, Syracuse, NY, USA.
Elisina Tyler's 1940–41 Diary.

Primary printed sources

British Parliament Diaries
Congressional Record
Foreign Relations of the United States
Documents on British Foreign Policy
Magyar Törvénytár
National Assembly Diary of Hungary
League of Nations. *The Financial Reconstruction of Austria. General Survey and Principal Documents*. Geneva, 1926.

Bibliography

League of Nations, *The Financial Reconstruction of Hungary. General Survey and Principal Documents*. Geneva, 1926.
League of Nations. *The League of Nations Reconstruction Schemes in the Inter-war Period*. Geneva, 1944.
League of Nations Journal *A History of the Peace Conference of Paris*. edited by H. W. V. Temperley, vol. 5. London: Henry Frowde and Hodder & Stoughton, 1921.

Secondary sources

Books

Ablonczy, Balázs. *Pál Teleki – The Life of a Controversial Hungarian Politician*. Wayne (NJ): Hungarian Studies Publications, 2007.
Aldcroft, Derek H. *From Versailles to Wall Street, 1919–1929*. London: Allen Lane, Penguin Books Ltd., 1977.
Andorka, Rudolf. *A madridi követségtől Mauthausenig*. ["From the Madrid Legation to Mauthausen"] Budapest: Kossuth, 1978.
Antalffy, Gyula. *A Thousand Years of Travel in Old Hungary*. Translated by Elisabeth Hoch. Budapest: Corvina Kiadó, 1980.
Baker, Leonard. *Brahmin in Revolt. A Biography of Herbert C. Pell*. New York: Doubleday & Co. 1972.
Barber, William J. Designs within Disorder: Franklin D. Roosevelt, the Economists, and the Shaping of American Economic Policy, 1933–1945. Cambridge: Cambridge University Press, 2006.
Barcza, György. *Diplomata emlékeim, 1911-1945*. [My Diplomatic Memoir] Vols. 1–2. Budapest: Európa História, 1994.
Barker, Elisabeth. *British Policy in South-East Europe in the Second World War*. London: Palgrave Macmillan, 1976.
Bácskai, Tamás, ed. *A Magyar Nemzeti Bank története*. vol. 1. Budapest: Közgazdasági és Jogi Könyvkiadó, 1993.
Bán, András D. *Pax Britannica. Brit külügyi iratok a második világháború utáni Kelet-Közép-Európáról, 1942–1943*. [Pax Britannica. British Foreign Policy Papers about Post-War Central and Eastern Europe, 1942–1943] Budapest: Osiris, 1996.
Beatty, Jerome. *Americans All Over*. New York: The John Day Company, 1938.
Beal, Richard B. *Sparrow. Sparrow Mission*. New York: Writers Club Press, 2002.
Benson, Robert Louis. *A History of US Communications Intelligence during World War II: Policy and Administration*. Fort Meade, MD: National Security Agency Center for Cryptologic History, 1997.
Berend, Iván T., and György Ránki. *Magyarország gazdasága az első világháború után, 1919–1929*. [The Economy of Hungary after World War I, 1919–1929] Budapest: Akadémiai Kiadó, 1966.
Berend, Iván T., and Miklós Szuhay. *A tőkés gazdaság története Magyarországon, 1848–1944*. [The History of Capitalism in Hungary] Budapest: Kossuth Kiadó, 1973.
Balogh, Béni L. *The second Vienna award and the Hungarian-Romanian relations, 1940–1944*. New York: Columbia University Press, 2011.
Borhi, László. *Dealing with Dictators. The United States, Hungary, and East Central Europe, 1942–1989*. Bloomington & Indianapolis, In: Indiana University Press, 2016.

Brown, Anthony Cave. *The Last Hero: Wild Bill Donovan.* New York: Times Books, 1982.
———. *The Secret War Report of the OSS.* New York: Berkley Publishing Corporation, 1976.
Cartledge, Bryan. *Mihály Károlyi & István Bethlen: Hungary.* London: Haus Publishing Ltd., 2009.
Butcher, Harry C. *My Three Years with Eisenhower. The Personal Diary of Captain Harry C. Butcher, USNR. Naval Aid to General Eisenhower, 1942 to 1945.* New York: Simon and Schuster, 1946.
Case, Holly. *Between States: The Transylvanian Question and the European Idea during the Second World War.* Stanford: Stanford University Press, 2009.
Clavin, Patricia. *Securing the World Economy: The Reinvention of the League of Nations, 1920-1946.* Oxford: Oxford University Press, 2013.
Clay, Henry. *Lord Norman.* London: Macmillan & Co. Ltd., 1957.
Coolidge, Calvin. *The Autobiography of Calvin Coolidge.* New York: Cosmopolitan Book Corporation, 1929.
Coolidge, Harold Jefferson, and Robert Howard Lord. *Archibald Cary Coolidge: Life and Letters.* Boston and New York: Houghton Mifflin, 1932.
Costigliola, Frank. *Awkward Dominion. American Political, Economic, and Cultural Relations with Europe, 1919-1933.* Ithaca, NY: Cornell University Press, 1984.
Csukovits, Enikő. *Magyarországról és a magyarokról. Nyugat-Európa magyar-képe a középkorban.* [About Hungary and Hungarians. The Hungary Picture of Western Europeans in the Middle Ages] Budapest: MTA, Bölcsészettudományi Kutatóközpont, 2015.
Czettler, Antal. *A mi kis élethalál kérdéseink – A magyar külpolitika a hadbalépéstől a német megszállásig.* [Our Little Life and Death Questions. Hungarian Foreign Policy from Entering the War until German Occupation] Budapest: Magvető, 2000.
Deák, Francis. *The Hungarian-Rumanian Land Dispute.* New York: Columbia University Press, 1928.
———. *Hungary at the Paris Peace Conference. The Diplomatic History of the Treaty of Trianon.* New York: Columbia University Press, 1942.
Discussing Hitler. Advisers of U.S. Diplomacy in Central Europe, 1934-1941. Edited and introduced by Tibor Frank, Budapest and New York: Central European University Press, 2003.
Duke, Florimond., and Charles M. Sawyer. *Name, Rank, and Serial Number.* New York: Meredith Press 1969.
Dulles, Allen. *The Secret Surrender.* New York: Harper & Row 1966.
Ehrman, John, ed. *Grand Strategy.* Vol. V., August 1943–September 1944. London: Her Majesty's Stationery Office, 1956.
Eichengreen, Barry. *Globalizing Capital. A History of the International Monetary System.* Second edition. Princeton and Oxford: Princeton University Press, 2008.
———. *Golden Fetters: The Gold Standard and the Great Depression, 1919-1939.* Oxford: Oxford University Press, 1996.
Fenyvesi, Charles. *Három összeesküvés.* [Three Conspiracies] Budapest: Európa Könyvkiadó, 2007.
Fink, Carole. *The Genoa Conference: European Diplomacy, 1921-1922.* Chapel Hill: University of North Carolina Press, 1984.
Gehl, Jürgen. *Austria, Germany, and the Anschluss, 1931-1938.* London: Oxford University Press, 1963.
Gergely, Jenő. *Gömbös Gyula. Vázlat egy politikai életrajzhoz.* [Gyula Gömbös. Sketches for a Political Biography] Budapest: Elektra Kiadóház, 1999.

Bibliography

Greiner, Helmut. *Kriegstagebuch des Oberkommandos der Wehrmacht, 1940–1945.* [The War Diaries of the Wehrmacht High Command] Frankfurt: Erster Helbband 1961–1965.

Gunst, Péter. *Magyarország gazdaságtörténete, 1914–1989.* [The Economic History of Hungary, 1914–1918] Budapest: Nemzeti Tankönyvkiadó, 1996.

Hamerli, Petra. *Magyar-olasz diplomáciai kapcsolatok és regionális hatásaik (1927-1934).* [Hungarian-Italian Diplomatic Relations and Their Regional Effects] Budapest: Fakultás Kiadó, 2018.

Hanebrink, Paul. *A Specter Haunting Europe: The Myth of Judeo-Bolshevism.* Cambridge, Massachusetts, London, England: Belknap Press of Harvard University Press, 2018.

Havas, Eugene. *Hungary's Finance and Trade 1928.* London: London General Press, 1929.

Heinrichs, Waldo H. *American Ambassador. Joseph C. Grew and the Development of the United States Diplomatic Tradition.* Boston and Toronto: Little Brown and Company, 1966.

Herring, George C. *From Colony to Superpower. U.S. Foreign Relations Since 1776.* Oxford: Oxford University Press, 2008.

Hoover, Herbert Clark. *The Memoirs of Herbert Hoover.* vol. 1–3. New York: The Macmillan Company, 1951–1952.

Hornyák, Árpád. *Magyar-jugoszláv diplomáciai kapcsolatok, 1918–1927.* [Hungarian- Yugoslav Diplomatic Relations, 1918–1927] Újvidék: Forum Könyvkiadó, 2004.

Horthy, Nicholas. *Memoirs.* Safety Harbor, FL: Simon Publications, 2000.

Howard, Michael, ed. *Grand Strategy.* Vol. IV., August 1942–September 1943. London: Her Majesty's Stationery Office, 1972.

In Memory of Roland William Boyden. Boston: Commonwealth of Massachusetts, 1933.

International Bank for Reconstruction and Development. *Fifth Annual Report, 1949-1950.* Washington, D.C. 1950.

Höttl, Wilhelm. *The Secret Front. Nazi Political Espionage 1938–1945.* New York: Enigma Books, 2003.

Jeszenszky, Géza. *Lost Prestige. Hungary's Changing Image in Great Britain 1894–1918.* Saint Helena, CA: Helena History Press, 2013.

Joó, András. *Kállay Miklós külpolitikája. Magyarország és a háborús diplomácia 1942–1944.* [The Foreign Policy of Miklós Kállay. Hungary and Wartime Diplomacy 1942–1944] Budapest: Napvilág Kiadó 2008.

Juhász, Gyula, ed. *Magyar-Brit titkos tárgyalások 1943-ban.* [Secret Hungarian–British Negotiations in 1943] Budapest: Kossuth Kiadó 1978.

——. Magyarország külpolitikája 1919–1945. [Hungary's Foreign Policy 1919–1945] Budapest: Akadémiai Kiadó, 1988, (Third edition).

——. *Magyarország nemzetközi helyzete és a magyar szellemi élet 1938-1944.* [The International Situation of Hungary and Hungarian Intellectual Life] Budapest: Akadémiai Kiadó, 1987.

Jones, Kenneth Paul, ed. *U.S. Diplomats in Europe, 1919-1941.* Reprinted edition. Santa Barbara, CA: ABC-Clio, 1983.

Kaser, M. C., and E. A. Radice, eds. *The Economic History of Eastern Europe, 1919-1975.* vol. 1. Oxford: Clarendon Press, 1985.

Katz, Barry M. *Foreign Intelligence: Research and Analysis in the Office of Strategic Services, 1942–1945.* Cambridge, MA: Harvard University Press, 1989.

Kádár, Gyula. *A Ludovikától Sopronkőhidáig.* [From the Ludovica to Sopronkőhida] vol. 1–2. Budapest: Magvető 1978.

Kádár-Lynn, Katalin, ed. *The Inauguration of "Organized Political Warfare": The Cold War*

Bibliography

Organizations sponsored by the National Committee for a Free Europe/Free Europe Committee. Saint Helena, CA: Helena History Press, 2013.

Kállay, Nicholas. *Hungarian Premier. A Personal Account of a Nation's Struggle in the Second World War.* New York: Columbia University Press, 1954.

Kelly, Catherine E. *Between Town and Country: New England Women and the Creation of a Provincial Middle Class, 1820–1860.* Ph.D. diss., Rochester: University of Rochester, 1992.

Kelly, Catherine E. *In the New England Fashion: Reshaping Women's Lives in the Nineteenth Century.* Ithaca: Cornell University Press, 1999.

Kennan, George F. *Memoirs, 1925–1950.* [1967] New York: Bantam Books, 1969.

Kerepeszki, Róbert. *A „tépelődő gentleman": Darányi Kálmán (1886–1939).* [The "Pondering Gentleman": Kálmán Darányi] Pécs: Kronosz Kiadó, 2014.

Keys, Barbara J. *Globalizing Sport. National Rivalry an International Community in the 1930s.* Cambridge, Massachusetts: Harvard University Press, 2006.

Komlos, John H. *Louis Kossuth in America, 1851-1852.* Buffalo, NY: East European Institute, 1973.

Lansing, Robert. *The Peace Negotiations: A Personal Narrative.* New York: Houghton Mifflin, 1921.

Laville, Helen. and Hugh Wilford, eds. *The US Government, Citizen Groups and the Cold War: The State-Private Network.* London and New York: Routledge, 2006.

Lewis, Cleona. *America's Stake in International Investments.* Washington, D. C.: The Brookings Institution, 1938.

Link, Arthur S., ed. *The Papers of Woodrow Wilson.* vols. 1-69. Princeton, NJ: Princeton University Press, 1987.

Lloyd, George. *The Truth about Reparations and War-debts.* London: William Heinemann Ltd., 1932.

Lojkó, Miklós. *Meddling in Middle Europe.* Budapest: Central European University Press, 2006.

Low, Alfred D. *The Anschluss Movement (1918–1938) and the Great Powers.* Boulder, Colorado: East European Monographs; distributed by Columbia University Press, New York, 1985.

Macartney, Carlile Aylmer. *Hungary and Her Successors. The Treaty of Trianon and Its Consequences, 1919–1937.* London: Oxford University Press, 1937.

Macartney, Carlile Aylmer. *October Fifteenth: A History of Modern Hungary 1929–1945.* vol. 1–2. New York: Frederick A. Praeger, Inc. 1956-1957.

Magda, Ádám. *A Kisantant és Európa, 1920–1929.* Budapest: Akadémiai Kiadó, 1989.

Martin, Geoffrey J. *The Life and Thought of Isaiah Bowman.* Hamden, CT: Archon Books, 1980.

Matheovics, Ferenc. *A magyar–román birtokper.* [The Hungarian-Romanian Optants Case] Budapest, 1929.

Matić, Igor-Philip. *Edmund Veesenmayer: Agent und Diplomat der nationalsozialistischen Expansionspolitik.* München: De Gruyter Oldenbourg, 2002.

Mauch, Christof. and Jeremiah Riemer. *The Shadow War Against Hitler: The Covert Operations of America's Wartime Secret Intelligence Service.* New York: Columbia University Press, 2003.

Márkus, László. *A Károlyi Gyula kormány bel- és külpolitikája.* [The Domestic and Foreign Policy of the Károlyi Government] Budapest: Akadémiai Kiadó, 1968.

Mendelsohn, Ezra. *The Jews of East Central Europe between the World Wars*. Bloomington: University of Indiana, 1983.
Nagy, Elek. *Magyarország és a Népszövetség*. [Hungary and the League of Nations] Budapest: Franklin Társulat, 1930.
Nagy, Zsolt. *Great Expectations and Interwar Realities. Hungarian Cultural Diplomacy, 1918-1941*. Budapest: Central European University Press, 2017.
Nasaw, David. *The Chief. The Life of William Randolph Hearst*. Boston and New York: Houghton Mifflin Company, 2000.
Neiberg, Michael S. *The Path to War. How the First World War Created Modern America*. Oxford: Oxford University Press, 2016.
Nicolson, Harold. *Curzon: The Last Phase*. London: Constable & Co., 1934.
Northedge, Frederick. International Intellectual Co-operation Within the League of Nations: Its Conceptual Basis and Lessons for the Present. London: University of London, 1953.
Ormos, Mária. *Az 1924. évi magyar államkölcsön megszerzése*. [Raising the Hungarian State Loan of 1924] Budapest: Akadémiai Kiadó, 1964.
———. *Magyarország a két világháború korában (1919-1945)*. [Hungary in the Age of the World Wars] Debrecen: Csokonai Kiadó, 1998.
———. *Merénylet Marseille-ben*. [Assassination in Marseilles] Second edition. Budapest: Kossuth Könyvkiadó, 1984.
Orzoff, Andrea. *Battle for the Castle: The Myth of Czechoslovakia in Europe, 1914-1948*. Oxford: Oxford University Press, 2009.
Peirce, Hayford. and Royall Tyler. *Byzantine Art*. London: E. Benn, 1926.
Peirce, Hayford. and Royall Tyler. *L'art Byzantin*. Paris: Librairie de France, 1932.
Pemberton, Jo-Anne. *The Story of International Relations, Part Two: Cold-Blooded Idealists*. London: Palgrave Macmillan, 2019.
Peterecz, Zoltán. *Jeremiah Smith, Jr. and Hungary, 1924-1926: the United States, the League of Nations, and the Financial Reconstruction of Hungary*. London: Versita, 2013.
Petersen, Neal H., ed. *From Hitler's Doorstep: The Wartime Intelligence Reports of Allen Dulles, 1942-1945*. University Park, PA: Pennsylvania State University Press, 1996.
Péteri, György. *Global Monetary Regime and National Central Banking. The Case of Hungary, 1921-1929*. Boulder, Colorado: Social Science Monographs, 2002.
———. *Revolutionary Twenties. Essays on International Monetary and Financial Relations after World War I*. Trondheim: University of Trondheim, 1995.
Pritz, Pál. *Magyarország külpolitikája Gömbös Gyula miniszterelnöksége idején, 1932-1936*. [The Foreign Policy of Hungary During the Premiership of Gyula Gömbös, 1923-1936] Budapest, Akadémiai Kiadó, 1982.
Püski, Levente. A Horthy-korszak szürke eminenciása Károlyi Gyula (1871-1947). [Gyula Károlyi, the Éminence Grise of the Horthy Era] Pécs-Budapest: Kronosz Kiadó - Magyar Történelmi Társulat, 2016.
Quint Howard H., and Robert H. Ferrel, eds. *The Talkative President. The Off-the-Record Press Conferences of Calvin Coolidge*. Amherst: The University of Massachusetts Press, 1964.
Roberts, Priscilla. *Frank Altschul, 1887-1981: A Political and Intellectual Biography*. unpublished manuscript.
Romsics, Ignác. *István Bethlen: A Great Conservative Statesman of Hungary, 1874-1946*. Boulder, Colorado: Social Science Monographs, 1995.
Roosevelt, Kermit, ed. *War Report of the OSS*. 2 vols. New York: Walker & Co. 1976.

Roosevelt, Nicholas. *A Front Row Seat*. Norman, Oklahoma: University of Oklahoma Press, 1953.
Rothschild, Joseph. *East Central Europe between the Two World Wars*. Seattle: University of Washington Press, 1974.
Sallai, Gergely. *Az első bécsi döntés*. [The First Vienna Award] Budapest: Osiris, 2002.
Salter, Arthur. *Personality in Politics*. London: Faber and Faber, 1947.
——. *Security. Can We Retrieve it?* London: MacMillan and Co., Ltd, 1939.
——. *World Trade and Its Future*. London: Oxford University Press, 1936.
Schubert, Aurel. *The Credit-Anstalt Crisis of 1931*. Cambridge: Cambridge University Press, 1991.
Schulzinger, Robert D. *The Wise Men of Foreign Affairs: The History of the Council on Foreign Relations*. New York: Columbia University Press, 1984.
Shirer, William L. *Rise and Fall of The Third Reich: A History of Nazi Germany*. New York: Simon & Schuster, 1998.
Smith, Bradley F. *The Shadow Warriors: O.S.S. and the Origins of the C.I.A.* New York: Basic Books, 1983.
Smith, Jeremiah. *The Preservation of the Peace*. Cambridge, MA: Harvard Law School, 1927.
Smith, Neil. *American Empire. Roosevelt's Geographer and the Prelude to Globalization*. Berkeley, CA: University of California Press, 2003.
Smith, Richard Harris. *OSS: The Secret History of America's First Central Intelligence Agency*. Berkeley, CA: University of California Press, 1972.
Soule, George. *Prosperity Decade. A Chapter from American Economic History, 1917–1929*. London: The Pilot Press Limited, 1947.
Spanish Art, An Introductory Review of Architecture, Painting, Sculpture, Textiles, Ceramic, Woodwork, Metalwork. Burlington Magazine Monograph 2. London: B. T. Batsford, 1927.
Steel, Ronald. *Walter Lippmann and the American Century*. Boston and Toronto: Little, Brown and Company, 1980.
Steiner, Zara. *The Triumph of the Dark. European International History 1933–1939*. Oxford: Oxford University Press, 2011.
Szabad, György. *Kossuth on the Political System of the United States of America*. Budapest: Akadémiai Kiadó, 1975.
Szegedy-Maszák, Aladár. *Az ember ősszel visszanéz... Egy volt magyar diplomata emlékirataiból*. [One Looks back in the Fall... From the Memoirs of a Hungarian Diplomat] vol. 1-2, Budapest: 1996.
Tanselle, G. Thomas. *Royall Tyler*. Cambridge: Harvard University Press, 1967.
Toniolo, Gianni. with the assistance of Piet Clement. *Central Bank Cooperation at the Bank for International Settlements, 1930–1973*. Cambridge: Cambridge University Press, 2005.
Tyler, Royall. *A Book of Forms, with Occasional Notes*. Brattleboro, VT: Joseph Steen, 1845.
Tyler, Royall. *The Emperor Charles the Fifth*. London: George Allen and Unwin, 1956.
Tyler, Royall. *One Name, Two Lives*. Blue-Tongue Books, Charlie's Forest, NSW Australia, 2017.
Tyler, William R. *The Castelvecchio Family*. Formatted and supplemented by Royall Tyler, New South Wales, Australia, 2014.
Ullein-Reviczky, Antal. *German War—Russian Peace. The Hungarian Tragedy*. [1947]

Translated by Lovice Mária Ullein-Reviczky. Saint Helena, CA: Helena History Press, LLC, 2014.
Vogeler, Robert A., with Leigh White. *I Was Stalin's Prisoner*. New York: Harcourt, Brace and Company, 1951.
Vonyó, József. *Gömbös Gyula*. [Gyula Gömbös] Budapest: Napvilág Kiadó, 2014.
Walterskirchen, Gudula. *Engelbert Dollfuß: Arbeitermörder oder Heldenkanzler*. Wien: Molden Verlag, 2004.
Wilford, Hugh. *The Mighty Wurlitzer*. Cambridge MA: Harvard University Press, 2008.
Winkler, Marx. *The Investor and the League Loans*. New York: Foreign Policy Association, Volume 4, June 1928, Supplement No.2.
Wiskemann, Elizabeth. *Fascism in Italy: Its Development and Influence*. 2nd edition. London: Palgrave Macmillan, 1970.
Wolff, Larry. *Inventing Eastern Europe: The Map of Civilization on the Mind of the Enlightenment*. Stanford, CA: Stanford University Press, 1994.
Zsiga, Tibor. *A szentgotthárdi fegyverbotrány*. [The Szentgotthárd Arms Scandal] Szombathely: Pannon Műhely Kft., 1990.
Zsigmond, László, ed. *Magyarország és a második világháború: Titkos diplomáciai okmányok a háború előzményeihez és történetéhez*. [Hungary and the Second World War: Secret Diplomatic Papers to the Antecedents and History of the War] Budapest: Kossuth Könyvkiadó, 1966.

Book chapters

Barker, Elisabeth. "Problems of the Alliance: Misconceptions and Misunderstanding." In *British Political and Military Strategy in Central, Eastern and Southern Europe in 1944*, edited by William Deakin, Elisabeth Barker, and Jonathan Chadwick, 40–53. London: Macmillan Press, 1988.
Berkes, Antal. "The League of Nations and the Optants' Dispute of the Hungarian Borderlands: Romania, Yugoslavia, and Czechoslovakia," In Remaking Central Europe. *The League of Nations and the Former Habsburg Lands*, edited by Peter Becker and Natasha Wheatley, Oxford, Oxford University Press, 2020, 283–311.
Crampton, Richard. "Edvard Beneš." In *Mental Maps in the Era of Two World Wars*, edited by Jonathan Wright and Steven Casey, 135–156. New York: Palgrave Macmillan, 2008.
Durin-Hornyik, Veronika. "The Free Europe University in Exile, Inc. and the Collège de l' Europe libre (1951–1958)." In *The Inauguration of "Organized Political Warfare,"* edited by Kádár-Lynn, 439–514. Saint Helena, CA: Helena History Press, 2013.
Gyula, László. "Fettich Nándor emlékezete." [Remembering Nándor Fettich] In *Cumania, 1, Archeologia*, edited by Attila Horváth and Elvira H. Tóth, 231–232. Kecskemét: Bács-Kiskun Megyei Múzeumok Közleményei, 1972.
Kimball, Warren F. "The Sheriffs: FDR's Postwar World," in *FDR's World: War, Peace, and Legacies*, edited by David B. Woolner, Warren F. Kimball, and David Reynolds, 91–121. New York: Palgrave, 2008.
Kovács, Zoltán András. "A Janus-arcú tábornok. Adalékok Ujszászy István vezérőrnagy pályaképéhez." [The Janus-faced General. Additions to the Career of Major General István Ujszászy] In *Vallomások a holtak házából. Ujszászy István vezérőrnagynak, a 2. vkf. Osztály és az Államvédelmi Központ vezetőjének az ÁVH fogságában írott feljegyzései* [Testimonies from the House of the Dead. The Notes of Major General István Ujszászy, Head

of Department 2 of Intelligence and Counterintelligence and State Security Center, during in his Captivity of ÁVH] edited by György Haraszti, 72–153. Budapest: Corvina 2007.
Lojkó, Miklós. "Railways and Diplomats. The Failure of the League of Nations to Settle the Manchurian Crisis, 1931–1933." In *At the Crossroads of Human Fate and History*, edited by Nóra Deák, 349–366. Budapest: Eötvös Loránd Tudományegyetem, Bölcsészettudományi Kar, Angol-Amerikai Intézet, 2019.
Peirce, Hayford and Royall Tyler. "Byzantine Art." In *The Encyclopaedia Britannica*, Fourteenth Edition, Vol. 4, London: The Encyclopaedia Britannica Company, Ltd., 1929, 488–492.
Peterecz, Zoltán. "SOE Operations in Hungary during the Second World War." In *Contemporary Perspectives on Language, Culture and Identity in Anglo-American Contexts*, edited by Éva Antal, Csaba Czeglédi, and Eszter Krakkó, 216–230. Cambridge: Cambridge Scholars Publishing, 2019.
Peterecz, Zoltán. "Hungary and the League of Nations: A Forced Marriage," In *Remaking Central Europe. The League of Nations and the Former Habsburg Lands*, edited by Peter Becker and Natasha Wheatley, Oxford, Oxford University Press, 2020, 145–165.
Romsics, Ignác. "Hungary's Place in the Sun: A British Newspaper Article and its Hungarian Repercussions." In *British-Hungarian Relations since 1848*, edited by László Péter and Martyn Rady, 193–204. London: School of Slavonic and East European Studies, University College London, 2004.
Steininger, Rolf. "12 November 1918–12 March 1938: The Road to the Anschluss." In *Austria in the Twentieth Century*, edited by Rolf Steininger, Günter Bischof, and Michael Gehler, 85–113. New Brunswick, NJ and London, UK: Transaction Publishers, 2009.
Taraszovics, Sándor. "American Peace Preparations during World War I and the Shaping of the New Hungary." In *20th Century Hungary and the Great Powers*, edited by Ignác Romsics, 73–97. Boulder, Colorado: Social Science Monographs, Atlantic Research and Publications Inc., 1994.
Tyler, William Royall. "A Young American Friend of Miguel de Unamuno." In *Homenaje a Julián Marías*. 713–734. Madrid: Espasa-Calpe, S.A., 1984.

Journal articles

Ablonczy, Balázs. "A frankhamisítás. Hálók, személyek, döntések." [The Franc Forgery. Networks, Persons, Decisions.] *Múltunk* 53, no. 1 (2008): 29-56.
Afinoguénova, Eugenia. "An Organic Nation: State-Run Tourism, Regionalism, and Food in Spain, 1905–1931." *The Journal of Modern History* 86, no. 4 (December 2014), 743–779.
Aguado, Iago Gil. "The Creditanstalt Crisis of 1931 and the Failure of the Austro-German Customs Union Project." *The Historical Journal* 44, no. 1 (Mar., 2001): 199-221.
Alvarez, David. "No Immunity: Signals Intelligence and the European Neutrals, 1939–45." *Intelligence and National Security* 12, no. 2 (1997): 22–43.
Aradi Gábor. "A San Remo-i tárgyalások magyarországi előkészülete." [The Hungarian Preparations for the San Remo Talks] *Levéltári Szemle* 52, no. 3 (2002): 24–38.
Bakay Kornél. "Fettich Nándor emlékére." [In Memory of Nándor fettich] Életünk 18, no. 1 (1981 January): 55–62.
Barcza, György. "My Memoirs as a Diplomat 1911–1945 (Excerpts)." *The Hungarian Quarterly* 36, no. 140 (1995): 81–101.

Bibliography

Bauer, Kurt. "Hitler und der Juliputsch 1934 in Österreich." *Vierteljahrshefte für Zeitgeschichte*, 59, no. 2, (2011): 193–227.
Beneš, Eduard. "The Little Entente." *Foreign Affairs* 1, no. 1 (September 1922): 66–72.
Berdahl, Clarence A. "The United States and the League of Nations." *Michigan Law Review* 27, no. 6 (April 1929): 607–636.
Berend, Iván and György Ránki. "German-Hungarian Relations Following Hitler's Rise to Power (1933–34)." *Acts Historica* 8, no. 3-4 (1961): 313–346.
Bethlen, István. "Hungary in the New Europe." *Foreign Affairs* 3, no. 3 (April 1925): 445–458.
Blackwell Marilyn S. "The Republican Vision of Mary Palmer Tyler." *Journal of the Early Republic* 12 (Spring 1992): 11–35.
Borbándi, Gyula. "A Teleki-Pelényi terv nyugati magyar ellenkormány létesítésére." [The Teleki-Pelényi Plan to Establish a Western Hungarian Counter Government] *Új Látóhatár* 9, no. 2 (March-April 1966): 155–170.
Clavin, Patricia. "The Austrian Hunger Crisis and the Genesis of International Organization after the First World War," *International Affairs* 90, no. 2 (March 2014): 265–78.
Császár Ildikó. "A szentgotthárdi fegyverszállítási botrány sajtóvisszhangja." [The Press Echo of the Szentgotthárd Arms Scandal] *Vasi Szemle*, 68, no. 6 (2013): 579–591.
Dessants, Betty Abrahamsen. "Ambivalent Allies: OSS' USSR Division, the State Department, and the Bureaucracy of Intelligence Analysis, 1941–1945." *Intelligence and National Security* 11, no. 4 (1996): 722–753.
Egressy, Gergely. "A Statistical Overview of the Hungarian Numerus Clausus Law of 1920—A Historical Necessity or the First Step Toward the Holocaust?" *Eastern European Quarterly* 34, no. 4 (January 2001): 447–464.
Graham, Jr., Malbone W. "The Elections to the New Hungarian Parliament." *The American Political Science Review* 21, no. 2 (May, 1927): 381–388.
Ferber, Katalin. "Lépéshátrányban: a magyar kormány kölcsönszerzési kísérlete 1930–1931-ben." [Handicapped: The Efforts of the Hungarian Government for a Loan in 1930–31] *Gazdaság* 22, no.1 (1988.): 89–108.
Frank, Tibor. "'...to fix the attention of the whole world upon Hungary.' Lajos Kossuth in the United States, 1851–52." *The Hungarian Quarterly* 43, no. 166 (Summer 2002): 85–98.
Glant, Tibor. "Herbert Hoover and Hungary, 1918–1923." *Hungarian Journal of English and American Studies* 8, no. 2 (2002): 95–109.
Götz, Norbert and Janne Holmén. "Introduction to the Theme Issue: 'Mental Maps: Geographical and Historical Perspectives.'" *Journal of Cultural Geography* 35, no. 2 (2018): 157–161.
Harmsworth, Harold Sydney (Viscount Rothermere). "Hungary's Place in the Sun." *The Daily Mail* June 21, 1927.
Huttlinger, Jim. "The First Field Offices." *Bank's World* 14, no. 7 (July 1995): 17–19.
Joó, András. "A 'Kállay Alap' története – tények es kérdőjelek." ['National Treasure.' The Story of the Kállay Fund: Facts and Questions] *Századok* 154, no. 2, (2020): 327–362.
Juhász, Gyula. "A német-magyar viszony néhány kérdése a második világháború alatt." [Some of the Questions of the German–Hungarian Relationship during World War II] *Történelmi Szemle* 22, no. 1–2 (1984): 269–78.
Kennan, George F. "The Sources of Soviet Conduct." *Foreign Affairs* 25, no. 4 (July 1947): 566–78, 580–82.
Kovrig, Bennett. "Mediation by Obfuscation: The Resolution of the Marseille Crisis, October 1934 to May 1935." *The Historical Journal* 1976, 19, no. 1 (March 1976): 191–221.

Kun, József. "Magyarország német katonai megszállásának előkészítése és lefolyása, 1943 szeptember–1944 március." [The Preparation and Execution of the German Occupation of Hungary, September 1943–March 1944] *Hadtörténelmi Közlemények* 10, no. 1 (1963): 37–84.

Lada, Zsuzsanna. "The invention of a hero: Lajos Kossuth in England (1851)." *European History Quarterly* 43, no. 1 (2013): 5–26.

Laqua, Daniel. "Transnational Intellectual Cooperation, the League of Nations, and the Problem of Order." *Journal of Global History*, 6, no. 2, (July 2011): 223–247.

Lojkó, Miklós. "The Failed Handshake over the Danube. The Story of Anglo-American Involvement in the Liberation of Central Europe at the End of the Second World War." *Hungarian Studies* 13, no. 1 (1998/99): 119–127.

MacPherson, Nelson. "Reductio Ad Absurdum: The R&A Branch of OSS/London." *International Journal of Intelligence and Counter Intelligence* 15, no. 3 (2002): 390–414.

Morrison, Rodney J. "The London Monetary and Economic Conference of 1933: A Public Goods Analysis." *The American Journal of Economics and Sociology* 52, no. 3. (Jul., 1993): 307–321.

Neale, J. E. "Calendar of State Papers Spanish. Vol. xiii, 1554-1558 by Royall Tyler." *The English Historical Review* 72, no. 282 (January 1957): 113–115.

Ormos, Mária. "Magyarország belépése a Nemzetek Szövetségébe." [Hungary's Entry to the League of Nations] *Századok* 91, no. 1 (1957): 235–49.

Paikert, Alajos. "A Népszövetségi Ligák jelentősége." [The Significance of the League of Nations] *Külügyi Szemle* 6, no. 1 (1929): 65–68.

Pelényi, John. "The Secret Plan for a Hungarian Government in the West at the Outbreak of World War II." *The Journal of Modern History* 36, no. 2 (Jun., 1964): 170–177.

Peterecz, Zoltán. "'A Certain Amount of Tactful Undermining.' Herbert C. Pell and Hungary in 1941." *The Hungarian Quarterly* 52, no. 202-203 (Summer-Autumn 2011): 124–137.

——. "Reflection of and about Hungary in the English-speaking World in the Interwar Years." *Hungarian Studies* 31, no. 2,(2017): 237–249.

——. "Sparrow Mission: A US Intelligence Failure during World War II." *Intelligence and National Security* 27, no. 2 (2012): 241–260.

Pogány, Ágnes. "Válságok és választások" [Crises and Elections] *Aetas* 15, no. 4 (2000): 27–41.

Reinisch, Jessica. "Internationalism in Relief: The Birth (and Death) of UNRRA." *Past and Present* 210, Supplement 6 (2011): 258–289.

Réti, György. "Gömbös és a Római Hármas Egyezmény, 1934." [Gömbös and the Rome Three Power Pact] *Történelmi Szemle* 36, no. 1–2 (1994), 135–65.

Romsics, Ignác. "Franciaország, Bethlen és a frankhamisítás." [France, Bethlen, and the Franc Forgery] *Történelmi Szemle* 26, no. 1 (1983): 67–86.

Scott-Smith, Giles. "The Free Europe University in Strasbourg: U.S. State-Private Networks and Academic 'Rollback'." *Journal of Cold War Studies* 16, no. 2 (Spring 2014): 77–107.

Stafford, Paul. "The Chamberlain-Halifax Visit to Rome: A Reappraisal." *The English Historical Review* 98, no. 386 (Jan., 1983): 61–100.

Street, Gordon M. "Memories of a Mission to Paris." *International Bank Notes* 15, no. 7 (July 1961): 3–5.

Tyler, Royall. "The Eastern Reparations Settlement." *Foreign Affairs* 9, no. 1 (October 1930): 106–117.

Vass, István G. "Bakach-Bessenyey György tárgyalásai az Egyesült Államok megbízottaival Bernben, 1943. augusztus 28. és 1944. március 19. között: A Kállay-kormány béketapogatózásainak újabb dokumentumai." [The Negotiations of György Bakach-Bessenyey with the Emissaries of the United States in Bern, between August 28, 1943, and March 19, 1944: New Documents of the Peace Feeling of the Kállay Government] *Levéltári Közlemények* 65, no. 1–2 (1994): 153–205.

Villemus, G. De. "Hungary To-day." *The Living Age* 332, no. 4305 (May 1, 1927): 785–787.

Weninger, László Vince. "Népszövetség." [League of Nations] *Külügyi Szemle* 6, no. 1 (1929): 102–111.

Zsiga, Tibor. A szentgotthárdi fegyverbotrány." [The Szentgotthárd Arms Scandal] *Vasi honismereti és helytörténeti közlemények* 35, no. 1 (2008): 14–23.

Internet sources

"Bliss-Tyler Correspondence." https://www.doaks.org/resources/bliss-tyler-correspondence

Susan Clair Imbarrato. "Royall Tyler (1757-1826)," *The Heath Anthology of American Literature*. Fifth Edition, Paul Lauter, General Editor, https://college.cengage.com/english/lauter/heath/4e/students/author_pages/eighteenth/tyler_ro.html, accessed September 6, 2018.

Kniefacz, Katharina. "Elisina Tyler, geb. Contessa di Castelvecchio." https://geschichte.univie.ac.at/de/personen/elisina-tyler-geb-palamidessi-de-castelvecchio, accessed August 17, 2019.

Newspapers

8 Órai Ujság
A Reggel
Budapesti Hírlap
Christian Science Monitor
Az Est
The Harvard Crimson
Honi Ipar
Magyar Hírlap
Magyar Iparművészet
Magyarország
Magyarság
Nemzeti Ujság
Neue Freie Presse
The New York Times
Népszava
Our World
Pesti Hírlap
Pesti Napló
The Times
Uj Barázda
Uj Nemzedék
Ujság
Városok Lapja

Index

Acheson, Dean, 252
Adams, John, 1
Alexander, King of Yugoslavia, 150, 155,
Anschluss, 171–73, 176, 184, 190
Antigny (France), 14, 21, 38, 51, 58, 63, 66, 70, 72, 74, 77, 78, 84, 93, 94, 96, 112, 134, 140, 150, 158, 175, 176, 194, 203, 204, 249, 258, 260
Apponyi, Albert, 89
Apponyi, György, 255
Assembly of Captive European Nations (ACEN), 254
Auer, Pál, 255
Avenol, Joseph, 147, 174, 204

Bakach-Bessenyey, György, 227–29, 242
Bandholtz, Harry Hill, 115
Bank of England, 32, 33, 39, 56, 58, 75, 76, 81, 111, 113, 148, 152, 153
Bank for International Settlements (BIS), 100, 107–11, 113, 121, 152
Baranyai, Lipót, 205, 222, 223
Barcza, György, 201
Barthou, Louis, 150, 155
Bárdossy, László, 209, 218, 219
Beneš, Eduard, 44, 47, 156, 172, 188, 231
Berle, Adolf A., 227, 230, 254, 256
Berlin, 9, 89, 102, 103, 106, 112, 186, 187
Berthelot, Philippe, 155
Bethlen, István, 42, 43, 45–50, 54, 60, 61, 67, 69, 82, 87, 92, 93, 97, 101, 106, 111, 112, 114, 116, 125–27, 135, 152, 230–32, 238

Bliss, Mildred Barnes, 38, 88, 102, 128, 139, 142, 146, 149, 155, 156
Bliss, Robert Woods, 11, 13, 252
de Bordes, Jan van Waltré, 113
Boyden, Roland William, 28, 37, 46, 49
Brentano, Theodore, 44
Bruce, Henry James, 118–20, 123, 124, 135–38, 146, 152, 161, 165–68, 178, 201
Bud, János, 75, 92, 153
Budapest, 25, 40, 41, 44, 49, 51, 54, 58–60, 63, 65, 66, 68–70, 72–74, 82, 83, 85, 87, 88, 92–96, 100, 101, 106, 111–15, 117–19, 121–23, 126, 134, 135, 138–40, 143, 145–47, 149, 150, 154, 158, 160, 166, 167, 169, 176, 179, 198–201, 205–8, 210, 215, 222, 224, 234, 237, 238, 240, 242, 267, 268
Bullitt, William C., 203, 207

Cadogan, Alexander, 226
Chamberlain, Neville, 143, 165, 189, 292
Charron, René, 52, 56, 73, 83, 110, 111, 210
Child, Richard W., 31, 32
Clapp, Gordon, 251, 253
Coolidge, Archibald Cary, 25
Coolidge, Calvin, 28, 29, 65, 88
Curzon, George, 47, 48

Darányi, Kálmán, 161, 171
Dollfuss, Engelbert, 149, 150
Donovan, William J., 219, 220, 232
Drummond, Eric, 97, 205
Dulles, Allen W., xi, 25, 217, 219, 220–23,

226, 227–30, 232, 239, 242, 248, 249, 252, 254, 255, 261

Eccles, Marriner S., 180
Eckhardt, Tibor, 155
Eisenhower, Dwight D., 225, 254
Esterházy, Móric, 154

Fabinyi, Tihamér, 166
Feis, Herbert, 180
Fettich, Nándor, 65
Financial Committee, 30, 32, 46, 48, 56, 58, 64, 68, 70, 72, 74, 76, 77, 81, 85, 93, 94, 97, 112, 117–22, 124, 127, 136–38, 142, 144, 162, 163–66, 174
Fish, Hamilton Armstrong, 54
Foreign Office, 6, 9, 46, 138, 145, 179, 182, 202, 225
Franco, Francisco, 190
Free Europe University (FEU), 256, 258, 259

Geneva, 29, 37, 58, 59, 61, 63, 67, 68, 70, 72, 78, 81, 86, 90, 93, 95, 97, 98, 109, 112, 116, 130, 138, 142, 151, 153, 154, 158, 169, 174, 176, 179, 181, 184, 185, 188, 193, 197, 198, 200, 203, 204, 208, 210, 211, 250, 272, 283, 293, 297
George, Lloyd, 25, 31, 33
Gömbös, Gyula, 131, 133–38, 145, 150, 153–55, 159, 161, 173, 235
Grant-Smith, Ulysses, 54
Grew, Joseph C., 25, 254

Halifax, Edward Frederick Lindley Wood, 189, 201
Hambro, Ronald Olaf, 96
Harding, William Procter Gould, 49
Harrison, George Leslie, 180
Harrison, Leland, 239
Hatvany, Lili, 155
Hearst, William Randolph, 24
Hevesy, Pál, 98
Hitler, Adolf, 103, 104, 109, 145, 150, 179, 180–82, 187, 190, 194, 197, 198, 205, 207, 214, 216, 224, 233, 268, 270, 272–75, 284, 291, 296

Hornsby, Bertram, 112
Horthy, Miklós, 42, 97, 106, 111, 112, 114, 125, 126, 153, 154, 219, 234, 240, 261
Höttl, Wilhelm, 232, 233
Hughes, Charles Evans, 29
Hull, Cordell, 143, 176, 180, 227, 234, 235

Imrédy, Béla, 75, 76, 137, 138, 147, 148, 152, 153, 154, 167, 179, 184, 235
International Bank for Reconstruction and Development (IBRD, or World Bank), 248, 249
International Monetary Fund (IMF), 248

Jackson, Charles Douglas, 256, 257, 259, 262
Joint Chiefs of Staff (JCS), 220, 227

Kállay, Miklós, 217, 219, 221, 222, 228, 229, 233, 240, 242
Károlyi, Gyula, 112, 114, 119, 120, 125, 126, 127, 130, 134, 154
Kennan, George, 140, 254
Knox, Geoffrey, 179
Korányi, Frigyes, 46, 120, 123, 153
Kossuth, Lajos, 53
Krebs, Ellen Curtis, 3
Kun, Béla, 40, 41

Lamont, Thomas, 28, 49, 50
Lansing, Robert, 23–25
League Council, 50, 63, 64, 72, 75, 85, 93, 166, 286
League of Nations, xi, 22–24, 26, 28, 29, 30, 32–40, 43, 44–46, 48, 50, 52, 55–57, 64, 67, 69, 71, 72, 74, 77, 78, 85, 86, 89, 90, 92, 97, 99, 103, 109, 112, 113, 115, 116, 118, 125, 128, 130, 131, 133, 134, 142, 150, 151, 155, 158, 160, 166, 167, 169, 173, 180, 181, 185, 191, 192, 197, 204, 211, 213, 241, 243, 247, 249, 262, 263, 285, 290, 291
Lester, Seán, 210, 217
Levi, Doro, 187, 188, 214
Licen, Livio, 52
Lippmann, Walter, 88
Lodge, Henry Cabot, 23
Logan, James Addison, 31, 32

London, 5, 9, 10, 11, 13, 20, 44, 47, 57, 72, 76, 77, 93, 96, 100, 112, 113, 142, 143, 144, 153, 163, 198, 201, 217, 220, 255, 268, 297
Loveday, Alexander, 112, 165, 167, 174, 182
Luce, Henry R., 254

McCloy, John, 249
Messersmith, George C., 180
Meulen, Carel Eliza ter, 30, 70
Morgan, John Pierpont, Jr., 37, 49
Morgenthau, Henry, Jr., 180, 185, 186, 189, 199, 200, 202, 267
Mussolini, Benito, 87, 134, 145, 149, 182, 185, 190, 200, 269, 270, 272, 273, 274, 275, 285
Norman, Montagu, 32, 33, 36, 39, 47, 56, 57, 76, 78, 102, 152, 153, 237, 259
National Bank of Hungary, 58, 71, 75, 76, 92, 110, 118, 128, 151, 153, 168, 222, 281
National Committee for a Free Europe, Inc. (NCFE), 254, 255, 256, 257
Niemeyer, Otto, 46, 102, 116, 117, 120, 148, 154, 165, 174

Office of Strategic Services (OSS), xi, 219
O'Malley, Owen St. Clair, 201
Ottlik, György, 222

Peace Conference (Paris), 23–26, 28, 34, 40, 41, 51, 56, 223, 263
Peirce, Hayford, 22, 24, 73, 74, 82, 84, 94, 113, 139, 140, 158, 198, 248, 260, 262
Pelényi, János, 206, 259
Pell, Herbert C., 218
Phillips, Frederick, 165
Popovics, Sándor, 56, 76, 92, 151, 152, 153
Pospíšil, Vilem, 112, 165

Quincy, Josiah Huntington, 3

Radio Free Europe (RFE), 254, 255
Radvánszky, Antal, 222, 223
Reményi-Schneller, Lajos, 179
Reparations Commission, 28, 29, 30, 31, 34, 36, 38, 46, 47, 51, 102
Rist, Charles, 112

Roosevelt, Nicholas, 25, 110, 111, 115, 116, 118, 120, 135, 140, 142, 152, 154, 238
Roosevelt, Franklin Delano, 133, 143, 144, 180, 185, 187, 192, 220, 221, 234
Rothermere, Lord (Harold Harmsworth), 82, 115

Salter, Arthur, 32, 38, 56, 61, 92
Sargent, Orme, 202
Schober, Béla, 153, 168
Seipel, Ignaz, 37
Siepmann, Harry Arthur, 52, 56, 68, 75, 76, 81–83, 92, 96, 111, 123, 151–53
Simpson, John Hope, 78
Sigray, Antal, 126
Smith, Jeremiah, Jr., xi, 49, 50–52, 55–65, 68, 69, 71, 72, 113, 115, 116, 125, 165, 166
Stimson, Henry Lewis, 121
Strakosch, Henry, 57
Suvich, Fulvio, 112
Szálasi, Ferenc, 240
Szegedy-Maszák, Aladár, 222
Széchenyi, László, 45, 121
Sztójay, Döme, 241

Tabakovics, Dusán, 56
Teleki, Pál, 192, 200–2, 204–10, 217, 235, 239, 242, 268
Teleszky, János, 153, 168
Tittman, Harold, 193, 204
Trianon Peace Treaty (Treaty of Trianon), 41, 42, 45, 86, 87, 234, 236, 277
Tyler, Elisina, 13–15, 20, 21, 34, 35, 51, 58, 66, 73, 78, 96, 138, 140, 154–56, 185, 194, 203, 204, 209, 210, 260, 262
Tyler, Mary Hunt Palmer, 1, 2
Tyler, Royall (1757–1826), 1, 2
Tyler, William Royall (1852–1897), 2, 3
Tyler, William Royall (1910–2003), 14, 262

Unamuno Don Miguel de, 8, 12, 264, 265
United Nations (UN), 243, 244, 247, 249, 272, 283, 290, 293, 294, 297
United Nations Relief and Rehabilitation Administration (UNRRA), 217, 247
University of Salamanca, 7

Varga, Béla, 262
Versailles Peace Treaty (Treaty of Versailles), 23, 26, 28, 41, 44
Vienna, 12, 34, 35, 36, 37, 51, 52, 61, 73, 100, 101, 106, 107, 141, 162, 189, 224
Vogeler, Robert, 261

Walko, Lajos, 101, 126, 153
Wekerle, Sándor, Jr., 95, 114

Welles, Sumner, 180
Wharton, Edith, 20, 210
Wilson, Woodrow, 19, 20, 22, 23, 24, 25, 26, 213
Wolff, Károly, 117

Zanuck, Darryl, 254
Zimmermann, Alfred, 37

Lyulph Mowbray Howard,
George Tudor Castle, and Royall Tyler

Royall Tyler and his father,
William Royall Tyler, Sr.

Royall Tyler as a school boy

William Royall Tyler, Sr.

Royall Tyler as a young boy

Ellen Krebs Tyler Quincy, Royall Tyler's mother

Royall Tyler with his favorite owl

Royall Tyler and his mother in Biarritz, 1903

1901 Census, Middlesex County, Great Britain

Royall Tyler as a League of Nations officer

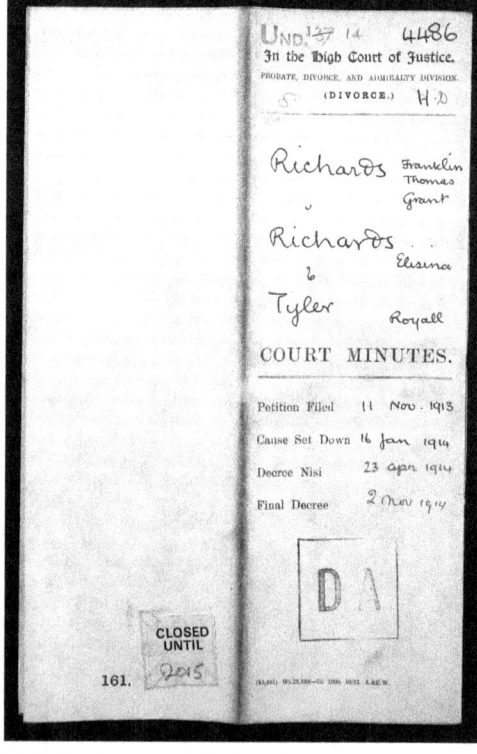

Elisina's divorce certificate, 1914

Elisina Tyler, Royall Tyler, and their son, William Royall Tyler

Elisina Tyler and Royall Tyler in Geneva as an older couple

Royall Tyler and Antal Sigray after World War II

Royall Tyler at summer in Budapest

Royall Tyler at a small Budapest restaurant (János-hegy)

Royall Tyler on New York Passenger Lists & Arrivals 1948

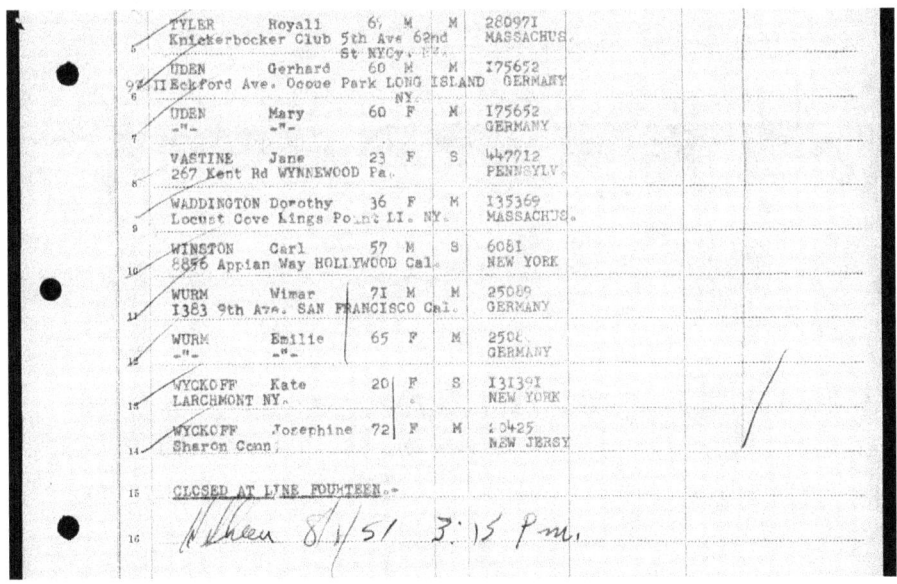

Royall Tyler on New York Passenger Lists & Arrivals 1951

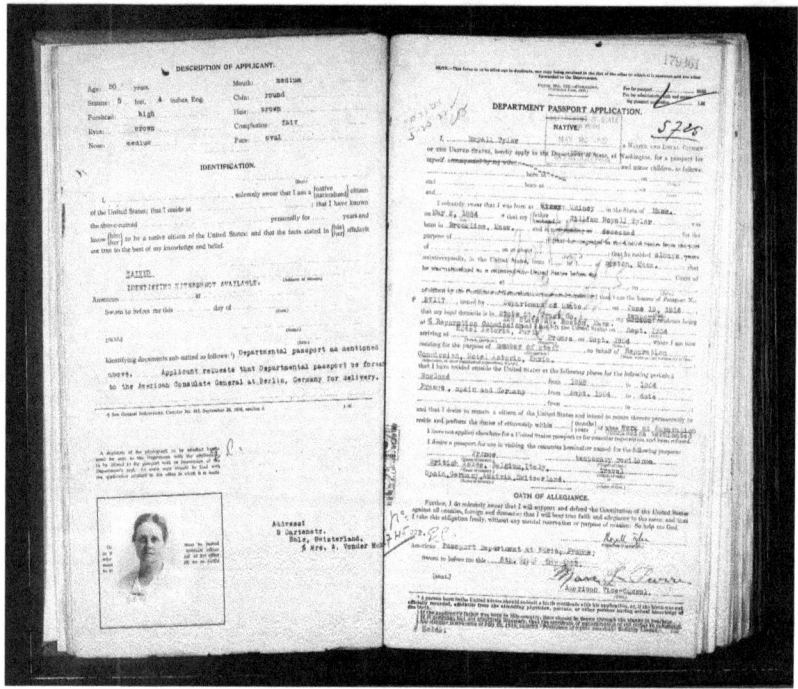

Royall Tyler's United States Passport Application, 1922

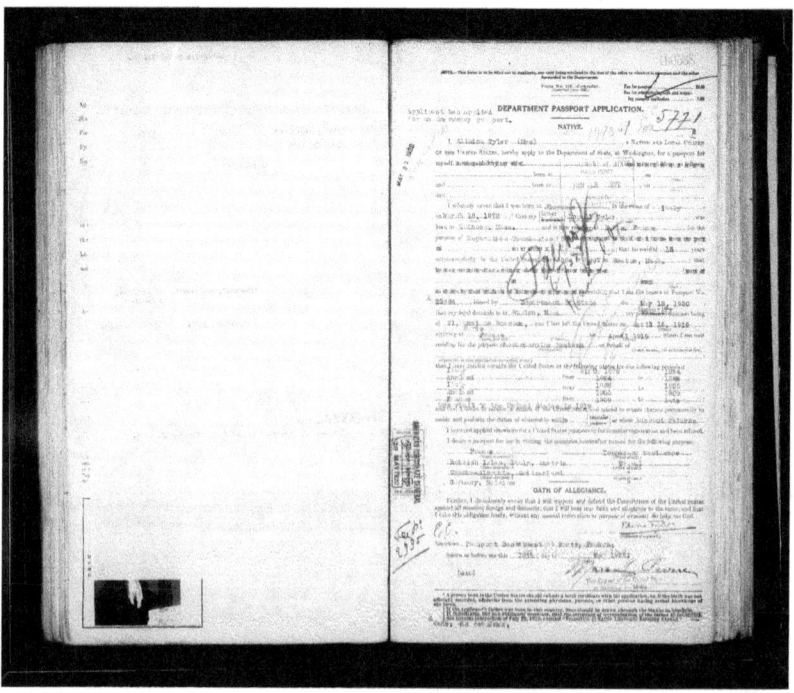

Elisina Tyler's United States Passport Applications, 1922

www.ingramcontent.com/pod-product-compliance
Lightning Source LLC
Chambersburg PA
CBHW070507240426
43673CB00024B/471/J